D1032354

Volkmar Gantzhorn

Oriental Carpets

Their Iconology and Iconography
from Earliest Times to the 18th Century

TASCHEN
KÖLN LISBOA LONDON NEW YORK PARIS TOKYO

Hohenzollernring 53, D–50672 Köln
This work was a dissertation originally titled
"The Christian Oriental Carpet"
for the Faculty of Cultural Studies at the
University of Tübingen
Layout: Volkmar Gantzhorn
Graphics: Claudia Reusch
Translated by Charles Madsen
English text edited by Robert Bartlett Haas
Cover design by Angelika Taschen, Cologne

Printed in Germany
ISBN 3–8228–0545–9
GB

Table of Contents

B. The High Middle Ages

Part Two: From the Late Middle Ages to Modern Times

Carpet-Group C V
Diamond-Form Cross Carpets and Step-Form Cross Carpets

Foreword

It is seldom, in our present generation, that the fresh eye of a contemporary scholar can throw new light on a field of research which has long been dominated by the eminent scholar of the past. But this is exactly what the author, Dr. Volkmar Gantzhorn, has done in this remarkable book. "The Christian Oriental Carpet".

What has qualified him to do this?

Dr. Gantzhorn has successfully combined in one lifetime the roles of teacher, painter, sculptor, traveller, art and cultural historian. His sharp eye for form, ornament, symbols and hidden meanings in the arts, plus his personal knowledge of public and private carpet collections around the whole world (and of the scholars who have studied them), give him the unusual advantage of being able to write about carpets with an almost global view of the field.

What is this book about?

In this book, two and a half thousand years of carpet history are analyzed and presented. It is the result of Dr. Gantzhorn's belief that we have long needed an entire revision of our former thinking about the history and symbology of the Oriental carpet.

He has therefore traced the patterns and motifs in historical carpets (most of which we can still find in the rugs of today) back to their earliest known sources. He discovered that they stem from very ancient traditions in the christianized Middle East which were carried forward, well into the beginning of the present century, by Armenian weavers.

These motifs sometimes allude to wordly power, sometimes they refer to special aspects of the Christian faith which was adopted early by the Armenians, or sometimes they served symbolic functions.

What are the findings?

The author convincingly demonstrates that the "oriental carpet", so called, had neither a nomadic origin, nor was its birthplace Central Asia – both previously–held scholary positions. It was born, rather, in the Armenian highlands. Carpets appeared in this area when Monophysite Christianity was flourishing there, long before the creed of Islam had appeared.

During those early times, the area also served as a crossroads for the oldest trade-routes – those from the east and the west, as well as those from the north and the south. Thus Armenian weaving reached the outside world early, as we know from the examples which are to be found today in the great museums and private collections of the world.

These carpets provide the basis for Dr. Glantzhorn's principal thesis in this book, namely that Christian Oriental carpets existed long before the Islamic culture made its appearance there. This thesis he further supports by a rich array of illustrations drawn from his own extensive travel and research.

What will you discover for yourself?

You will find here for the first time in any carpet history, for example, photographs of every carpet type discussed in the text, along with examples showing the stages of its development. Other illustrations provide comparative examples from related fields in the decorative arts. architectural ornament, book illumination, metalwork, frescoes and floor tiles. These make clear parallel but often previously unrecognized stages in the complex history of carpet development, as well as the hitherto neglected contribution of Armenian Christian craftsmen to it, and thus to world arts generally.

Readers of this book may also well find, as I did, that Dr. Gantzhorn's greatest contribution has been to teach us how to look at carpets more systematically, with sharpened eyes for the details of their design and ornament, for their colour and texture, their symbols and ultimate meanings.

These are the very special skills which can help us to become more literate appreciators of the historical carpet –both as an art form, and, as in the case of the Christian Oriantal carpet specifically, as a new category in the world's textile history to be consciously studied and enjoyed.

In this new work, Dr. Gantzhorn has provided us all with an entirely new way to look at carpets, both historically and as compelling art forms. The approach to seeing is made immeasurably easier for the reader by the splendid graphic pattern-drawings by Claudia Reusch, which amplify the text.

Dr. Robert Bartlett Haas
Los Angeles and Nürtingen

For Claudia

ACKNOWLEDGEMENTS

This work is, after F. R. Martin 1908 and Kurt Erdmann 1955, the third attempt in writing a comprehensive history of the oriental carpet.
The Christian Oriental Carpet is the result of decades of fundamental research work, and at the beginning there was neither an idea nor any knowledge about its Christian origin. Until the manuscript of this book was finished, the author intended to write about the Islamic oriental carpet as well, but unfortunately there are but few capets until the 19th century which can, with certainty, be attributed to Moslem use. The most important of these are illustrated in this book for comparison.

The original German edition has been published unchanged, as well as has the English and the French translation, from the manuscript finished in 1987 and accepted as a dissertation by the Department of Cultural Studies at the University of Tübingen.

With nearly 1,000 reproductions, 600 of which appear in colour, this book is unique in its field. It not only brings together those carpets of antiquity most important for the history of carpets, but also presents those considered to be the most beautiful, drawing for this on both public and private collections from around the world. Much of this material is presented here for the first time to a wider audience, and this in a completely new context. Even particularly knowledgeable readers may be surprised to find themselves unfamiliar with much of it.

It is the author's aim to free the oriental carpet of the harmful reputation of being merely a floor covering to be walked on to the point of being worn out – since 'barbaric' Europeans were the first to destroy it with their shoes. Indeed, the author would like to create the awareness that these textiles, woven by devout Christians, are in fact icons with no utilitarian purpose. As cult objects of Christian oriental churches, these carpets, along with other textiles, constitute what may well be the most important Armenian contribution to the history of world art. This book attempts to make good the injustice done to a people who, in the course of their more than two thousand year history, have suffered more than any other as a result of their geographic location between the Orient and the Occident. The Armenians have countless times been divided, exploited, robbed, exiled, deported, enslaved, murdered and mistreated. They have even been robbed of their art, the authorship for which has been attributed to the conquerors during the years which followed, either due to an ignorance of the facts involved, or to the manipulation of these facts. This unique collection of patterns and designs, characteristic of oriental carpets, is a part of the Armenian heritage and identity, and it should now be understood as such.
The author would like to thank the innumerable museums and collections in Europe, Asia and the United States which shared their carpets and textiles, often opening their otherwise inaccessible deposits for my viewing. One can not possibly mention by name all those museum directors, curators, colleagues, collectors and dealers who gave him clues and support, provided him with photographs, or allowed him to examine and take pictures of the carpets in their collections or care. It was in discussions with them, which often went on for hours, that he found valuable stimuli and the strength to persevere.
A very special word of thanks indeed must be said to my life companion, Mrs. Claudia Reusch, who through all the years has shown extraordinary self-sacrifice by offering the spiritual, personal and material help required for making this book possible. To her the author dedicates this book.

Volkmar Gantzhorn

Introduction

Comparatively speaking, the history of oriental carpets is a new field of scholarly research. Although the earliest publications appeared 110 years ago, the first attempt to show any historical development was not undertaken until 1908 by F.R. *Martin.*[1]

Just how difficult it was in those early years to categorize the work correctly, or even to agree on a set terminology, might best be illustrated by citing Ignaz Schlosser[2], the former Director of the Österreichisches Museum für angewandte Kunst in Vienna:

"Even in the early 19th century it was still common to give oriental carpets in general the collective name 'Turkish', in the same manner that we later find only the term 'Persian' being used."

This very significant shift in terminological usage clearly points out a dependence on the market situation. Midway into the 19th century, dealers from western countries (that is, primarily the English, Germans and Americans) had begun to have the carpets they had purchased in Istanbul copied in large quantities in Persia, in order to meet the demand for such carpets in their domestic markets. As a result, the sheer number of Persian carpets increased to such an extent that, by comparison, the production on Turkish territory became almost insignificant. A well-organized industry had commercialized the Persian Carpet, thus creating another standard.

By the time the first scholarly studies were conducted, this new Persian Carpet industry already had a 50-year tradition. Since dealers played an essential role in naming the various kinds of carpets, the centres of production during the second half of the 19th century became equated with the origin of the rug designs. And, because Persians, who were of Aryan descent, were, in accordance with the ideological climate of that time, considered capable of greater cultural achievement than, for example, the Turks, carpets bearing the name 'Persian' were also assured greater commercial success.[3]

We must also remember that as a result of the First World War far-reaching changes were taking place in eastern Europe and the Near East with respect to political conditions and population structures. These changes included the reduction of the Ottoman Empire to the area of what is now Turkey; the Christian persecutions at the end of the last century; the ethnocide of the Armenians from 1894–1915, and in 1923 the deportation of the Greek population – all serving to change the picture from previous centuries. All field-research carried out after this time must, of necessity, have resulted in an utterly incorrect and misleading outcome, which in no way corresponded to the actual conditions which existed to the end of the 19th century. Not until 1955, with *Kurt Erdmann,* was an attempt made to establish a new history of the oriental carpet.[4] It is clear that Erdmann was searching for new answers to questions whose old answers he, too, appeared to be dissatisfied with. This is particularly apparent in his book 'A History of the Early Turkish Carpet.'[5] The fact that this search took him to Turkish territory shows that he was on the right track.

But Erdmann's history of carpets was flawed by two premises: the myth of the Seljuk carpet and (deriving from this) the hypothesis that such carpets had originated in nomadic tribal settings.

Since these premises are of decisive significance for the entire literature on carpets, they must be dealt with at this point. The basis for these considerations seems to have been Yule's English translation[6] of Marco Polo's account[7], which, in addition to Pope's interpretation[8], Erdmann was familiar with. As the research on Marco Polo indicates, Yule's translation did not proceed from the French original, but from the much later Italian Ramusio version of 1559. This is actually the case with most of the more recent translations as well. Let us examine the critical passage available to us, in H.E. Rübesamen's modern German translation:[9]

"About the Turkmen Nation

The Turkmen population consists of three classes. The Turkomans, who worship Mohammed and follow his laws, are a crude people, completely uneducated. They live in the mountains or other virtually inaccessible places which offer good grazing land for their cattle, their sole livelihood. Here there is an outstanding breed of horses, called Turks, and handsome mules, which are sold at high prices. – The other Turkmen classes are made up of Greeks and Armenians, living in cities and in permanent settlements and earning their livelihood from commerce and trade. It is here where the best and most beautiful carpets are produced as well as silk of crimson and other splendid colours. Among the most important cities are Konya, Khazar and Sevastopol, where St. Blasius attained the glorious martyr's crown. They are all subject to the great Khan, the ruler of the eastern Tatars, who appoints their governors."

Compelled by his premises, Erdmann altered even literal quotations[10] in order to supply proof for the nomadic-Turkmenian origin he desired. The dispute as to a possible ambiguity in the Ramusio version proves superfluous, since there are much earlier versions of the passage above, including earlier German versions. The so-called Ottimo-manuscript, a 'Milione'-manuscript dating from 1309 in the Biblioteca Nazionale in Florence[11] (ill. 1), might well be the earliest.

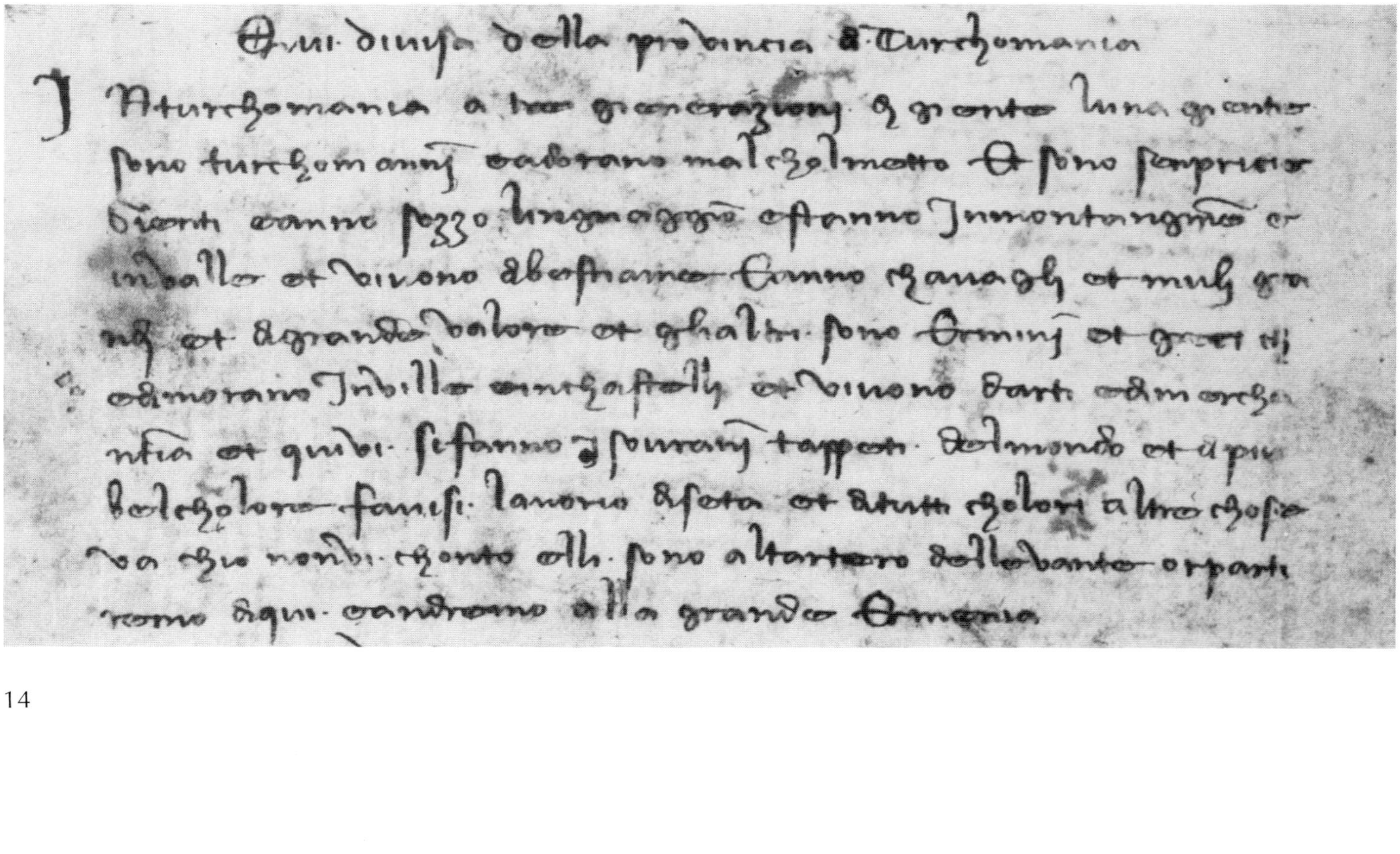

Ill. 1: Marco Polo: El Milione; so-called 'Ottimo-manuscript' from 1309. Biblioteca Nazionale in Florence, codex no. II.IV.88, F. 5v.

The 'Ottimo-manuscript' is the oldest surviving version of the Marco Polo text and at the same time the first translation into another language of the lost French original – here into Italian. It was written 12 years after the original.

Von turchoma
Turchomania ist ein
gelegen bi den zwen
armenien. In der wonen
dri secten. Di ersten heist
man turchomanni di
halden machameti e
unde habin eyn besun
dir sprache und eyn sito
de. unde sint eynueldic.
unde lebin von deme
vie. Do sint gar gute
pfert unde mule. Di
andirn unde di dritten
sint kriechin und armi
ni dy wonen czu same
ne in den stetin und in
den vestin der do vil sint
unde lebin von kunstin
unde von koufinschacz.
ouch macht man do di
bestin unde di schonstin
teppte von der werlde.
unde siden gewant.
unde von golde tzhelt
chin gewurcht schone
und gar geneme. Sy
sint undirtenik ouch
den tartern. Do ist sa
balten di stat do gemar
tirt wart sente blasius

Ill. 2 (above): The 'Medieval Marco Polo'; c. 1370.
Stiftsbibliothek in Admont, Codex Admont, 504, F. 2vb, 3ra.

The Admont Codex is the oldest surviving German version. It corresponds word for word to the Ottimo-manuscript, being expanded only to include a geographic description of the location and a reference to St. Blasius.

The German translation, on which the following is based, is by Ulrich Köppen:[12]

"The following can be said of Turkmenia: the Turkmenian population is divided into three groups. The Turkomans are Muslims characterized by a very simple way of life and extremely crude speech. They live in the mountainous regions and raise cattle. Their horses and their outstanding mules are held in especially high regard. The other two groups, Armenians and Greeks, live in cities and forts. They make their living primarily from trade and as craftsmen. In addition to the carpets, unsurpassed and more splendrous in colour than anywhere else in the world, silks in all colours are also produced there. This country, about which one might easily tell much more, is subject to the Khan of the eastern Tatar Empire."

One of the earliest German versions is available to us in the Middle German Marco Polo, the Codex Admont. 504[13] from c. 1370, where the following, rendered into current English, can be read (F. 2vb-3ra; ill. 2):

"Of Turkmenia

Turkmenia is located near the two Armenias. It is inhabited by three sects. The first are the Turkomans. They worship Mohammed and have a special language and are characterized by a certain coarseness. They are simple and obtain their livelihood raising cattle. They have very good horses and mules. The second and third sects are composed of Greeks and Armenians, who live together in the towns and forts, of which there are many. They work as craftsmen and traders. Here the world's best and most beautiful carpets are made, and lovely and appealing silken garments as well, richly woven with gold. They are also subject to the Tatars. Here is the town where St. Blasius died a martyr."

These texts coincide to a large extent with the first printed German versions of the Marco Polo text, these being 'Das puch des edeln Ritters vnd landtfarers Marcho polo, das do sagt von mangerley wunder der landt und lewt,' Nuremberg 1477[14] (ill. 3) or the 'Chorographia Tatariae oder wahrhafftige Beschreibung der vberaus wunderbahrlichen Reise,' printed in Leipzig in 1611[15] (ill. 4).

IR vernumē habt von dem kleynē ermīnia· Nun wol-
len wir sagen von dem grossen | in dem wonet dreyer-
ley volck | vn̄ peten machomet an | vn̄ sein vō grober
zungen | vn̄ wonen in dem gepirg oder eben dar nach sie dan̄
weyd zu dem viech finden · Si haben auch gar schöne pfer-
de vnd mewler · Die andern zwey geschlechte oder volck
das seyn ermini vnd kriechen die wonen pey eynander | vnd
leben von iren hantwercken vnd kauffmanschacz | do mach-
et man die schönsten tebich vnd auch guldene tücher · In
dem landt seyn vil schöner stett · In dem landt ward auch
gemartert sandt Blasy | das landt ist vntertan dem keyser
der tartarey von dem auffgang der sunnen | das ist der groß
Cham von Cathay | der peseczte das land vnd stett mit
hernn nach seynem willen ·

Ill. 3 (right): Das puch des edeln Ritters vnd landtfarers Marcho polo, das do sagt von mangerley wunder der landt und lewt. . . printed by Fricz Creußner, Nuremburg 1477. Bayrische Staatsbibliothek in Munich, no. 2° Inc.c.a.652ᶜ, F. 7v, 8r.

A mere 22 years after the completion of the Gutenberg Bible and the invention of the art of printing, the Marco-Polo text was printed. This is the best proof of how current this work still was 180 years after it was originally written down.

Quotations of passages from Abulféda and Ibn Battuta[16] suffered a similar fate with their content being altered as well. The meaning of Ibn Battuta's account was actually stood on its head, and rendered as saying that even the 'Aksaray carpets' were exported to 'the land of the Turks.'

We should emphasize the importance of the term 'Aksaray carpets', which was a trade name[17], having nothing to do with Konya.[18] In the 13th as well as perhaps the 14th century, Aksaray was the residence of the Mongolian Khans in central Anatolia. To this day, not a shred of evidence has been found to substantiate the contention that Seljuks produced carpets in Anatolia. The fact that a few carpets were found in the Alâeddin-Mosque in Konya[19] is insufficient proof.

It is surprising that Kurt Erdmann paid no attention whatsoever to the most important sources for his research on early carpets. There is a collection of material, which first appeared between 1942–1951 in the periodical ARS ISLAMICA and is of central importance for this work. Here, all oriental sources – in this case primarily Arabian – from the 6th to the 13th century and beyond are assessed:[20]

R.B. Serjeant: ISLAMIC TEXTILES
Material for a history up to the Mongol Conquest

The importance of this book lies in the fact that it allows us to understand the true meaning of frequently cited sources. The source material considered thus far consists predominantly of Arabian texts in the English 19th century translations. The term *'carpet'* used in these translations, and automatically rendered *'Teppich'* by German authors, is altogether unsatisfactory. True, in the present author's linguistic community of southern Germany one finds the everyday term 'Teppich' serving to describe any number of things that might be used as coverings, ranging from bedspreads or table cloths to wall-hangings and including all kinds of cloth floor coverings. These items correspond generally to all those for which the term *'carpet'* is used to refer in the translations. For this reason alone many references based on translations into English are irrelevant.

In this connection the lexical combinations incorporating the word 'mahfur' deserve special attention. 'Mahfur' is the participle of 'hafara'. 'Hafara' means literally in English 'to dig,' 'to dig up', 'to engrave'. In his translation Serjeant used the words 'raised' and 'in relief'. The word 'mahfur' can have both a negative and a positive meaning spatially. 'Dug up' can likewise be used to mean 'raised up', or 'roughed up'. Since the lexical combination 'Armani mahfur' is a synonym for 'Armeniatica stronglomaletaria', 'mahfur' could be translated (when used to describe textiles) as 'long-fibred', or 'long-pile'.

In any case the word *'mahfur'* was used especially in order to distinguish and mark floor textiles exhibiting a 'raised', 'raised up', 'roughed up' surface – characteristics which can only be appropriately applied to *knotted-pile carpets.*[21]

In fact the English word *'carpet'* stands for the Arabian expressions listed below with the following meanings:

in die Tatarey / das I. Buch. 31

Von dem Land Turcomania, vor zeiten Cilicia, vnd Caramania, genandt.

Das 12. Capitel.

TVrcomania iſt eine Landſchafft von einem geſamleten Volck zu ſammen geleſen / aus Griechen / Armeniern / vnd Caramanien. Sie haben ein eigne Sprach / vnd geleben des verfluchten Mahomets geſatz. Es iſt ein vngeſchickt grob Bäwriſch Volck / das wohnet hin vnnd wieder in Bergen vnd Thälern / ſonderlich erwehlen ſie jhnen wohnungen / da gute Weid iſt / dann ſie haben viel Viehes / Schaff / Kühe / Säw / vnd Camelthier / die ſind bey jhnen in groſſen werth. Die Griechen vnd Armenier die bey jhnen wohnen / die haben Städt vnd Flecken / da haben ſie jhr arbeit im ſeiden Werck / da macht man die köſtlichen vnnd ſchönſten Teppichen in der Welt. Sie haben viel Städt / vnter denen ſeind die fürnembſten / Cogno / (vorzeiten Iconium genant) Cæſarea / vnd Sebaſte / da S. Blaſius vmb Chriſtus willen gelitten hat / Vnd haben einen Herrn / der iſt dem Keyſer der Tartarn / vnterthänig.

Ill. 4 (above): Marco Polo: 'Chorographica Tatariae oder warhafftige Beschreibung der vberaus wunderbahrlichen Reise'; Leipzig, 1611. Württ. Landesbibliothek in Stuttgart, no. Geogr.8° 5479, F. 31,32.

This version, printed 134 years later, conforms to the original in content. The geographic explanation 'once called Cilicia, and Karamania' is a reference to Armenia (Cilicia was the Kingdom of Armenia Minor); 'Karamania' shows the current affiliation to the Sultanate of Karamania.

Armanī: frequent abbreviation for maḥfūr
Armanī maḥfūr: Armenian *knotted-pile carpets*
Arminiya: a special kind of Armenian *knotted-pile carpets*
bisāṭ (Plural: busut): textile floor covering
busut *maḥfūra:* knotted-pile
busāṭ: large textile floor covering
darānik (dūrank, durnūk): two-coloured cover, blanket, cloth
Djahramī: material for covers, blankets, cloths
farsh: material for covering (i.e. upholstery)
fursh: material for covering, furniture cover
ḳālī: floor carpets, used as later abbreviation for:
ḳālī-hā-yi-*maḥfūrī:* Armenian knotted-pile carpets
maḥfūrī (Pl. āt): knotted-pile carpets
miṭraḥ (Pl. maṭāriḥ): Armenian rectangular carpet
nakhkh (Pl. nakhākh, nikhākh, ankhākh): runner, probable frequent synonym for *Armanī maḥfūr*
namaṭ (Pl. anmāṭ): blanket, coverlet, bedspread
naṭ' (Pl. anṭā'): embroidered covers, blankets, cloths
shādurvān: large wall-hangings
ṭinfisa (Pl. ṭanāfis): Greek or Byzantine cover, blanket, cloth
zarbīya (zurbīya): Armenian (?) flat-weave
zīlū: Armenian flat-weave, quite possibly today's 'Zili' and 'Sileh', also used in place of 'ḳālī'
zullīya (Pl. zalālī): Armenian flat-weave, quite possibly today's 'Soumak'

The acceptability of the term 'prayer-rug', translated as 'Gebetsteppich' in German, to stand for the Arabian expression *'musalla'* (pl. musallayat), is also questionable. This Arabian expression, similar to 'carpet' or 'Teppich', can be used to refer to a variety of things. A 'musalla' can be a piece of embroidery, (brocaded) velvet or any kind of flat-weave. No lexical combination with 'mahfur' could be found in Serjeant's book, making it impossible to prove that knotted prayer-rugss were in existence during the time preceding the Mongol invasion.

An analysis of Serjeant's book with regard to these 'mahfuri' provides us with an exact overview of the propagation of knotted-pile carpets from the 6th up to the 13th centuries and even later. They are first mentioned in *Ibn Khaldun,* a summary of the lists of taxes paid in kind from a book entitled *Djirab al-Dawla* by one Ahmed ibn

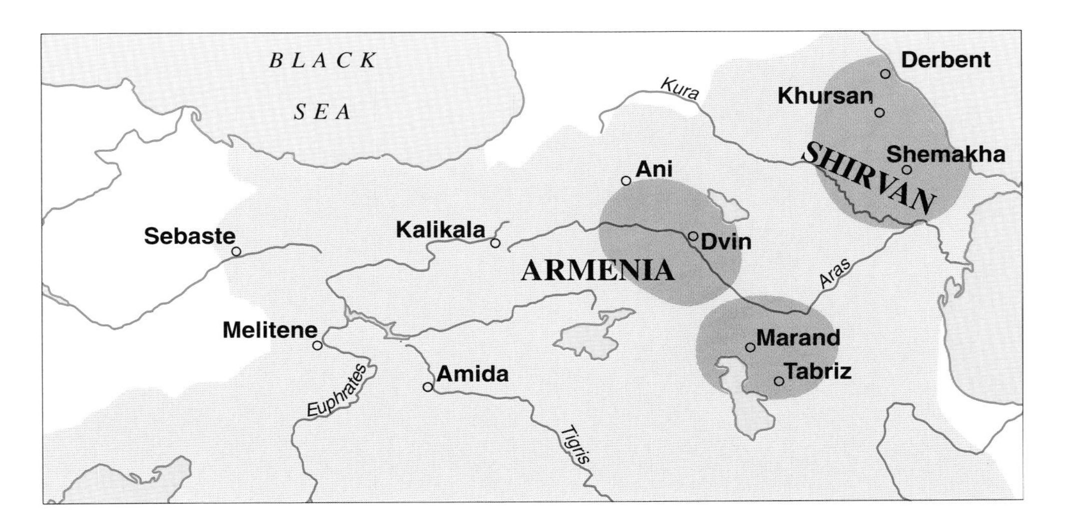

Ill. 5 (right): Production centres of knotted-pile carpets within the region influenced by Armenian culture during the 10th century.

The map, based on information provided by Serjeant's work, shows the Armenian weaving centres from as early as the 10th century. These, today located in Russian Armenia, Azerbaijan, Persia and Turkey, remained the most important Armenian weaving centres for 1,000 years, or up until the genocidal acts of this century.

'Abd al-Hamid, from the time of Ma'mun's reign *at the end of the 8th century.* Here his lists indicate that Armenia *had to deliver 20 carpets* (busut mahfura) *annually to the caliph of Baghdad as tax.* This is further elaborated on by *Tha'alibi* (prior to 1021), who reports that *at this time* Armenia was required to deliver, in addition to other taxes, *30 carpets* (busut mahfura) to the Bujidian Sultan. In the year 768 *Tabari* mentions an *Arminiya,* an Armenian carpet.

Károly Gombos cites the Arabian historian Muhammed *Barishini,*[22] who writes that in 911 Emir Jusuf Abu-Sadsch sent, among other items, *seven Armenian carpets* to his caliph Muhtaschir.

A very early reference to Armenian knotted carpets can be found in the 'Enzyklopädie des Orientteppichs.'[23] Iten-Maritz quotes *N. Adontz* to the effect that in 813 the Bulgarian King Krum took *Armeniatika Stronglomaletaria* (Armenian woollen pile carpets) as booty while scouting in the Orient. This same source also mentions the historian *Bayhaki,* who in 1025 writes that *Mahmoud of Ghazna* presented the ruler of East Turkestan, Kadir Khan, with valuable *Armenian carpets.*

Further Armenian pile carpets are cited in 'ISLAMIC TEXTILES': in the *Hudud al-'Alam* and by *Makdisi* (Mukaddisi) as well as *Ibn Haukal,* the latter two in the 10th century. *Ibn Haukal* associates the production of the *Armani mahfur* with certain locations: *Marand, Tabriz, Dabil* (Dwin) and other districts in Armenia. The *Province*

Ill. 6: Armenia from around 70 B.C.

The map shows the greatest extent of the state territory of Armenia at the time of Tigrane II.

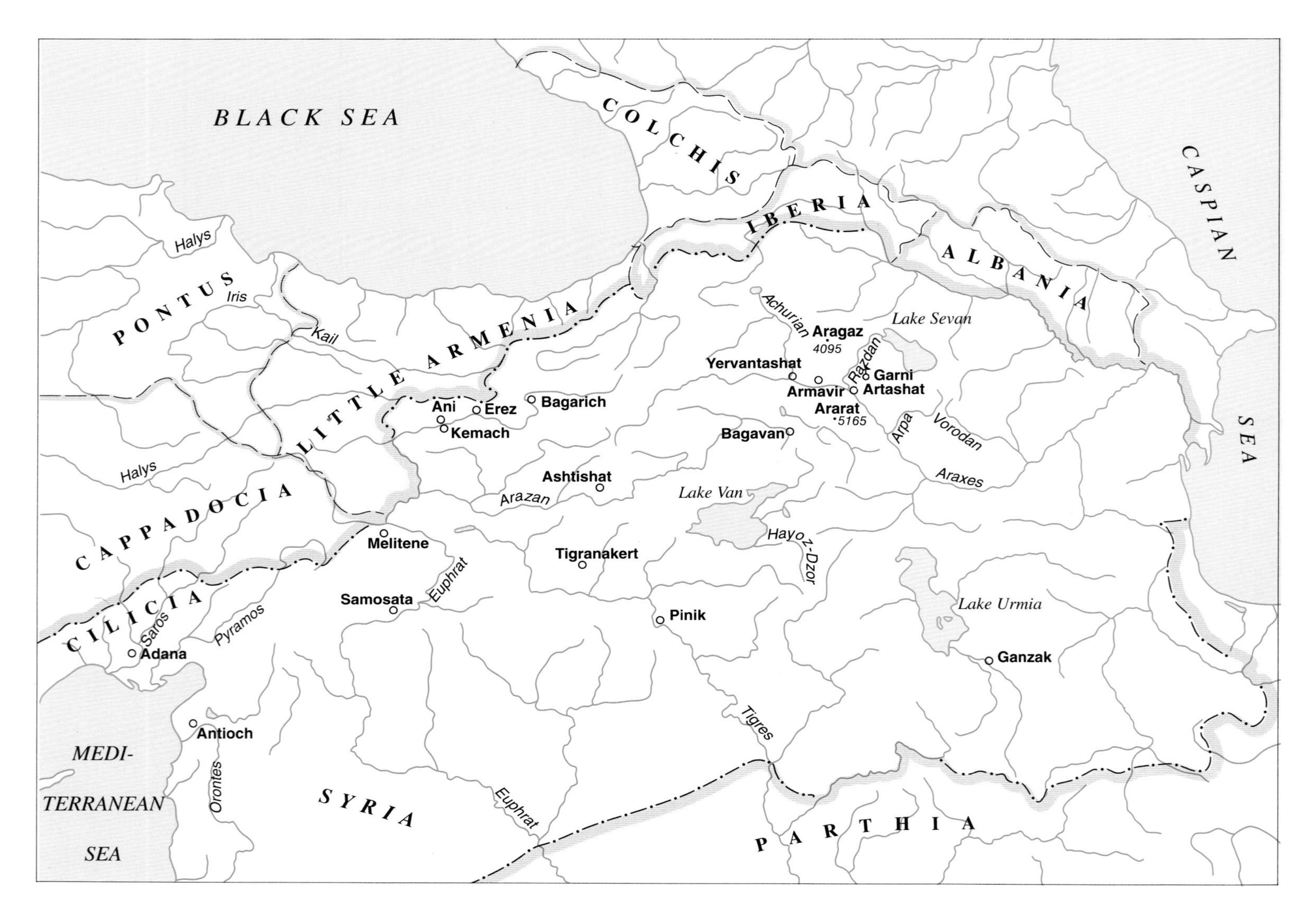

of Shirvan in *Hudud* is mentioned by name, with the towns *Shirvan, Khursan* and *Derbent* being specified as production centres for *mahfuri.*

The invasion of the Seljuks in 1071 appears to have seriously impaired and partially destroyed the majority of the weaving centres in Armenia. In the region of West Armenia only *Kalikala,* Arzan-al-Rum (Erzerum), is mentioned. This may well have been the only weaving centre on the territory of the Ikonium Sultanate. The Arabian expression *kali* for Armenian carpets, becoming *hali* in Turkish, is derived from this. The production centres of *Dwin* (Dabil), famous for the purple carpets[24] produced there, *Tabriz,*[25] and those in the *region of Shirvan* seem to be the only ones in the region of East Armenian cultural influence to have survived.

For the time up until the High Middle Ages, these remain the only references pertaining to the production of knotted-pile carpets. They take into account the entire region of the Orient, including the Near East and Asia, where Arabs did their trading.

Ibn Haukal writes that outside of the Orient knotted-pile carpets *(mahfur) were produced in Andalusia* in the *10th century* and that these resembled the best of the very expensive Armenian knotted carpets. The production centre was located in the district of *Murcia,* in the city of Murcia, in Tantala and in Alsh. This is the area of the Greek colony Hemeroskopeion, which was later to become the western Gothic province of Theodemir. As the Province of Todmir, this area was able to maintain its independence and its bishopric seat even under the Umayyaden.

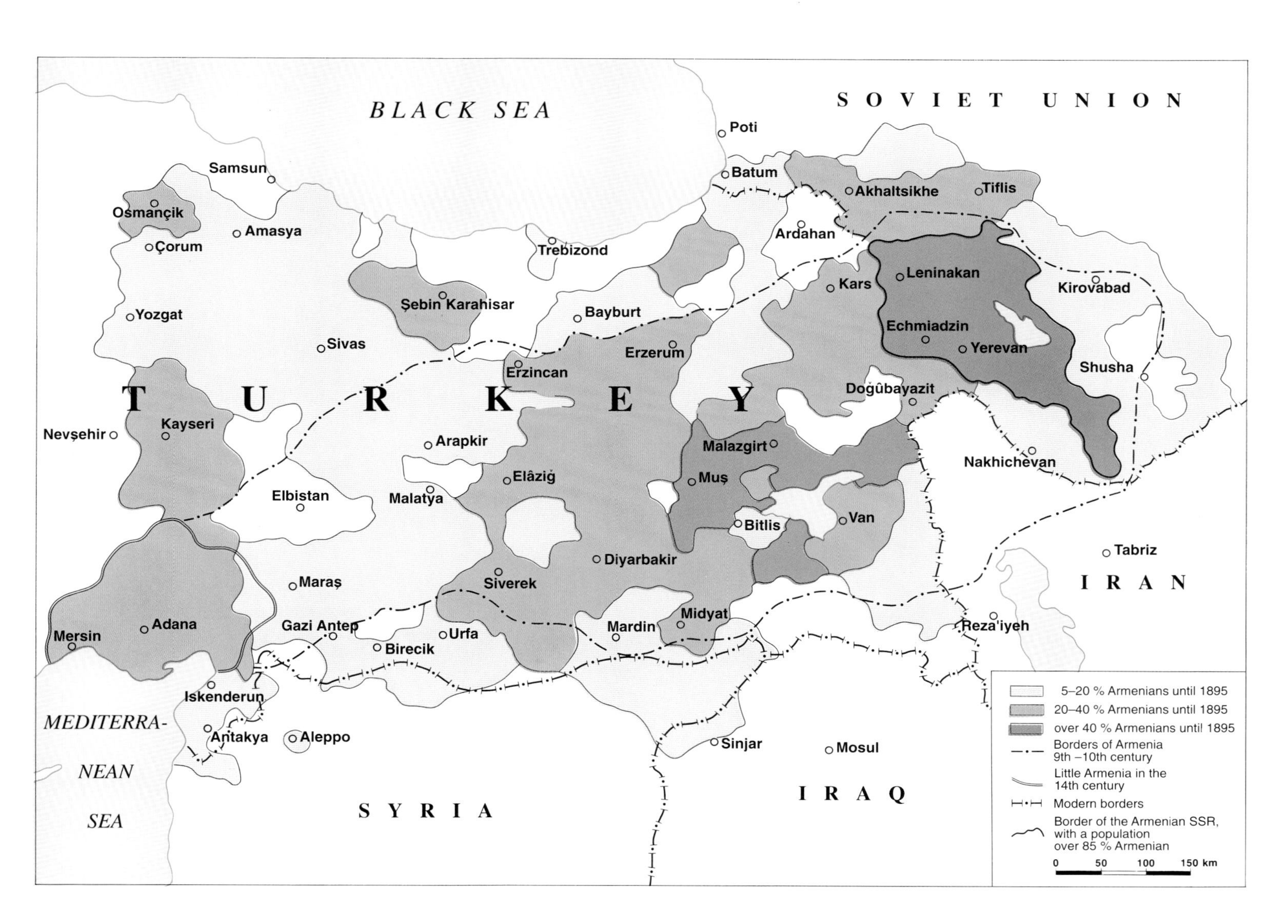

Ill. 7 (below): The distribution of Armenians in the Caucasus, central and western Anatolia before 1895.

A comparison with the map in ill. 6 shows that even after 2,000 years the Armenian area of culture and settlement was still preserved. The denser population in the west, i.e. in the regions of Karahisar, Osmancik, Kayseri and in Cilicia, can be attributed to the big wave of emigration during the 10th and 11th centuries, which was brought on by the Seljuk invasion. More than half of the Armenian population found new homes here and in western Anatolia.

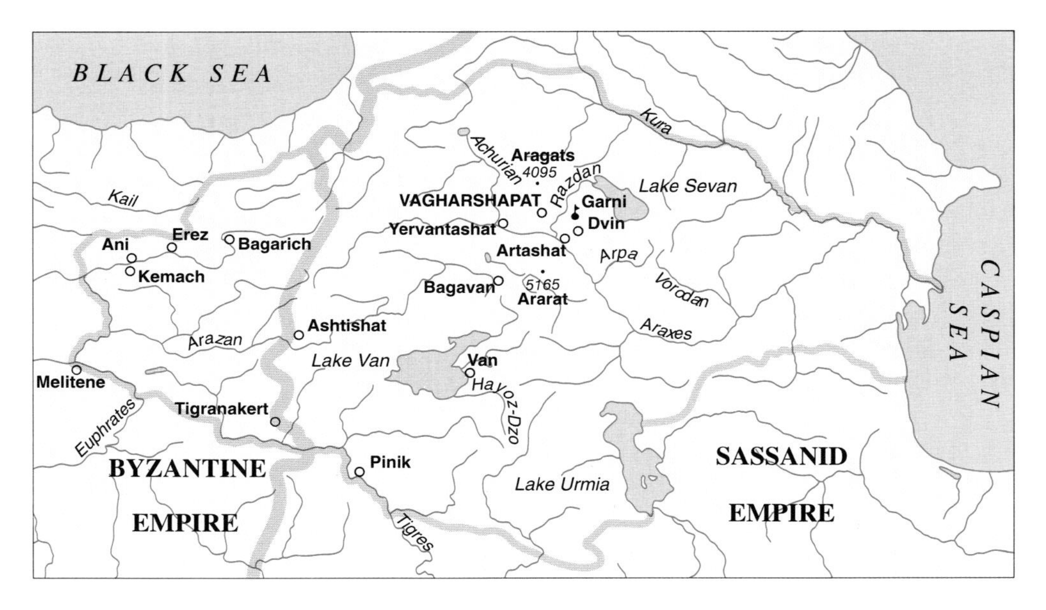

Ill. 8 (left): The division of Armenia between Byzantium and Persia in the year A D 387

Most of what made up the core of the Armenian territory belonged to Persia after the division of 387. This fact along with the rejection of a Byzantine hierarchy of the 'God-Emperor-Church' facilitated quite considerably the formation of an independent Armenian state church.

If we now pause a moment to summarize what has thus far been said, we clearly see that through the High Middle Ages pile carpets were produced exclusively in the cultural sphere of Armenia and in Spain. The ancient historians make no mention of carpets being produced in West Turkestan, something Erdmann was quite convinced of, although goods from as far away as China and India were certainly not uncommon.

The expression 'Armenian sphere of cultural influence' should be talken to mean the geo-ethnological area of Armenian settlement before 1895, not a political state. As may be seen on the maps in ills. 6 and 7, at the beginning of this century there was

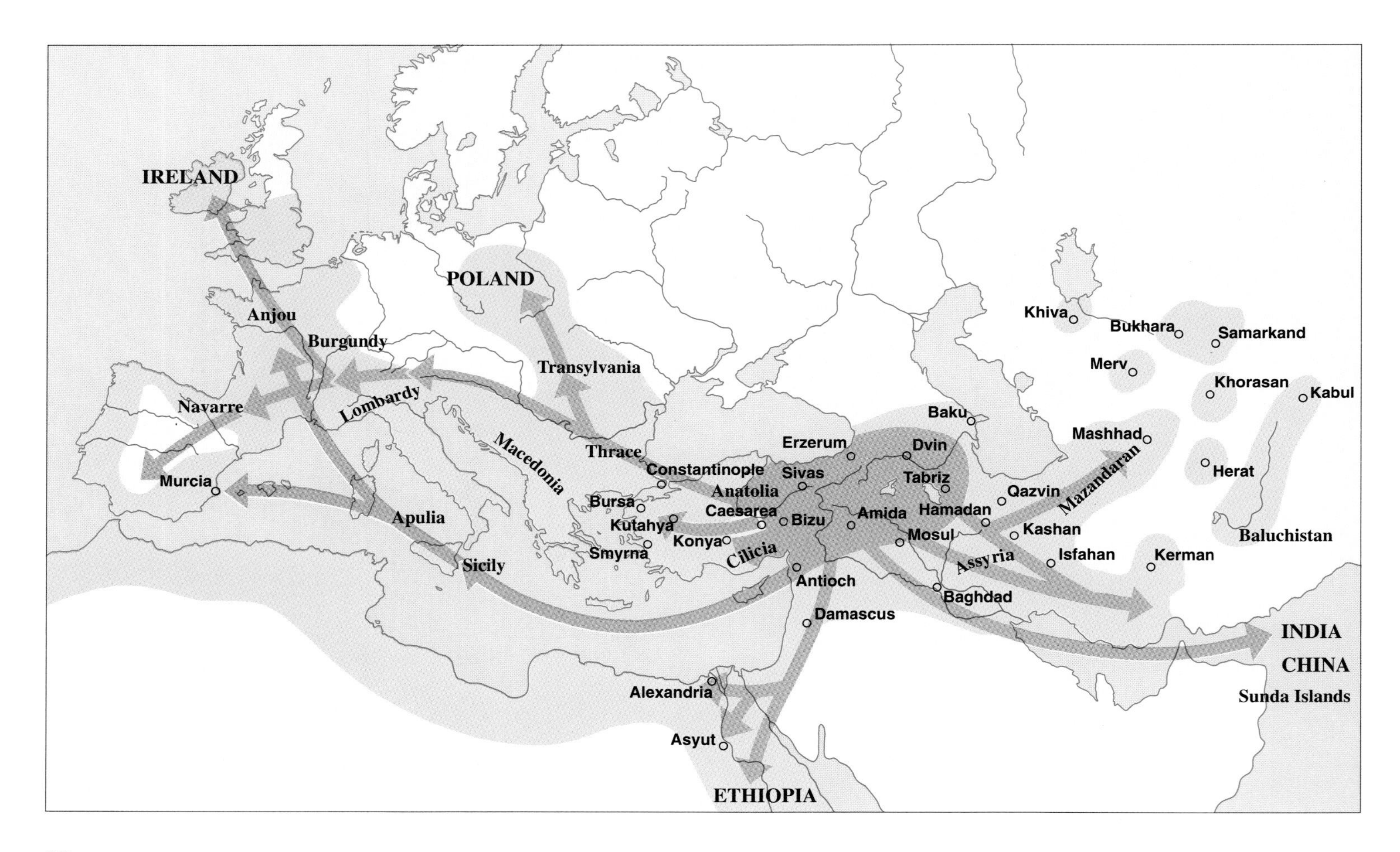

still a large degree of correspondence with the Armenian territory under Tigran II, under whom the geographical expression Armenia became firmly established. In addition to the policies of enforced resettlement to southern Persia and the regions of northern Greece, there were three great waves of emigration, the result of which was that Armenians settled not only in Asia Minor but also in Italy, France and Spain. The threat of the Seljuks resulted in large numbers of people emigrating to the west, where the Wilayet Sivas, the area around of Kayseri, Smyrna (Izmir), the Taurus mountains and Cilicia, northern Greece, and the Carpathian countries became centres with a high concentration of Armenian inhabitants. Beyond this we not only find Armenian emigrants in Syria, Egypt, all the coastal cities of the Mediterranean, but also in Persia, India, on the Sunda Islands and in China. Blood relationships in France and Sicily[26] resulted from numerous marriages made during the first crusade of 1095.

Erdmann's second premise, the nomadic-tribal hypothesis, claims a nomadic origin for carpets. The central idea here is that the knotted-pile carpet was created by the nomads as a way of replicating the hides of animals, of which they had an insufficient supply, in order – as the story goes – to compensate for the lack of felt carpets. Both assumptions, shortage of animal hides and the absence of felt carpets, are obviously false. Those members of the population providing for themselves exclusively by raising cattle were well supplied with hides at all times. The hides resulting from the slaughter of these animals alone, necessary as a source of food for the nomads, provided them with more than enough to meet their own needs. Likewise, the assertion that felt carpets were to be found only in the east proves untenable once we consider Serjeant's material. On the contrary, it must be emphasized that felt carpets had been distributed widely, from Armenia to parts as far away as China. Their alleged absence in West Turkestan cannot have been the reason for the emergence of the knotted-pile carpet.

If, hypothetically, carpets were to have replicated hides, then certainly not as proposed by Erdmann: as hide-substitute floor coverings. In fact, the idea that one might have sought to help one's guests keep their feet clean of the dirt of the floor by covering it with a carpet does not seem an entirely plausible explanation. It was actually just the opposite: one expected one's guests to remove their shoes before stepping on the carpet in order to keep it clean.

One might possibly regard the famous mythical 'Golden Fleece' as a hide imitation; however, in that case the hide substitute was *a symbol, a sign of power and authority*. Were this true of the hides discussed above, the substitute would be an intensification of the symbolic means of the hides of predators by value of which gods and heroes in the images on Greek vases and in mosaics demonstrate their strength and superiority.

Ill. 9 (left): Resettlement and emigration up until the High Middle Ages.

The map is the result of decades spent by the author studying the source material he was given access to on Armenian history. It takes into account all the waves of emigration, the relocation, deportation and new settlements from the beginning of the first millennium to the 12th century. See also ill. 345.

Even one of the oldest, though indirect, references to carpets points in this direction: when Christ entered Jerusalem, his apostles spread their clothing out before him, not having any carpets at their disposal, and announced his coming by calling, "Hosanna to the Son of David."[27] Regarding the carpet as a royal attribute is closely tied to references made to innumerable rulers, for example Chosroes II, whose carpet, however, was definitely not woven. A further example dates back to 1255, when the population of London was dismayed at the excessive number of carpets spread out on the floor for Eleonora of Castille's entrance into Westminster Abbey.[28]

The account of Sharaf al-Din Ali Yazdi in the 'Zafar name', writing of Timur's imperial carpet and throne-carpet, takes us another step. In Timur's absence the carpet functioned as deputy, meaning that foreign legations were permitted to kiss and pay homage to it. This leaves no further doubt: *carpets had the status of the office of the ruler.* In the provincial capitals carpets symbolized the presence of the ruler, having at the same time the character of today's embassies – they were extraterritorial. The special protection of the owner was bestowed on refugees who succeeded in reaching the carpet.

Even the red (!) carpet, which we today roll out when receiving visitors of state and stand on while listening to the national anthem, is our way of symbolically paying tribute to the authority of our guest.

Having said all this, the author finds it difficult to attribute any other function to carpets in the early times or the Middle Ages, or up through the Renaissance. They were in all likelihood *symbols of both worldly and spiritual power.*

The oldest depictions of carpets (though probably felt carpets) preserved for us in the Turfan Frescos served to portray religious and spiritual power and the glorification of Buddha (ill. 10).

Ill. 10 (left): Kyzil/East Turkestan, 6th/7th century: sermon scene; fresco. SMPK, Museum für Indische Kunst, Berlin.

The preaching Buddha is characterized by the halo, the gloriole and the (felt) carpet. This is one of the earliest representations in which a carpet is used to symbolize spiritual power.

Ill. 11 (right): Manichean book page from Cotscho, 8th/9th century: representation of the Bema festival, painting on paper; 25.5 x 12.4 cm, detail. SMPK, Museum für Indische Kunst, Berlin; MIK III 4979 v.

It is suspected that the splendrous furnishing of Manichean cult rooms, as well as the appealing vividness of illustrated manuscripts (as in this case with the depiction of a carpet) had a great influence on their Christian counterparts.

Whereas in the late Hellenistic period of the Christian cult religious and spiritual power were symbolized quite early on by depicting an empty throne, Manichean illuminated manuscripts of the 7th century show (analogous to the Turfan-Frescos) the carpet in this symbolic function (ill. 11). If we are right in assuming that early Christian illuminated manuscripts represented an answer to the challenge of the Manichean tradition of illumination,[29] then we cannot exclude the possibility that in Asia Minor, an area where Manichean traditions were indigenous, the Manicheans adopted the carpet as a symbol of spiritual power. It is quite conceivable for them to have then taken this concept from there via Mani to East Turkestan. Although we cannot provide a definitive proof for this question here, it is, however, a fact that the Armenian textile tradition offered nearly perfect conditions for this to happen: carpets serve as excellent symbolic vehicles regardless of the technique used in their production, and as such the knotted-pile carpet stands out as particularly precious.

In light of the preceding discussion it comes as no surprise that in the early Middle Ages carpets were used to characterize not only worldly power, but also spiritual meaning (ills. 12–15). Innumerable pictures show the places of worship of the Christian cult decorated with carpets: on the altar, as antependium, on the steps to the altar, and draped decoratively over the lectern. The importance of church dignitaries, the Virgin Mary as well as the saints, was stressed by the use of carpets. We also notice that in Sienese and Florentine painting from the close of the 13th century to the beginning of the 15th century, the Eucharist began to appear against the backdrop of a carpet at precisely the time that the expression INRI at the top of the cross – Jesus of Nazareth, King of the Jews – came into use (ills. 137, 138).

This gives rise to the question as to whether it would not be reasonable to entertain the possibility that the carpets used and depicted so plentifully in the Christian cult might not actually have been produced for this very purpose. It is clear that this idea would stand in opposition to the previous practice of attributing them only to Islamic art, something which their assumed Turkmen-Seljuk production had never called into question. On the other hand, it is not merely a matter of just one or two examples, but rather of a relatively large number, it is documented that Armenian Chris-

Ill. 12 (above): 'Girart-Master', Burgundy, c. 1447/50.
Illumination in: 'Die Taten des Girart von Roussillon', F. 6r: Jean Vauquelin presents his book to Duke Philip the Good of Burgundy.
Nationalbibliothek, Vienna, Austria, codex 2549.

The 'coat-of-arms carpet' of the Duke of Burgundy may have been a knotted-pile carpet. It is more important, however, that the carpet in this miniature symbolizes temporal power. The correspondence in form with the paintings of the Madonna in ills. 13, 169, 171 and 173 is clear.

tians produced carpets from the 8th century up to the beginning of the present century. Furthermore, we will see that carpets showing patterns which fulfil the requirements of Christian ornamentalism predominated, and that the message they convey is unequivocally Christian.

This book represents the first attempt to write a history of the Christian oriental carpet. In specifying *Christian oriental carpets,* it is to be understood that the author is referring to carpets made by Christians, most likely by Armenians and later possibly by Syrians and Greeks, for Christians – or, to be more exact, quite possibly only for the Christian cult until the late Middle Ages.

Since the references and sources above confirm the existence of knotted-pile carpets for the first millenium in Christian Armenia, and there only, there is no need to provide justification as to why these carpets can or must be Christian or, furthermore, why the crosses and symbols found on them do not represent meaningless decoration. Should the author succeed in showing that the carpets handed down from the past make up part of a long chain of traditional pattern and design, a chain unbroken in its development within the Armenian sphere of cultural influence from the first

Ill. 13 (above): Hans Memling: The mystical wedding of St. Catherine. 1479. Memlingmuseum in Bruges.

Analogous to the 'coat-of-arms carpet' in the preceding illustration, this Christian carpet makes the same claim to symbolize spiritual power.

millennium B.C. until the present, being spread from there into far reaches of Asia and Europe; and should the author furthermore succeed in showing that the symbolism present in these carpets is explicitly Christian, then the thesis of this study will have been borne out.

The distinction between the carpets we are discussing here and those produced for Islamic customers is easily defined (ills. 16–21).

At this point let us juxtapose two carpets: the 'Gohar carpet' (ill. 17, see also p. 350) and one in the Österreichisches Museum für angewandte Kunst, Vienna (ill. 16).

Ill. 14 (above): Hans Holbein the Younger: Georg Gisze; 1532. SMPK in Gallery of Paintings, Berlin.

The carpet in the portrait of a merchant demonstrates the worldly honor and the importance that representatives of trade had attained within the empire.

Ill. 15 (page 27): Master of St. Gilles: Mass at St. Gilles; c. 1500. National Gallery, London, no. 4681.

For the decoration of the Christian place of worship carpets with Christian symbols were also always in use. These, along with other devices and furnishings of splendour, were to make the unusual spiritual significance of this room obvious to all.

Ill. 17 (right): 'Gohar' carpet, 351 x 178 cm. In private ownership.

The 'Gohar' carpet is dated 1680 and bears an Armenian inscription. In its centre we see the cross incorporated into a 'tree of Jesse' composition.

Ill. 16 (left): WÖMAK no. T OR 348, 263 x 168 cm, Österr. Museum für angewandte Kunst, Vienna.

The Viennese carpet is one of the very few early Islamic carpets. Though in its centre it has kept its much deformed cruciform, the field has been filled with the 'names' of Allah and thus marked as Moslem. It must have been produced during the 16th century by Armenians who had converted to Islam.

Ill. 18 (page 30): TIEM no. 760, Turk ve Islam Eserleri Müzesi, Istanbul.

In contrast to the Christian arch-form or paradise-gate carpets (cf. especially ill. 683) this Moslem prayer rug foregoes all Christian symbols and instead shows an illustration of the Kaaba in the middle arch panel. The carpet was presumably made during the 16th century.

Ill. 19 (page 31): 'Gorzi' carpet, missing.

Although, in terms of the evolution of designs, the 'Gorzi' carpet is a relatively late Armenian arch-form carpet, it stands as a document of great importance because of its inscription and the date it shows (cf. caption to ill. 680).

Ill. 20 (left): TIEM no. 287, TIEM, Istanbul.

This Moslem prayer rug, too, shows the Kaaba in order to distinguish itself clearly from Christian carpets, whose Armenian border it kept.

Ill. 21 (right): MMA no. 17.120.124, 162 x 107 cm. Metropolitan Museum of Art, New York. The Fletcher Fund.

The Moslem prayer rug from what was formerly the Fletcher Collection likewise does without Christian symbolism, even though the 'cloud-bands' still remind us of the original design; instead, its pediment field is filled with the 'names' of Allah. The carpet is thought to have originated during the first part of the 16th century, although the time of production itself is still a subject of controversy.

Ill. 22: Crosses: Basic form types A-D_2

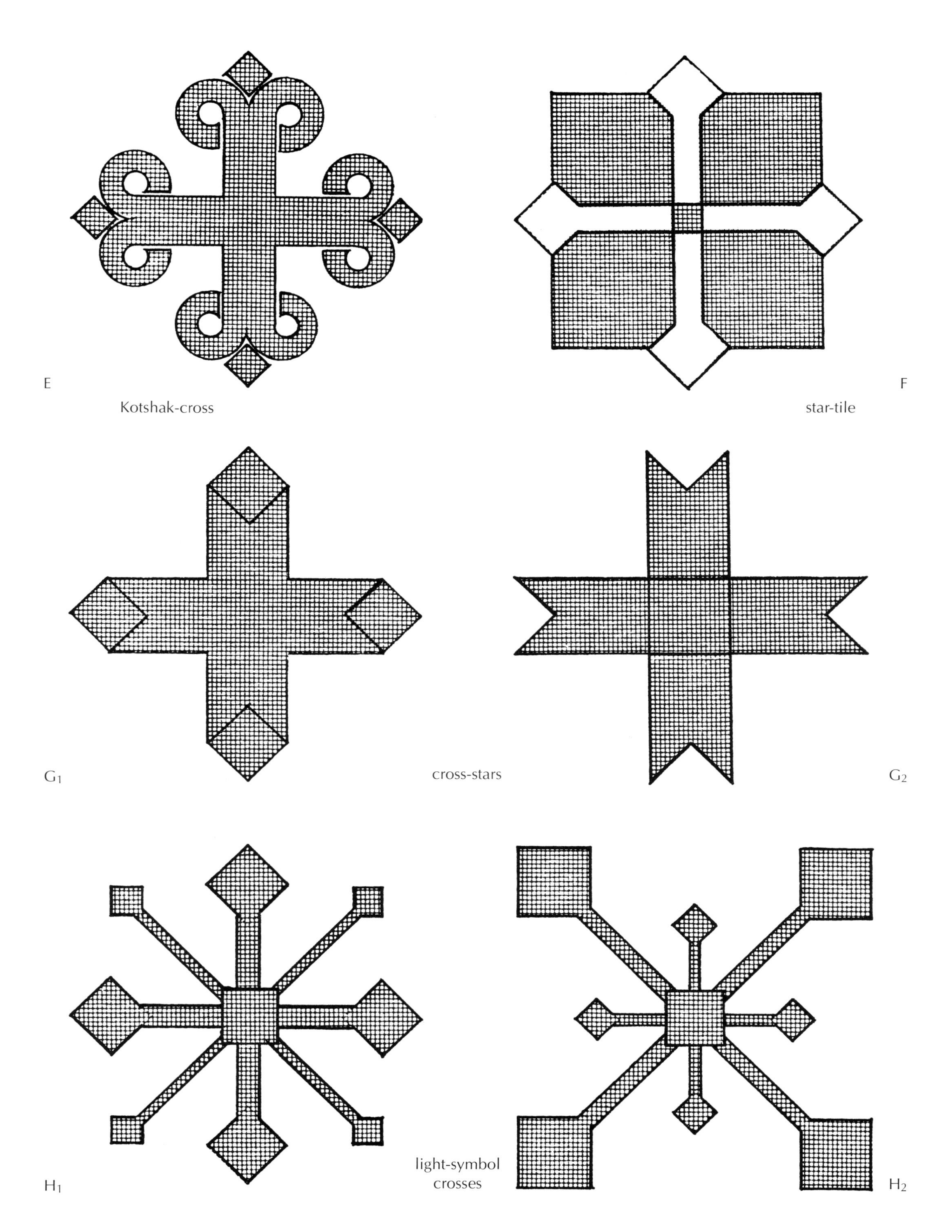

Ill. 23: Crosses: Basic form types E-H_2

Ill. 24: Boteh from a south Persian carpet fragment (Afshari region south of Kirman), 125 x 110 cm, 17th/18th century. Owned privately.

So far the earliest known boteh design in a carpet is a 'tree of Jesse' composition, in the centre of which an Armenian cross is located.

Ill. 25: Boteh from a south Persian carpet (Qashqai region of the Fars province), 274 x 194 cm, 18th century. Kunstauktionshaus Dr. Fritz Nagel, Stuttgart (297/3392).

The cruciform is still clearly visible; the 'tree of Jesse', however, has become more floral. Worthy of note here are the two sets of two Armenian ԴԴ -letter-number symbols (four all in all), separated by a cross.

Ill. 26: Boteh from a south Persian carpet (Qashqai region of the Fars province), 132 x 96 cm, 19th century. Eberhart Herrmann, Munich.

In c. 1800 the boteh was transformed into a wonderful florid composition, which, however, nonetheless contains all the plant symbols pertaining to the Virgin Mary.

Although in the case of the latter piece the original cross composition can still be recognized as such, the carpet has been inscribed with the 99 names of Allah in order clearly to define it in its Islamic function. We find that the same thing has happened when we compare the 'Gorzi carpet' (ill. 19, see also p. 484), an Armenian arch-form carpet of Christian origin, with Islamic prayer carpets (ills. 18, 20, 21). Islamic prayer carpets avoid the use of obvious Christian symbolism and colour, replacing them instead with what are equally clear Islamic symbols such as the representation of the Kaaba or the name of Allah. The same is true of carpets produced for the Jewish faith. In the wake of the continuing, repeatedly enforced Islamization during the 18th century, many symbols lost their original meaning and began to lose their impact, only to be given new vitality, and to be imbued with new life, at the conclusion of this phase. Thus, among other things, what had once been half crosses became birds; cross-rosettes were transformed into flowers, and the 'tree of Jesse' into 'botehs' (ills. 24–27) – a phenomenon that can be observed from Anatolia and Persia to Turkestan, and is reflected in the purely descriptive taxonomy of numerous designs.

Ill. 27: Boteh from a south Persian carpet (Fars region), 155 x 105 cm, 19th century. Private collection.
The boteh design can appear in a more animated form in rare cases from the 19th century. The meaning of this new bird design still remains a mystery.

Despite their myriad appearances, the actual number of symbols found in these Christian carpets is very limited. The cross designs are derived from a limited set of basic designs (ills. 22, 23), with the cross-star G_2 and, by extension, the light-symbol cross H_1 being of central importance. As symbols they represent the epiphany, divine vision.
Characteristic, specifically Armenian symbols are also the S-and E-shapes. The S-shaped symbol is the first letter of the Armenian word տեր, which means God

Ill. 28: 'S'-symbol from a central Anatolian arch-form carpet, 194 x 106 cm, late 19th century. Kunstauktionshaus Dr. Fritz Nagel, Stuttgart (319/3447).

Despite the fact that the lilies of grace, located above the arch field in earlier carpets (cf. ills. 675, 679), are now positioned head down underneath – thus showing a certain ignorance of traditions – the red colour of Christ in the arch panel complements the Armenian S-symbol for God. For this reason this late example is also clearly identifiable as Christian.

the Almighty (ills. 28, 29). The E-shape is both the Old Armenian short form for 'HE', meaning the Almighty, and at the same time the first letter of the word **Յիսուս** , which means 'Jesus'[30] (ills. 30, 31).
These symbols are almost always used apotropaically, in keeping with pre-Christian traditions. Since their interpretation and meaning are closely tied to an awareness of the Armenian alphabet, and furthermore, since, in addition to carpets, they appear in all branches of the visual arts, we can assume that they were used only by Armenians copies notwithstanding.

These two Armenian letter-symbols, to which apotropaic powers are ascribed, have meaning at different levels. Presumably it was precisely on account of these inner meanings, derived from pre-Christian traditions of the 4th century, that they became connected with the most important words in the Christian cult at the time the Armenian alphabet was created. In this way it was possible for the new cult to preserve the form and content of symbols handed down through time without a break in continuity.
In representations of the 'S', Armenians see not only the sign of God, but also the representation of the dragon. To our western way of thinking this is contradictory and difficult to relate to. Whereas in almost all European, Oriental and even late

Ill. 29 (above): 'S'-symbols in a central Armenian carpet, 250 x 108 cm. 18th century or earlier. Eberhart Herrmann, Munich.
Ill. 30 (middle): 'E'-symbols from a central Armenian Kilim, 192 x 113 cm, 'light' diamond-detail, end of the 19th century. Owned privately.
Ill. 31 (right): 'E'-symbols and 'S'-symbols on the body of the phoenix, detail from ill. 294.

Armenian myths, the dragon is an evil creature of darkness and water, only to be defeated with God's help, in Armenia there is a second, older dragon, whose attributes are the complete opposite. It symbolizes goodness and wisdom as guardian of the water, personifies power, and affords projection against injustice and evil.[31] The idea of the dragon as the divine incarnate can be traced back to the old mythologies of rulers, which were common in Mesopotamia and the Caucausus and most certainly among the Parthians as well. Yet there are also connections with the east, with China, very likely as a result of the transfer of metallurgy to that part of the world. There the dragon symbolizes for the masculine, positive Yang principle,

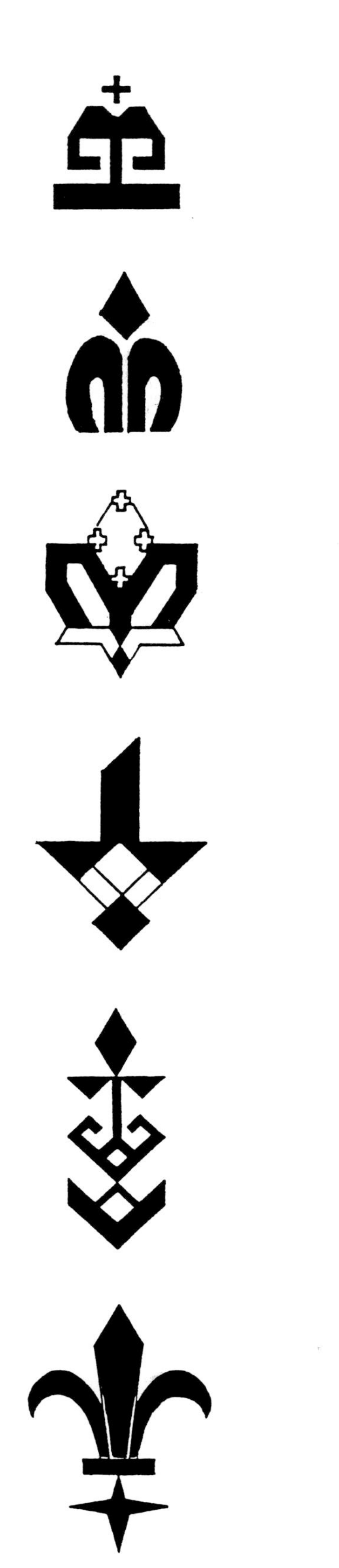

Figure 1 a-f: E-symbol designs

The series of figures in the margin above shows the evolution of the E-designs beginning with the 'tau'-'omega' from the turn of the millennium, then the lily of the 11th-13th centuries, followed by the 'acorn blossom' of the 14th/15th century, ending with the 'tree of Jesse' from the 16th century, which is followed by the tree of life.

bringing good luck.[32] In this sense the 'S'-shaped dragon was used in exactly the same way as the 'S' – as a symbol for God, often replacing the cross. In the 'S'-shape two dragons appear on the tau-shaped crutch of Armenian patriarchal staves, which appear later sometimes crowned by a cross.[33] In this design the dragon adorns the liturgical robe of the patriarch, as, in the picture of dedication of Codex 197 dating from 1287 in the Matenadaran.[34]

The 'S' and 'E'-symbols are related in a way not readily visible. The word for God begins with the Armenian 'T', which is 'S'-shaped. As a symbol, it is identical in content to the 'tau', the Hebraic symbol for the righteous, which likewise as an early Christian symbol is related to Christ[35] and to the Old Armenian 'E' which stands for HIM and means the Almighty. And in this vertical E-shape we find the Armenian 'Y', the first letter in 'Jesus'.

In early carpets we find this 'E'-shape as it appears in Fig. 1 a, in later carpets as shown in Fig. 1 b. The present author was repeatedly offered the 'lily' as an interpretation of this symbol. Due to the numerous instances of concurrence with the symbolism and thought of the Far East, the author considers, beyond the symbolism of letters, that the inclusion of the symbol for 'source', 'giving life', 'begetting' to be very probable, not only because of their visual identity, but also because of the correspondence in content with the oldest symbol of Christ, the Egyptian cross of the Copts (ill. 64). This cross adapted the Egyptian hieroglyphic for 'giving life' into the symbol of the new, Christian cult.

The 'lily' is a symbol of both Christ and the Virgin Mary. In its trifoliate shape it is a Christ-related symbol of the grace of God, as well as a formalized, abbreviated representation of the tree of life.[36] It corresponds to the Armenian design of the 'tree of Jesse.' In its early form it appears as an omega-shaped 'E' or 'root' for the cross in all Katchkars, as well as in architectural reliefs from the 7th century on – and thus as a symbol of the resurrection. Jesus, then, is the root of the cross, the beginning of new life, and so the way to paradise. Due to the interchangeable nature of concepts, we frequently find the 'tree of Jesse' in the form of the tree of life or the 'tree of paradise' in place of the cross in the illuminated manuscripts and the carpets of the early and High Middle Ages. It is usually either crowned by the cross or connected to it, or to like symbols. Once this had been brought to Europe, it began to take on figural representations, although in the case of what is probably the oldest depiction, the bronze relief of the door of San Zeno, Verona, the compositional connection to the Katchkars can still clearly be recognized.

The 'lily', as a symbol of the Virgin Mary in this form, is likewise a symbol of the Mother of God,[36] the 'panagia', the Holy Virgin, 'Our Blessed Lady.'

When all is said and done, is it a symbol of Christ or of the Virgin Mary? In contrast to the way orthodoxy or Catholicism view the use of images, to the Monophysites symbols are not related to individuals, standing instead for 'the ONE', the 'Divine'. They are all equally interchangeable. For this reason it is quite possible that the actual appearance of a symbol can encompass seemingly contradictory elements in expressing a given thought.

For example: the symbol of the fountain = source of life ('I am the life') = source of revelation ('I am the truth') = Jesus = lily symbol = divine grace = 'panagia' (Holy Virgin) = Mary = 'tree of Jesse' = omega symbol = end = beginning = resurrection = tree of life.

These explanations are, in the tantric sense, intended to promote further thought; once outside the Monophysitic region, these symbols became clearly connected to specific figures in the *Salvation legend* because they were incorporated into western ways of thinking or were superimposed on them. Hence, the lily for example, as a symbol for 'Notre Dame' = 'Our Blessed Lady', first achieved broad acceptance as a symbol for the Virgin Mary with the Templars.

The 'E'-shapes, which in the course of development to the 16th century can take on the form of any of the images presented in figures 1 a-f (see also ills. 29, 30), change subsequently to what are more or less floral designs: the 'tree of Jesse' (ills. 24–27, 305–310) or the tree of life (ills. 696, 697). For the periods during which they developed, they represent overlapping generic designs.

A further Armenian letter-symbol can be found on carpets produced in the region from East Armenia to central Asia: › ԴԴ ‹ = ›dd‹ (ills. 32 a, b). Armenians tended to use letters to stand for numbers. Thus, the Armenian letter › Դ ‹= ›d‹ is what would be for us the fourth letter of the alphabet and is used for the number '4', which, in Armenia, is a sacred number. It is always used in conjunction with statements about the relationship of the divine with the world. In like fashion we see a doubling of the '4' in an evangelistary dating from 1304[37] combined with the representation of the sun (ill. 32 b). This symbol appears four times in the central square of the 'Salor gul' (ill. 559), which is divided into four parts. In the corners of this square there are three-armed 'cloverleaf multiple crosses' opposed along the diagonal. These are located in place of the usual central cross composition, where we would normally expect to find light beams. These conceptually link the cross-multiple with the four gospels of the evangelists, in accordance with the message of the Pentecost, Matt. 28:16–20, and mean 'the pouring out of the Spirit' and/or 'proclaiming the faith.'[38]

In later, 19th century examples this symbol comes to life as a nondescript animal, sometimes with three or more legs.

A very important group of symbols depicts the 'conception of the world', the world-picture. The Armenian church was the first Christian church able to unite symbols in their physical form with their content. This is true of the cross (cf. p. 56) as well as of the cruciform domeshaped church. In the cathedral in Echmiadzin (ill. 35) a prototype was developed that is said to go back to the conception of Gregory, the founder of the religion. The floor plan is astonishing in its correspondence to a Buddhist mandala (ill. 37), in terms of both its composition and its content. Mandalas, too, can be referred to as simplified world-pictures, tantras laid out on a surface. Mandalas are to be 'walked on', either in thought or on foot. They are to be regarded as aids for those seeking revelation, the essential, 'divine' way to experience a new reality. In the mandala both the experience of the world and its subjugation are concentrated.[39] This is the first example to show clearly that very early on a spiritual connection between the tantric ideas of India and the early Christian ideas of Armenia existed. With the help of tantric modes of thought, many of the problems we Westerners have in comprehending the message of the old Oriental – and in particular the Armenian church – could be overcome.

The question has seldom been raised as to why the old conception of the world according to Aristarchos, from the 3rd century B.C. (which already assumed a spherical shape for the earth and which had the planets – including the earth – revolving around the sun), was superseded during the 2nd century A.D. by the Ptolemaic system, and then finally by the 'Christianike Topographia' of Kosmas Indikopleuste, the 'traveller to India', in the 6th century.[40] Tantric thought seemed much better suited to the mystical tendency of the Old (and New) Testament than did the empirical logic of Greek natural scientists. Eastern symbolism interpreted from a Christian perspective was easier to understand than inscrutable science.

Ill. 32a: › ԴԴ ‹-symbol

› ԴԴ ‹-symbol from the so-called 'Salor gul', detail from ill. 559.

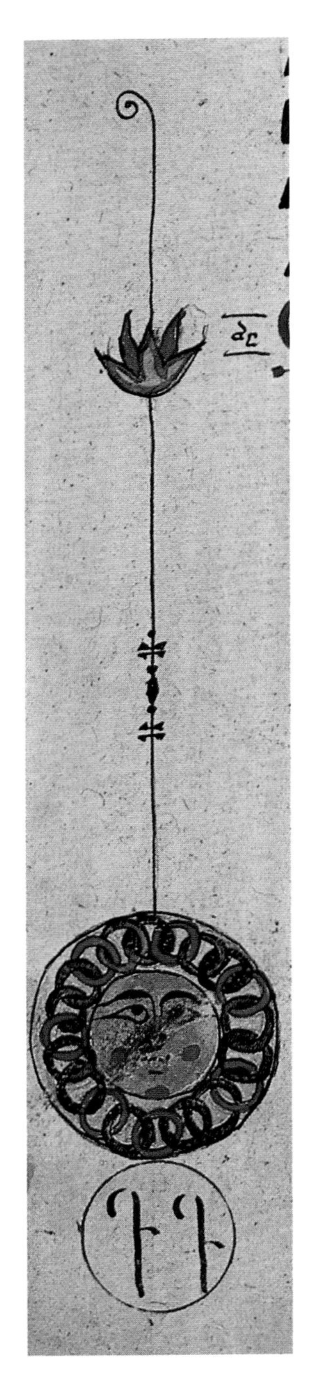

Ill. 32b: › ԴԴ ‹-symbol

› ԴԴ ‹-symbol as marginal drawing in an Armenian evangelistary from Nakhichevank dated 1304. Erivan, Matenadaran, codex no. 3722.

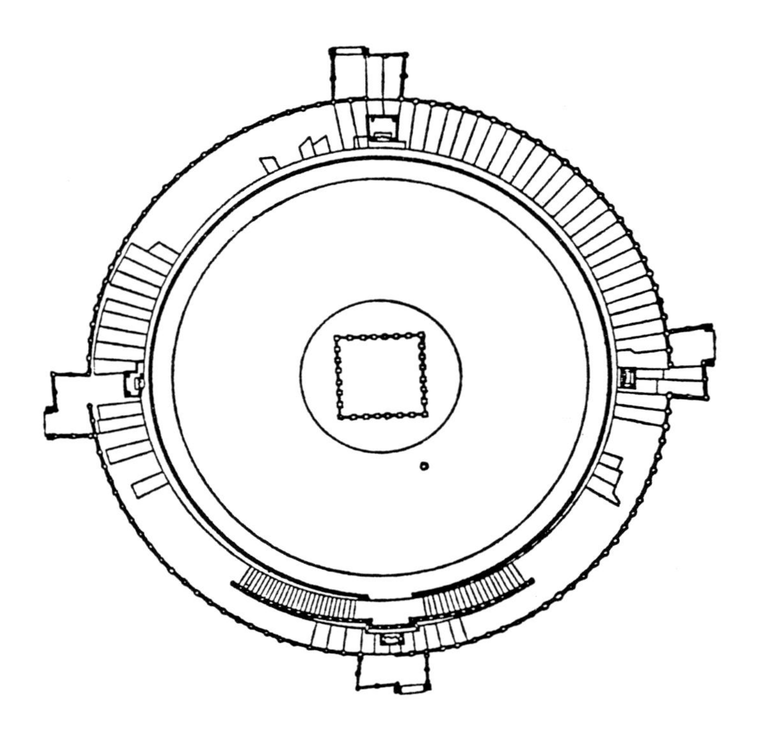

Ill. 33: Sanchi (India), stupa 1;
2nd-1st century B.C.

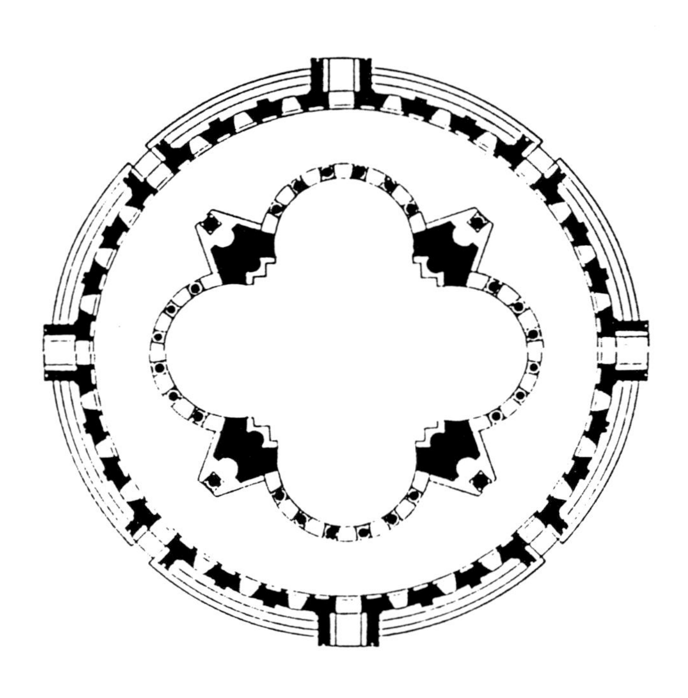

Ill. 34: Swartnoz (Armenia), Palace Church;
643–652; initial state prior to additions.

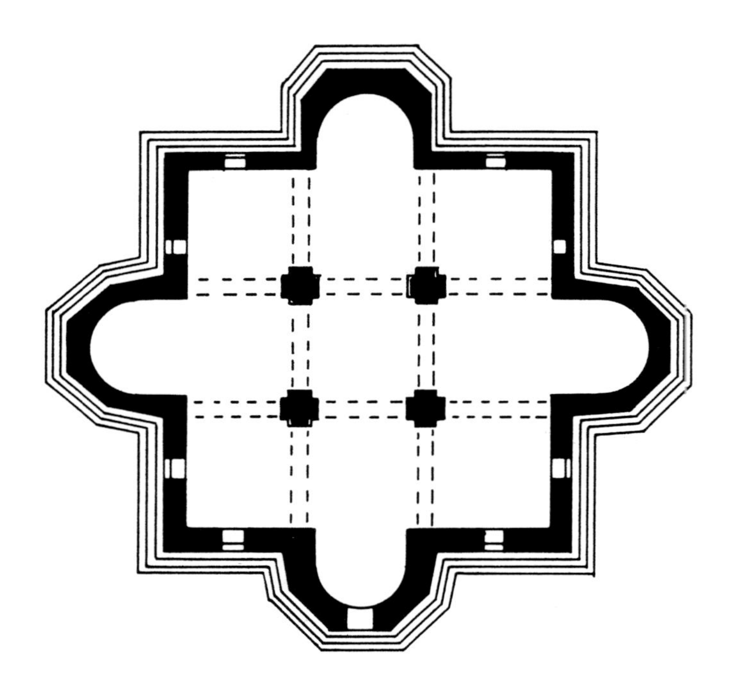

Ill. 35: Echmiadzin (Armenia), cathedral;
301–303/484; initial state without
changes or additions.

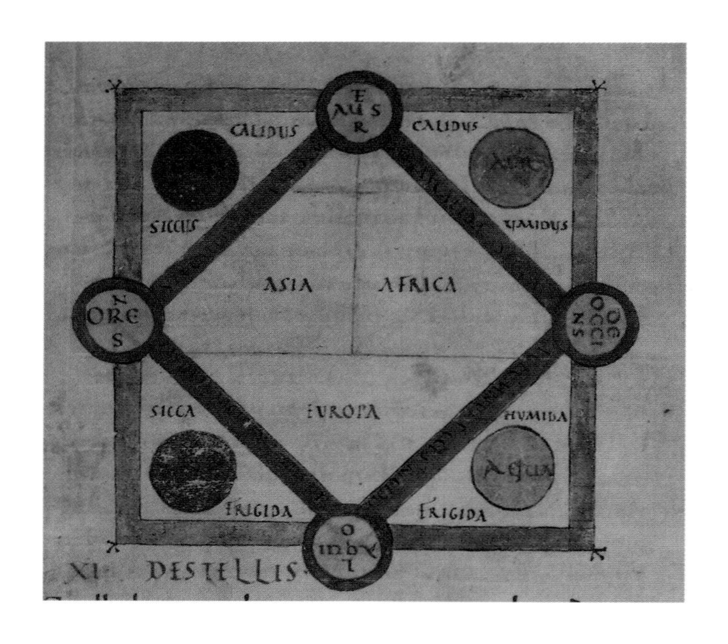

Ill. 36: Diagram of the world,
from an almanac, Salzburg, c. 818.
Österr. Nationalbibliothek,
Vienna, codex 387, F. 1341.

Ill. 37: Mandala of the Vasudhara; Nepal, dated 1400. Private collection, currently SMPK, Museum für Indische Kunst, Berlin.

Kosmas refers expressly to the authority of the Nestorian Katholikos Patrikios (Mar Aba, active 540–552), who represented the tradition of the Nestorian conception of the world[41] adhered to by the academy, which was moved from Edessa to Nisibis. This tradition seems to be in agreement on the essential points with that of Armenia. Whereas, however, the illustrations of the Kosmas manuscripts[42] strive for clarity, in keeping with the Greco-Byzantine tradition, the world-pictures depicted in the Armenian carpets remain, as do the mandalas, abstract, geometric symbols (ills. 37, 38). The Carolingian diagram of the world (ill. 36) shows a drastically simplified design of the same general idea. There are even illustrative parallels in the early Middle Ages, as a comparison of the world-picture of ill. 38 with the Mappamondi in the Camposanto of Pisa (ill. 39) shows. The difference lies in the external shape of the earth, which make clear the opposing views of the world.

Ill. 38: World cosmogram from the knotted-pile carpet MBN no. 10/294. Bayrisches Nationalmuseum, Munich.

The detail from ill. 251 shown here can also be traced back to the same basic design and the same cosmological content. A comparison with Ill. 39 shows the contrast with the Central European concept, where the round earth-disc is located in the centre of the world cosmogram.

It must be pointed out that a good many of the symbols that are used in Armenian art, and consequently also in the carpets of that country, concur in part with those used in the art of other Monophysitic cultures of the Orient, those of the Copts for example. They share a meaning diametrically opposed to that found in the art of western and central Europe.

Even within the various spheres of influence in Armenian art itself there were contradictions. Two camps were invariably at odds with each other. One, which the present author would like to refer to as traditionally Armenian, manifested itself in its disdain for purely representational art, preferring instead the richly symbolic sign language of surface ornamentation characteristic of Katchkars, carpet pages and carpets themselves. The other camp, which can be understood only in terms of its Byzantine influence, is responsible for the profusion of images that alone have become the subject of any work done on Armenian illuminated manuscripts. It is important to understand the inner tension between these two camps in order to clarify certain contradictions. Of foremost importance for the traditionalists was the maintenance of all things uniquely Armenian: language, Monophysitism, hostility towards images and a predisposition for ornamental drawing. In certain significant points this attitude resulted in manifold concurrence with Islam. In contrast to this, the Byzantine scholars among the Armenians were prepared to accept reform from outside and, to a certain extent, even to question their own national identity during times of difficulty, in order thus (by identifying with the Byzantine or Catholic church) to be protected against possible Islamic attacks.

Here it is only possible to touch on a few of the problems. As yet there is no authoritative study providing sufficient treatment of the iconography and iconology of the oriental church in the Christian tradition or of the Armenian church in particular. However, Ernst Badstübner and his colleagues have been doing preliminary work on such a study. This explains the author's special gratitude to his colleagues in eastern Europe and Armenia, for only with their help was it possible to shed light on difficult iconological issues and the interrelationships between them.

The difficulty of presenting things in their proper historical context lies in the fact that carpets are seldom dated. The earliest dated carpets go back to the 16th and

Ill. 39: The world map of Pietro di Puccio d'Orvieto in the Camposanto in Pisa, c. 1350.

17th centuries, and of these there are very few. The carpets shown in paintings represent termini ante quem, yet give no hint as to their actual age. They could be the results of quite recent work or, by the same token, hundreds of years older. We do not yet know how old the carpets handed down to us really are. The only way, scientifically, of determining an object's age is by means of carbon dating, which has achieved a high degree of accuracy even when using small samples.[43] With very few exceptions, for which the present author is in part responsible, only individual carpets amongst those considered to be oldest have actually been tested for their age. Yet even here experience has shown that with respect to a negligible C^{14}-age considerable sources of error can arise as a result of storage and other environmental factors, such that a discrepancy of 500 years one way or the other can easily be the consequence. We are still primarily, indeed solely dependent on stylistic features. Not until there is correspondence between carpets and comparable datable specimens from, for example, illumination, ornamental architecture, pottery or the crafts will dating be possible. Here we are assuming that the ornamental content of the carpets had parallels in the other art of the day. Yet at this point we should not forget the difficulty resulting from the fact that in all ages – and this was true of the icons – old designs are drawn on for the completion of new pieces of art.

The idea of using colour as a way of determining age is completely restricted to the last 110 years. The practice of fixing the use of red dyes derived from insects to the time only following the discovery of America and thus arriving at an approximate method of dating is based on ignorance. In actual fact dyestuffs have been derived in this way from ancient times when the 'Armenian kermes' provided a way of dying material red – Kurdian[44] mentions the year 714 B. C. and also the first exact description by Ghazar Parbetzy in the 5th century. The dye of the oriental kermes, often referred to as cochineal, is also well documented, beginning in at least the 8th century. One problem appears to be the fact that on into the High Middle Ages the craft of dying was in the hands of the Jews,[45] who were in sole possession of the privilege of collecting insects needed for this purpose. For this reason even the early Arabian sources reflect the same inexactitude in their usage of terminology as do those of this century.

The insect of the 'Armenian kermes', *Porphirophora Hamelii B.,* lives as larvae on the roots of a variety of grasses – a conclusion which both Parbetzy and Parrot,[46] a 19th century traveller, arrived at in their own independent descriptions. This Armenian species lives only in the relatively damp regions of the Araxes valley. The Kirmiz dyeing centre was at Ardashad near Dwin, for which Pelakori in the 8th century synonymously uses the place name 'al-Kirmiz', while Baladhuri refers to it as 'karyat al-kirmiz' ('village of Kermes') in the 10th century. It appears that, although Ardashad along with Dwin were destroyed by Timur in 1386–87, the tradition of producing kermes continued.

In 1985, the present author received samples of *P. hamelii,* and thus became the first person in the western world to be provided the opportunity to analyze the dye. Commenting on the results of the thin-layer chromatography of *P. hamelii B.*, Dr. Helmut Schweppe (BASF) concludes[47] that *hamelii* contains the dye crimson acid and possibly large amounts of protein compounds of crimson acid, which similarly occur in lac dye as so-called lacciferous acid (laccainic acid protein compounds). Since, as of November 1986, Dr. Schweppe's work on the dye analyses was still in its preliminary stages and the results from the spectrographic analysis conducted by Prof. Max Saltzmann (Los Angeles) are as yet not available, we will have to wait until their work has been published.

Porphirophora (Margarodes) polonica, the so-called 'Polish kermes', is closely related. The question as to whether this species is identical to *P. monticola* or to *P. triciti,* both of which are also indigenous to Armenia and were introduced to eastern and northeastern Europe through emigration, has yet to be answered. These species likewise live in the form of larvae at the roots of lower plants.

The widest distribution was enjoyed by *Kermococcus vermilio,* the 'oriental kermes' (often mistaken for Coccus ilicis), whose larvae live above ground on the kermes oak (Quercus coccifera). Already in the 8th century Djahiz mentions the three main dispersal areas of that time: the Maghrib, Andalusia and Tarum in Fars.[48] He was not able to distinguish between P. *Hamelii* and K. *vermilio* and suspected the latter also to be on grass. He wrote of K. *vermilio* that it was completely unknown except to the members of a Jewish sect, who were also able to locate it. On the other hand, Makkari[49] already knew that the larvae lived on oak trees. This species lived in the warm, dry regions of the entire Mediterranean, Armenia and Persia. In addition, Ya'qubi[50] mentions it in upper Egypt in the 10th century. Basically, *Porphirophora* and *Kermococcus* are impossible to confuse. They each live in different climates, one underground and the other above the ground.

They are far less likely to be confused with the fourth species, the Mexican cochineal or *Dactylopius coccus,* which lives on the prickly pear Opuntia coccinellifera indica. This species is correctly associated with America; it comes from central America (Mexico, Honduras) and is frequently mistaken for the Andalusian *Kermococcus vermilio.* Although cochineal quickly became a much sought–after commodity following the discovery of America, the insect along with its host plant were not introduced into the region of the Mediterranean until the 19th century.

Another red dye, possibly similar to the Armenian kermes, is 'Lac dye', made from the insects *Laccifer lacca (Lacca indiana)* and *Lakshadia communis,* both indigenous to India and southern Asia. The lac insects live on the Acacia catecu, Ficus and Butea frondosa.[51]

Even though we may determine that certain raw materials were used, this will not necessarily provide us with a means of dating these carpets. This is especially true in the case of cotton. There are authors who would have us regard the use of cotton in carpets as an indication that they were made quite late. Though there are certain to have been regional differences, it must be pointed out that in the entire region of Armenian cultural influence cotton had been grown since antiquity. For this reason alone, it is to be expected that cotton should be present in basic materials. In addition, cotton is more suitable, especially for fine work, because it can be twined tighter and, in relation to the thickness of the thread, possesses a much higher resistance to tearing.

From the available material, over 20,000 carpet slides alone, only a fraction could be chosen for this book. The author has therefore chosen only those which seemed typical of carpet development. Iconography and iconology are so inextricably meshed in carpet study that it would be pointless to try to separate the two. Often it is only by appreciating the meaning of what is presented that it is possible to perceive a change in design.

Christian oriental art is an art of signs and symbols from its inception. In this respect it stands in stark contrast to the representational art of ancient Classicism and the traditions it was built upon.

Ill. 40: Mevl. no. 859, detail. Mevlana Museum, Konya.

The detail from the carpet fragment of Ill. 449 shows in the centre of its so-called 'Memling gul', a design wide-spread throughout the entire region of Armenian cultural influence, a cross, (cf. ill. 56) typical of the early Christian art produced under this influence. It is composed of four divine 'lilies of grace' and referred to in carpet literature as 'Kotshak (= horned) cross'. It grew out of an Urartian-Hittite-Phrygian proto-design (ills. 55, 385, 451, 452) and also constituted a permanent feature of the European design tradition during the Middle Ages.

Part One: From the Beginnings to the High Middle Ages

The Christian Oriental Carpet

A: The Early Middle Ages

B: The High Middle Ages

Ill. 41: 'Pazyryk carpet', 200 x 183 cm, Hemitage, Leningrad.

The 'Pazyryk carpet' is the oldest surviving, nearly complete, knotted-pile carpet known today. For the time being there is no definite answer to the question as to whether the symbols in the upper left represent 'rosettes' or Urartian sun symbols (cf. ill. 54) at the beginning of a procession of riders or, instead, wheels for a burial ritual at the end of the procession.

This find would thus contradict all the assumptions which those engaged in the study of carpets, including myself, have always taken for granted. One would now have to conclude that the knotted-pile carpet did not grow out of simple nomadic conditions, but was rather the product of old oriental high cultures.

Kurt Erdman 1955 and 1959
in 'Der orientalische Knüpfteppich'

The Pazyryk-Carpet and the Emergence of the Knotted-Pile Carpet

The oldest known carpet today is the 'Pazyryk' carpet, which was found by Rudenko in kurgan 5 of Pazyryk in the Altai mountains in 1949 (ill. 41). Ulrich Schürmann[52] devoted a monograph to this carpet, the content of which coincides to a large extent with the ideas to be found here.

The Pazyryk carpet originated sometime during the 4th or 5th century B.C., measures 200 x 183 cm and is symmetrically knotted, exhibiting a density of 3600 knots/sq dm. Even by today's standards this can be considered very fine knotting. Both ground weave and pile are wool.

In this oldest carpet there is none of the long-pile hide substitute of the nomads, as Erdmann would have us believe. Rather, it is a highly cultivated, intricately patterned, short-pile piece of work created by experienced craftsmen. Schürmann assumes that this carpet was made in Sakis, the capital of Scythia in the country of Urartu south of the Urmia Sea, commissioned by a Scythian king, and carried out in the workshop of Proto-Armenian craftsmen.

Ill. 42: Phrygian-Archaic roof-tile frieze. Archaeological Museum, Istanbul, no. 5937.
The 'light-symbol crosses' in the carpet and on the ornamental tiles are identical; a feature of the Armenian design tradition until the end of the Middle Ages. Even in Europe this cross was used as a symbol for light in the biblical depictions from St.Kastor of 'God as world creator.'

Figure 2 a:
'fiat lux', detail from F. 2r: God as creator of the world
Bible from St.Kastor, Koblenz, 10th century(?). Graf Schönbornsche Schloßbibliothek, Pommersfelden, codex 333, F. 2r.

Figure 2 b:
'Pazyryk carpet', detail light-symbol cross.

Yet are the figures depicted here really Scythians? If we look at the Persepolis reliefs for how the Armenian delegation is depicted (ill. 45), we see that they look precisely like those shown on horseback on the 'Pazyryk'carpet (ill. 46) in terms both of the men's head covering as well as the size of their horses. Scythians wore pointed bashliks, which eliminates them from here. And a further consideration: was the carpet in fact a ceremonial burial object ordered years in advance? The agreement between what Herodotus wrote on the subject and the conditions surrounding the actual discovery of the Kurgan at Kostromskaja Stanica[53] seem convincing.
And yet there remain doubts. Certainly the carpet possessed symbolic character. At that time carpet borders had a protective function for the living and for the dead, as has always been the case. Death was frequently followed by the very situation that had marked life. Why call this a death march if it might possibly be a procession of tribute? Moreover, if Schürmann's interpretation of the other symbols proves to be true – rosettes as wheels and two-toothed ornaments as poles – they could stand for faithfulness until death. But they could also be symbols of the sun at the beginning of the riders' procession, and tables of ritual between the symbols of light. This is more likely, in view of what we know about Urartian symbols. It may have been a throne carpet to be buried along with the deceased. Elements of the design suggest it was made farther to the west. We encounter the same design of the inner panel on Phrygian-Archaic roof-tile friezes as well (ill. 42). Carpet patterns similar to these, sculpted from stone, can be found before entering the royal halls at the Palace of Nineveh and are likely to have been imports, as were the Phrygian garments of splendor.[54] This seems all the more likely when we consider the array of Urartian elements contained in them. The fallow bucks are Urartian in any case, and correspond to the representation on the stele in the Museum of Urfa (ills. 43, 44). The griffin representations are also Urartian. If we can correctly assume Armenians to be a Phrygian-Urartian people, then the figures represented here could well be Phryg-ian Armenians, for whom the head covering is typical. The kurgan of Pazyryk might not have been Scythian either, but rather Phrygian-Armenian, for the Phrygians built tumuli of the same type and size, as the excavations in Gordion show.[55]

Ill. 43 (above): Late Hittite-Urartian stele; Museum, Urfa.

The fallow buck, on the back of which rides a godhead, has the same characteristic marking on its shoulder-blade as do the fallow bucks in the carpet. The occurrence of fallow bucks is restricted to southeastern Europe and the Near East. For this reason alone it is unlikely that this carpet originated farther to the east.

Ill. 44 (right): 'Pazyryk carpet', detail from ill. 41.

Ill. 45: The Armenian delegation; Persepolis, 5th century B.C. Stairs on the east side of the Adapana.

The Armenian delegation is also represented on the reliefs of the stairs on the east side of the palace in Persepolis. The segment shows a man leading a horse. A comparison here tells all. One need only note the headdress of the rider, the size of the horse and the knotted tail.

Ill. 46: 'Pazyryk carpet', detail from ill. 41.

Thus the Pazyryk carpet will have to be regarded as one of the first testimonies to early Armenian work, quite possibly produced in the vicinity of the old textile centre of Ardashad in the south-western Caucasus. The connection with the Phrygians paves the way for a further hypothesis. It is a well-known fact that the Phrygians are thought to have invented the mosaic. Less well known, however, is the fact that the hitherto oldest Soumak was found in the hills of Gordion (8th century B.C.). The production of Soumaks has a great deal in common with the production of knotted-pile carpets, and in extreme cases they may even be identical.

The purpose of illustrations 47–53 is to explain the technique. A jufti knot involving two sets of two warp strings is identical to the loop construction of a Soumak when abrupt colour changes are made. It is for this reason that the author sees the intricately patterned Soumak as the prototype of the knotted-pile carpet. The purpose of the knots is simply to fix the incorporated looped strings to the warp. The smaller the thread loop and the fewer the number of warp strings used, the faster a change of colour can be achieved. And it is this quick colour change that makes a greater precision in pattern possible. The reason behind the emergence of the knotted-pile carpet was not that it functioned as a hide-substitute, but rather that an existing technique was refined, making possible an improved medium for illustration.

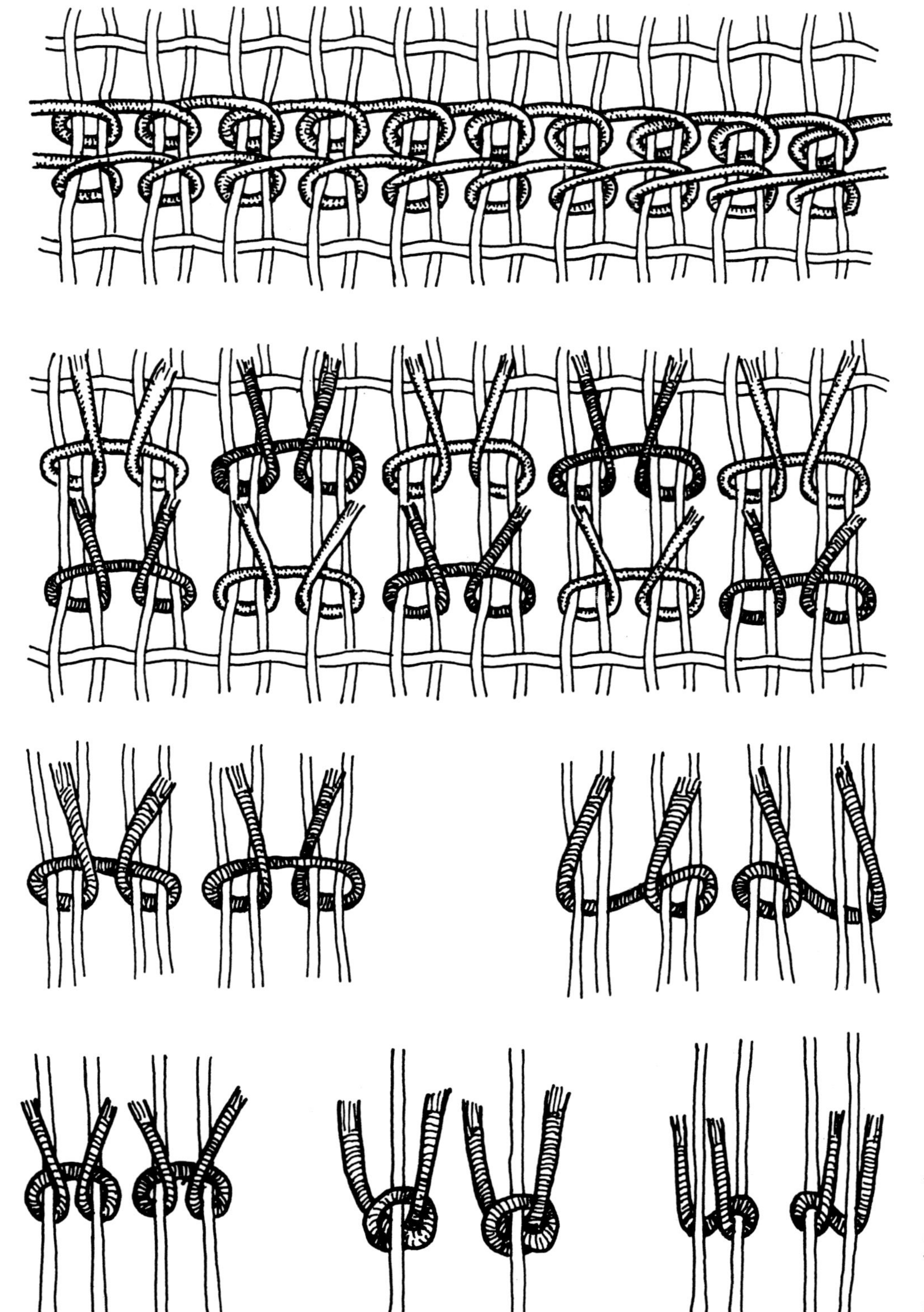

Ill. 47: Soumak-weave with no colour change.

Ill. 48: Soumak with extreme colour change = knotted-pile carpet using the symmetrical jufti knot.

Ill. 49 (left): Symmetrical jufti knot.

Ill. 50 (right): Asymmetrical Jufti knot.

Ill. 51 (left): Symmetrical knot over two warp strings.

Ill. 52 (middle): Symmetrical knot over one warp string.

Ill. 53 (right): Asymmetrical knot: left open – right open.

Traditional Designs

A period of more than 1,000 years lies between the Pazyryk carpet and those next in line to have survived. This period of time can be filled only hypothetically by identifying a chain of traditional designs. In this connection we are only interested in how these traditional designs evolved in what has been defined above as the 'sphere of Armenian cultural influence,' and here we will confine ourselves to the motif of the cross and its variants. The early Christian populace of this area made conscious use of the rich variety of design from the pre-Christian age, which grew out of the art of the Hittites, the Urartians and the Phrygians.

The treatment of the motif of the cross in art history has resulted in a good deal of controversy at times, with two camps being at odds: the one intent on seeing in the cross purely decorative ornament, the other certain of its symbolic import. Matters are complicated by the fact that even decorative motifs can have symbolic meaning.[56] In Christian oriental art, everything that was represented in a picture – here even carpets or mosaics are to be included – was never without reason or purpose. In contrast to Hellenistic art, preference was given to a language of signs and symbols rather than to a representation with man as its point of reference.[57] A predilection for forms of encipherment suggestive of secret codes had its place here as well. Taken together, such things, given our way of thinking fashioned by western tradition, can be recognized and comprehended only with a great deal of effort. Hence, 'communication problems' have often resulted in a kind of resistance, not so terribly far removed from the attitude characteristic of the witch hunts in the Middle Ages.

Ill. 54: Urartian: detail of a connecting piece (for furniture). British Museum, London, no. 91251.

This connecting piece for furniture, presumably from a throne-chair, shows two important Urartian symbols of light: the rosette and the proto-design of the 'Armenian cross', known in Europe as 'paw cross'.

In the Armenian sphere of cultural influence the cross symbolized what was regarded by Monophysites as the partial or regional divinity of the sun. It was at the same time the symbol of light, life and truth.

We find them as a single motif on Hittite and Urartian cult objects (ills. 54, 61, 62); one after the other and constantly varied on the garments of Hittite divine kings (ills. 59, 60); in the endlessness of filled surfaces for the earliest period in Urartu (ill. 58);

Ill. 55 (left): Urartian: wooden plank from the back part of a wagon, found in the Sevan Sea. Historical Museum, Erivan.

The wooden plank shows the early Urartian designs of the so-called Kotshak cross and the wave band (running dog). Both designs were handed down in Armenian art and are characteristic of it.

then in Phrygian works in particular – monumentally in Midas Seheri (ill. 57) and ornamentally in the inlay work on furniture fragments from Gordion (ill. 452).

The Phrygians are considered to be the inventors of the mosaic. And it was precisely in mosaics, even during the reign of the Greeks and later the Romans, that the richness of pattern and design was able to survive nearly unchanged. Granted, art historians have paid more attention to the Hellenistic figural representations found there, rather than to the 'geometric designs' surrounding them. Nonetheless, the latter constitute important links in our chain of traditional designs. In Roman times, anti-Hellenistic sentiments appear to have gained sway. From Antioch, the variety of pattern and design in the mosaics of the entire Roman empire spread. This was also true in the subsequent period of early Christianity.

Whereas Constantine introduced the Christogram (ill. 65) and the Copts united the 'Egyptian cross' with the sun dial (ill. 64), the symbol for light and life, the region under the influence of Armenian culture adopted the 'light-(sun)-cross'(ills. 62, 63) which symbolized light, life and truth. What could have been more natural for the new cult than to embrace a symbol whose purpose was to express the same ideas? After all, it was Christ himself who is reported to have said: "I am come a light into world . . ." (Joh. 12, 46). New religions spring from the same source. Might this explain why, in this area more than anywhere else, early missionaries were so successful; why, in fact, Armenia was to become the first country anywhere in the world to establish Christianity as its state religion?

Ill. 57 (inside right): Phrygian wall relief, detail, Midas Seheri; 7th century B.C.

The Phrygians were masters of the ornamentation of large surfaces. The composition with crosses, of which a segment is shown here, has been handed down by Armenians on into the 20th century.

Ill. 58 (outside right): Urartian stele from Adiljevaz, garment detail (according to Brentjes).

The pattern here on the garment of an Urartian godhead appears identical with Ill. 57.

Ill. 59 (inside right): The Hittite King Warpalawas, garment detail; relief in Ivriz, second half of the 8th century B.C.

The garments of the Hittite King Warpalawas also contain details of design that we will encounter later in Armenian carpets and textiles.

Ill. 60 (outside right): The Hittite King Warpalawas, garment detail; relief from Bor, second part of the 8th century B.C.

Ill. 56 (left): Early Christian relief panel, fragment, St. John's Basilica, Ephesus.

On this early Christian relief panel, presumably from a parclose, we find both of the cross designs typical of Christian-Armenian art: left the 'Kotshak' cross, right the 'Armenian' (Tatzen) cross.

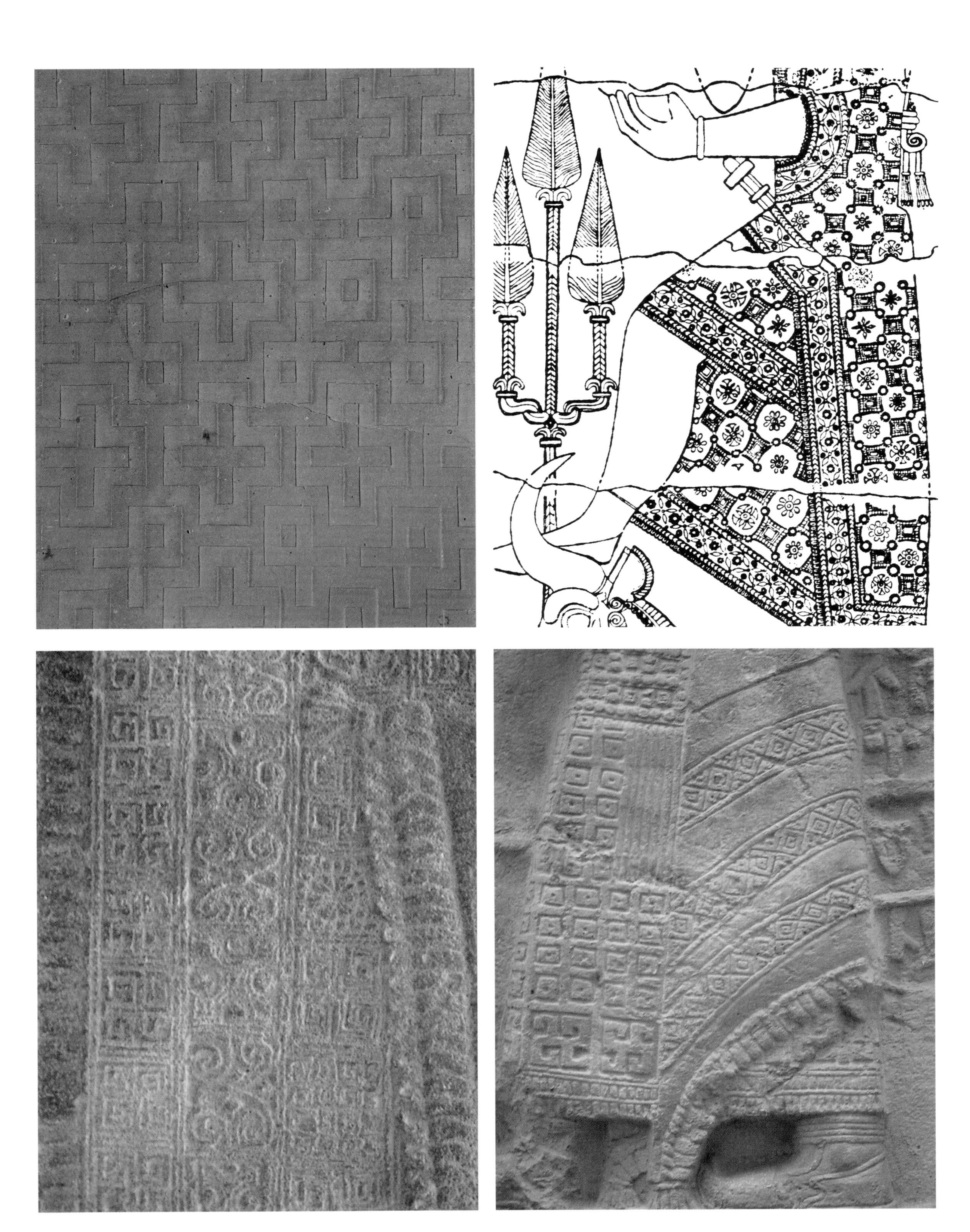

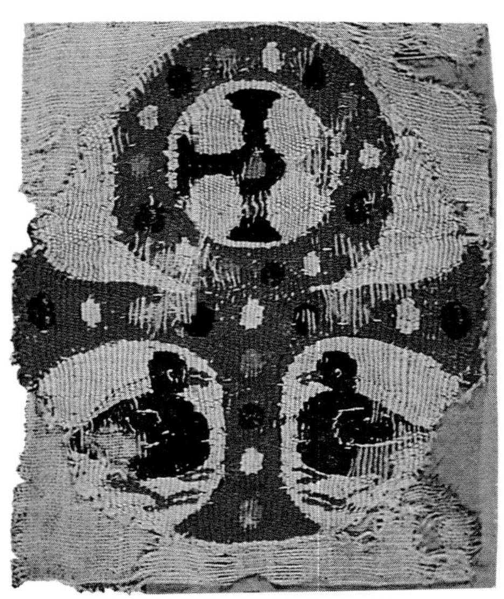

In the Byzantine Empire the Monophysite Anastasios I (491–518) replaced the Christogram (ill. 65) with the cross. This cross was not the symbol of suffering but one of triumph instead. Early coins depicted Victoria, the goddess of victory, (ill. 66) next to the cross in order to illustrate this. Under Justinian it gained acceptance as a symbol of Christ and Christianity. It is no mere coincidence that in every age, certain exceptions notwithstanding, in the region of the Monophysitic Church, there was strong resistance to the 'cross of suffering.' This interpretation stood in contradiction to the inner message of the symbol. This view was most consistently embraced by the eastern Syrian Nestorians, who placed their entire mission unter the sign of the 'cross of victory.'

Ill. 61 (outside left): Ceremonial standard from Alacahöyük, bronze. Anatolia, early bronze period, second half of the 3rd century B.C. Museum of Anatolian Civilizations, Ankara.
Geometrical cross compositions on the ceremonial standards in central Anatolia are probably connected with a sun cult. They make up part of a migration of designs from the Caucasus, which occurred along with the metallurgical transfer.

Ill. 62 (inside left): Urartian talisman from Aparan, bronze, 10th-8th century B.C. Historical Museum, Erivan.
Cruciform talismans were thought to have an apotropaic significance even at the beginning of the first millennium B.C.

Ill. 63 (outside left): Armenian, cross of Achz, A D 361.
In contrast to Byzantium, in Armenia, as a result of the pre-Christian tradition, the cross was the symbol of the new state religion from the very beginning. The cross of Achz possesses other features which make it typically Armenian: its 'plant-like' character, making it a prototype for Katchkars and the 'tree of Jesse'; partridges as a symbol of believers; rosettes as light symbols of 'inspiration'.

Ill. 64 (inside left): Coptic Egyptian cross on a textile fragment; 4th/5th century (?). Kaiser Friedrich Museum in Berlin, Early Christian Collection no. 9301. Destroyed in the Second World War.
The Coptic 'ankh' cross was adopted as a symbol for 'life' from the Old Egyptian hieroglyphics and connected with the cross as in this example here. The ducks on either side are probably in place of the partridges, which do not exist in Egypt.

Ill. 65 (outside left): Byzantine bronzefollis; 383–392.
Until the end of the 5th century Byzantium trusted in the Chi-Rho symbol without exception, as shown here on this coin.

Ill. 66 (left inside): Solidus of Anastasio, 491–518.
The Solidus of Anastosio shows the cross for the first time: the goddess of victory, Victoria, with a standard crowned with a cross.

Ill. 67 (right): Church of Zahrani, floor plan of the third stage of construction, dated A D 541. (according to Chéhab).
The order and the arrangement of the mosaics as shown in the plan give the impression that textile floor coverings, carpets for one, may have served as models.

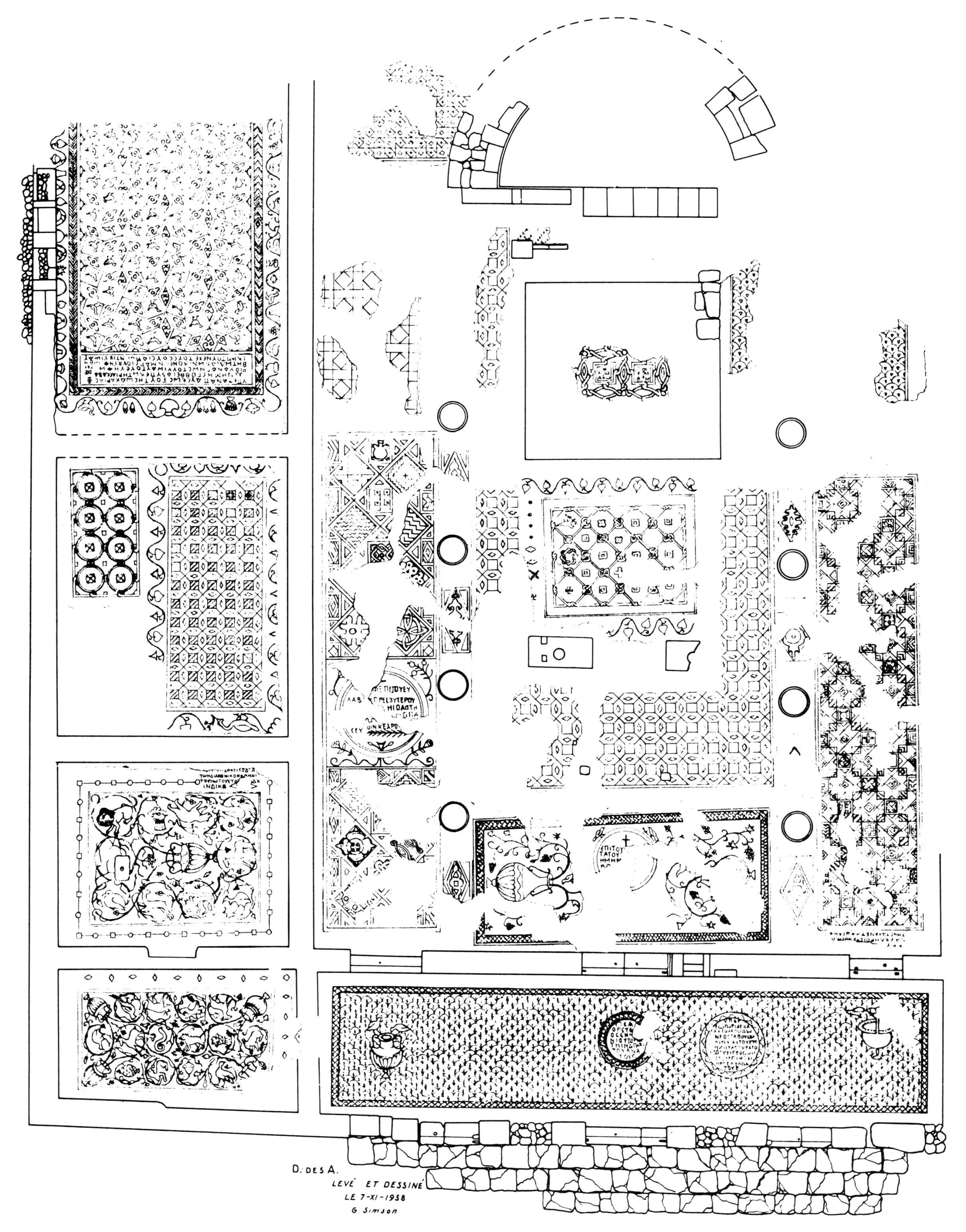
D. DES A.
LEVÉ ET DESSINÉ
LE 7-XI-1958
G Simson

For the time being, however, let us assume the following: that in the 4th century, Christians from both Armenia[58] and Syria had already adopted the pre-Christian 'light-symbol cross' as a symbol of continuing significance. Thus in its geometric-ornamental use, a tradition known to us primarily in the mosaics from the north-western part of Syria and Cilicia, the continuity of this symbol was not lost. This now raises the question as to whether it was the aforementioned region which influenced the entire sphere of what was in turn under the cultural influence of Armenia in terms of the history of design, or whether it was, in fact, the region located farther to the north which influenced the south. This question will now be considered.

Before turning to the mosaics, the author would like to present the floor plan of the church of *Zahrani*.[59] This small church, erected prior to 541 and located in what we know today as South Lebanon, does not actually belong to the region we will be dealing with; yet contained within it we find in condensed form all those patterns that can be seen farther north in Antioch,[60] in Gerasa[61] or in Misis-Mopsuhestia (Cilicia).[62] The plan shows the third phase at the beginning of the 6th century (ill. 67). If we were unaware of the fact that this drawing depicts mosaics, we would simply automatically assume that what we were looking at was a floor covered with carpets of completely different types. That is to say, we would see carpets of stone, mosaic carpets – each suggesting a unit unto itself complete with inner panel and border, strictly geometric carpets, vase carpets in the shape of runners, or main carpets, a kaleidoscope of possibilities. In viewing such variety, do we not feel compelled to ask: Who or what actually influenced whom? Were lasting, imperishable textiles – carpets – created here in these mosaics, or are our carpets no more than a transportable, textile substitute for just such lasting mosaics? There may well never be a complete answer to these questions for the simple reason that carpets dating from this period are not available to us. Despite this, however, we should re-examine the plan with these questions in mind. Even if we take into consideration different dates of manufacture, the mosaics do not strike us as subordinated to the room in their composition. They do not seem to take the room into account. In actual fact it is more the case that they appear to extend in accordance with their own spatial needs, as if real carpets had been spread out in the church to serve as models. The present author believes that this would favour the conclusion that the mosaics are duplications of the textiles rather than vice-versa.

The mosaic representations give us an idea of the richness of pattern and design common at that time. Yet there is one question which they leave open: were the models used knotted carpets or flat-weaves, pieces of embroidery or appliqué-works? If we allow the assessment of Serjeant's material to serve as our point of departure, we have to assume that we are dealing largely with flat-weaves or possibly embroidery in the case of 'vase carpets'. The variety in design is really quite amazing, even in what on the one hand often prove to be combinations of disparate stylistic elements – Hellenistic and anti-Hellenistic geometric motifs. Yet, on the other hand, in the Katchkars and other carpets we will see later, there is a recurring joy in the use of continuous variation on what remain unchanging compositions.

Each of the mosaics could be regarded as design forerunners for carpets still in existence today. It is truly astonishing that this collection of designs has changed so little over the centuries. Some examples of this are provided in the following without further commentary. Another will demonstrate how the chain of traditional design may be extrapolated from the mosaics to the carpets. Illustrations 72/73 show mosaics from Misis-Mopsuhestia and Zahrani. The overall surface pattern is the same for each, based on two types of organization: one diagonal and the other along horizontal and vertical axes, both of which, upon intersection, generate a multitude of various kinds of crosses: Greek crosses, a sort of key-cross and, of particular

Ill. 68: Floor mosaics in the House of the Red Pavement, Antioch (according to Levi).

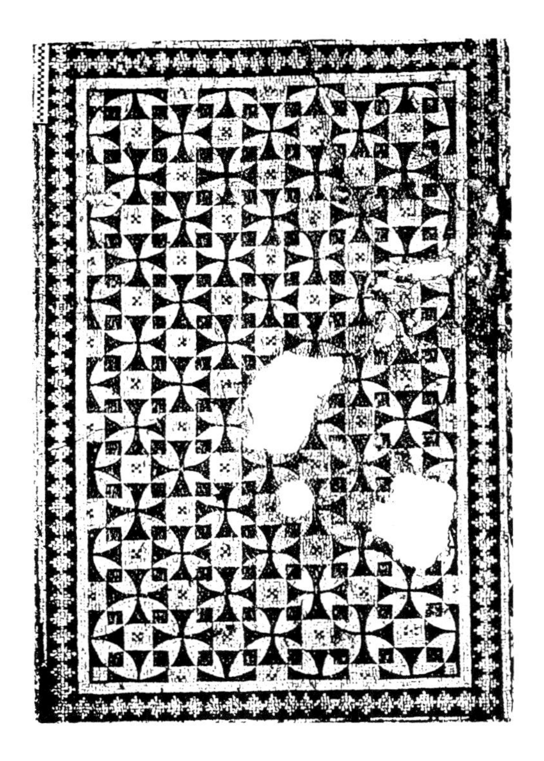

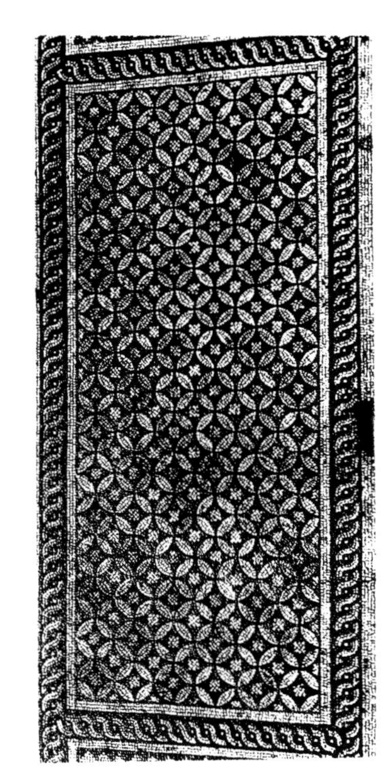

Ills. 69–71: Floor mosaics in the House of the Porticoes, Antioch; ills. 69 and 70 today in the museum of Antakya, ill. 71 according to Levi.

The mosaic floors presented here reflected, even at the time they were made, carpets with designs that continued in production, very nearly unchanged, into the 20th century.

importance, a cross-star inscribed in a Greek cross. The composition here, as compared with ill. 57, has become more refined and complex, with the basic conception of its spatial organization having been expanded along a diagonal component. The mosaic from Zahrani enriches the 'negative' squares between the cross-stars, or the centres of the light-symbol crosses of the basic form type H_1, depending on one's perspective, as well as the corner squares with numerous inscribed designs. Of these the various kinds of crosses in the 'negative'-squares give us an idea of how widely varied the cross types were in the 6th century. We find similar compositions in the mosaics (ills. 74, 75) as well as in the panels in *Khirbat al Mafjar* near Jericho. R.W. Hamilton[63] correctly states that these mosaics, which he finds to be more 'linear' in their design conception, can be distinguished from similar ones in Antioch and Gerasa – which were, after all, produced 200 years later. The present author agrees with this assessment. In closing, Hamilton comes to the following conclusion:

"I think we can fairly suppose that these rectilinear designs, perhaps some others in the next groups to be described, were more or less faithful copies of patterns commonly to be seen in the rug markets of the Near East during the eighth and earlier centuries." [64]

Ill. 72: Floor mosaic of the church, in Misis-Mopsuhestia; 5th century (according to Budde).

This mosaic is the classic prototype for a multitude of carpet genres, combining as it does cross stars with Greek and stepped crosses as well as the possibility of a central medallion, diagonal stripes and compartments.

Ill. 73 (page 61): Floor mosaic of the church in Zahrani; dated 541 (according to Chéhab).

This mosaic, identical in its composition to ill. 72, already exhibits characteristics from the same period, which were to become typical of Armenian carpets: joy in the varying of details, often, as in this case, variations on the central theme of the 'cross'.

+ΚΥ
ΝΑΥΚΛΗͰΡΟΙΕΥΞΑΜΕΝΟΙ
ΤΗΝCΤΑΥΑΝΕΨΗΦWCΑΝ+

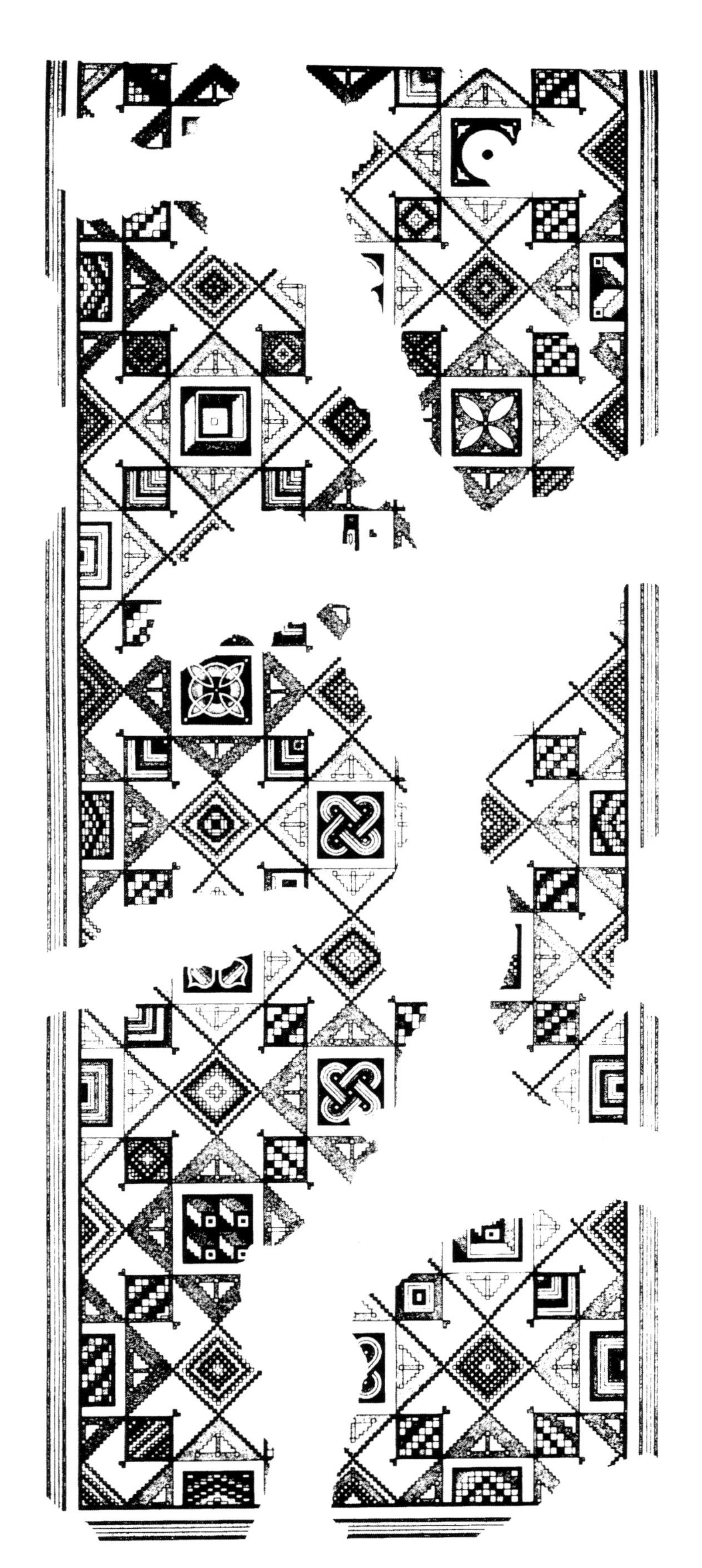

In their continued development of designs, the mosaics of Khirbat al Mafjar demonstrate the continuity of design evolution still evident in the 8th century and already familiar to us from the Armenian-Syrian sphere of cultural influence. Working on commission for an early Islamic ruler, Christian artisans allowed this established wealth of designs to influence their work. And yet even so, these are designs that we find not only here, but also throughout the entire Byzantine Empire. The correspondence with the carpet designs, which Hamilton believes exists and very certainly does, can be established, presuming the inclusion of Serjeant's material, only with those designs from the Armenian-Syrian sphere of cultural influence.

Ills. 74–75: Floor mosaic in the so-called 'Bath-Hall', Jericho-Khirbat al Mafjar. Courtesy of the Israel Department of Antiquities.

Yet another series within this realm of traditional designs strikes the author as very worthy of our utmost attention: in the 'Propylaea Church' in Gerasa[65] there is a medallion mosaic dated 565 (ill. 76) which unites all those elements cited in connection with ill. 73 and which is quite plainly being used as a symbol. An inscription present in the mosaic makes reference to the 'Diaconia', which took place under this symbol. We find the same symbol in the 'Procopius Church' from 526, likewise in Gerasa[66] (ills. 77a, b). Here the medallion is incorporated into a long mosaic 'runner'. The composition of the medallion corresponds to a large extent with those in Misis-Mopsuhestia from the 5th century (ill. 78) except that here everything proves to be richer, more complex in its multiple permeations. This symbol is developed further in Khirbat al Mafjar as well[67] (ill. 79). The designs filling the medallion are more difficult to make out as a result of the increase in interlacing designs.

Ill. 76: Propylea Church, Gerasa: Diaconia mosaic, dated A D 565. Yale University Art Gallery.

The Diaconia mosaic can be regarded as the prototype for a number of central medallions: The eight-pointed star, composed of two diagonally overlapping crosses and cross stars and interwoven by two bands of interlace, is, like a mandala, both a symbol of the world and a holy place.

Ill. 77 a, b: Procopius Church, Gerasa: floor mosaic in the northern nave, A D 526. Yale University Art Gallery.

Whereas in the Diaconia mosaic in ill. 76 the relationship to a greater context has been lost, the mosaic in the Procopius Church shows a similar medallion set into the 'mosaic carpet' in the same way that this was done 1,000 years later with the medallion carpets. The origins are to be found here.

Ill. 78: Floor mosaic of the church in Misis-Mopsuhestia; 5th century (according to Budde).

Ill. 79: Floor mosaic in the so-called 'Bath-Hall', Jericho-Khirbat al Mafjar. Courtesy of the Israel Department of Antiquities.

Ill. 80: Floor mosaic of the church, Misis-Mopsuhestia; 5th century; (according to Budde).

The centre consists of the well-known cross-star, which is extended into two crosses that are interlocked, and into whose beams stemmed drinking glasses have been worked.

The present author considers such traditional designs so important because, in connection with Armenian illuminated manuscripts of the first half of the 2nd millennia, they set standards for those carpets which are always described as typical of the Persians.[68] This is in reference to the carpets of group C VIII. In these, and in ill. 77b in particular, we can clearly see how the central, medallion-shaped symbol was simply superimposed on the ground. A further development of this is found, for example, in ills. 128, 129, 181 and 188.

Individual cross-stars, later incorporated into carpet designs, can be found on the baptismal font of Edessa, (ill. 81) and on the ceiling in the church of the Saghmosavank monastery (c. 1250).[69]

Ill. 81: Baptismal font of Edessa, 5th/6th century(?). Museum, Urfa.

In four of its five arch panels, the baptismal font shows variants of the eight-pointed star from ill. 76, with the cross in the centre in each case. The large cross of victory was removed from the fifth arch panel during the time of the Moslems, leaving the kneeling animals on either side, presumably a bull and a ram, still just discernible.

The Christian Oriental Carpet

The Beginnings: Carpet Pages

The carpet designs present in the mosaics have conveyed an idea of what we can, with justification, assume – though it must remain hypothetical – to be the traditional designs of early Christian carpets. We still know nothing about the materials used, and can but guess that the proportion of knotted-pile carpets was quite small. There is much to indicate, and the designs of the original carpets seem to bear this out, that the majority of the designs were not conceived especially for the pile carpet, but instead stem from a long tradition of embroidery and appliqué-work.

The author considers it important to have recourse to other textiles and to other possible sources of patterns when design development is at issue, if for a given period no pile carpets are available to document this. Developments in design are frequently an expression of the time, a current fashion, an attitude of mind, and are less frequently restricted to a certain technique. On the contrary, we encounter such developments in all possible techniques of the applied arts as well as in almost all materials.

Ill. 82 (left): Book of Durrow, c. 680; carpet page F. 1v; Trinity College Library, Dublin, codex no. 57.

The composition of the carpet's inner panel is identical to that shown in ills. 72 or 73. The use of pole-like crosspieces, a different colour from the ground, results in a double cross.

If from a certain period no original carpets have survived, then we must rely on other evidence able to convey a feeling for the originals lost. The mosaics discussed above represent one such possibility, though there is another. The present author touches on this here, despite well-meant advice that it be left out. Though it is not his intention to see the Nordenfalk – Meyer Schapiro[70] dispute flare up again, he does agree with Carl Nordenfalk to some extent. The author, too, sees in the Armenian-Syrian tradition of designs the model for the '*carpet pages*' in early Irish manuscripts. We continually hear of the Egyptian influence on Irish illumination when in fact it is the very tradition of designs that we are seeing. It is all really quite self-evident: Prior to 669 there were no carpet pages in Ireland. It was then that *Theodore of Tarsus* came to Ireland as papal legate. Theodore had had to flee the Arabs in Tarsus, the religious centre of Cilicia, found shelter in Rome with the Pope, was ordained Archbishop in Ireland and a few years before his death in 690 consecrated the church in Lindisfarne. The fact is that all the carpet pages in question were produced during Theodore's time of office. Even so, there may be only a few examples that take up the tradition just where their oriental models left off without already having been altered by the Celtic tradition (ills. 82–85 show these). The carpet page F. Iv of the *Book of Durrow*[71] (ill. 82) shows us the very same compositional scheme in its interior panel that we are already familar with from the carpet mosaic in Misis-Mopsuhestia. The use both of different colours to allow portions of the 'negative' areas to come together to form a bright yellow patriarchal cross as well as the bands of interlace result in a phenomenon quite common to these carpets – this being that abrupt changes in the visual make-up are often achieved quite simply by altering the colour without, on the whole, changing the composition. The same compositional scheme is also exhibited by carpet page F.2v of the *Book of Lindisfarne*[72] (ill. 83). Unlike the preceding example, here only a two-armed cross resulted. The squares or rectangles set into the 'negative-areas' of the cross, not unlike appliqué-work, suggest the influence of combined techniques such as possibly embroidery, together with weaving. This too is not new. The Cilician mosaics provided us with sufficient examples. The border outline has already undergone alteration in keeping with the Celtic tradition, and is thus no longer original. This is equally true of two further carpet pages from the same codex, F. 94v and F. 183v (ills. 84, 85), both of which do proceed from the same basic scheme, only then to combine this with the central medallion. Both are also similar in their basic design to those already shown from Cilicia (ill. 72).

Ill. 83 (page 70): Book of Lindisfarne, before 698; carpet page F. 2v. British Library, London, Cotton Ms. Nero D.IV.

The inner panel again follows the same compositional scheme as in ill. 82. Superimposed in the negative areas, in the manner of appliqué-work, are 'textile pieces' (Kilims?) with stepped crosses. The frame is already Irish.

Ill. 84 (page 71): Book of Lindisfarne, before 698; carpet page F. 94v. British Library, London, Cotton Ms. Nero D.IV.

Only a few sections of the ground show the original surface composition, which now, in reduced form, reemerges to fill the central medallion. Here too, along the outer edges of the negative areas, we find 'appliqué-work' with cross motifs.

Ill. 85 (left): Book of Lindisfarne, before 698; carpet page F. 138v. British Library, London, Cotton Ms. Nero D.IV.

An imposing Kotshak cross dominates this carpet page. The motifs of the ground are reminscent of the garments of Hittite godheads (ills.59, 60), which were typical of flat-weaves.

We encounter the compositional scheme of ill. 72 yet again in illuminated manuscripts from around 980 (ill. 86). They provide backgrounds of a textile-like nature for the depictions of evangelists and saints, and also serve as opening pages in the *Egbert-Codex*[73] and in the *Egbert-Psalter.*[74] Both codices are linked to the name of the Archbishop of Trier, Egbert. Egbert was an intimate friend of the Empress Theophanu, the wife and later widow of Otto II, who, following his death, assumed the regency for Otto III. The Byzantine Princess Theophanu was the niece of the Greco-Armenian Emperor John I. Tzimiskes (969–976) and there is much to indicate that as a result of this marriage close ties were maintained not only to Byzantium, but

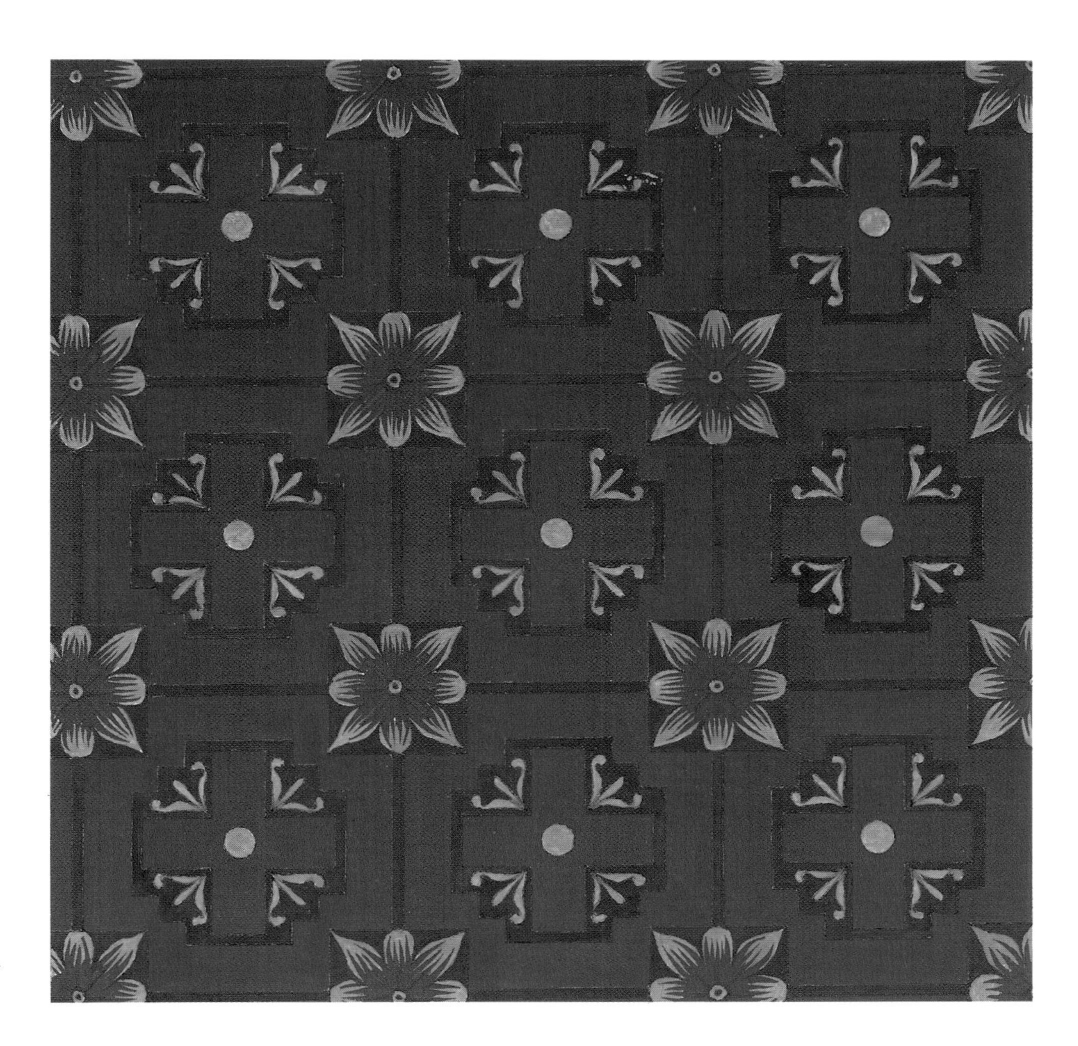

Ill. 86 (right): Egbert codex, c. 980; pattern of the background carpet from F. 6r. Stadtbibliothek, Trier, codex 24.

The composition is a variant of the composition in ill. 72.

also to Armenia in particular. This tradition was to be of great consequence under Bernhard von Hildesheim, Egbert's successor. Considering this background, the present author believes it possible that the 'textile' examples cited above might well be representations of Armenian carpets from the 10th century. In connection with these illuminated manuscripts, Gabriel Mandel mentions that they clearly show the influence of early Christian models from the 5th century, which now, surprisingly, are gaining recognition once again in this region.[75] One wonders whether this 'early Christian' influence might not also have had its origin in the Armenian-Byzantine region during the 10th century.

Early Fragments

As has already been mentioned, between the Pazyryk carpet and those carpets next in line, there is a gaping void of more than 1000 years. Erdmann assigns the carpet fragments found by Aurel Stein and Grünwedel in the Turfan Oases to some time between the 3rd and 6th centuries,[76] without ever offering any evidence in support of this. No attempt was ever made to determine their age and sample-analyses are not possible due to their limited size. Moreover, the circumstances of the find[77] cannot rule out the possibility that we may actually be dealing with the remains of dwelling-furnishings destroyed in the course of the Mongolian campaigns, which did not take place until the 13th century.

On the other hand, a fragment of pile-weaving (ill. 87) from the Keir Collection, published in 1982 by Edmund de Unger,[78] appears to be of the utmost importance. This textile fragment is not an actual knotted carpet, but instead lies in its development somewhere between a Soumak and a knotted carpet (cf. p. 52). The reconstruction carried out by de Unger exhibits in its design a certain relationship to the Pazyryk carpet as well as to the carpets of groups B III and C VII. Most stunning, however, is the agreement with the carpets in ills. 200 through 223.

It is a differentiated, coffered form with a square centre. The central cross shape, hardly recognizable now, is inscribed in a square that is surrounded by clearly visible S-symbols. This is in turn set in an octagon and, through the addition of points, has been modified to a cross-star. This is then enclosed by a panelled square frame in which eagles are quite clearly depicted. The square coffers of the border as well as of the two panels are filled in by a cross composition of the basic form type A (ill. 22), which itself must be viewed as the prototype for the border in TIEM no.

Ill. 87 a, b: Fragment of cut-loop weave, 6th-8th century(?). The Keir Collection.

a: present state, composed of fragments pieced together,
b: reconstruction of the original design.

The cut-loop weave, a coffered-form composition with central medallion, shows even in the remnants that have been preserved the surprising variety of cruciforms in the central octagons of the basic form type A of the cross.

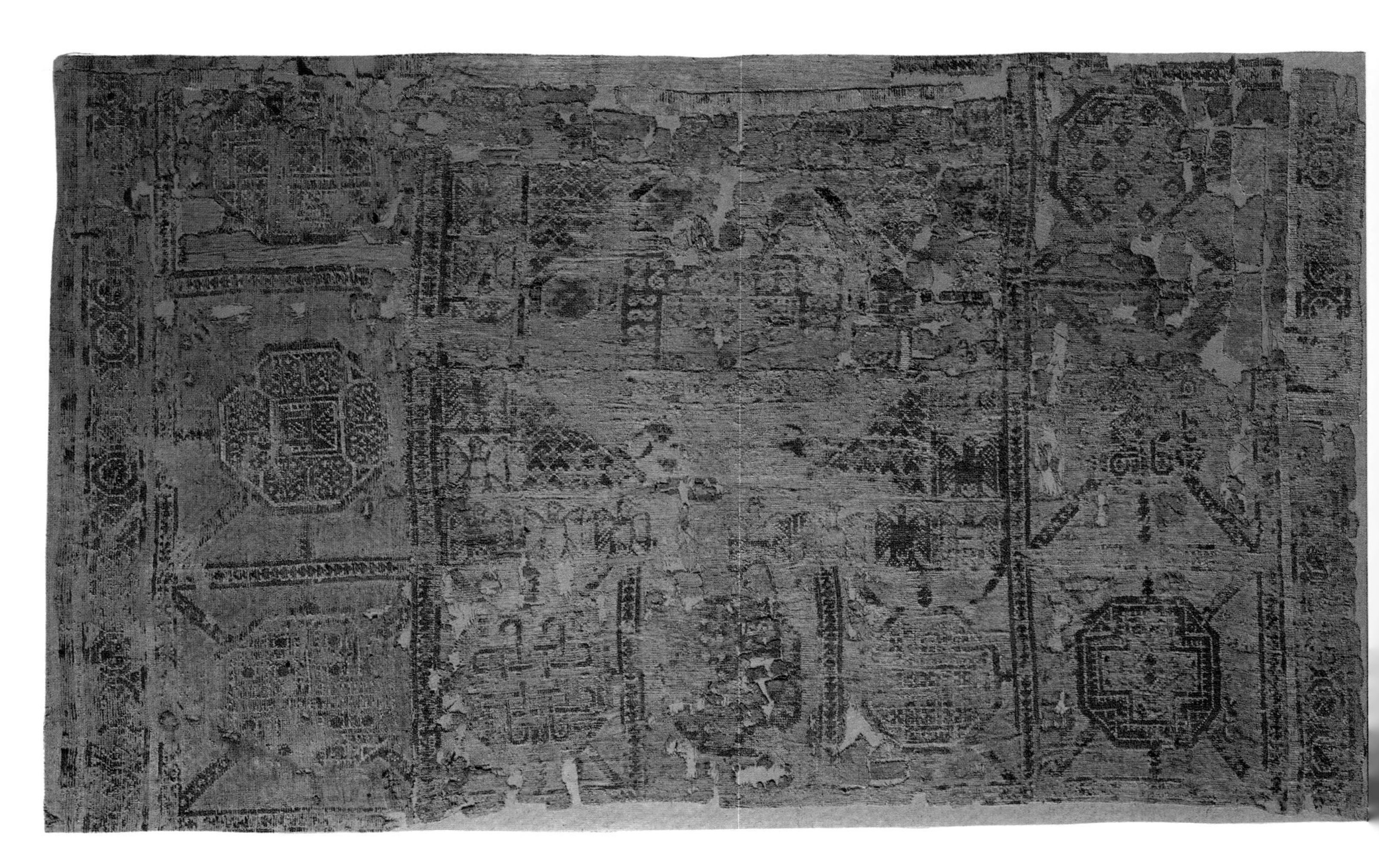

Ill. 88: Fragment of cut-loop weave, The Keir Collection: cross details. Montage from ill. 87 a, diagram and basic A-form.

685 as shown in ill. 99. However, unlike this latter example, in the fragment from the Keir collection we do not find the eight-pointed cross-star in the centre, but rather modified crosses inscribed in octagons. And these we are familar with from the collection of mosaic designs from the ornamental architecture of the Near East (ill. 88). The outside border is made up of stylized heads reminiscent of Coptic art. The question of when and where this Keir fragment was originally produced cannot be answered with any certainty. A comparison with corresponding ornamental designs would seem to suggest dating it to some time between the 6th and 8th centuries. De Unger's proposal that we consider Egypt its country of origin remains a

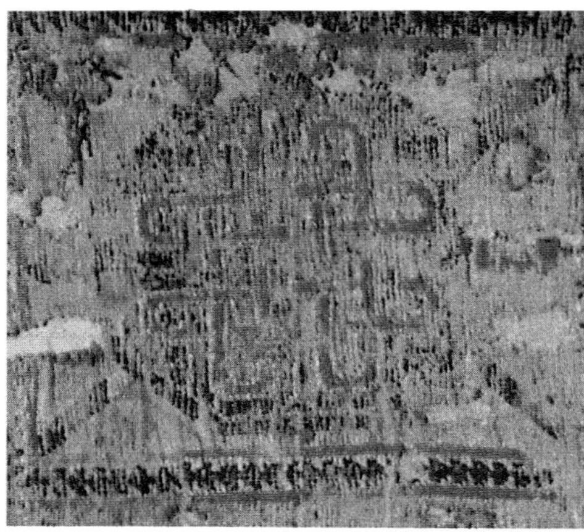

possibility, though not imperative. Since our processing of the available material is still in its infancy (that is, our attempt to distinguish Syrian, Armenian and Byzantine material from what is actually Egyptian-Coptic), the comparative material provided by de Unger is of no help in clearing up those questions still left open.
There can, however, be no doubt that this textile has a place in what we are calling the chain of traditional designs, acting as an important link, as a design itself. This is likewise true of several other pieces related to this one, such as that in the Metropolitan Museum of Art in New York (ill. 89).

Ill. 89: Knotted-pile and woven carpet fragment, 6th-8th century(?), 111 x 102 cm. Metropolitan Museum of Art, New York, no. 31.2.1. The Rogers Fund, 1931.

Ill. 90 (below): Anagram carpet, 7th-9th century. The Fine Arts Museum of San Francisco, San Francisco, no. 1986.4. Artist's realization of the anagram carpet from this illustration.

Number 31.2.1 of the MMA shows pieces knotted with the symmetrical knot which are raised above the ground-weave like a relief (*mahfur!*). The fragment found in Akhmin might well prove that production was carried out in Akhmin/Sohag, an Armenian settlement in upper Egypt.

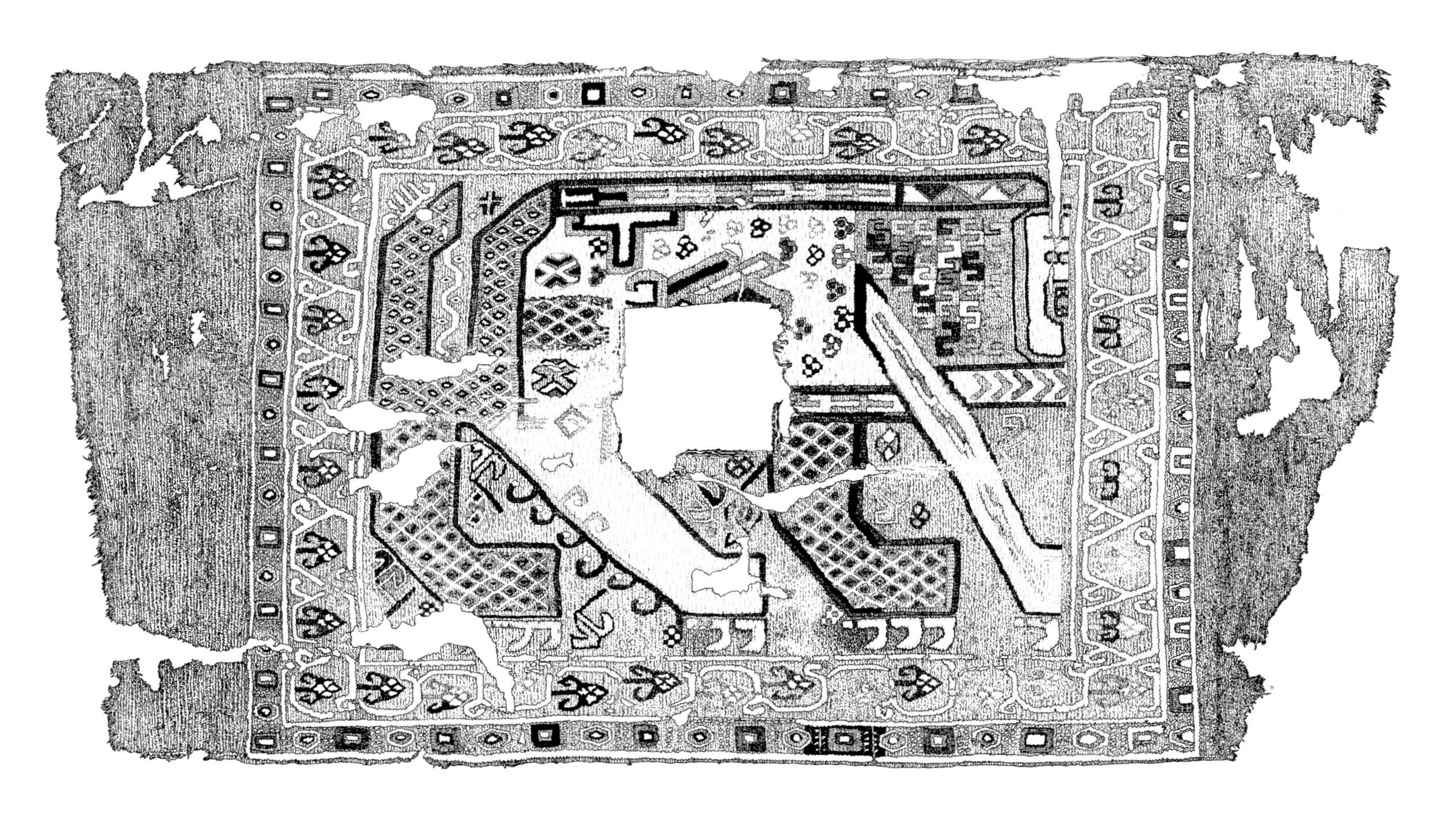

Ill. 91 (page 77, below): Anagram carpet, 7th-9th century. The Fine Arts Museum of San Francisco, San Francisco, no. 1986.4.

This carpet is possibly the most exciting rediscovery of a knotted-pile carpet during the last few years. The anagram consists of the letters in the Armenian word 'Յիսուս', meaning Jesus. These are arranged so that the 'image' of a lion results, an old symbol for Christ.

The recently rediscovered carpet in The Fine Arts Museum of San Francisco (ill. 91), which was allegedly found in Fostat 60 years ago, indeed appears unusual in its design. The results of radiocarbon dating showed that this carpet must have been produced no earlier than the 7th century and no later than the end of the 9th century. In the first study published on this carpet[79] the representation is interpreted as a 'gigantic animal, possibly a schematic lion.' It is in any case striking that in representing the animal there was no attempt made whatsoever to arrive at a realistic design that one might be able to reconstruct for oneself. Indeed, the animal appears to have been put together from differently sized and structured elements.

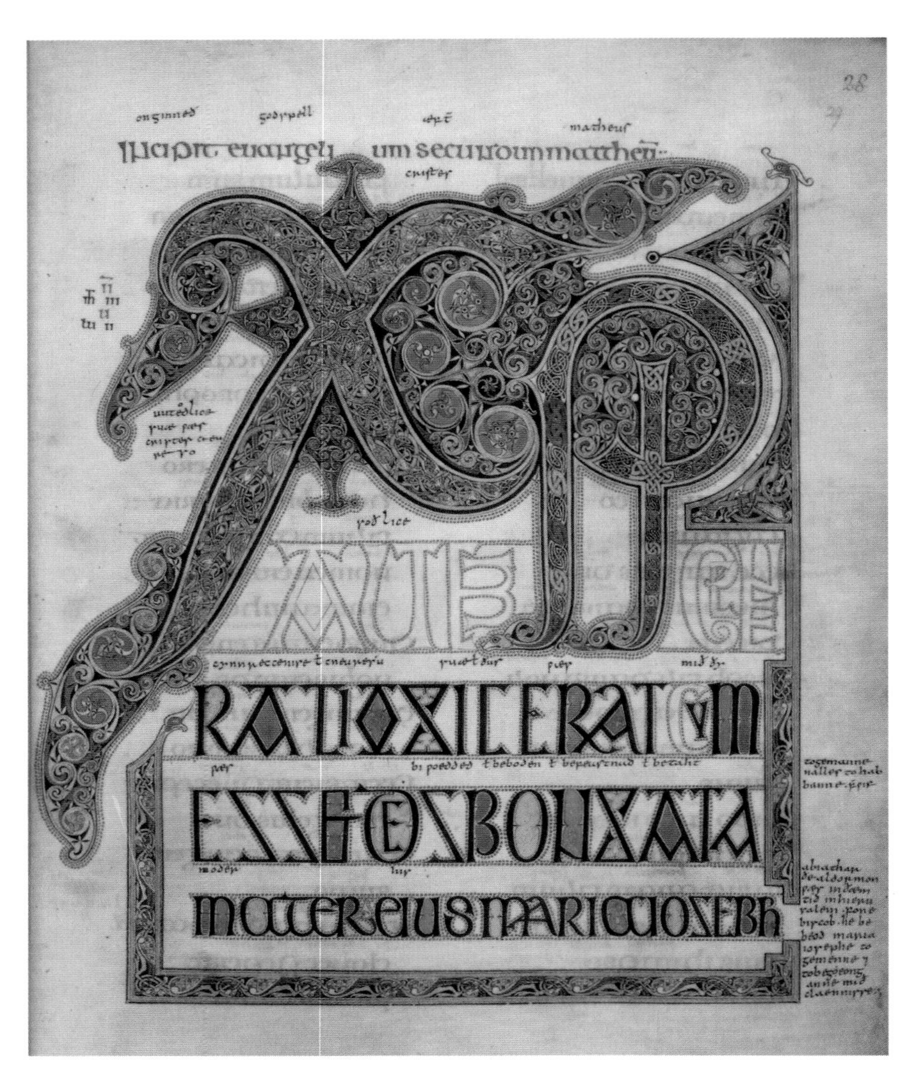

Ill. 92 (right): Book of Lindisfarne, before 698; incarnation initial on F. 29r. British Library, London, Cotton Ms. Nero D. IV.

Analogous to the carpet in ill. 90, the Chi-Rho anagram in this 'incarnation' initial likewise takes on the form of an animal, thus becoming a comparable symbol of Christ.

In our discussion of the likely beginnings of the Christian oriental carpet, our attention was drawn to the carpet pages of Irish illuminated 7th century manuscripts (cf. 69). And it is precisely here that we find the key to deciphering the meaning of this carpet. At first glance there is a similarity between this animal-like representation and the anagrams on the initialled pages of Irish manuscripts, such as page 130 r of the Book of Kells (ill. 93). Upon closer examination of such initialled pages the present author succeeded in finding a direct parallel: the 'incarnation' initials XPI (F. 29r) in the Book of Lindisfarne (ill. 92). Here, too, the anagram takes on the shape of an animal with – and this question remains open – two or three legs. The anagram in the carpet contains the letters of the Armenian word Յիսուս, meaning 'Jesus'. XPI, likewise, is the nomen sacrum for 'Jesus'. It is hard to conceive of a closer correspondence. Even the 'lion'-interpretation from above appears quite probable. The lion is used as one of the symbols of Christ[80] and beyond that symbolizes the power and strength of rulers. One might also be reminded that the S-shaped motifs can be used as an abbreviated form for 'God' as mentioned above (p. 37). And thus this carpet serves as an important document in a number of ways: First of all, it verifies the assumed connection between the ornamental designs of Irish illumination and the art of the combined spheres of Armenian and Syrian cultural influence; secondly, it is to date the oldest Christian oriental knotted-pile carpet and at the same time the oldest Armenian carpet; thirdly, it is a manifest symbol of spiritual power; fourthly, it is the immediate forerunner of the graphic 'animal carpets' of group B II, and finally, it stands as a striking example for the richly symbolic content of oriental textiles in the Christian tradition.

Ill. 93: Book of Kells, c. 800; opening page of the Gospel according to Mark, F. 130r. Trinity College Library, Dublin; Ms no. 58.

This anagram page shows little more than the scant traces of the former Cilician influence. What is striking is the transformation from four-part compositions to triple round, whirling forms, which is typical of the Celtic art of Ireland.

The matter is not as clear cut with respect to a fragment considered by Johanna Zick to be the oldest surviving remnant of a carpet knotted during the Islamic period[81] (ill. 94). Zick comes to the conclusion, following a technical analysis indicating the use of Z-spun wool and a red weft, that the carpet could not have been produced in Egypt. Unfortunately the remaining portion of the representation itself offers so very little in the way of clues as to its own identity that conjecture is resorted to in trying to establish what the composition in its entirety might have been. One such possible piece of guesswork is the palmette as proposed by Zick. A comparison of the Arabic lettering remaining from a line of text with the lettering of the 7th to 9th centuries makes it reasonable to attribute this piece to that time. The high quality of the fragment, 2294 knots/sq dm, the intensive glow of colours (the penetrating kermes-scarlet in particular), and the sophisticated layout – all of which Ms. Zick was able to determine when comparing this fragment to Egyptian products of the same period – led her to weigh the possibility that it was produced in the Arabian province of Armenia. Such a conclusion dovetails with the historical sources of the time, yet it is difficult to assign a place in our chain of traditional design to this textile because of its poor physical condition. While there may be similarities with Byzantine and Syrian models, they cannot easily be reconstructed.

Ill. 94: Fragment of a knotted-pile carpet, 7th-9th century, 32 x 19 cm; Museum of Islamic Art, Cairo, inv. no. 14680.

The fragment, the pattern of which is no longer identifiable, might be part of one of the carpets expected to accompany the annual payments of tribute to the caliphs.

A: The Early Middle Ages

Group A encompasses a wide array of surviving carpets or fragments, many of which often look radically different from one another. Having been found in the mosques of Konya, Beysehir and Divrigi, these were thought to be Seljuk (compare pp. 13 ff.). Similarities in borders or composition led the present author to subdivide these into the groups AI-AIII.

Group A I: Carpets with Cross-Block Borders

At the beginning of our discussion on carpets from the early Middle Ages let us place a carpet[82] (ill. 96) which is kept in Istanbul today. On a blue ground, linked together to form a net, there are offset coffers in the centre of which in each case there is a

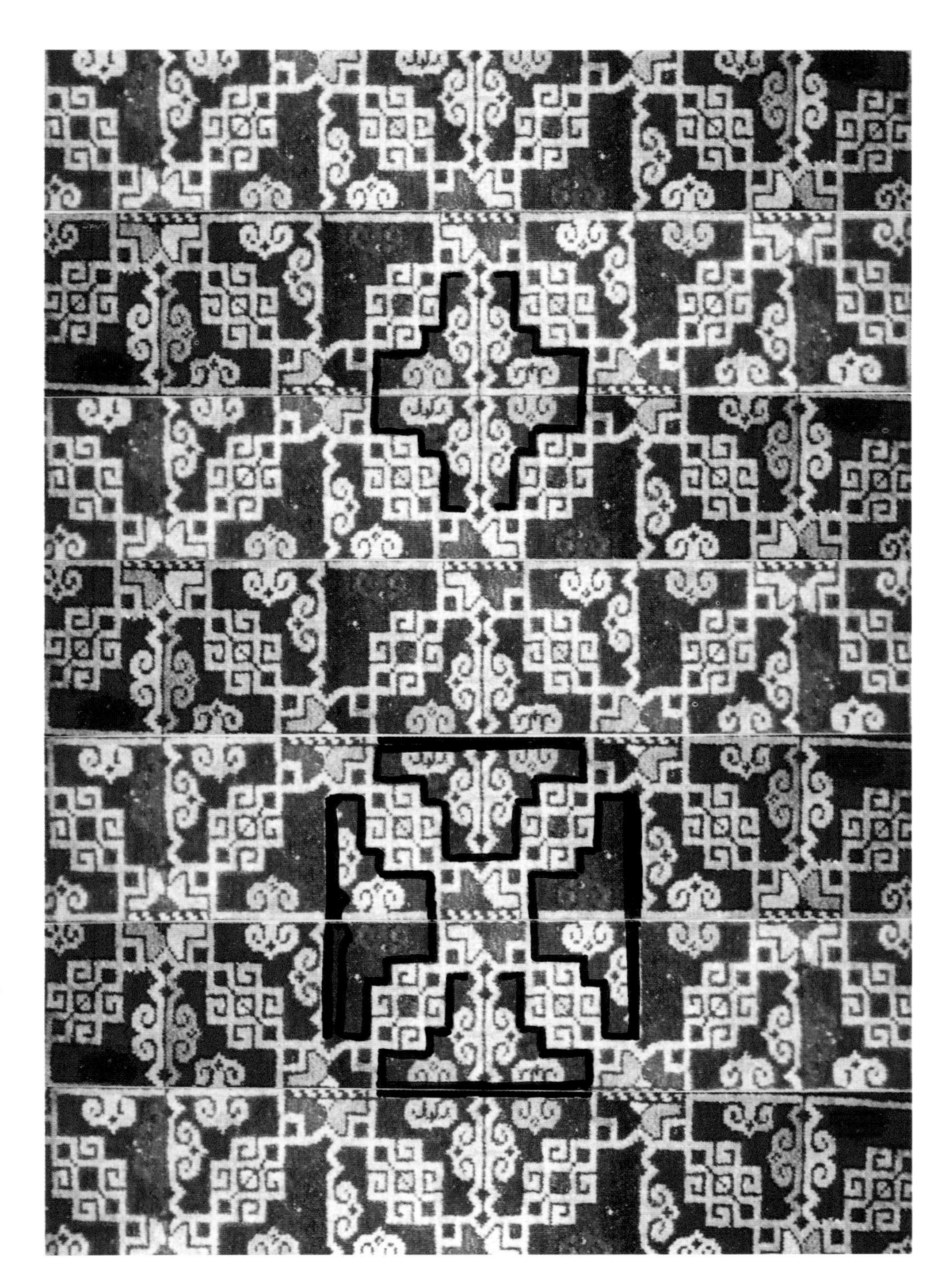

Ill. 95: Invented panel design, photographic collage consisting of borders of the C II a-type.

Borders frequently grew out of stripes of design from the inner panel. In this case the process was reversed: by laying border stripes side by side a panel composition was achieved that corresponds to that in ill. 72.
The elements of design they contain are the cruciforms of ills. 97 a and b.

Ill. 96 (left): TIEM no. 685, 320 x 240 cm. Türk ve Islam Eserleri Müzesi, Istanbul.

Ill. 97 a, b (right): Details from ill. 95: the two cruciforms determining the pattern.

red cross-star set in an eight-pointed star. The extension of this is seen in reduced cross arms. The invented panel design (ill. 95) demonstrates the original form. The main border (ill. 99) consists of coffers exhibiting the same motif as well. It lends more clarity to the old cruciform, the basic form type A, which we already know from the textile in ill. 88. The old pattern, though really very sketchy, has been preserved. A comparison with the decoration of the inner panel (ill. 98) shows that this underwent considerable reduction. We find an adequate silhouette of this cruciform on a Katchkar in Yeghegnatsor dating from 1041 (ill. 131a).[83] This is our first point of reference when it comes to providing a possible date. The yellow figures of the secondary border (ill. 101), too, point to a relatively early design. For the first time only a part, that is a half, of the cross was depicted. This practice was not actually new. A similar development can be found in manuscript illuminations dating from early Christian times. In these early days borders always had an apotropaic purpose, and we must assume that every detail was of significance, with every symbol carrying a number of different meanings. We can also assume that the belief

Ill. 98 (inside right): TIEM no. 685, detail from ill. 96: cross composition of the field design.

A comparison with the border in ill. 99 is helpful in recognizing the basic form type A.

Ill. 99 (outside right): TIEM no. 685, detail from ill. 96: cross composition of the main border and diagram.

in the exorcizing power of symbolic shapes must have played a role, judging from the fact that it still does today.[84] This is especially the case in oriental art, but even more so in the art of Armenia. And yet, why this reduction, which actually comes quite close to being an encodement? Was it a way of adapting to a non-Christian environment in which 'readability' was to be reserved only for the initiated? In other words, was it a kind of secret language? One suspects this, considering the S- and E-shaped symbols, the interpretation of which requires a knowledge of the Armenian alphabet (cf. p. 37, ill. 709).

The border of the TIEM carpet mentioned above, no. 865, introduces the development of a very small group of fragments, consisting thus far of three or four. Of these, three are related in their main or secondary borders, with two being identical in their design of their inner panels or originating from similar principles of patterning (ills.

Ill. 100 (outside left): TIEM no. 685, detail from ill. 96: detail of the field design.

Ill. 101 (inside left): TIEM no. 685, detail from ill. 96: secondary border and diagram.

A comparison with ill. 99 shows the division in half of the cross composition in the main border.

Ill. 102 (outside left): Mevl. no. 1034, detail from ill. 104: cross composition from the main border.

Ill. 103 (inside left): TIEM no. 688, detail from ill. 105: cross composition from the main border.

102–106). This development in borders is tentatively completed with the border of a carpet, Vakf. E 344, whose geographical attribution and dating are more exact (ill. 106). We find a nearly identical border design on the portal of the Mausoleum of Mu'mine Khatun, erected in 1186 in Nakhichevan, a town located south-east of Dwin on the Araxes.[85] This correspondence provides us with a second clue in our attempt to date these textiles, making it quite possible to assume that carpets TIEM no. 685, Mevl. no. 1034 and TIEM no. 688 are to be dated earlier than Vakf. E 344, possibly to the end of the 11th or the beginning of the 12th century. The question as to the province of these carpets must remain unanswered. Their designs suggest an origin in West Armenia. Whether they represent the 'kali'[86] of Kalikala (Erzerum), or whether they were already being knotted in central Anatolia, cannot be definitively established at this time. Vakf. E 344, however, represents the established set of designs characteristic of the eastern region of central Armenia.

Ill. 104 (right): Mevl. no. 1034, 112 x 49 cm, fragment. Mevlana Museum, Konya.

Ill. 106 (inside right): Vakf. no. E 344, detail from ill. 108: main border and diagram. A comparison with ill. 99 shows the reduction and the modification along one side, i.e. the sacrifice of the hook forms (hasten) originally derived from the diacritical marks on Kufic writing, and the creation of new cruciforms, which typically involves what is left over.

Ill. 107 (outside right): Mausoleum of the Mu'mine Khatun, Nakhichevan; detail from the relief decor of the portal, constructed in 1186.

Ill. 105 (left): TIEM no. 688, 230 x 114 cm. Türk ve Islam Eserleri Müzesi, Istanbul.

A carpet from the 13th century, the inner panel of which quite clearly demonstrates the Chinese influence in the restructuring of the individual designs. Ill. 124 shows a section.

Ill. 108 (right): Vakf. no. E 344, 380 x 230 cm. Vakiflar Carpet Museum, Istanbul.

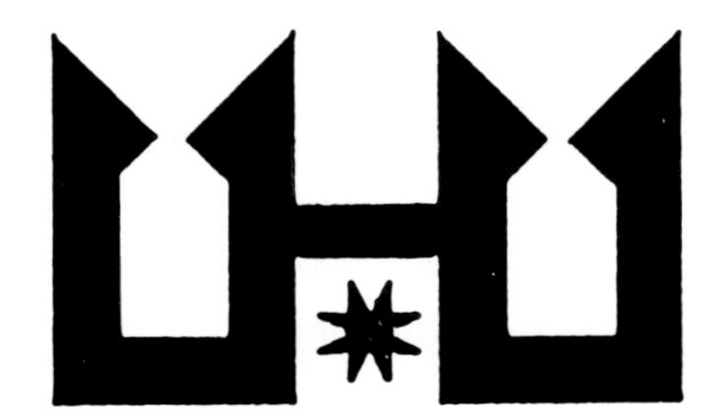

Group A II: Carpets with Pseudo-Kufic Borders

This group likewise encompasses only a few fragments, six all in all, each exhibiting disparate designs in their inner panels. Common to all of them, admittedly, is what can be identified as a large border of varying patterns, which the literature has come to term 'Kufic'. One can, indeed, determine a superficial, formal correspondence with Kufic lettering (ill. 106). Yet after studying these designs more carefully, this hypothesis proves to be without support. Illustration 109 shows the detail of a border from TIEM no. 689. This detail shows only half of the basic form type D_1 – very much simplified, for example half of the cross found in the border of TIEM no. 685 (ill. 98). In the border of TIEM no. 684 (ill. 111) the cross-star has been preserved, though how this originally fitted into the whole is no longer clear. A flatweave (ill. 110) in which the entire pattern remains intact[87] clarifies this. Here we find nearly the same phenomenon that we encountered with regard to the secondary border of TIEM no. 685. It appears that this use of demi-cruciforms has a rather long tradition, possibly going back as far as the 10th century. We find these designs in relief bands in Greece (ills. 114, 115), primarily on buildings showing the greatest Armenian influence. Examples of this can be found in the ornamental frieze of the apse of St. Mary's Church in Hosios Loukas, as well as on the sarcophagus of the donor Romano II (959–963), a Byzantine Emperor of Armenian descent; in the decorative band on the head piece

Ill. 109 (right): TIEM no. 689; detail from ill. 117: main border and diagram.

Ill. 110 (left): Vakf. no. YD 872, 'Zili'. Vakiflar Kilim Museum, Istanbul.

Right: detail of the field design, covered for comparison.

This illustration is intended to help in understanding the reduction to half of the original cruciform (e.g. ill. 99).

Ill. 111: TIEM no. 684, detail from ill. 120: main border.

This border has been able to keep the cross star from the central square of the cross basic form-type A.

Ill. 112: TIEM no. 692/693, detail from ill. 122: main border.

Ill. 113 a,b: TIEM no. 681, details from ill. 121: main borders.

Both illustrations from the same carpet show very well how a pseudo-Kufic border can develop from a cross half.

of Jesus of Navi[88] or much farther afield, in northern Spain on the wall arch of the apsis of Santa Maria de Tahull.[89] G. Lampakis[90] compiled the brick decorations used in Hellenistic churches. A large number of these are based on the design of the demi cruciform. Lampakis attempted to base his interpretation of these designs on writing, always arriving at variations of the letter combinations IX and IC. This interpretation, however, does not seem to be in accordance with how these designs evolved. It is important to note that in so doing, Lampakis wanted to demonstrate that Christian rather than Islamic traditions were in evidence here. The question as to whether the formation of similarly designed Kufic writing might not have been influenced by such Christian ornamentation at this point remains unanswered.

Ill. 114 (left): Lower church, Hosios Loukas: sarcophagus of Romano II, 10th century: ornamental frieze from the lid.

Ill. 115 (left): Apse of St. Mary's Church in Hosios Loukas, 10th century: ornamental frieze from the outside wall.

Ill. 116 (left): Frieze of writing from a window jamb in Ghasni; detail, 12th century. Lindenmuseum, Stuttgart, Inv. no. A 35 904 L.

It is striking that the ornamental friezes of Christian origin correspond much more closely to the borders than does the much later 'florid' Kufic. This gives rise to the suspicion that the influence may possibly have run in the opposite direction.

If carpets were being done by Christian weavers for the Seljuk or Mongolian occupying power, then some of them may be found in these groups, whereas the so-called 'hoof-mark pattern' in the carpets TIEM no. 689 (ill. 117) represents yet another example of the continuation of the Armenian-Syrian tradition of designs,[91] and the cross-stars in Mevl. no. 862 (ill. 118) certainly presume a Christian background as common knowledge. We do notice particularly with respect to TIEM no. 692/693,

Ill. 117 (right): TIEM no. 689, 608 x 246 cm. Türk ve Islam Eserleri Müzesi, Istanbul.

The inner panel consists of Kotshak crosses set in octagons, which are laid out like tiles to form a composition familiar from early Christian mosaics in Antioch.

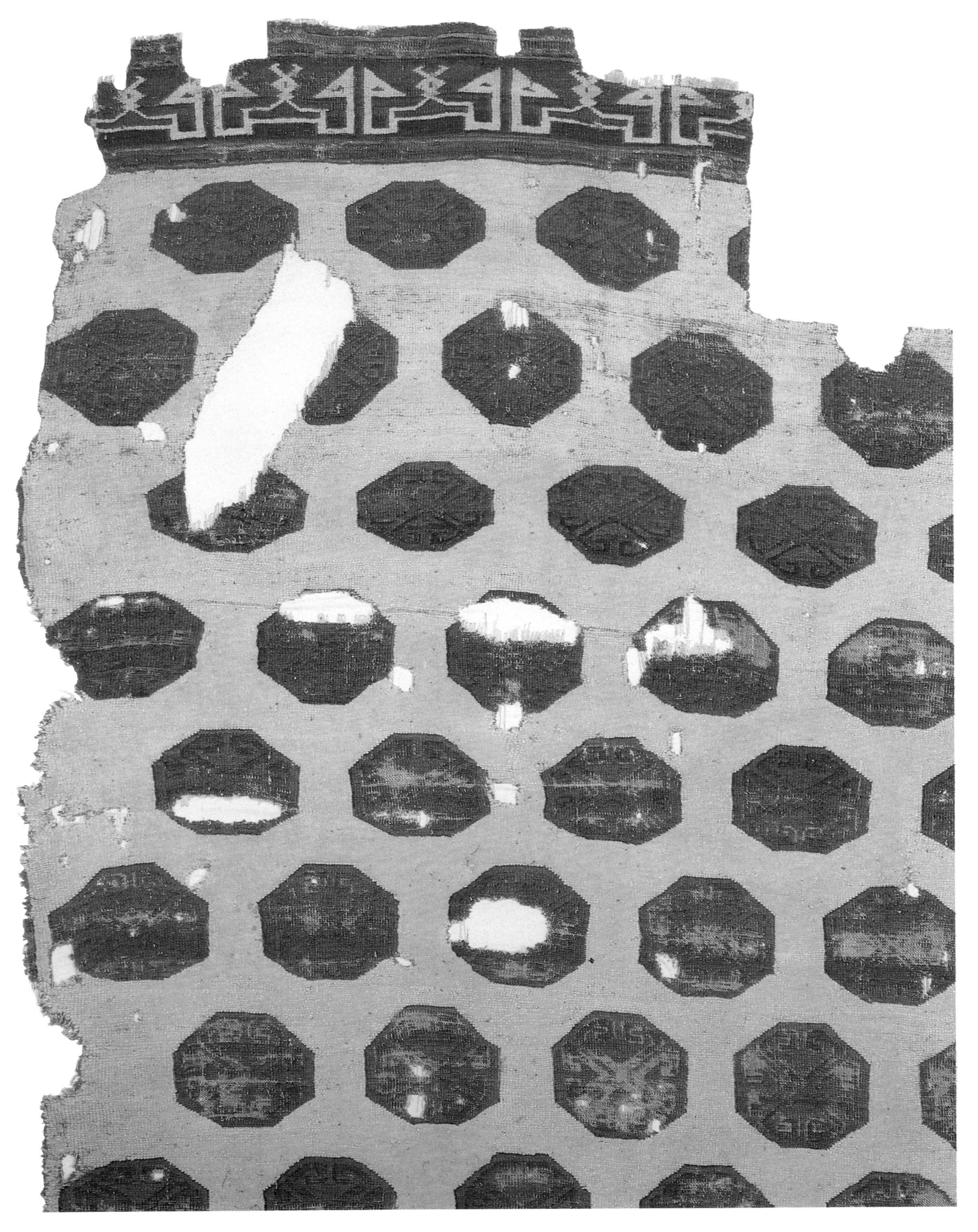

Ill. 118 (right): Mevl. no. 862, 255 x 90 cm, fragment. Mevlana Museum, Konya.

The design elements of this inner panel are particularly typical of Armenian carpets: the diamond-form crosses in endless repeat are composed so that they share certain elements, e.g. lilies and 'S'-symbols. The cross star, symbolizing the epiphany, is located in the centre.

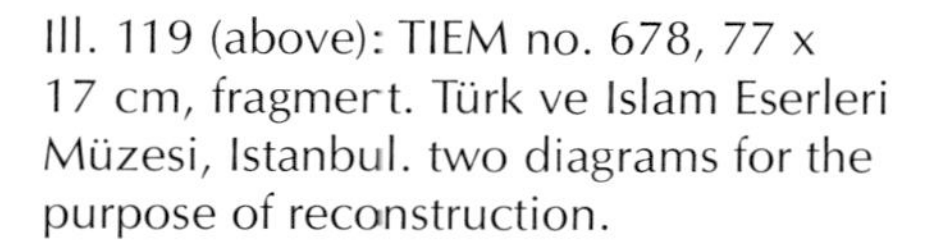

Ill. 119 (above): TIEM no. 678, 77 x 17 cm, fragmert. Türk ve Islam Eserleri Müzesi, Istanbul. two diagrams for the purpose of reconstruction.

The hooked diamond in the centre of the hexagonal star could have originated from ill. 118. The star is encircled by six S-shaped symbols standing for God.

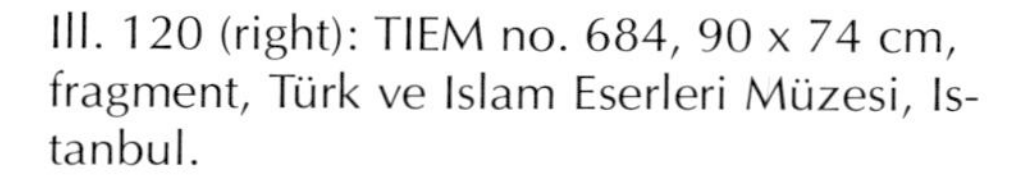

Ill. 120 (right): TIEM no. 684, 90 x 74 cm, fragment, Türk ve Islam Eserleri Müzesi, Istanbul.

The former Kotshak cross of the basic E-form undergoes here, for the first time, a 'floral' transformation on one side and is decorated with the S-symbol in the centre. This very likely represents an early design of the 'tree of Jesse'.

Ill. 121 (right): TIEM no. 681, 520 x 285 cm. Türk ve Islam Eserleri Müzesi, Istanbul.

The fact that the border along the sides differs from that at the top and bottom clearly shows the development from the half-cross to its misinterpreted modification. The author has so far been unable to interpret the design of the field; however, it appears in this form on the opening pages of Armenian codices as well.

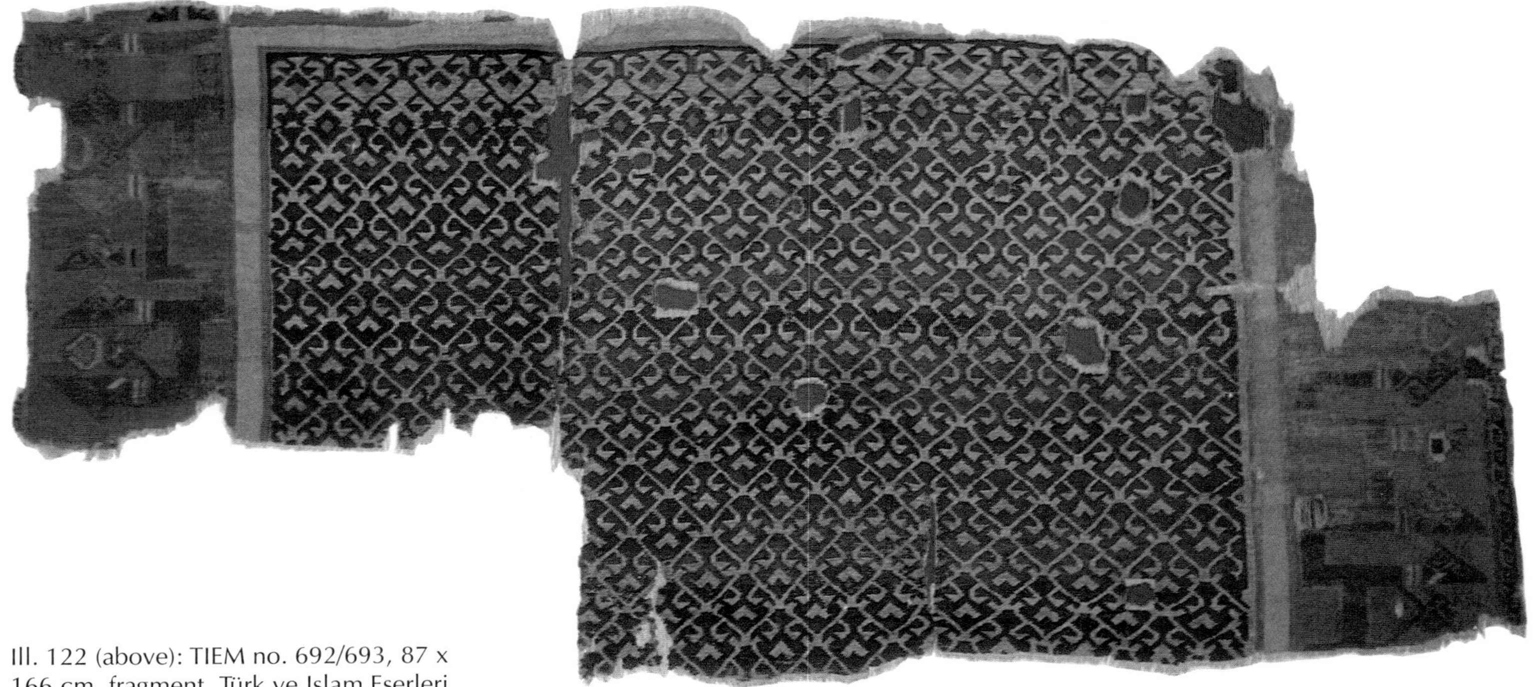

Ill. 122 (above): TIEM no. 692/693, 87 x 166 cm, fragment. Türk ve Islam Eserleri Müzesi, Istanbul.

Each of these detail photographs clearly shows the change and restructuring that have taken place in the former ground design, which was quite similar to that in ill. 118.

Ill. 123 a,b (right):TIEM no. 692/693, details from ill. 122 a: the field design, b: the beginning of the repeat pattern.

but also in the case of TIEM no. 681, that Christian symbolism was obviously changed. This is well shown in ill. 120, where we see that while in the first one and a half rows the original concept repeated itself with virtually no change, subsequent rows show that, as work progressed, the design was modified. TIEM no. 681 (ill. 121) represents a further development in this design, which also appears in Armenian illuminated manuscripts.

Ill. 124 (right): TIEM no. 688, detail from ill. 105: field design.

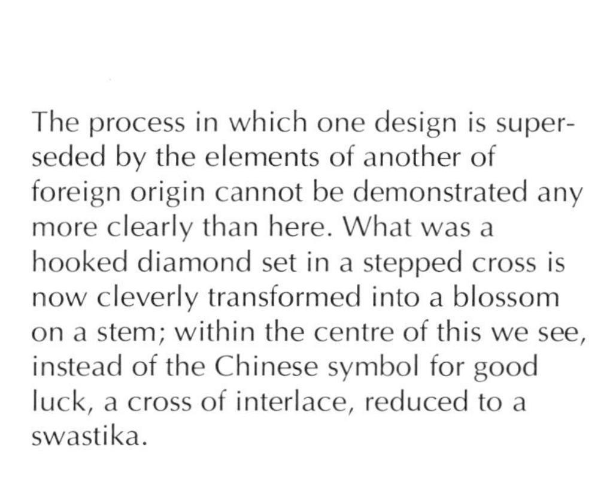

The process in which one design is superseded by the elements of another of foreign origin cannot be demonstrated any more clearly than here. What was a hooked diamond set in a stepped cross is now cleverly transformed into a blossom on a stem; within the centre of this we see, instead of the Chinese symbol for good luck, a cross of interlace, reduced to a swastika.

Modifications in design may also have been stimulated by outside influences, in the ground design of TIEM no. 688 of the Group A I (ill. 124). Here the Greek cross outlines of the Kotshak crosses give way to floral designs, with the Kotshak crosses themselves becoming blossoms filled with crosses, recalling the influence of Chinese textiles such as the silk on display at the Metropolitan Museum of Art, New York (ill. 125).

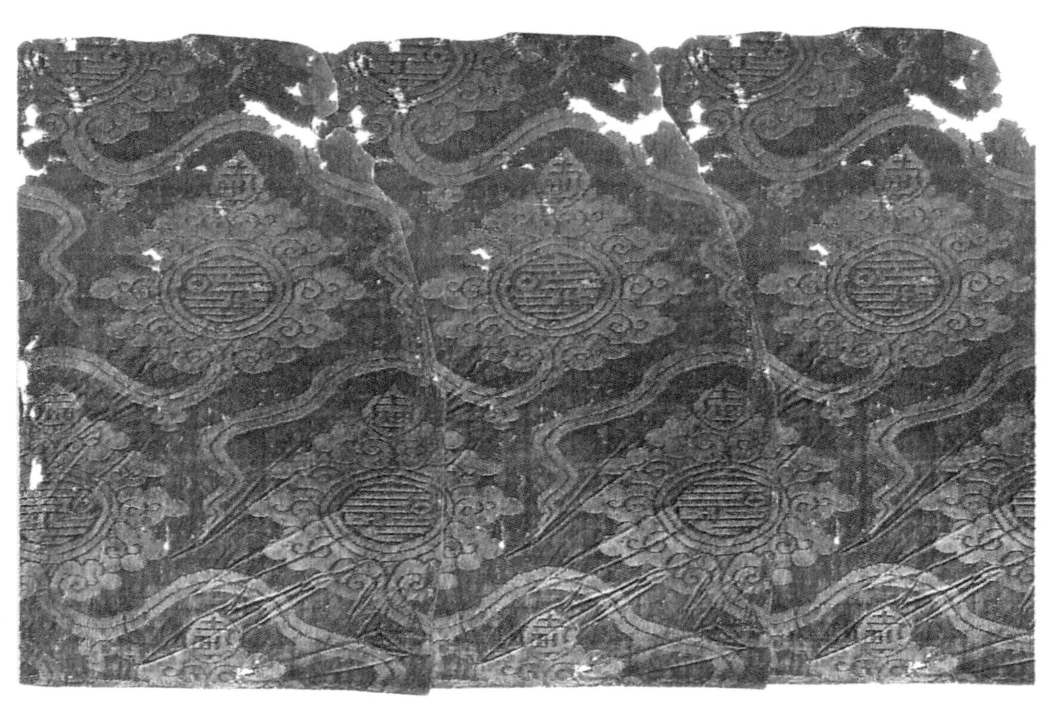

Ill. 125 (right): Chinese silk, MMA no. 46.156.20. The Metropolitan Museum of Art, New York. The Rogers Fund.

A more complete picture of the pattern repeat is achieved by using a montage of photographs of the same fragment.

Ill. 126 (right): Vakf. no. A 217, fragment, 195 x 185 cm. Vakiflar Carpet Museum, Istanbul.

Group A III: Coffered-Form Medallion Carpets I - Large-Pattern(LP) Holbein Carpets I

This group contains those carpets which could be considered to mark the beginning of the series labelled by Erdmann 'Holbein carpets of Type III/IV'[92] known in England as 'Large-Pattern Holbein carpets'.

To date the present author has seen only one carpet from the 12th century, fragment Vakf. A 217 (ill. 126). Two large medallions fill the inner panel. They carry on the design tradition which we are familiar with from Cilicia (ill. 79), in the Diaconia-Mosaic (ill. 76) and Khirbat al-Mafjar (ill. 78); it is a tradition we encounter again in the design of the opening pages of the Armenian evangelistaries (ills. 128, 181, 182). This tradition plays an important role in Armenian metalwork. Illustration 129 shows us an example, a granulated box made of gold-plated silver. The extension of components from the Diaconia-Mosaic (ill. 76) is obvious; the manner in which the panels are filled to look carpet-like is typical and definitive for Groups A III, B II and C VI. The border of Vakf. A 217 (ill. 130) represents a very interesting intermediate stage between TIEM no. 685 (ill. 99) and MBN no. 10/294, a carpet in the Bavarian National Museum in Munich (ills. 251, 261, 263, 265, 267) to which we will return. The design of this border is comparable to the Katchkar-borders from around the 11th or 12th century, such as those in Yeghegnatsor and Kodaik, Havoots-tar[93] (ill. 131) or Noraduz (ill. 132).

Ill. 127 (right): Vakf. no. A 217, detail from ill. 126: medallion.

Ill. 128 (left): Armenian evangelistary, dated 1232, from the Horomos Monastery near Ani: detail of the title page of the Gospel according to Mark, F. 29r. Matenadaran, Erivan, codex no. 1519.

Granted, the carpet panels on the opening pages can only rarely be compared directly with carpets; yet they do have a good deal in common when it comes to details and the general concept of the surface layout.

Ill. 129 (left): Small Armenian metal box made of granulated, gold-plated silver, 23 x 29.7 cm, used as a reliquary for the heads of St. Matthew and St. Helen, as well as for Lazarus' head later. 10th/11th century(?) or earlier. Domschatzkammer, Trier.

The structure of the granulated surface establishes the connection between the Diaconia mosaic in ill. 76 and Vakf. A 217. Crosses of interlace and knot-crosses together form yet another light-symbol cross composition, which we encounter in numerous carpets, especially those of the Groups B II and C VI. The interlace cross in the medallion bears a striking similarity in how it is put together with the proto-designs of the later Holbein guls (ills. 357, 359).

Ill. 130 (right): Vakf. no. A 217, detail from ill. 126: main border.

The border calls to mind that found in ill. 99, based on the basic A-form – with the exception that here bands of interlace are used in a way that suggest a single, continuous design. This can be observed in the Katchkars of this time in much the same way.

Ill. 131 (right): Katchkars: inside left dated 1041, Yeghegnatsor; outside right dated 12th century, Kodaik, Havoots-tar.

The crosses of the basic A-form and the S-symbol present in the stone border of the Katchkar on the left are worthy of note.

Ill. 132 (right): 12th century Katchkar, border detail; Noraduz.

B: The High Middle Ages

Whereas up to now the assumption that we were dealing with a steady, though oftentimes interrupted, development of designs has been more hypothesis, the documentation for this improves markedly from this point on. Because the carpet was first a symbol of supremacy and then one of status, certain information has been handed down to us which does not otherwise survive in its original form. Paintings, frescos and panel paintings recorded what was of import in their time. As of the 11th century, we find carpets represented in paintings of worldly or spiritual rulers, or saints.

A good deal of attention has been focused on the depictions of animal carpets.[94] However, just why this was not done with regard to other carpets is unknown.

Carpets in European Painting

The earliest depictions of carpets are to be found in the second half of the 13th century in paintings from northern Italy, Tuscany, the area surrounding the cities of Sienna, Padua, Florence and in Lombardy. It is Giotto to whom we owe thanks for most of these paintings, his being the most accurate as well. Might this be due to the fact that Giotto, as a youth, completed an apprenticeship in weaving? The carpets

Ill. 133 (right): Giotto: The Bishop of Assisi's Vision of St. Francis; before 1300. Upper Church, Assisi. Fresco.

depicted by Giotto vary greatly in their design and most probably do not stem from his period; in part, they are very likely to be considerably older.

Illustration 135 shows a detail of the inner panel of the carpet belonging to the Bishop of Assisi,[95] painted by Giotto before 1300. It is comparable to TIEM no. 685 (ill. 96) and yet is based on a variation of the cross basic form type E (ill. 23). This is characteristic of a fashion that was predominant in Armenia during the 10th century and in the greater area of Byzantium subsequent to the loss of the Armenian regions during the 11th and 12th centuries. Between the circles a 'negative area' took shape, which in turn made room for a further cross motif. Erdmann illustrated a carpet

Ill. 134 (right): Detail of the carpet depicted in ill. 133.

Ill. 135 (right): Carpet design from ill. 133.

In its structure the carpet possesses obvious similarities to textiles from the 10th to the 12th century. Cf. ills. 175, 161–165.

Ill. 136: St. Karapet, Norawank; detail of the Tympanon from 1261.

The madonna is shown seated on a carpet as a sign of her importance.

Ill. 137: Master of S. Francesco: Crucifix, 1272. Pinacoteca, Perugia.

Whereas this painting by the Master of S. Francesco also shows a carpet on the piece of wood under Christ's feet, probably in its original form, in all later examples the carpet is only found under the body of Christ, for greater effect.

similar in composition,[96] which appears in a fresco from Bojana dated 1259 and describes a scene from the life of St. Nicholas.

We find the next stage of development in various different paintings by Giunta Pisano, Duccio, and Cimabue, as well as by Giotto and his school. They provide backgrounds for the large crucifixes and, in the present author's view, have the character of carpets in terms of both function and design. In the work of Berlinghiero Berlinghieri there is a small carpet under Christ's feet,[97] similar to those commonly found in the depictions of the evangelists. Not until the closing decades of the 13th century did the eucharist begin to appear against the background of a carpet, something that was also being done by painters in Armenia at the same time with depictions of the Mother of God[98] (ill. 136). This analogy may be entirely coincidental and yet this use of carpets does seem to bespeak a shared attitude. Such 'background'-carpets reflect the evolution in design of a group of carpets from the 13th or 14th century. In ill. 139 we have a detail from the background carpet by Giunta Pisano (c. 1260)[99] and in ill. 140 one by Cimabue (c. 1270).[100] A comparison with ill. 135 reveals that the circular medallions were omitted. Retaining only their

Ill. 138: Cimabue: Crucifix, 1260/70. San Domenico, Arezzo.

Ill. 139: Giunta Pisano: Crucifix; c. 1260; S. Domenico, Bologna. Design of the background carpet.

During the first part of the 13th century the circular medallions give way to diamond-form compositions.

Ill. 140: Cimabue: Crucifix; c. 1260/70; Design of the background carpet from ill. 138.

Ill. 141: Duccio: MAESTRA, Offering in the Temple; c. 1290/95, detail. Cathedral Museum, Siena.

Ill. 142: Carpet design from ill. 141.

At the end of the 13th century so-called 'four-lobed' cruciform designs replace the diamonds. The former may resemble cosmograms (ill. 144).

change in colour, 'positive' and 'negative' areas take up equal amounts of space in what is now dominated by a lattice-work of diamonds. Among Duccio's paintings one carpet is depicted with an almost identical design; it was used as an antependium (1290/95).[101] Illustrations 143 and 147 present two further variations which emerged during the last third of the 13th century. The latter, which stems from a Lombardic fresco completed between 1270 and 1290,[102] is most certainly from a floor carpet. We find very similar designs in carpets depicted in illuminated manuscripts: one such being Armenian from the 11th century (ills. 175, 176) and one French from the 15th century.[103] Such designs also exist in surviving carpets proper.[104] The background carpet by a master of San Francesco from 1272[105] (ill.

Ill. 143 (left): Cimabue: Crucifix; c. 1270. San Francesco, Arezzo. Design of the background carpet.

Ill. 147 (right) Carpet design from ill. 145.

The carpet represents the very next step in the further development of the Gagik throne carpet from ills.175, 176. A comparison clearly shows the similarities to the original dating from the first half of the 11th century.

Ill. 144 (left): Master of San Francesco: Crucifix; c. 1272. Pinacoteca, Perugia. Design of the background carpet from ill. 137.

144) strikes us as somewhat unusual. The design, which we frequently see in ornamentation from the 1300s in both Italy and France (Limoges!), can be regarded as transitional, tying the later cross-star tiles (ills. 150, 151) to the earlier cross-circle compositions (ill. 135).

The cross-star tiles of ill. 150 are also to be found in a carpet which Giotto depicts on the steps leading up to the altar below the ciborium in the fresco of Christmas Mass at Greccio[106] (ills. 148, 149). The compositional correspondence with the carpets shown in ills. 250 and 251, which represent the same type in original, is striking. Again we find the same 'cross-star tile design', to a greater or lesser degree of clarity, in the background carpets of the crucifixes, an example being the one by Giotto in Florence (c. 1300, ill. 151). This cross-star tile design is of the utmost importance for our evolution of designs since it embodies the prototype of the 'Holbein gul' (ills. 357, 359), one of the types of the later Holbein carpets of Group C II. The carpet belonging to Bonifacius VIII, which hangs in front of him from the balustrade of the balcony when he announces the year of the jubilee in 1300[107] (ill. 154), is nearly identical. Giotto's depiction here, which attributes to a carpet such representational significance by showing it hanging over a balustrade, is the earliest known to the present author.[108]

Ill. 145 (above): Lombardian, c. 1270/90: Madonna with Child and Saints, Madonna detail. San Vincenzo, Galliano.

Ill. 146 (left): Detail of the carpet depicted in ill. 145.

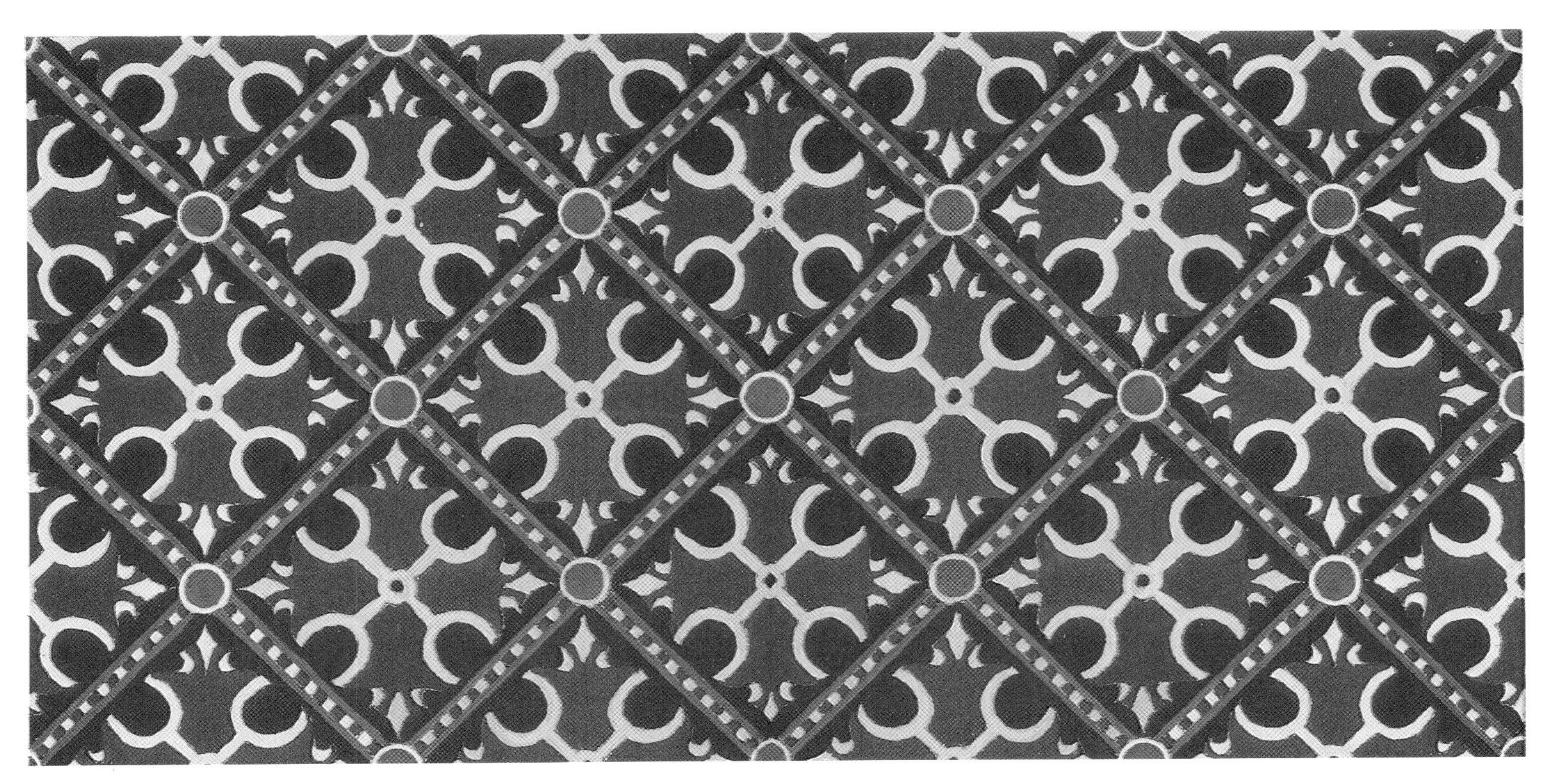

Ill. 148: Giotto: Christmas Mass at Greccio; before 1300. Upper Church, Assisi. Fresco.

Ill. 149: Detail of the carpet depiction from ill. 148.

Ill. 150: Carpet design from ill. 148.

The depiction of this carpet is of utmost importance, as it shows the carpet type in its function. Up to now, two such examples have survived (ills. 250, 251).
The design itself, cross and star-tile, marks the beginning of a design evolution that extends into the present century.

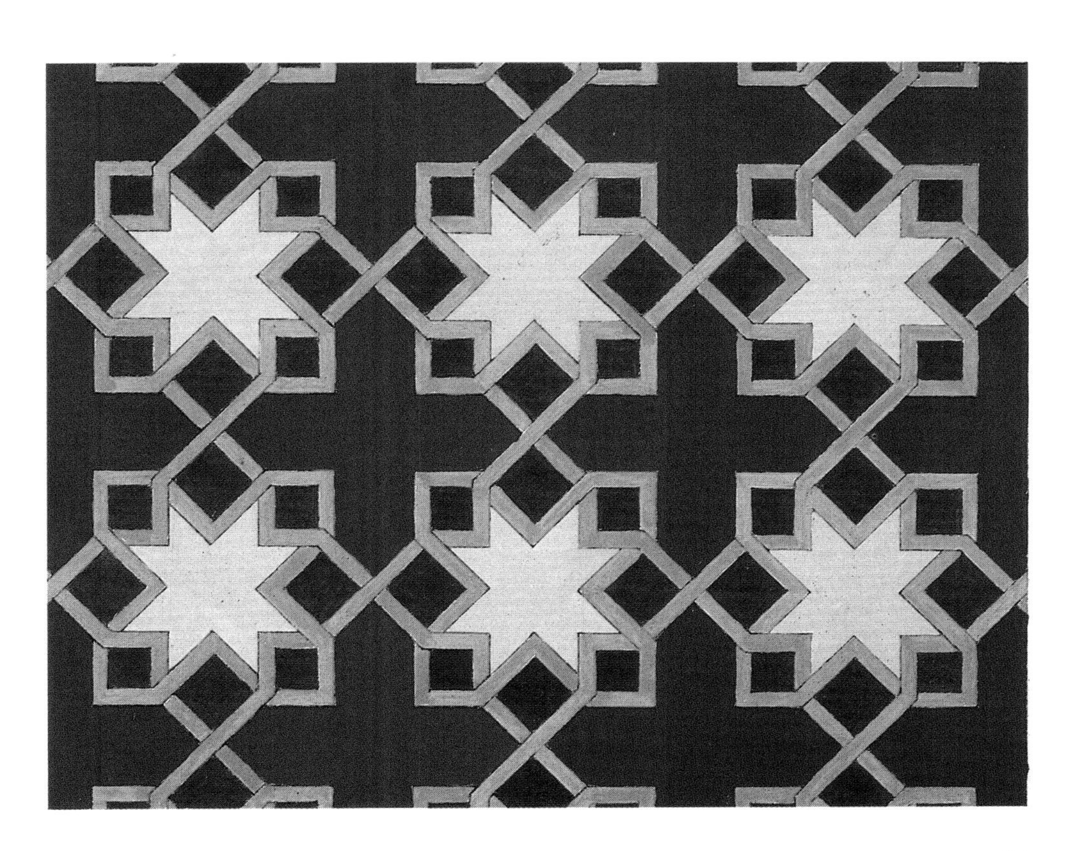

Ill. 151: Giotto: Crucifix; c. 1300. Santa Maria Novella, Florence. Design of the background carpet.

Ill. 152: Giotto: Madonna; San Giorgio alla Costa, Florence.

Ill. 153 (left): Carpet design from ill. 152.

Ill. 154 (left): Giotto: Boniface VIII Announces the Year of Jubilee, c. 1300. San Giovanni, Rome. Detail.

Ill. 155 (below): Giotto: Pope Gregory IX's Vision of St. Francis; c. 1300. Upper Church, Assisi. Carpet design.

It takes a close look to see that this design is based on the same construction as found in ill. 150.

The ease with which this very impressive design can be modified by one simple trick is shown in the carpet of Pope Gregory IX, depicting the vision of St. Francis[109] (ill. 155). The design adheres exactly to the same scheme of construction as that shown in ills. 150 and 151. Numerous modifications of this design emerged in a similar manner in the 14th century.
Further designs used by Giotto warrant our attention. Behind the Mother of God in the painting 'Madonna with Child and Angels'[110] (ill. 152) there hangs a textile which might well be a carpet because of the fact that carpets were frequently so depicted to Armenian Madonnas of the same time. The composition of these carpets (ill. 153) is an extension of the chain of traditional designs discussed above (cf. p. 58 ff, ills. 72, 73) and is also to be considered the prototype of the composition of the so- called later 'Holbein carpets.'

Ill. 156 (left): Giotto: The Sermon to Honorius III; c. 1300; Upper Church, Assisi. Carpet design.

This example demonstrated how, even during the early period of design evolution, there was always a tendency toward asymmetrical cross designs.

The carpet showing Pope Honorius III is a long 'runner',[111] the ornamentation of which (ill. 156), at first glance, seems to have hardly anything to do with carpets mentioned previously. Yet if we compare one of what appear to be seven cartouches with a medallion from the carpet of the Bishop of Assisi (ill. 135), we see that this design is in fact a further development of the former. The symmetrical cruciform with its four equal arms was changed into an asymmetrical design which, particularly in the 15th and 16th centuries, represents a sort of model design for the gul, which the author has come to call 'arabesque cross'. Here this symmetrical cruciform is to be regarded as the partial proto-design of what later became asymmetrical.

Another of Giotto's background carpets is of interest for the position it takes in the line of evolution leading up to the 'Holbein carpets': in ill. 157 we see a detail of its ground. Here the overall concept of the design in the transitional phase between the cross-star tile design and the small-pattern Holbein carpets is clearly discernible. The cruciforms give way to what later are to become 'arabesque crosses'. The interlacing still works together to form part of the design. The separation of these two elements has not yet occurred at this stage.

Illustration 158 also clearly shows a stage in this line of evolution. About the year 1345 Vitale da Bologna presented a carpet that served as a covering for a coffin.[112] The designs create a combination of different stages of development running parallel to one another, similar to what we have already seen in ills. 144,151,152 and 157. They belong to a series that we must consider to have been parallel developments of the period rather than part of a straight line of evolution.

In addition to these more geometric carpets, there are a significant number of others which have taken their place in the literature as 'animal carpets'. This term, like so many others, is not entirely appropriate, though in many cases animals are, in fact,

Ill. 157 (right): Giotto: Crucifix; before 1310. San Felice, Florence. Carpet design.

represented.[113] The reference here is to a group of carpets with figural depictions, thought by some authors[114] to be the oldest altogether. One can say in all certainty that this is incorrect.[115] We cannot help but notice that among these carpets some are unmistakably heraldic in function. Others show, for example, two birds on either side of a tree, and yet again others present individual birds, animals with heads

Ill. 158 (right): Vitale da Bologna: A Story of St. Antonius; c. 1345. Pinacoteca Nazionale, Bologna. Carpet design.

turned looking back, or the dragon-phoenix motif. Mills lists 60 examples of animal carpets. The largest number of these served to glorify the Virgin (34 all in all), only two represent popes (ill. 160) and on only one do we also find a worldly person depicted: Robert von Anjou.[116] The remaining carpets are reserved for a wide range of different saints.

The carpet in the 'workshop' of St. Eligius, decorating the table in front of him (ill. 159), appears revealing to the present author. Here, in diagonal alternation, we see crosses of varying designs and some extraordinary two-footed beasts. The crosses identify this carpet as Christian, which is also the case of the carpet in the Annunciation in the Schlossmuseum in Berlin.[117] For the bird-tree image Erdmann drew on Anagni's choir robe (ill. 162) and on the dignitary from the Chrysostomos codex of Nicephoros Botaniates[118] (ill. 161) for the animals as a basis for comparison. It is very likely that the fabric in both cases is Armenian.[119] Both show the alternating cross-animal combination which is likewise to be found on fabrics attributed to early Italian silk weaving.[120] In the Christian cult the use of the animal symbols was widespread, extending from Armenia to Anatolia, Byzantium, Italy and even as far as Spain during the High Middle Ages. We find early examples in stone reliefs in Achtamar at the beginning of the 10th century.[121] Mention should also be made at this point of exhibits in the museums of Konya, Iznik, Istanbul and of the floor mosaics in San Miniato al Monte (Florence) (ills. 165–168).

The present author sees a very close connection between these 'animal carpets' and the heraldry that had become fashionable in the 13th century. It originated in the kingdom of Armenia Minor possibly due to the fact that with crusaders present there, one had to have a way of distinguishing them one from the other. But first of all it is necessary to differentiate between heraldic and non-heraldic carpets. Illustration 12 provides an example of a heraldic carpet in use.
At the same time, however, we also see to what an extent the secular function of these carpets went hand in hand with their spiritual function. What, then, could be

Ill. 159 (left): Taddeo Gaddi: The Workshop of St. Eligius. Prado, Madrid.

This is the only example showing cross variants and animal depictions in alternating compartments.

Ill. 160 (above): Giovanni di Paolo: St. Catherine of Siena requests Pope Gregory XI to return to Rome from Avignon, 1447–49. Stiftung Thyssen-Bornemisza, Lugano.

more obvious than to assume that the same process also applies to 'animal carpets', namely that animal symbols in the Christian tradition were adopted instead of the coats-of-arms? This also applies to the dragon-phoenix motif, which always has its place in Christian art (cf. p. 194).

Erdmann includes several examples in his Group IV of 'occidental copies of oriental carpets'.[122] Although these represent work from a later period, including them in the present discussion is appropriate. These carpets, with very few exceptions, hang from open windows in which people are seen; in other words, they must have been status symbols. It is quite possible that some of these may actually be heraldic. In the case of others, however, the author is reminded of an anecdote told of Giotto by Sacchetti in his sixty-third novella, the 'Trecentonovelle'. It closes with the following comment: "Every scoundrel claims to have a coat-of-arms and a long-established family tradition and yet their fathers were probably raised in orphanages."[123] That is to say, there was very possibly a great deal of commissioned work done in which the identity of the client could not be established after the fact. In addition, it is also problematic that from the 15th century on production may have been carried out in western Europe. Although this is likely, it is not of significant concern to us in the High Middle Ages.

Ill. 161 (left): Collection of the sermons of Johannes Chrysostomos of the Emperor Nicephoros III Botaniates (1078–1081). Bibliothèque Nationale, Paris, codex Coislin 79. F. 2r.

Figure 4 (below): Detail of the dignitary (according to v. Falke).

The attire of the dignitary corresponds to that of King Gagik Ardsruni (ill. 165) as well as that of Gagik of Kars (ill. 175). It is not clear whether the figure depicted here, described as the highest judge and highest curator of the vestiary, is an Armenian, which the headdress would indicate. Beginning in 1022, after the incorporation of Armenian regions, numerous Armenian princes stayed at the Court of Byzantium, among them King Gagik II of Ani.

Ill. 162 (right): Pluviale, detail; Cyprus, 11th/12th century or earlier (before 1295). Treasure vault of the cathedral, Anagni.

Cyprus at this time was closely allied with the Kingdom of Armenia Minor. The piece of embroidery can be regarded as representative of early Armenian pieces.

Let us complete this brief overview by looking at some carpets depicted in paintings from the beginning of the 15th century, the originals of which, however, we can certainly attribute to the 14th century. They are further developments of the prototypes shown in ills. 139 and 140 as well as in 150, all of which, in representations of the Virgin Mary by Jan van Eyck, decorate the floor in front of the throne.[124] Illustrations 169 and 171 contain design variants of the same type: diamond-designs, both with and without colour changes; field separation by many-coloured stripes and medallions of different sizes filled with cross-stars or rosettes at the points of intersection. There are differences with respect to what the diamonds can be filled with: in one instance eight-pointed stars and in the other knotted-crosses and rosette crosses. Illustration 173 connects ill. 150 with those carpets later referred to as 'Lesghian' (ills. 347, 348). The ground is made up of large yellow cross-stars while the 'negative areas' are filled with light-symbol crosses of the basic form type H_1, the centres of which are enclosed by squares.

Ill. 163 (left): Half-silk Samitum, fragment. Deutsches Textilmuseum, Krefeld, Inv. no. 00044.

A montage of photographs completes the repeat pattern.

Ill. 164 (right): Silk fabric, 10th century(?); courtesy of the Cooper-Hewitt Museum, The Smithsonian Institution's National Museum of Design/Art Resource, New York, Acc. no. 1902–1.222. Gift of J.P. Morgan (from the Badia collection)

A similar fabric is to be seen on the floor in front of King Gagik of Kars' family (ill. 175). The elefant fabric of the cathedral treasury in Aachen takes up a motif of this fabric; however, it was presumably not produced until after the conquest of the Armenian regions by the Seljuks and the relocation of artisans to the Court of Byzantium.

Ill. 165 (left): Achtamar, Church of the Holy Cross; 915–921. Detail from the garment of King Gagik Ardsruni of Waspurakan.

Ill. 166 (below): Relief with the depiction of the 'tree of Jesse', flanked by two hares facing each other. 4th/5th century(?). Archaeological Museum, St. Sophia, Istanbul.

The depiction of hares as a symbol for the believer was already in use in the Hittite Empire (Gate of Alaca-Hüyük, c. 1200 B C) and among the Urartians (relief of Adiljevaz, 8th century B C – Ill. 451). From here it was adopted into Christian symbolism.

Ill. 167 (right): Marble relief with depictions of symbols of life and peacocks. Presumably from St. Sophia, Nicea, 4th century. Museum, Iznik.

The peacock is regarded as a symbol of immortality.

Ill. 168 (left): San Miniato al Monte, Florence: detail from the floor mosaic in the central nave. 11th/12th century.

As with the baptistry, the floor mosaics in San Miniato attest the strong influence that was exercised by Armenian fabrics and carpets and their design layout.

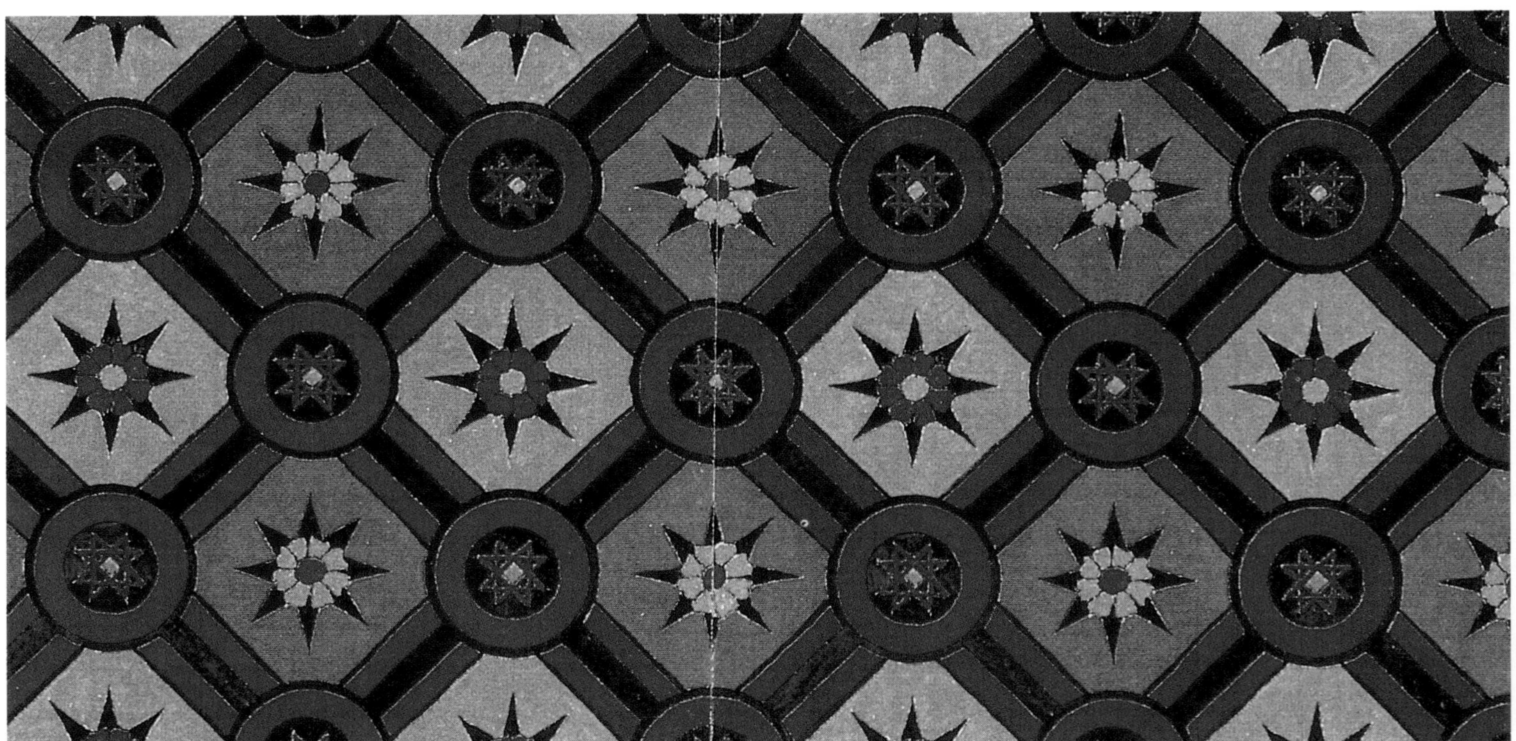

Ill. 169 (left): Jan van Eyck: Madonna; 1441–1443. The Frick Collection, New York.

Ill. 170 (below left): Field design of the carpet in ill. 169.

The carpets depicted by van Eyck are prototypes of the diamond-form cross carpets of Groups C V and C I as well.

Ill. 171 (right): Jan van Eyck: Lucca-Madonna; before 1441. Städelsches Kunstinstitut, Frankfurt.

Ill. 172 (below): Field design of the carpet in ill. 171.

Carpets in Armenian and Syrian Painting

Of that which has survived in the way of Armenian and Syrian painting, it is primarily manuscripts – excepting individual frescos – that, through their illuminations, provide us with insight into the decorative art of the period. Carpet depictions as such do exist, yet they are restricted to the few known Cilician and Anatolian codices. And since so far no study of these sources has been undertaken, it is amply conceivable that, among the abundance of material in the Matenadaran in Erivan, the Mechitarist congregation in Vienna, the San Lazzaro monastery in Venice, the patriarchate in Jerusalem, or the collections in Europe or overseas, there may still be important examples. In addition to the representations of the apostles, in which carpets are commonly shown, the opening pages of the gospels are of particular interest. Here we usually find entrances or doors depicted, the upper panels of which often resemble a carpet, perhaps even being copied from old carpet 'remnants'. Furthermore, the marginal notes and sketches are revealing in their design detail. At the moment the author finds it quite problematic that those engaged in the study of Armenian illuminated manuscripts should, without exception, be Byzantine scholars, for clearly they will be interested in studies which reveal a strong Byzantine influence, as the figural depictions characteristic of Byzantium do. Since, however, there have in all periods been strong nationalistic tendencies which, for purely ideological reasons, have rejected Byzantine influence, one can assume that there are paintings amidst the existing material that reflect these tendencies – as was, for example, the case with the Katchkars, which continued to follow their own national traditions without succumbing to Byzantine influence in any significant way.

Carpets in Armenian Illuminated Manuscripts

The earliest recorded depictions of carpets can be found in two manuscripts dating from the 11th century. One is the evangelary of King Gagik of Kars,[125] portraying him seated on the throne (ill. 175), the other is an evangelary in the Matenadaran[126], which shows an apostle sitting on a carpet (ill. 177). Both carpets are geometric in design and red, a tradition typical of Armenia, still common today for state occasions. The Gagik throne carpet exhibits a very fine pattern (ill. 176). We recognize the simultaneous use of squares and diamonds which allow leaf-form crosses to take shape, and are roughly similar to those in ill. 147. The carpet depicted in the Matenadaran illustration is also based on the same principle of design, incorporating squares and diamonds. In the latter instance, however, cross-stars are positioned in the squares, such that their pointed ends fill in the corners. From this scaled-down cluster emerge larger patterns, whose designs, as noted above, correspond in turn to the borders of the Katchkars in ills. 131 and 132. This agreement with the source material used by Serjeant on the one hand, and between illuminated manuscripts and the Katchkars on the other – and this 100 years prior to the Seljuk invasion – provide incontestable evidence for the correctness of the hypotheses presented in this book.

Another evangelary is of importance in more than one respect. Ma XIII 1 at the university library in Tübingen, originally from the Drasark monastery in Cilicia in 1193, and based on an older drawing from 893, shows carpets in the representations of three evangelists:[127] F. 73r (ill. 178) presents a carpet with a design incorporating a grid of diamonds into which step-form crosses have been inscribed. And despite the strong simplification, this design is certainly comparable to the basic design in ill. 95. Here again we have step-form crosses in a lattice-work of diamonds. The carpet found in F. 142r (ill. 179) corresponds in terms of its design to a carpet we have already noted in ill. 150. It contains a simplified rendition of the 'cross-star' tile

Ill. 173 (above left): Jan van Eyck: The Madonna of Kanonikus van der Paele; 1436. Municipal Gallery, Bruges.

Ill. 174 (below left): Field design of the carpet in ill. 173.

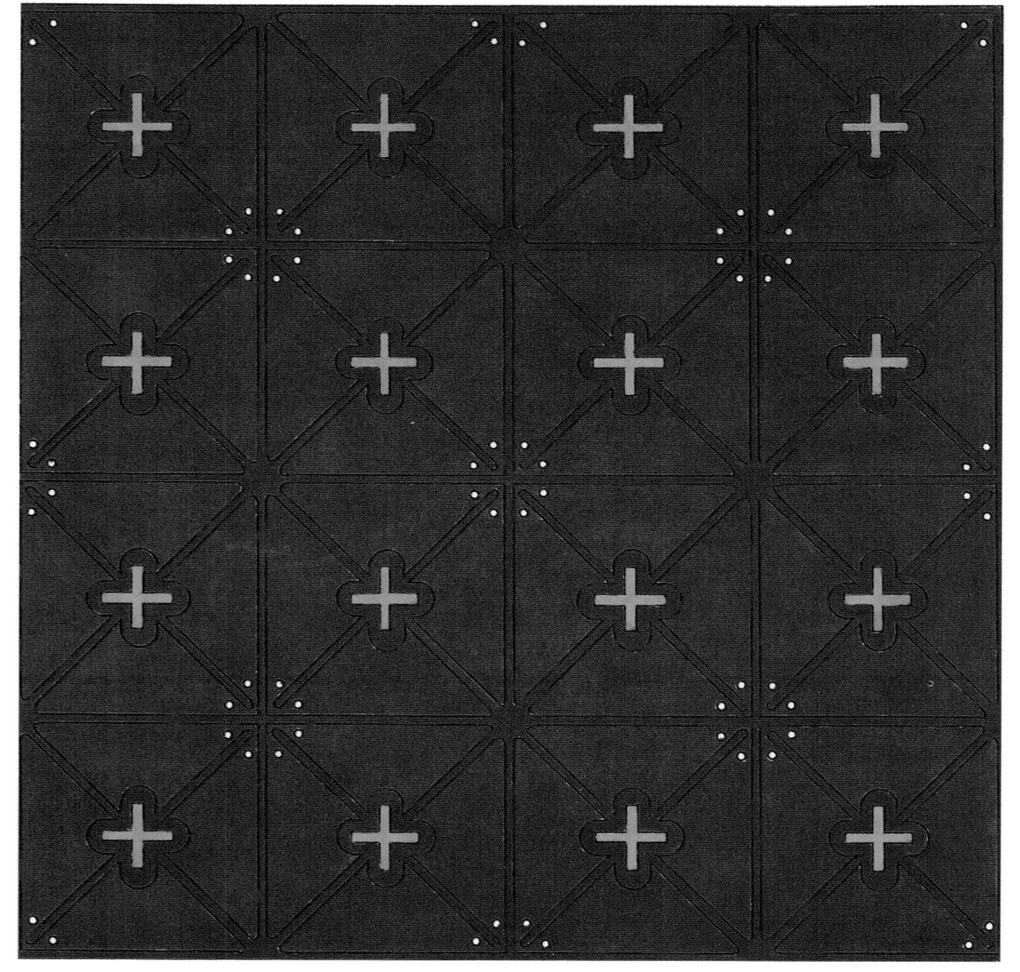

Ill. 175 (above): Evangelistary of Gagik of Kars: first part of the 11th century. F. 135v: depiction of the king, his wife Gorandoukht and his daughter Marem. Armenian Patriarchate, Jerusalem, Ms. 2556.

We notice here that in contrast to the Byzantine Emperor (ill. 161), the Armenian king and his family are shown sitting cross-legged, as was customary in the Orient, on a red carpet on which a silk fabric reminiscent of ill. 164 is spread.

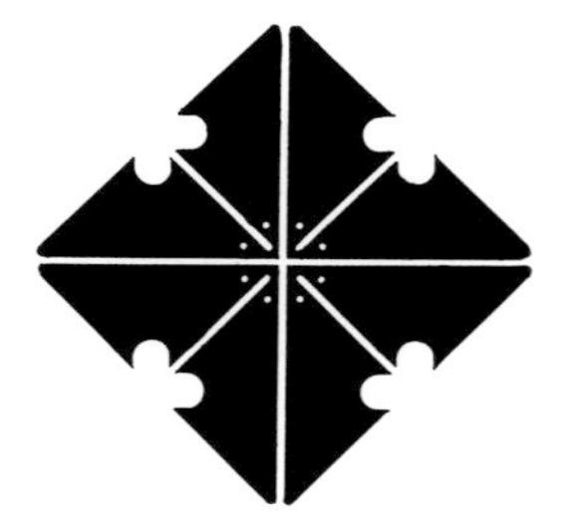

Ill. 176 (left): Field design of the carpet in ill. 175 and diagram.
A classical compositional scheme that incorporates nearly all the possible Armenian carpet compositions: the coffer with the cross within a cross and the four-part diamond-form cross (diagram) along the diagonal. The carpet in ill. 146 stands in direct succession to this one, those in ills. 172 and 174 are derived from it as well.

design. The shades of golden ochre, interestingly enough, also match. The carpet shown in F. 260r (ill. 180) also features a well-defined diamond-design, though it can only partially be made out.

Illustrations of three opening pages will now be presented since they exhibit a wide array of design details that are of significance for Armenian carpets. The upper part of the first page of the Gospel according to Luke, from the evangelistary XIII 1, F. 143v (ill. 181–183) at the university library in Tübingen, shows a panel which – though it does not actually depict a carpet – stands as an example in the evolution of medallion carpets. The medallion closely resembles the inner portion of that of Vakfl. A217 (ill. 127) or those in Group B II (ills. 283–290). The diamond-design, arranged here in stripes, recurs frequently in later carpets within the Armenian design tradition. Certain details are of particular importance: to begin with we find the S-shaped symbol in the border as a cipher for the Armenian word › **տեր** ‹ meaning God. This occurs similarly in many carpets of Armenian origin.[128]

Another symbol visible on the leg of the P-initial is the 'E'-design, the Old Armenian short form for 'Him', which means 'God the Almighty', and is represented in Armenian by 'Y', the short form for › **Յիսուս** ‹, which means 'Jesus' (cf. pp. 37 ff.).

In the university library, Tübingen: Ma XIII 1, F. 261v (ills. 184–186) there is a marginal sketch illustrating a cross of the same type as those shown in ills. 17 or 56. The panel shows almost all of a medallion carpet. Whereas within the medallion a cross composed of interlace fills the circle, the opposed lanceolar leaves in the corners are typical elements of designs used to fill the area above the pediments in a group of arch-form carpets decorated with coupled-columns.

In the panel at the university library, Tübingen: Ma XIII 4, F. 7r[129] (ill. 187), the upper part of a table of canonical rules, the pseudo-Kufic language of symbols is discernible. This we already found present in the border from the Vakfl. A 217 (ill. 130). Yet another panel deserves our attention: F. 129v from the evangelistary of Theodosiopolis, dating from 1232[130] (ill. 188). Here we have a semblance of the design used 70 years later by Giotto in one of the background carpets of his large crucifixes[131] (ill. 151). The 'lilies' in the ground of TIEM no. 681 (ill. 121) appear here in the medallion as well.

Ill. 177 (right): Evangelistary, 11th century; depiction of apostle, detail carpet. Matenadaran, Erivan, Ms. 7736, f. 18v.

Ill. 178 (page 128): Evangelistary, Drasak/Cilicia 1193: F. 73r: Evangelist. University Library, Tübingen, Ma XIII 1.

The carpet at the feet of the apostle contains small stepped crosses as in ill. 70 or 462.

Ill. 179 (page 129): Evangelistary, Drasak/Cilicia 1193: F. 142r: Evangelist. University Library, Tübingen, Ma XIII 1.

Here we see cross compartments similar to that shown in ill. 69.

Ill. 183 (above): P-initial from ill. 181.

Ill. 181 (right): Evangelistary, Drasak/Cilicia 1193, F. 143r: beginning of the Gospel according to Luke. University Library, Tübingen, Ma XIII 1.

To be noted here is the cruciform in the medallion. It is the proto-design for numerous carpet medallions, cf. ills. 127, 551, 554, and the 'S'-border.

Ill. 182 (right): Carpet panel from ill. 181.

Ill. 180 (left): Evangelistary, Drasak/Cilicia 1193: F. 260r: Evangelist. University Library, Tübingen, Ma XIII 1.

Ill. 184 (right): Evangelistary, Drasak/Cilicia 1193: F. 261v: beginning of the Gospel according to John. University Library, Tübingen, Ma XIII 1.

Ill. 186 (above): Cross detail from ill. 184.

Ill. 185 (right): Carpet panel from ill. 184.

Here, too, the medallion variants are noteworthy. It is, however, important to notice the spandrels filling the upper corners of the panel. A design similar to this recurs in the arch-form carpets (ill. 679).

Ill. 187 (page 133): Evangelistary; Carpet panel from F. 7v. University Library, Tübingen, Ma XIII 4.

One of the many possible permutations in the depiction of the 'tree of Jesse.'

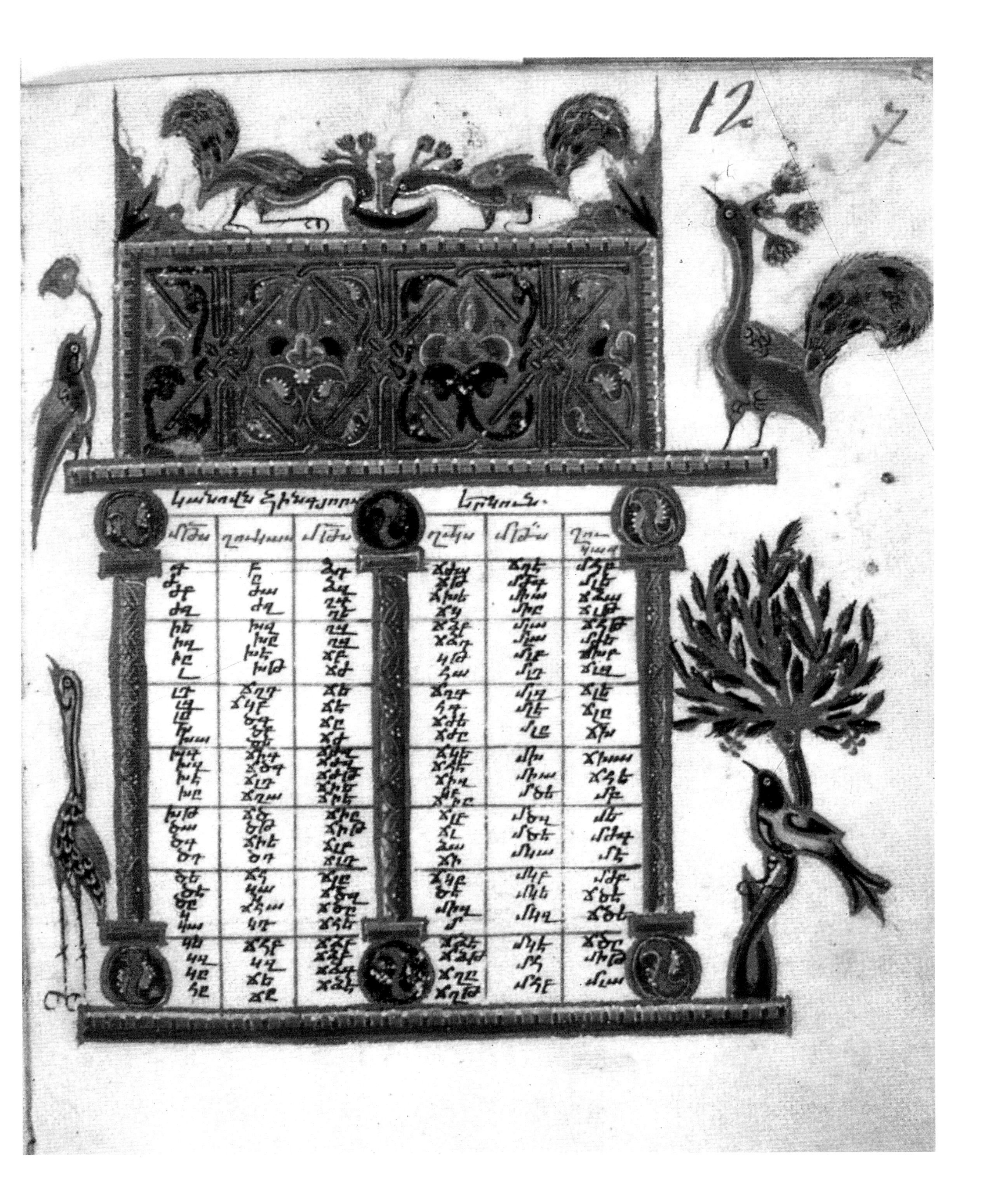

Ill. 188 (right): Evangelistary from Theodosiopolis: Karin 1232. Carpet panel from F. 1r. San Lazzaro, Venice; no. 325/129.

Ill. 189 (right): Evangelistary from 1235: depiction of apostle. Courtesy of the Freer Art Gallery, Smithsonian Institution, Washington D.C., Acc. no. 44.17, F. 14 verso.

Ill. 190 (page 135): Lectionary from Cilicia from 1286: St. Basil, F. 6v. Matenadaran, Erivan, codex 979.

The figure of the church father has been impressively worked into the arch field of the carpet. The cross rosette border of this miniature might easily have been a prototype of the borders of early arch-form carpets (ills. 675, 679, 680).

Ill. 191 (left): Evangelistary from 1315: Mark the Evangelist, carpet detail from F. 99v. (single sheet, glued on). Library of the Mechitarist Congregation, Vienna, codex 460.

The design on the textile under the seat cushion represents a different part of the design spectrum common at that time: spiralling leafed vines of the kind familiar to us from metalwork (ill. 192) and from reliefs (ill. 136).

In the evangelary from 1253 of the Freer Gallery of Art (FGA 44.17)[132] a carpet with a large cross-block border is represented on which an evangelist is depicted (ill. 189). Unfortunately the inner panel was painted so carelessly that an analysis cannot provide us with any certainty as to its exact origin. Presumably this is a further development of the design we are already familiar with from ill. 178, thus making it a precursor of what we know today as 'ak-su' (ill. 601). In a Cilician lectionary dating from 1286 the image of St. Basil, the Church father, has been impressively incorporated into the arched-field of a carpet (ill. 190). The cross-rosette border of this miniature could be regarded as the prototype of borders in early arch-form carpets (ills. 675, 679, 680).

Ill. 192 (right): Travelling altar, c. 1300; treasure vault of the cathedral, Echmiadzin.

There is yet another evangelary, dated 1315,[133] in the library of the Mechitarists in Vienna, which – unlike all other manuscripts known to us – shows Mark the Evangelist sitting on what would appear to be a carpet of non-geometric design. We recognize the scrolling pattern of leafy vines, though nothing beyond that might cause us to consider this textile a carpet (ill. 191). And yet, despite this, it does represent part of what at that time was the common range of design. We see similar designs not only in the metalwork (ill. 192), but also in the building tiles of the Mongolian period.[134] The opening page belonging to this manuscript has in its panel the early form of the cross which makes up the subsidiary gul (ill. 246) in the carpet Mevl. no. 860/861/1033.[135] This is an organic variant of the cross-star tile design which was of very great importance for the evolution of designs. Off to one side, at the top, we find another cross completing the marginal floral design (cf. ills. 184, 186). This, too, has its parallel in the carpet just mentioned, thus providing us with a point of reference for positing a possible date.

Ill. 193 (left): Evangelistary from 1315; carpet panel from F. 100r. Library of the Mechitarist Congregation, Vienna, codex 460.

In the carpet panel we find what served as the model for the cross composition of the secondary gul in ill. 246. The crown of the cross on the 'tree of Jesse' on the right margin also warrants our attention.

Ill. 194 (right): Syrian evangelistary, c. 1220. F. 197v: Pentecost. British Museum, London, codex add. 7170.

Carpets in Syrian Illustrated Manuscripts

Presumably the depictions of carpets in Syrian illustrated manuscripts are no less frequent than what we have now seen with Armenia. And yet, the material that the author was actually able to see was quite limited. The pictures of the Pentecost, from the codices BM add. 7170 in London and BA. Syr. 559 in the Vatican, use the 'star-tile design'[136] (ills. 194 and 195) common in the 13th century and familiar to us from Italian and Armenian art. Both codices contain further depictions of carpets which show agreement: in the illustrations accompanying 'Jesus instructs his disciples' and 'Jesus and the Samaritan' (ills. 196, 197) we find in each instance small carpets with geometric designs such as the cross or rosette diamonds, arranged diagonally.[137] Often the borders of the paintings are more important, especially considering the fact that what was said above in connection with our treatment of Armenian codices (p. 125) also applies here. We will look more closely at some of these borders in our discussion of the relevant carpets. In concluding, the author would like to consider one more carpet page, which, though it did not originate until 1577, goes back to a preliminary illumination from the year 1285.[138] It represents a further development in the designs familiar to us from ills. 72 and 73, which will provide a transition to subsequent groups such as the small-pattern Holbein carpets.

Ill. 195 (right): Syrian evangelistary, 1219–1220. F. 181v: Pentecost. Biblioteca apostolica, Vatican, codex Syr. 559.

The carpets depicted in Syrian illustrated manuscripts often have small cross-star tile compositions that find their extension in the 'Baluch' carpets. This migration of designs begins here.

Ill. 196 (left): Syrian evangelistary 1219–1220. F. 180r: Jesus instructs his disciples. Biblioteca apostolica, Vatican, codex Syr. 559.

Ill. 197 (left): Syrian evangelistary, 1219–1220. F. 183r: The Samaritan. Biblioteca apostolica, Vatican, codex Syr. 559.

Ill. 198 (right): Syrian evangelistary, 1285/1577. F. 40: carpet page. Biblioteca apostolica, Vatican, Ms. Borgia 169.

This carpet page still shows quite clearly the design tradition of early Christian codices, which have the same source as the Irish illuminations of the 7th century (ills.82,83). The latter, at the same time, provides a bridge to the SP-Holbein carpets of Group C II.

Carpets in Chinese Sung Dynasty Painting

Ibn Battuta, who in 1333 reported that carpets from Aksaray were being exported to China, has been frequently cited.[139] The next research step therefore was to try to find carpets depicted in Chinese painting. The effort paid off. In fact in the meantime, independent of the research carried out by the present author, other reports have been published of carpet representations discovered in Sung painting.[140] The number of such carpets appearing in the existing work of the Sung school, as well as the length of time during which they were produced, was very limited. It occurred only in the 13th century and is restricted in amount to two scrolls and two single paintings, now located in the National Palace of Taipei in Taiwan[141] and in the collection of the Metropolitan Museum in New York.[142] The subject of each of these paintings is the same: they illustrate the life of the lady Wen Chi. This story, which is thought to have taken place as early as the 5th century, gained new relevance as a result of Mongol rule in China. Lady Wen Chi is said to have been abducted and taken off to Mongolia and years later, after an eventfull life, was released and allowed to return to her home, lavished with gifts. This story was given repeated treatment in Chinese art. The Boston museum owns two versions, one from the 6th century, and one from about 1230. Neither rendering (and this is something the author would like to draw special attention to) shows a carpet. The paintings in Taipei and New York cited above, dating to the middle or latter part of the 13th century, are the only ones with carpets. These paintings are clearly of the period. Therefore, the assumption that what they show, specifically the carpet representations, was contemporaneous is a justifiable one. This is important. There are altogether 12 carpets represented in these paintings, and they will be described in what follows.

As all of these representations developed from older models such as the Boston scroll-fragment, most of the paintings are similar in their composition. There are three different versions of the same motif (ills. 200–205). The carpet representations we are considering show medium-sized carpets, approximately 2 x 1.5 m, the colour predominantly red. They all share this same red colour regardless of whether they are runners in front of tents (ills. 206 and 209), carpets inside these tents or beneath sunshades (ills. 210–221) or even those that have been reduced to use as saddle blankets (ills. 222, 223). Common to them all are the cross motifs, whether they appear as imposing Greek crosses, leaf-form crosses, or a combination of the two in the centre as cross-block borders or panels. One finds nothing in these carpets that might not be ascribable to a Christian origin nor, by the same token, anything that might rule this out.

Another question is whether the carpets represented here are in fact what are referred to by both Ibn Sa'id and Ibn Battuta as 'Aksaray carpets'. There is no definitive answer here, though there is nothing to disallow the assumption. The design details are elements of an established set of designs that originated within the region of Armenian cultural influence, with the red colour which made the Armenian carpet famous. Unlike Hanna Erdmann, the present author is unable to discover anything Chinese about these carpets. A look at ill. 210 clearly shows the lack of correspondence between the pillow covered in Chinese silk and the carpet it is placed on.

Hanna Erdmann compares such carpets as described above with those once known as 'Damascus-carpets' or today, as a result of Kurt Erdmann's work,[143] called 'Cairene carpets', which were attributed to the Mameluks. A discussion of these carpets will follow later. For the sake of comparison let us now, without further elaboration, simply juxtapose one of the most beautiful of these latter carpets – one of similar design – with those discussed in this section (ill. 224). Again, Hanna Erdmann attempted to call the carpets represented in these Chinese paintings

Ill. 199 (left): Chen Chü-Chung (second part of the 13th century): The Return of Lady Wen Chi. National Palace, Taipei. Part of a scroll of pictures.

Ill. 200 (above): Detail from ill. 199: Lady Wen Chi seated on the carpet.

Ill. 201 (below): Carpet from ill. 199.

The Armenian collection of designs is especially clear here in the details, e.g. in the 'S'-secondary border or in the crosses of the basic A-form. The relationship to carpets from Group B II is also clear.

Ill. 202 (above right): Li Tang Wen (2nd part of the 13th cent.): The Return of Lady Wen Chi, detail. National Palace, Taipei.

Ill. 203 (below right): Carpet composition from ill. 202.
The Greek cross composition in this carpet can hardly be surpassed in its clarity. Its appearance is not as pronounced even in ill. 224, despite its size.

Ill. 204 (page 146 above): Wen Fong (2nd part of the 13th century): The Story of Lady Wen Chi, detail from episode 11: Watching Wild Geese Fly South. MMA, New York, no. 1973.120.3. Gift of the Dillon Fund, 1973.

Ill. 205 (page 146 below): Carpet composition from ill. 204.

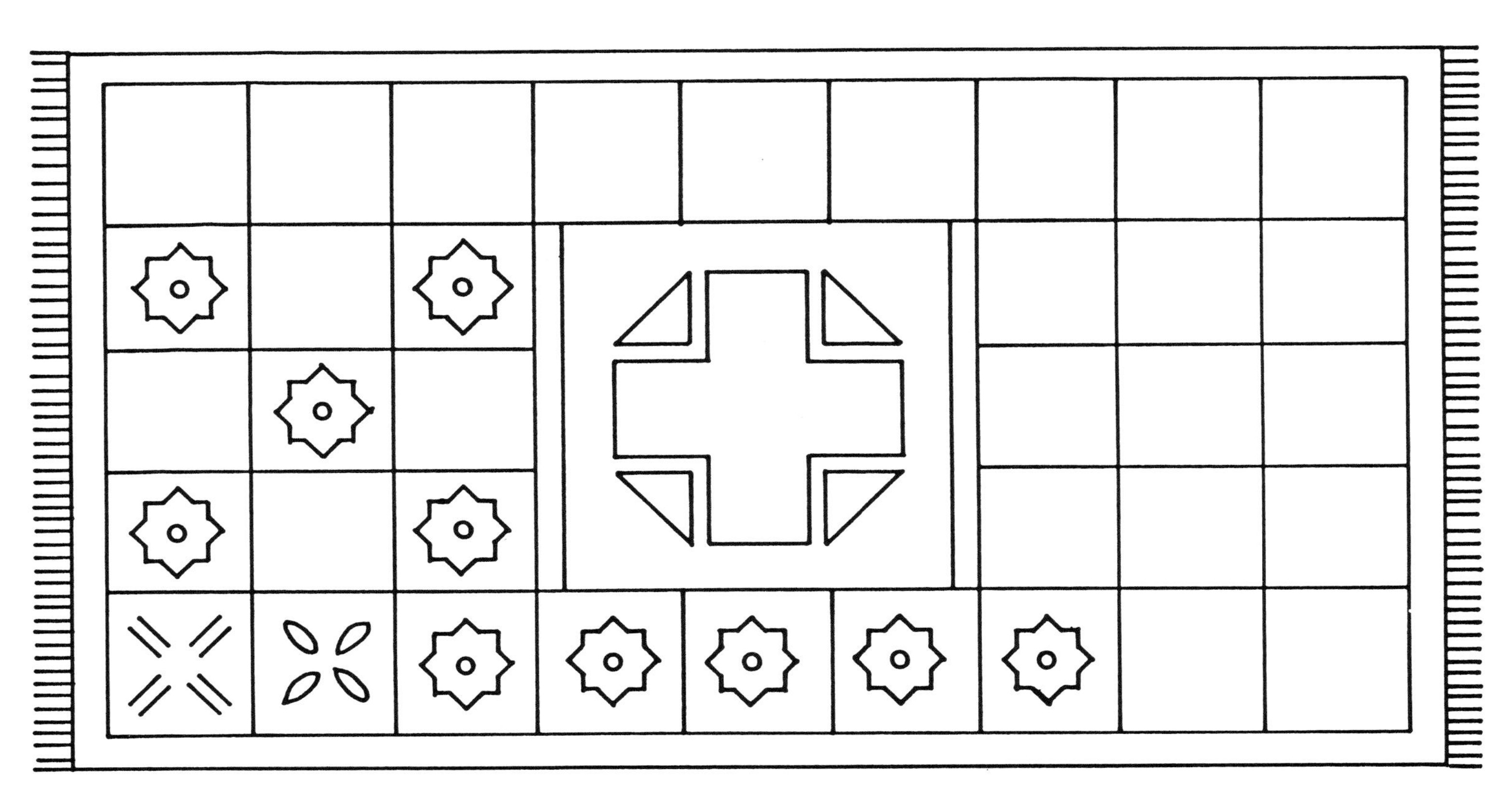

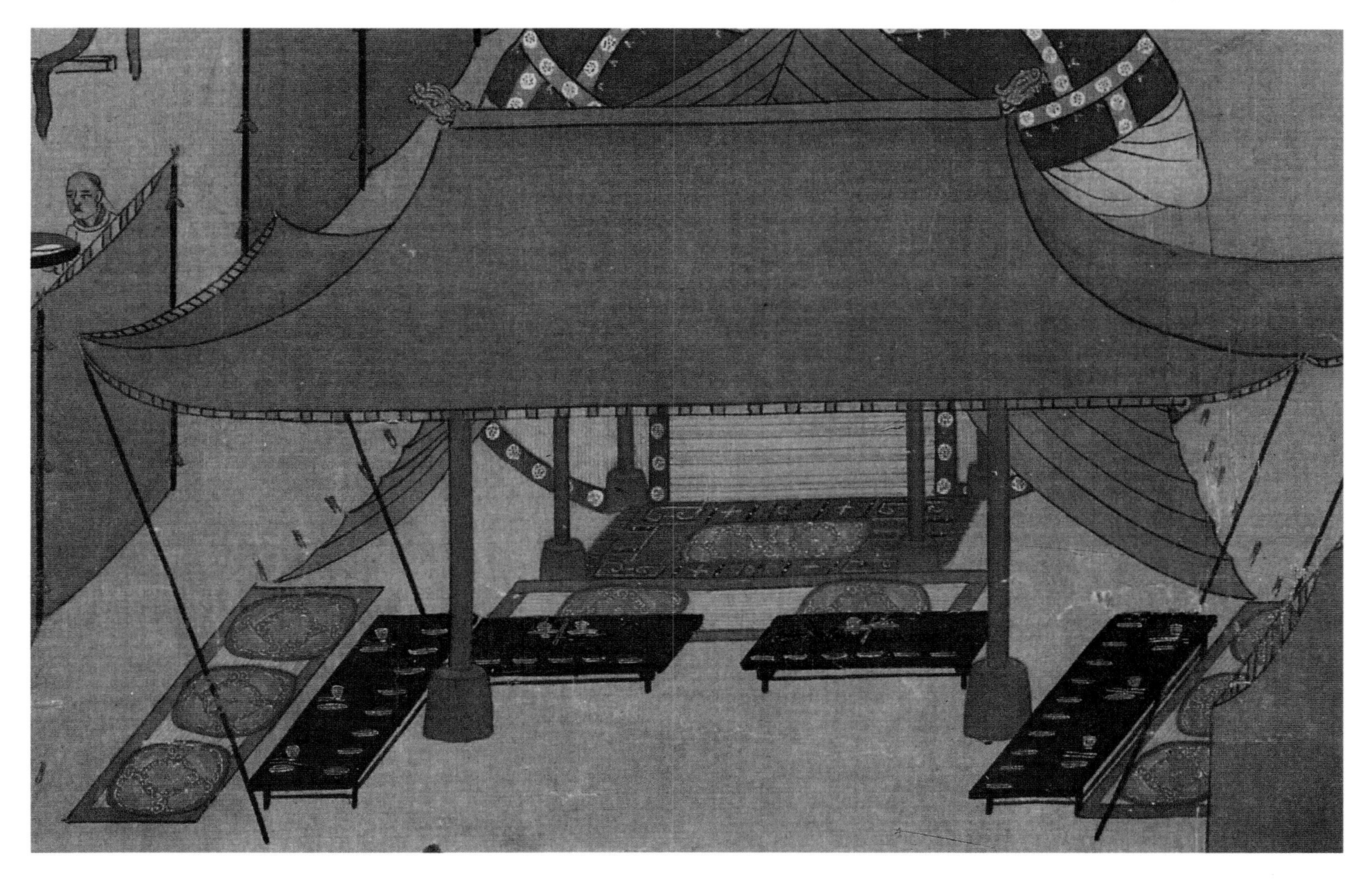

Ill. 206 (page 147 above): Sung Hui-Tsung (2nd part of the 13th century): The Story of Lady Wen Chi, detail; National Palace, Taipei.

Ill. 207 (page 147 below): Carpet composition from ill. 206.

Ill. 208 (page 148 above): Wen Fong (2nd part of the 13th century): The Story of Lady Wen Chi, detail from episode 10: A Child is Born. MMA, New York, no. 1973.120.3. Gift of the Dillon Fund, 1973.

Ill. 209 (page 148 below): Carpet composition from ill. 208.

Ill. 210 (above): Wen Fong (2nd part of the 13th century): The Story of Lady Wen Chi, detail from episode 13: Parting. MMA, New York, no. 1973.120.3. Gift of the Dillon Fund, 1973.

Ill. 211 (below): Carpet composition from ill. 210.

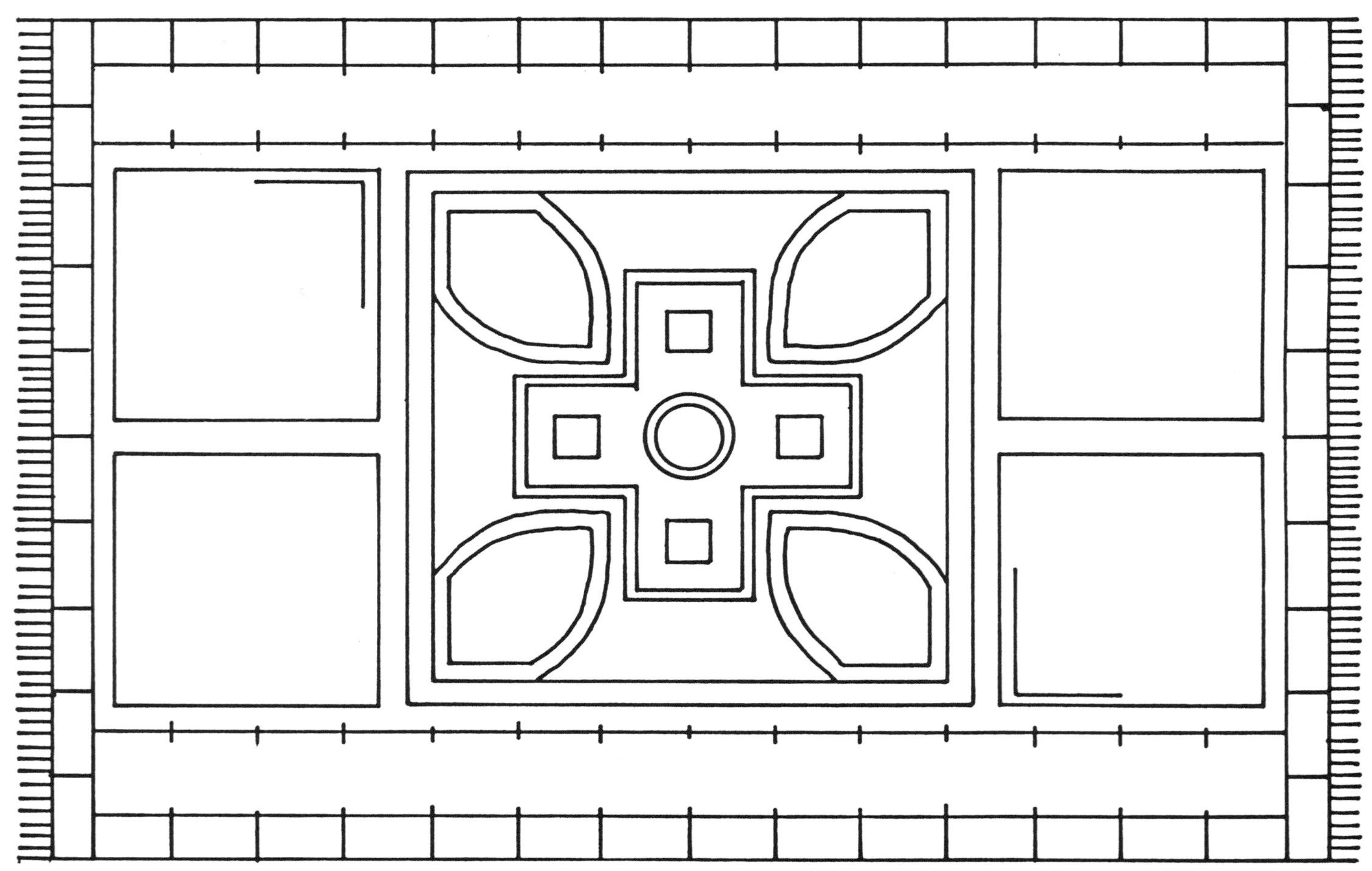

Ill. 212 (above left): Wen Fong (2nd part of the 13th century): The Story of Lady Wen Chi, detail from episode 5: Camp at the River. MMA, New York, no. 1973.120.3. Gift of the Dillon Fund, 1973.

Ill. 213 (left below): Carpet composition from ill. 212.

Ill. 214 (above): Wen Fong (2nd part of the 13th century): The Story of Lady Wen Chi, detail from episode 3: Camp in the Desert. MMA, New York, no. 1973.120.3. Gift of the Dillon Fund, 1973.

Ill. 215 (right): Carpet composition from ill. 214.

Ill. 216 (above): Wen Fong (2nd part of the 13th century): The Story of Lady Wen Chi, detail from episode 9: Lady Wen Chi Writes Home. MMA, New York, no. 1973.120.3. Gift of the Dillon Fund, 1973.

Ill. 217 (below): Carpet composition from ill. 216.

Chinese and, in so doing, was led to posit a Chinese influence on Turkoman and Turkish carpets.

At this point it is perhaps appropriate to draw attention to a commonly-held misconception: of the tribes with which Genghis Khan set out to establish his empire by force, the Kereit, Naiman, Ongut and some of the Kara Khitai were of the Christian-Nestorian faith, while the remaining tribes were partly Buddhist and partly Shaman. A Kereit became Genghis Khan's head wife. Likewise a Kereit by the name of Sorchachtani beki, the Doquz Chatun and grand-daughter of Ong Khan, first became Tolui's head wife and then Hulagu Khan's. She was Möngke and Kublai Khan's mother, a Christian whose vast influence has not been appreciated to this day. Her authority was immense, and she is to be credited in particular with the spread of the

Nestorian faith in Asia on the one hand, and also with the Khans' anti-Moslem sentiments, something which caused the Mongols to regard the Moslems with fierce enmity.[144] Her influence as 'first lady' on the other women and also on the children only comes out indirectly in the source material. Following her death in 1265, her niece succeeded in continuing her aunt's mission work until the death of Kublai Khan in 1294, whereas in the area of the Golden Horde Berke Khan was the first to become Moslem, while Ilchan Arghun was Buddhist and his son Ghazan converted to Sunni Islam in 1295. The Christian influence in the Mongol empire was limited

Ill. 218 (above): Sung Hui-Tsung (2nd part of the 13th century): The Story of Lady Wen Chi, detail. National Palace, Taipei.

Ill. 219 (below): Carpet composition from ill. 218.

in time to the authority of the main women of the Kereit tribe, and terminated at the death of Kublai Khan. Without exception, the paintings presented above stem from this time. The present author considers it quite possible that, as in the story about Lady Wen Chi, women of high standing who were allowed to return home could in fact have been given a Christian carpet. Such a carpet would then have become a symbol on two counts: first, it would have come to symbolize dignity and rank – once again note here who it is that was permitted to step on or use the carpet – and, secondly, it would have come to symbolize the faith. As we can be sure that these were imported carpets made of wool, the likelihood that they were Christian is greater. For wool, which was not held in high regard as a material in China,[145] could only have attained a function as manifest as this as a result of its special content and function.

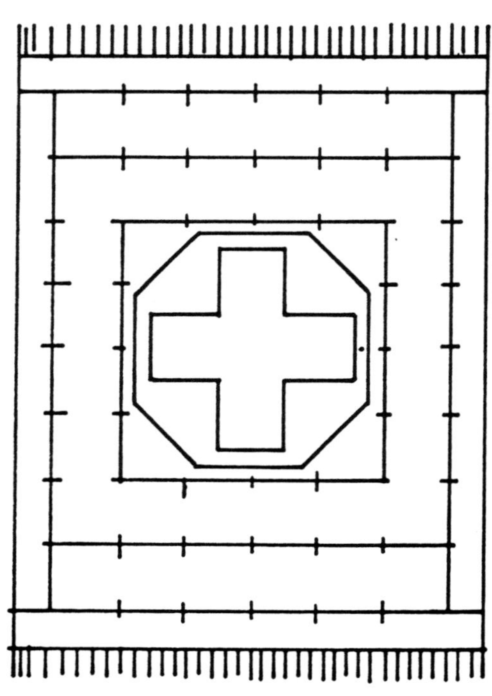

Ill. 224 (right): Silk carpet, 540 x 290 cm. Österr. Museum für angewandte Kunst, Vienna, no. T 8332.

The carpet is the most beautiful and at the same time the best preserved of its genre (B III, C VII); it was in the possession of the German imperial family.

Ill. 220 (outside left): Sung Hui-Tsung: (2nd part of the 13th century): The Story of Lady Wen Chi, detail. National Palace, Taipei.

Ill. 221 (inside left): Carpet composition from ill. 220.

Ill. 222 (outside left): Wen Fong (2nd part of the 13th century): The Story of Lady Wen Chi, detail from episode 13: Parting. MMA, New York, no. 1973.120.3. Gift of the Dillon Fund, 1973.

Ill. 223 (inside left): Carpet composition from ill. 222.

This detail is a very interesting document, clearly showing how part of a carpet was reused as a saddle blanket.

Carpets in Islamic Painting

What can be said about the infrequent occurrence of figural representations in Islamic painting applies to the representations of carpets in particular. The earliest have survived from the 14th century. We find a considerable number in manuscripts from the 15th and 16th centuries, and of these we will concern ourselves for the most part with those from the Timurid period, that is, dating from the 15th century.

Ill. 225 (page 157): Firdausi: Shah Namah; Baghdad 1330/1336. Iskander's Deathbed. Courtesy of the Freer Gallery of Art, Smithsonian Institution, Washington D.C., Acc. no. 23.5.

Of special interest, in addition to the carpet, are the two outer decorative panels above the hanging lamps; they resemble those in ill. 201.

To begin with let us look at two miniatures from the so-called 'Demotte Shahnameh'.[146] In ill. 225 we have the miniature 'The Laying-out of Iskandar', with ill. 227 depicting the 'Arabian Zohhak on the Iranian Throne'. In each case a carpet which is only visible in part is shown in the lower third of the miniature. In the Iskandar carpet (ill. 226) the design is geometric. The Zohhak throne carpet (ill. 228), on the other hand, is one of the so-called animal carpets, to which Richard Ettinghausen devoted an essay.[147] We have seen the geometric design of the ground elsewhere. The Katchkars in ills. 131 and 132 exhibit it in their borders. The outside, 'pseudo-Kufic' border has also been discussed previously.[148] The secondary borders are stripes consisting of rows of hooked-'S' designs in different colours, such as are to be found in Armenian illuminated manuscripts from the 13th century.[149] From Ettinghausen we have an illustration of the reconstructed throne carpet. The octagons, encircled by the S-design and enclosed within squares, contain animal symbols of which we see too little to allow interpretation. The squares themselves are

Ill. 226 (below): Carpet from ill. 225.

The carpet shows a design in its ground that corresponds to the borders of the Katchkar in ills. 131, 132.

Ill. 227 (page 158): Firdausi: Shah Namah; Bagdad 1330/1336. Sohhak on the Throne. Courtesy of the Freer Gallery of Art, Smithsonian Institution, Washington D.C., Acc. no. 38.3.

Ill. 228 (page 159, above): Carpet from ill. 227 (according to Ettinghausen).

The animal carpet is closely related to Group B II.

outlined by a stripe of alternating half-crosses, something we have also seen in the Armenian codices. Adjacent to this is a zig-zagged line, which is in turn followed by a stripe to which Ettinghausen directs our attention.

He refers to this stripe as "a cross on a stepped base," which, when put side by side in alternating colours, makes up one of the bordering stripes, analogous to the S-designs. Needless to say, what we have here is clearly a Christian symbol, in fact it is one of the most common among the Monophysites in Armenia, Cilicia, as well as in Syria during the 13th century. This simplified and yet concentrated example represents a further step in the development of the secondary border in TIEM no. 685. Without realizing the connection, Ettinghausen has even provided us with an intermediary step in the design evolution. The in-and-out T-stripe which comes next is also a part of this established set of designs[150] just as is the one after that with its pseudo-Kufic ornamentation. Both Iskander's carpet and Zohhak's throne-carpet were, then, probably produced in the kingdom of Armenia Minor sometime around the end of the 13th or the beginning of the 14th century.

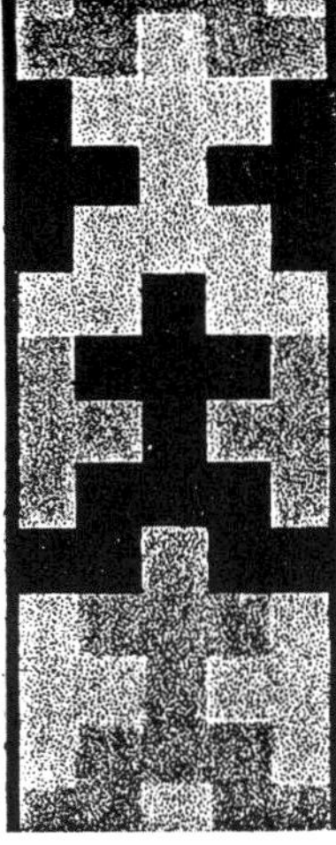

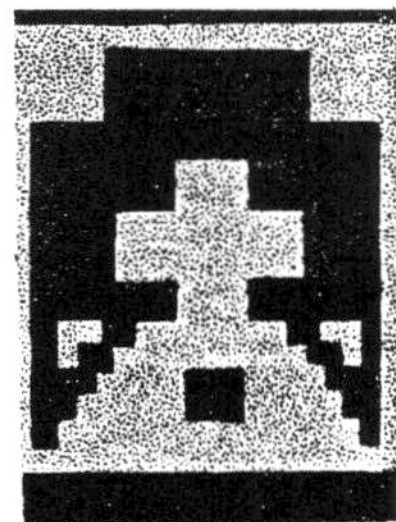

Figure 5 (above):
Of these border details the upper one comes from ill. 228. The one in the middle forms the connecting link with TIEM no. 685 (ill. 101) – it is a detail from TIEM no. 299 (no illustration).

Ill. 230 (above): Shah Namah c. 1450: King Piruz' Court. Eustache de Lorey Collection. Carpet design (according to Briggs).

Compositions constructed around the number 3 are rare within the region influenced by Armenian culture and suggest foreign influence, in this case Latin.

The carpets in the *Timurid illustrated manuscripts* have been correctly and thoroughly analyzed and presented.[151] In what follows, the author will merely provide a brief summary of Amy Briggs' work and then go on to investigate to what extent the carpet types listed there correspond to the designs from the region of Armenian cultural influence, thus making plausible the assumption that they originated in this area. Amy Briggs classifies these carpets into types (ill. 229): Type I is based on squares; Type II on star-crosses; Type III on octagons; Type IV on hexagons and Type V on circles. In addition, there are carpets closely related to these: those exhibiting a repeated pattern over a larger area which do not coincide with this classification, and a few showing a non-repeating geometric pattern. If we now compare the types described above with those presented in the preceding chapters, the results will leave no question as to overall agreement. Not only is it possible to find a correspondence in Armenian illuminated manuscripts for each of the types mentioned here, but there are also actually correspondences for almost every single illustration. And, furthermore, the Armenian examples are almost all dated to an earlier time.

Throughout this material there is but one example that on first glance is not obviously Christian: fig. 55 of Briggs, (ill.230), a carpet representation that Briggs assigns to Type IVa. According to Briggs drawing, three-footed forms and triangles together with hexagons appear to be portrayed here. However, a comparison with the original miniature,[152] dating from approximately 1450, leaves this interpretation looking doubtful at best. And yet such a design would be conceivable for Armenia. In actual fact, the number 4 is predominant in the sphere of Armenian cultural influence – contrary to the 3 which is more common in nothern Germanic or Celtic regions,[153] though in Cilicia the triangle does occur as a numeric symbol. It is the European or, perhaps more likely, the Minorite influence that is manifest in the triangle and that Prince Hetum was in sympathy with. For this reason the triangle inscribed in a circle,[154] symbolizing the harmony between the divine and the cosmic, appears on the first page of the 'Prince Hetum Lectionary' from 1286 as a symbol equivalent to the cross (ill. 233).[155] The surface ornament also contains designs corresponding to fig. 54 of Briggs (ill. 234), a carpet of Type IIIc from a Timurid representation of approximately 1440, and to fig. 49, of Type IIIa (ill. 237) from a representation from around 1450. Thus fig. 55 of Briggs could be a further step in the development of the design from the 'Prince Hetum Lectionary', provided that the Briggs drawing is correct. The present author is inclined, however, to see in the miniature precisely the design from the lectionary.

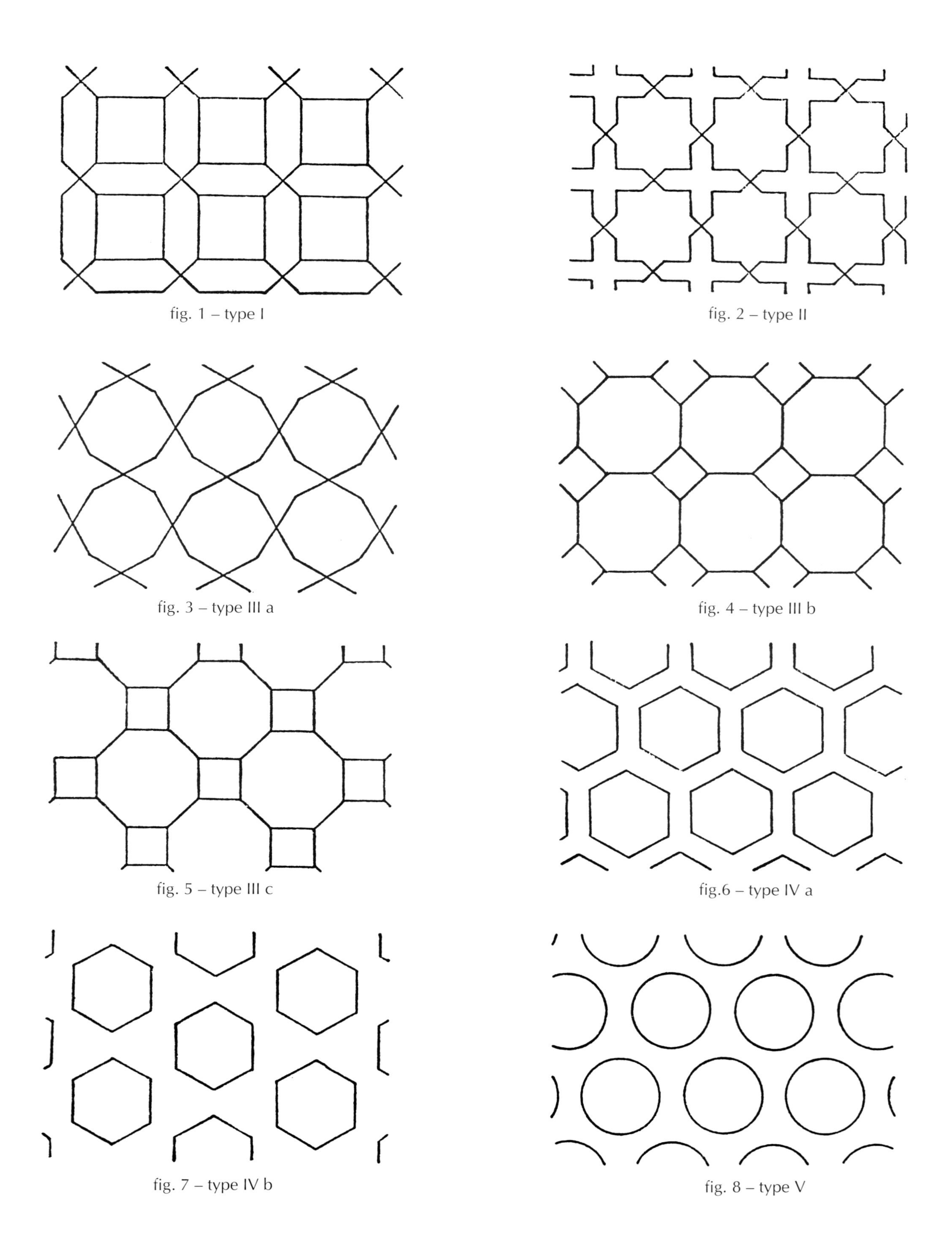

Ill. 229: Basic types of carpet designs in Timurid painting (according to Briggs).

Ill. 231 (right): Khusrau wa Shirin manuscript, 1396–1430. Freer Gallery of Art, Washington, no. S 368_2 B (31.34): carpet design (according to Briggs).

The opening page of an evangelary from approximately 20 years before[156] corresponds to Fig. 53 of Briggs, of Type III b (ills. 235, 236).

Each of the field compositions is based on the cross-star tile design. They show the connection that exists between carpets produced in the west (Anatolia: Groups B I, C II) and in the east (Central Asia: Group C X).

In accordance with these examples, the designs were already present roughly 150 years earlier in Armenian illustrated manuscripts. They may have found their way into the carpets later, perhaps not until the middle of the 14th century. Fig. 42 of Briggs strikes the author as the most interesting in terms of the design evolution in carpets. It is an example of Type IIIb in a representation from 1429 or 1430 (ill. 239) and could indeed be a prototype for the carpets later to be produced in Turkestan. For this design, too, the equivalent is to be found in the Armenian illustrated manuscripts from the 14th century.

Ill. 232 (right): Sultan Husain Mirza in the Garden, miniature from c. 1485. Gulistan Palace Museum, Teheran. Carpet design (according to Briggs).

Ill. 234 (left): Shah Namah, c. 1440: Tahmina Visits Rustam. Royal Asiatic Soc., London. Carpet design (according to Briggs).

The exactness with which this carpet replicates the cruciforms from the Hetum lectionary, which is 150 years older, is astounding.

Ill. 236 (left): Shah Namah of the Sultan Ali Mirza: Scene from the Court; 1393–1405. TIEM, Istanbul. Carpet design (according to Briggs).

Here, too, Armenian illuminated manuscripts, more than 100 years older, served as the model for the carpet design.

Ill. 233 (right): Prince Hetum Lectionary, Cilicia 1286. Matenadaran, Erivan; codex no. 979, F. 59r. Carpet panel.

Ill. 235 (right): Evangelistary, Cilicia c. 1250–1275. Matenadaran, Erivan; codex 9422, F. 162r; title page to the Gospel according to Luke.

Ill. 237 (left): Shah Namah from c. 1450: King Piruz' Court. Eustache de Lorey Collection. Carpet design (according to Briggs).

This design variant is presumably the prototype for the gul design in ill. 536.

Closer examination of the designs of those 'Timurid carpets' presented by Amy Briggs makes it clear that such designs were already all in existence in the 14th century, that is, before Timur's invasion. They are therefore 'pre-Timurid', making the term 'Timurid', as introduced by Briggs, superfluous. Of course this leaves open the question as to when and where these carpets may have been produced. For the most part, what we are here referring to as the region of Armenian cultural influence belonged to the empire of the Il-Khans. Only the southern part, the kingdom of Armenia Minor in Cilicia, was subjugated by the Mamluks during the second half of the 14th century. This of course limits our area of investigation. Yet, on the other hand, we know of numerous Christian, Armenian and Syrian communities within

Ill. 238 (left): Khamsa of Emir Khusrau of Delhi, dated 1485; Dancing Dervishes. MMA, A. Chester Beatty Collection, New York. Carpet design (according to Briggs).

this entire empire. The above-mentioned 'Florentine Diatessaron'[157] from 1547 speaks of Christian communities emerging in Khorezm and Mazandaran as a result of deportations at the hands of the Mongols during the time from 1220 to 1230. It is further indicated that minorities continued to live on in these communities into the 16th century. These people were continually in contact with their ancestral home, which gives us reason to assume that designs were passed on to them. It is therefore quite possible that these carpets may not only have been produced in the region that was traditionally within the sphere of the Armenian cultural area extending from Erzerum to Tabriz, but also in the diaspora of the 14th and 15th centuries. We will return to this problem in greater detail when we discuss carpets from Turkestan.

Ill. 239 (above): Shah Namah from 1429/30: Luhrasp Hears of Kai Khusrau's Disappearance. Gulistan Palace Museum, Teheran. Carpet design (according to Briggs).

Despite the fact that no colour separation had yet been attempted in the guls, the composition bears a strong resemblance to Ersari gul designs (ills. 560/562, 579–584).

Carpets from the High Middle Ages

The survey provided thus far of the carpet representations in paintings from Europe to China has prepared us for what we can now expect in the originals from the Middle Ages. Whereas we have been exposed to surprising variety, we have also witnessed a remarkable assiduousness in design, despite some degree of conformity to fashion trends of the day, which account for variations and modifications. And this is something we should reflect on. In the opinion of Ernst H. Gombrich,[158] "one must consider that a craving for change is not experienced where rituals are at stake. Ritualistic art is based on the desire for repetition and constancy rather than for new stimuli." We have experienced this in Egyptian art and are aware of the same problem when it comes to icon painting. And here in the 'textile-icons' created for the Christian cult we have a suitable form of expression which would lose its integrity the instant its function were changed. For symbolism is rooted in function. In this context we must avoid the temptation not only of wanting to equate this highly symbolic, ornamental language of symbols in Armenian art with (western) European ornamentalism; we must also resist the desire to apply to it the same western standards of assessment. Here the symbol takes over the significance and the function otherwise held by the picture. Hence, it is important to seek explanations for why changes in the symbolic content occur. Over the course of time, the more a religious symbol was transformed into a predominantly or purely decorative motif, the more certain it became that such a symbol would no longer serve any use in ritual.

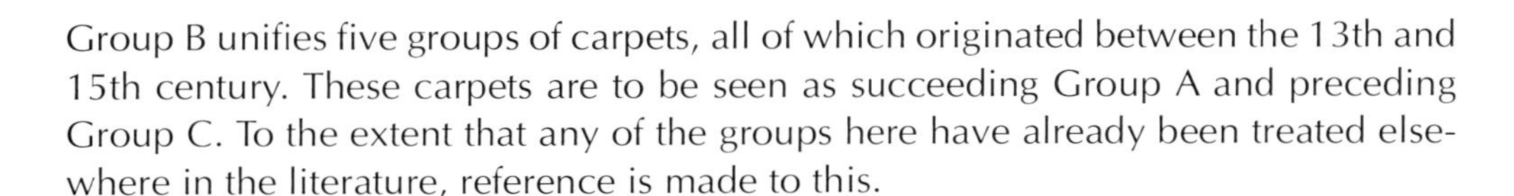

Group B unifies five groups of carpets, all of which originated between the 13th and 15th century. These carpets are to be seen as succeeding Group A and preceding Group C. To the extent that any of the groups here have already been treated elsewhere in the literature, reference is made to this.

Group B I: Holbein Carpet Prototypes

The last carpet to be mentioned from Group A I was Vakf. A 305 (ill. 240). It is to be located along the line of evolution from Group A I to Group B I. On the one hand it is an extension of the old, familiar traditional design, and yet it also stands at the beginning of a series of designs that continue into the 16th century and beyond. Large Greek crosses fill the red ground with alternating colours such that crosses filled with cross-rosettes take shape in the negative areas. We even rediscover the familiar cross-star in the Greek cross – this time in a square which, flanked on each side by a lily, takes on the shape of a cross. The design of the Greek cross is a very significant intermediate stage in the development of the so-called 'Holbein gul' design, which itself is a component of what are later to become the 'Holbein carpets'.

A second carpet is Mevl. no. 860/861/1033 (ill. 249). Diamond-shaped Greek crosses are shown on a blue ground. Their pointed shapes are reminiscent of the cross-star tile designs of the 12th or 13th century. As in Vakfl. A 305, we find in these Greek crosses small cross-stars, the extensions of which likewise form cross arms. More important for the design evolution are the diamond-crosses which are found in rows between, later to become a part of the 'arabesque crosses'. Illustrations

Ill. 240 (left): Vakf. A 305; 175 x 157 cm.
Vakiflar Carpet Museum, Istanbul.

241 (above) 243 (below)

242 (above) 244 (below)

245 (above) 247 (below)

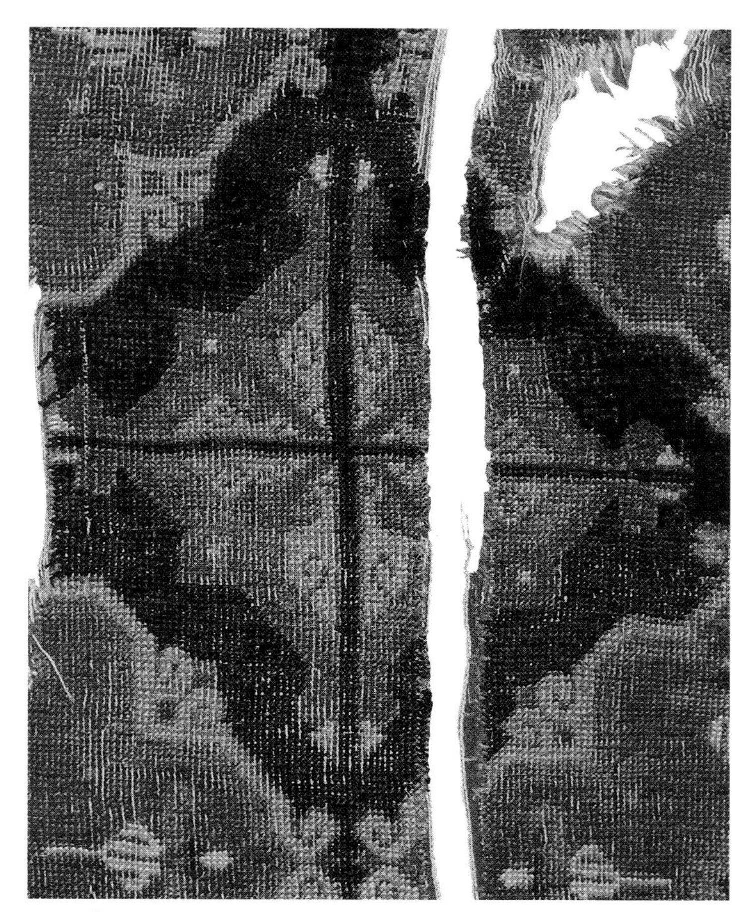

246 (above) 248 (below)

Ill. 241 (page 168): Vakf. A 305; main border from ill. 240.

Though the border does appear to be somewhat disjointed structurally, it has its equivalent in the illuminated manuscripts of the 12th century: in evangelistary no. 7737 of the Matenadaran.

Ill. 242 (page 168): Vakf. A 305; main gul of the field design from ill. 240.

Ill. 243 (page 168): Mevl. no. 860/861/1033; main gul of the field design from ill. 249.

Ill. 244 (page 168): Holbein carpet, Stuttgart; main gul of the field design from ill. 360.

Ill. 245 (page 169): Mevl. no. 860/861/1033; main border from ill. 249.

The dark blue design in each case is one fourth of the central cross composition.

Ill. 246 (page 169): Mevl. no. 860/861/1033; secondary gul of the field design from ill. 249.

Ill. 247 (page 169): Private collection; secondary gul of the field design from the carpet used to cover a Renaissance chair.

Ill. 248 (page 169): Holbein carpet, Stuttgart; arabesque gul of the field design from ill. 360.

Ill. 249 (right): Mevl. no. 860/861/1033; 293 x 127 cm. Mevlana Museum, Konya.

246–248 show this development clearly. Illustration 247 shows part of a more recent carpet, of which several fragments exist in various collections.[159] If we put this design together with the proto-design in the medallion of the runner of Pope Honorius III (ill. 156), we come up with the exact 'arabesque cross' of the Holbein carpets (ill. 248).

Because of their designs, each of these carpets can be assumed to have originated between the end of the 13th and the beginning of the 15th century. In looking at their secondary borders, we can actually place Vakfl.A 305 at the beginning of this period and Mevl.no. 860/861/1033 at the end. Both are likely to have originated in the Armenian homeland, with the first one exhibiting a western influence and the second an eastern. This could indicate their production in the western or eastern part of the country respectively.

Group B II: Coffered-Form Medallion Carpets II
Large-Pattern (LP) Holbein Carpets II

This group is the continuation of Group A III, referred to as medallion carpets, or also 'large-pattern Holbein carpets,' whose development over the course of several centuries we have already considered. To the Vakf. A 217 (ills. 126, 127) discussed earlier we can now add two carpets: one of these, part of a private collection in Geneva, only appeared in publication[160] in August, 1986, but has never been made available for viewing (ill. 250); the other, MBN no.10/294, in the Bavarian National Museum in Munich, is well known from exhibitions and publications[161] (ill. 251). The Genevan carpet is complete, whereas the one in Munich has been pieced together in the middle, leaving us uncertain as to its original appearance. Each is based on the same cross-star tile design familiar to us from a small section of Giotto's work (ill. 150) and from various other miniatures. Specifically, the carpet shown on the steps to the ciborium in the Christmas Mass at Greccio by Giotto demonstrates a striking similarity in composition, even with regard to its dimensions. In the inner panel of the Genevan carpet there is a row of four large star-tiles flanked on either side by cross halves. The star-tiles are beautiful examples for the depiction of world-pictures, already referred to on page 39 ff. The appearance of the Munich carpet is altered by the fact that the two outside star-tiles have been left out and replaced on each end by octagons filled with cross variants.

The borders are important, showing us a total of three designs and one design variant in their development. Interestingly enough, there are two different designs for each carpet. In the case of the Genevan carpet, a shorter end and the two long sides as well as the second shortened end are framed by a border that contains almost all the elements found in TIEM no. 685 (ill. 99), though it may seem at first sight as if new designs had emerged as a result of the different parts merging. There are two possible ways of reconstructing how these borders must have evolved, both requiring that we refer back to our basic form type A (ill. 24). The first possibility involves turning the main cross-tile by 45 degrees about its own axis. In addition to this, the cross arms of two adjacent crosses come together to enclose a cross-star, forming an interlace octagon where they join (ill. 258). The second possibility would have the central cross-star enclosed in an interlace octagon (ill. 265), the upper and lower cross arms were lost (we observed this reduction in ills. 102/103) and though the two remaining were complete, they joined with those contiguous with them to form a new whole resulting from a different cross-knot (ills. 261, 263).

Ill. 250 (left): Cross star tile carpet, 543 x 228 cm. Private collection.

This carpet, closely paralleled in a fresco by Giotto (ill. 148), can be regarded as one of the best preserved and most important carpets of the High Middle Ages.

The illustration clearly shows the cross-star tile composition as well as the arrangement of the world cosmogram.

Ill. 251 (right): MBN no. 10/294, 305 x 217 cm. Bayrisches Nationalmuseum, Munich.

The Munich carpet, of a somewhat later origin, is certainly very similar to the previous one in many details; yet, despite its significance, it remains a poorly-preserved fragment, not permitting any statements as to its former size

Ill. 252 (left): TMW no. 1961.2.1., 300 x 176 cm. Textile Museum, Washington.

This carpet, too, is a fragment which, years ago, was reworked using the Soumak technique with the result that until recently it was in fact thought to be one.

Ill. 253 (right): TIEM no. 417. Türk ve Islam Eserleri Müzesi, Istanbul.

Ill. 254 (left): TIEM no. 701. Türk ve Islam Eserleri Müzesi, Istanbul.

Ill. 255 (right): PHAM no. 43.40.67. Museum of Art, Philadelphia. McIlhenny Collection, bequest of John D. McIlhenny.

Ill. 256 (left):
TIEM no. 468.
Türk ve Islam
Eserleri Müzesi,
Istanbul.

Ill. 257 (right):
TIEM no. 700.
Türk ve Islam
Eserleri Müzesi,
Istanbul.

Ill. 258 (page 180): TIEM no. 704, Türk ve Islam Eserleri Müzesi, Istanbul.

Ill. 259 (page 181): BOIM no. I.29, 170 x 113. Staatliche Museen zu Berlin, Islamisches Museum, Berlin.

The second design in the development of these borders is to be found along three sides of the Munich carpet. At one point it undergoes modification, resulting in the variant mentioned above (ill. 263) and finally, at the upper, short end where it changes into the third design (ill. 267) in a way similar to what was observed in Group A II (cf. pp. 87 ff.). Now the composition is no longer based entirely on the basic form type A, but instead on only half of it. As was previously the case with the entire design, this part is now connected to the cross. The evolution of the borders within Group B II and the transition to Groups C II and C III is clearly shown in ills. 267–272.

The development of border designs in their original form corresponds to such designs in the Katchkars from the 12th/13th century,[162] making it possible to assume an origin for the border designs discussed here in the 13th or early 14th century. This coincides with the occurrence of carpets in the paintings and illuminated manuscripts of this time.

TMW no. 1961.2.1.(ill. 252) moves one more step in this development. It is a fragmented woven carpet which was presumably restored a few centuries ago using the Soumak technique. It has already been cited in our discussion of the evolution of borders (ill. 269). The cross-star tile design is in part still discernible as a 'negative area'; the panels have become wider and now accommodate four stars with cross tile-shaped guls in between. This is much like what we have seen in Mevl. no. 860/861/1033 (ill. 249) as well as in the fragment in illustration 247. Aside from the proportions, the cross-star tile design is clearly preserved in the panels. The border constitutes an extension of the design found in the Munich carpet (ill. 267), the halves have again become a whole and form a rectagonal frame, which looks very nearly square. The interlace knots themselves are once again cruciform (ill. 269) and they go on to enclose plainer crosses, which are now more obvious as such.

As there is commonly a vast array of parallel developments for any given period, it is only possible to follow one of these at a time. TIEM no. 468 (ills. 256/262) contains a somewhat later extension of the second design from above (Geneva/Munich, ill. 261) dating from the latter part of the 14th century (ill. 262). In contrast to the Washington carpet, the individual designs were reduced to such an extent that the original design is hardly recognizable. The border is continued and further reduced in TIEM no. 701 and TIEM no. 714 (ills. 264 and 266), both of which are to be attributed to a slightly later period, quite possibly to the first part of the 15th century.

We encounter a special form of the so-called 'Kufic-Border' in PHAM no. 43.40.67 (ills. 255, 268). This carpet, having the same secondary border, stems from approximately the same time as BMIK no. 83.522 (ill. 272). Its border (ill. 268) represents a late design in the line of evolution that branches off from Vakf. no. E 344 (ill. 106).[163]

The other line of evolution for borders takes us from MBN no. 10/294 (ill. 267) to BMIK no. I 5526 (ill. 271) and finally to BMIK no. 83.522 (ill. 272), all of which likewise probably originated during the 15th century. The main border in ill. 271 finds a *terminum ante quem* in Mantegna's fresco in Mantua:[164] 1465/1474.

The borders of the remaining carpets in the group are independent of these evolutionary tendencies: two of three are in part identical. In both BMIK no. 79.110 and TIEM no. 704 (ills. 273 and 274) we again find the cruciform halves arranged opposite one another. It was the early form of this that we encountered in the Lombard fresco from the end of the 13th century (ill. 147). Based on its secondary border, the carpet in Berlin is the older of the two, though both are to be dated to the 15th century. TIEM no. 700 (ill. 276), sharing the same border stripe with TIEM no. 704 (ill. 274), is even older than this.

Ill. 260 (left): BMIK no. 79.110, 182 x 123 cm. SMPK, Museum für Islamische Kunst, Berlin.

Ill. 261: MBN no. 10/294: main border from ill. 251.

Ill. 262: TIEM no. 468: main border from ill. 256.

Ill. 263: MBN no. 10/294: main border detail from the lower left of ill. 251.

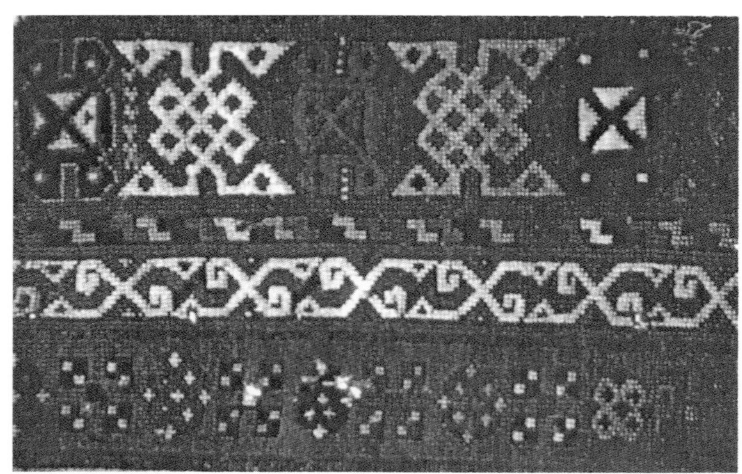

Ill. 264: TIEM no. 701: main border from ill. 254.

Ill. 265: MBN no. 10/294: interlace octagon of the main border from ill. 251.

Ill. 266: TIEM no. 417: border from ill. 253.

Ill. 267: MBN no. 10/294: reduced hook-form (hasten) design of the upper border from ill. 251

Ill. 268: PHAM no. 43.40.67: border from ill. 255.

Ill. 269: TMW no. 1961.2.1.: border from ill. 252.

Ill. 270: TMW no. R 34.2.1.: border from ill. 292.

Ill. 271: BMIK no. I.5526: border from ill. 291.

Ill. 272: BMIK no. 83.522, 158 x 112 cm: border detail.

Ill. 273: BMIK no. 79.110: border from ill. 260.

Ill. 274: TIEM no. 704: borders from ill. 258:

Ill. 275: MBN no. 10/294: star tile from ill. 251.

Ill. 276: TIEM no. 700: border from ill. 257.

Ill. 277: TMW no. 1961.2.1.: central medallion from ill. 252.

Ill. 278: MBN no. 10/294: octagon from ill. 251.

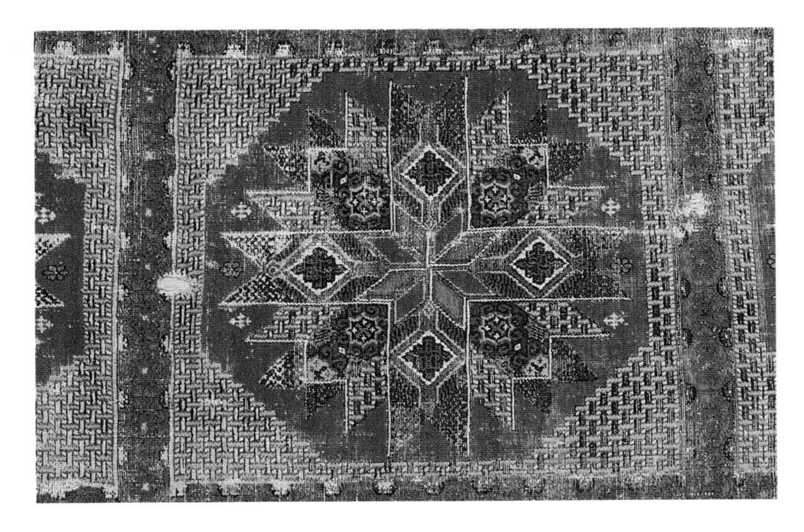

Ill. 279: MMA no. 13.193.2.: medallion from ill. 336.

Ill. 280: BMIK no. 83.522, 162 x 122 cm: medallion I.

Ill. 281: BMIK no. 79.110: medallion from ill. 260.

Ill. 282: BMIK no. 83.522, 162 x 122 cm: medallion II.

Ill. 283: TIEM no. 417: medallion from ill. 253.

Ill. 284: BOIM no. I.29: medallion from ill. 259.

Ill. 285: PHAM no. 43.40.67: medallion from ill. 255.

Ill. 286: BMIK no. I.5526: medallion from ill. 291.

Ill. 287: TIEM no. 694: medallion.

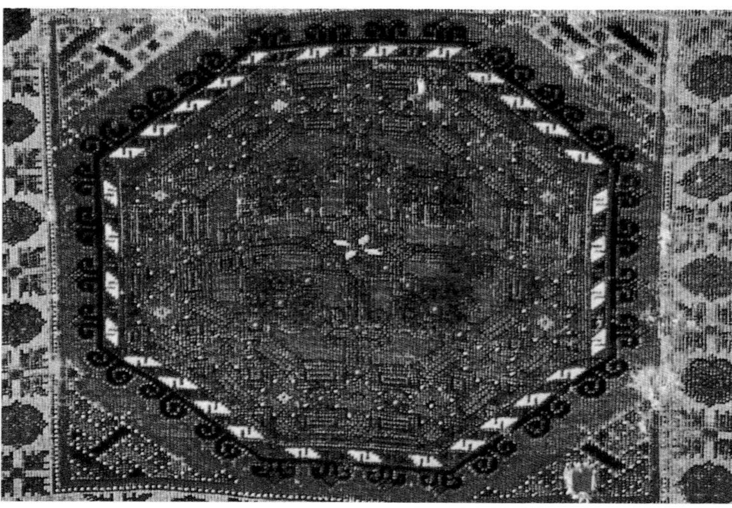

Ill. 288: TIEM no. 704: medallion from ill. 258.

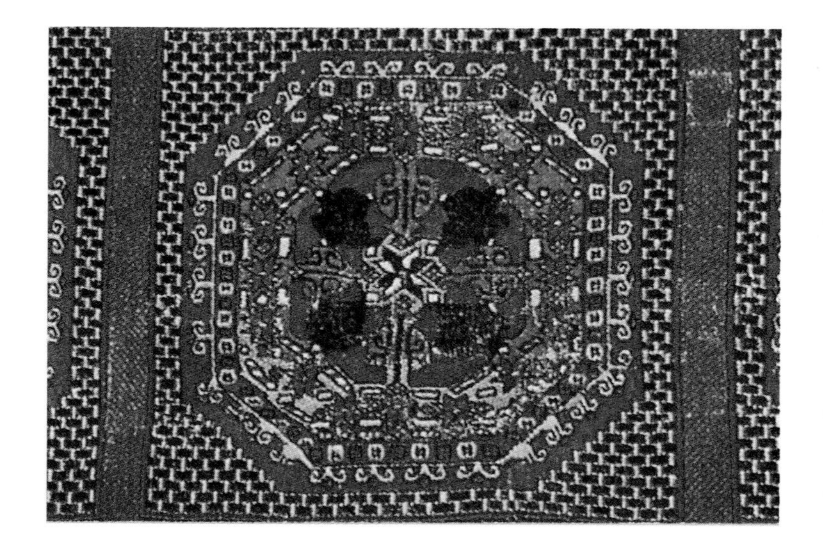

Ill. 289: CLAM no. 52.511: medallion from ill. 342.

Ill. 290: TIEM no. 701: medallion from ill. 254.

The medallion details of ills. 275–290 show the development over a period of time of almost 200 years: from the world cosmogram to light-symbol crosses and single-star crosses and finally to the 'Gloria Crucis'.

Ill. 291 (right): BMIK no. I.5526, 430 x 200 cm. SMPK, Museum für Islamische Kunst, Berlin.

Ill. 292 (page 190): TMW no. R 34.2.1. Textile Museum, Washington.

Ill. 293 (page 191): ARM no. 1975–147, 185 x 135 cm. Rijksmuseum, Amsterdam.

The central medallion is connected to four smaller octagons by cross-pieces in such a way that a highly expressive cross emerges as a new composition.

In one border stripe we see Greek crosses between cross-rosettes; the beams of the former are formed by 'acorns' in the earlier design and oak leaves in the more recent design. TIEM no. 700 exhibits both types in its borders. The cross-rosettes mentioned here will be discussed later (cf. p. 266). For the time being, suffice to say that they constitute a motif used in Armenian carpets and flat-weaves down to the present century. The border stripe referred to here can also be found in a painting by Crivelli dating from the latter part of the 15th century.[165]

Two carpets which, in terms of the evolution of their borders, are so problematic that they virtually resist classification are first of all TMW R 34.2.1. (ills. 292, 270), the ground of which is identical to BMIK no. 83.522 (ill. 272), and secondly BOIM no. 1.29 (ill. 259), from which the borders are missing except for a narrow stripe. Both of these carpets are 15th century, in any case. The one on display in Berlin may even date back to the 1300s.

As was shown in Figs. 1 a-f on page 38, the development of the lily-acorn-tree of Jesse provides us with a way of dating carpets. The design of the 'acorn' in Fig. 1 d was used from the middle of the 14th to the beginning of the 15th century, and for this time it represents what might be considered a 'prototype'.

Illustrations 275–290 provide us with a chronological sequence of the medallions in the early 'LP-Holbein carpets'. This progression, too, is informative with regard to changes in the motifs. As already mentioned on pp. 39 ff., the world-picture is still preserved in its unadulterated form in MBN no. 10/294 (ill. 275). We see the square of the earth with the four cardinal points, surrounded by the divine symbols; within this (or above it) stripes of light green and red are used to symbolize the glassy sea and fire, in other words, heaven. Continuing, we see the orbiting stars in the *super caelos,* the highest sphere, at the centre of which appears the cross-star as a symbol of the *caeli spirituales.*[166] One can trace a certain development in which the cosmogram evolves over time into a depiction of the heavenly spheres, with the light-symbol cross becoming increasingly dominant, in order, finally, free of the mythical cosmology of the early Middle Ages, to function once again exclusively as the pure symbol of the Christian faith, as 'Gloria Crucis'.

With its Greek cross composition, in which what remains of the world-picture forms an integral part, the fragment in the Alanya museum (no. 411, ill. 495) represents a transition in design to ARM no. 1975–147 (ill. 293). In this latter carpet vestiges of multiple-row coffered-form medallion carpets and the large-cross composition culminate so as to prepare the way for the central medallion-carpet of the late 15th century. Three sets of three octagons fill the field such that the central octagon, plainly larger than the others, embraces the Gloria Crucis, with the remaining octagons being filled with cross-stars. The octagons in the middle were then joined to the centre by means of crosspieces and set apart in colour, thus resulting in the emergence of a clearly visible, expressive cross. Whereas the border is in some ways related to that of BMIK no. 79.110 and TIEM no. 704 (ills. 273, 274), it does at the same time appear to predate Mevl. no. 860/861/1033 (ill. 245) in its development. On all four sides the border shows a row of what is a quarter of the original diamond leaf-form cross and still it gives us an impression of the relationship between the alternating half-crosses, set apart as they are in colour.

The animal carpets still remaining to us make up a special type of cross-block carpet. Here, in place of the cross, the world-picture or the Gloria Crucis, we see a figural representation. The so-called Berlin "Dragon-Phoenix carpet" (BOIM no. 1.4, ill. 294) contains the depiction of the 'dragon-phoenix' which gives it its name; the 'Marby carpet' (STSHM no. 17786, ill. 296) shows two birds facing one another.

Ill. 294 (right): BOIM no. I.4., 172 x 90 cm. Staatliche Museen zu Berlin, Islamisches Museum, Berlin.

The famous 'Dragon-Phoenix carpet' symbolizes the immortality of the divine and the triumph of life everlasting. The phoenix, flying above the 'S'-shaped, 'divine' dragon, bears the symbols for Jesus and God (ill. 31).

These carpets are the legitimate successors of the anagram carpets discussed on page 77 (ill. 90). That is, here we find figural representations of what has already been examined in the Christian carpets of this latter group. It was in 1981 that Lemyel Amirian[167] pointed out for the first time that in the phoenix of the above there were Armenian letters (ill. 31). Though this struck Donald King[168] as fantastic, he did at least mention it. In our discussion we have already looked at the S- and E-shaped symbols (pp. 37 ff.). These are the ciphers for 'God' and 'Jesus' on the body of the phoenix. Furthermore, knowing that the phoenix is an earlier symbol for Christ, which was, in truth, not first introduced into the Islamic world by the Mongols but had instead actually been used in the Christian world of the Orient as a symbol since the first (!) century, we can posit the following interpretation. To symbolize the triumph of eternal life over death, the resurrection,[169] the phoenix is suspended above the 'S'-shaped or 'divine' dragon.[170] Thus the divinity is used in association with Jesus, explained by Jesus:

> *Jesus, God, resurrected from the dead, triumphant victor of eternal life, is the manifestation of the 'divine'.*

Ill. 295 (above): Church of the Holy Cross. Achtamar; 915–921. Relief from the south side wall.

The relief here shows in its depiction of the eagle (as a symbol for Christ, it signifies the resurrection) and the dove (for believers) a compositional equivalent of the 'Dragon-Phoenix carpet'.

An interesting correspondence is to be found among the reliefs on the wall of the Church of the Holy Cross on Achtamar.[171] Here, identical in its composition, we find the depiction of an eagle above a dove (ill. 295). The eagle too, in symbolizing Christ, is likewise a sign for the resurrection. The dove, on the other hand, symbolizes those on earth who seek salvation in God by living pure and peaceful lives.[172]

Two birds appear directly opposite each other in the Marby carpet. Anyone who has spent time studying the codices of the Christian Orient will be aware that these birds are among those indispensible motifs available to Christian symbolism in signal form. Whether they be peacocks (immortality), partridges (honesty), cocks (watchfulness and passion), cranes (devotion) or others, they are symbols of the Christian faith, and were widely distributed in the Middle Ages through the innumerable writings of Physiologus[173] in the Greek, Coptic and Armenian languages. Illustration 187 shows us a detail from the table of canonical rules of an Armenian evangelary which again gives an impression of such symbolism – the peacock as well as the cock. If we now compare these representations with those of the Marby carpet, taking into account the textile quality, the correspondence becomes clear. The double-T-shaped construction we can take to be a tree composed from the parts of a cross that has been pulled apart. The visual fusion of the tree of life, the cross, and the peacocks means:

> *Immortality and eternal life in the Christian faith.*

The borders indicate that the origin is Armenian. In contrast to the Berlin carpet, the Marby carpet exhibits an Armenian 'S'-border that is quite old, bringing to mind that of TIEM no. 688 (ill. 103). The leaf-form cross quarter border is more recent than the one in ARM no. 1975–147 (ill. 293), making an attribution of both carpets to the 15th century plausible.

For the purpose of elaboration, let it be said here that both carpets are from churches, the one in Berlin having been found in central Italy, and the Marby carpet, as the name implies, in Marby, Sweden – quite some distance apart. There is as yet nothing to show what exactly their liturgical purpose was. The fact that they are in relatively good condition makes it unlikely that they were used as floor coverings. It is, however, certainly conceivable that they may have occasionally been used as antependiums during Pentecost, or as hangings on the lectern, something we find numerous examples of even in this century.

Ill. 296 (right): STSHM no. 17786, 145 x 109 cm. Statens Historiska Museum, Stockholm.

The 'Marby carpet', too, symbolizes immortality, with a peacock on either side of the tree of life.

Whereas the representative carpets of this group just discussed were based, in very simplistic terms, on a division of the ground into square or rectangular coffers, this last example takes us back to the diamond pattern, which likewise belongs to the older traditional designs. We already encountered this principle of design in Group B I in Mevl. 860/861/1033 (ill. 249), specifically in the proto-design series of the 'SP-Holbein carpets.' In this case we are dealing with one of the forerunners of diamond-form carpets, up to now also attributed to the Bergama region. To date no comparable piece or successor to this carpet has been found, although the designs contain elements we have become familiar with in the above. The early border design makes it likely that this originated before the Mevl. 860/861/1033 (ill. 245) and the ARM no. 1975–147 (ill. 293) and also the Marby carpet (ill. 296). The presence of the 'acorn crosses' limits this time of possible production to the period between the middle of the 14th and the beginning of the 15th century.

Ill. 297 (left): Private collection, 199 x 151 cm.

There are of course parallel developments, as is so frequently the case. We have carpets such as the one Domenico Ghirlandaio spread at the feet of his 'Enthroned Madonna'[174] (ill. 482) or the 'Pohlmann carpet' (ill. 493).[175] These carpets will both receive our attention in section C of Part Two.

The question as to where the carpets of this group may have been made is yet to be answered. Without justifying his decision, Erdmann attributes them to the region of Bergama in western Anatolia. When viewed in the context of other material at our disposal, it seems more possible that they may have originated in the Wilayet Sivas of north-central Anatolia, for example, because there was a strong concentration of Christian communities there up to the 20th century. Equally as possible, however, is their production in eastern or south-eastern Anatolia. Indeed, their obvious correspondence in design to the 'Mamluk carpets' more than anything makes this seem possible. And yet, because this carpet type was so widespread among Christians living in the region of Armenian cultural influence, which had shifted to the west, an area of production for the group as a whole cannot yet be determined. It seems possible that early examples might have been produced in the south-west, and the later work in the northern, central or western regions of Anatolia as a result of emigration from Cilicia to the west, northwest or the north due to the Mamluk conquests. It should be noted that among those carpets referred to today as 'Kasaks' or also as 'Akstafas' – carpets, in other words, whose origin in the Caucasus is not disputed – there are some which correspond in their composition to those presented in this group. This is likewise true of the carpets from the Bergama region. There a large portion of the population was Armenian until the turn of the century. Whether or not this was due in part to an influx of emigrants from Cilicia cannot be determined, though it would appear likely.

Group B III: Damascus/Mamluk Carpets I

This group includes the early examples of the genre referred to as 'Damascus carpets' up until 1939, which were then renamed 'Cairene carpets' by Erdmann.[176] In his writing on the subject, Erdmann attempted to prove that these carpets had been produced in Cairo. He justified this by referring to the injunction of Murat III[177] which, thanks to Sarre, resulted in so much confusion. Erdmann believed that this document provided him with evidence to the effect that in Istanbul, Bursa or elsewhere, no manufactory had produced carpets for the Ottoman Court before 1585. Despite the fact that Erdmann himself frequently contradicted his own hypothesis in what he said elsewhere in his writing, and despite the fact that new material in the form of military pay records[178] shows both his assumption and conclusions to be incorrect. The label 'Mamluk carpet' has become established, as is so often the case with misnomers, without the new evidence being considered.

The study of Egyptian textiles is still in its infancy. There is as yet no set chronology and the existing material has not really been organized. We do know that as a consequence of its geographic location, Egypt served as an area of retreat for the Monophysitic Christians during times of war-like conflicts in Asia Minor. When, after the council of Chalcedon, the Armenian and Syrian monasteries in Cilicia, Syria and Palestine had to be vacated in the face of the advancing Byzantine armies, those fleeing were provided refuge and homes in the Armenian and Syrian monasteries, which had been in existence in Egypt since the 4th century. The same was true during the Mongol invasions: again a number of the Monophysites emigrated to Egypt. The Armenians made up a significant proportion of those emigrating, their numbers being estimated at 120,000. That we must not underestimate their contribution to Coptic art becomes clear when we view the material that has survived. At the end of the 12th century the Armenian Abu Salih wrote a book on the churches and monasteries of Egypt[179] confirming this. In the vicinity of Cairo and in upper Egypt, there were high concentrations of Armenians; in Assiut there was a textile

Ill. 298 (left): WÖMAK no. T 8348, 550 x 223 cm. Österr. Museum für angewandte Kunst, Vienna.

centre. Strzygowski published Armenian inscriptions found in the apses of the White Monastery near Sohag, which attest to the fact that in 1073 Armenian artists and craftsmen were at work there.[180] In the present author's view, it is easy to distinguish the Coptic and Armenian-Syrian approaches to art. This would apply to textiles as well. We can assume with certainty that those textiles found in Egypt exhibiting a geometric design are not originally Coptic. To this day, it has not been proven that Armenians actually produced carpets in Egypt, nor that they were responsible for cultivating the kermes-type kermococcus vermilio in upper Egypt (Assiut) for the production of dyes, for which there is evidence in the 10th century. We should be aware of these facts before we set about comparing designs.

Anyone who has worked as a photographer with these carpets will have noticed from the differences revealed through the lens that, in fact, there are two groups. In photographing the carpets belonging to the one group, there is no problem achieving very clear results with colour slides, whereas pictures of those in the other group always appear somehow blurred. In the absence of any results from scientifically substantiated analyses, there appear, nonetheless, to be two groups. The first of these (clear picture) reveals a very large number of purely Armenian designs, ones we find recurring in a similar form in carpets from both Anatolia and the Caucausus. Concerning our evolution of designs, these are older, earlier.

Unfortunately the author was successful only to a very limited degree in taking pictures of carpets himself. This group can thus be expected to expand once the appropriate material is available.

First of all our discussion will focus on WÖMAK no. T 8348 (ill. 298), a fragment in the Österreichisches Museum für angewandte Kunst in Vienna, which in its details reveals an astounding degree of correspondence to MBN no. 10/294 (ill. 251) – and that is without considering the colours. Although this fragment consists of several different parts, its format and composition can easily be reconstructed. In the centre of the rectangle extended lengthwise there is a square, in which, one after the other, a Greek cross, an octagon, a cross-star and a cosmogram of the world were all forced in together. One finds this design repeating itself out to the ends on both sides. The remaining space is filled in with light-symbol crosses of various compositional patterns.

The main border stripe contains a very filigreed variant of the pseudo-Kufic design elements (ill. 303) which received our attention much earlier (pp. 88 ff.). The inner border stripe with designs often interpreted as 'beakers' can also be traced back to the same origin (ill. 114). There are cypresses between the goblets and on either side of the large cosmogram, we find stripes filled with palm trees and symbols of life, possibly depicting paradise. Surrounding the cosmogram are light-symbol crosses (ills. 301, 302) which are formed from the 'tree of Jesse', this time in accordance with the design in fig. 1 e (ill. p. 38). This contains the 'life-giving' elements of the 'tree of Jesse' in repetition (ill. 307). The prototype of this symbol appears in Vakf. E 344 (ills. 108, 305), along the vertical extensions of the cosmogram of the world in MBN no. 10/294 (ills. 251, 308), in an early Caucasian carpet (ills. 473, 310) and now here in this Viennese example crowned with what can barely be made out as a cross, which is itself flanked on both sides probably by two acorns. The 'tree of Jesse' as shown here is a design element of Groups B IV and the more floral C V c (ill. 309). The symbol can take various different forms, and at times has a heart-shaped element in its root.

Ill. 299 (left): WÖMAK no. T 8348: medallion from ill. 298.

Ill. 300 (left): WÖMAK no. T 8348: central medallion from ill. 298.

The central medallion contains a cross-star and a world cosmogram. It resembles a mandala.

Ill. 301 (above): WÖMAK no. T 8348: star tile from ill. 298.

Ill. 302 (above): WÖMAK no. T 8348: star tile cross from ill. 298.

Ill. 303 (above): WÖMAK no. T 8348: main border from ill. 298.

Ill. 304 (below): WÖMAK no. T 8348: secondary border from ill. 298.

Ill. 305 (above): Vakf. no. E 344: prototype of the 'tree of Jesse' from ill. 108.

Ill. 306 (above): WÖMAK no. T 8348: goblet design in the secondary border from ill. 298.

Ill. 307 (above): WÖMAK no. T 8348: 'tree of Jesse' from ill. 298.

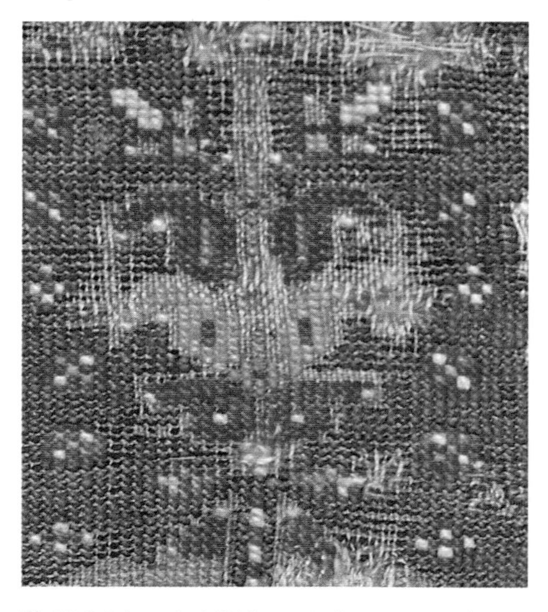

Ill. 308 (above): MBN no. 10/294: 'tree of Jesse' from ill. 251.

In the small secondary borders we find a design with the 'S' we recognize, which again is common to the Caucasus, Anatolia and Cilicia: it is a scroll vine with an alternating symbol of the cross, which as the 'wood of life' can also be a symbol for the community of Christ[181] (ill. 303 above) and in some carpets has cruciform leaves.[182]

A second carpet is preserved as a fragment: LV & A no. 150–1908 (ill. 311), considered by some authors[183] to be the oldest remaining 'Mamluk carpet'. Though its ground does contain all the individual details listed above, it exhibits very significant differences in its borders. The main border consists of contiguous interlace variants of the 'Holbein gul' (ill. 313), whereas the outside border is quite reminiscent both of MBN no. 10/294 (ill. 267) and PHAM no. 43.40.47 (ill. 268). In developmental terms, however, it is between these two that it must be placed. Due to the borders, the fragment takes on a definite 'Anatolian' character, at odds with its having been ascribed to Egypt. The outermost border stripe, visible only in sections and consisting of symbols of life in opposition, is new as well, as is the accompanying stripe next to the octagon which represents a later variant of the secondary border familiar to us from TIEM no. 685 (ill. 101).

The S-border, a common Armenian design, makes an Armenian origin for this carpet likely, and the ornamentation it exhibits identifies it as Christian. What sets these carpets apart technically from those done in Anatolia or the Caucasus deserves our attention. The knots are asymmetrical, which suggests that they were produced

Ill. 309 (p. 202, lower left): TIEM no. 904: late form of the 'tree of Jesse' from a 'dragon carpet' of Group C V c.

Ill. 310 (p. 202, lower right): Private collection: 'tree of Jesse,' reflected in the border from ill. 466.

The 'tree of Jesse' has its parallel in the marginal drawings of illuminated manuscripts. It usually appears in connection with a symbol: either the lily of grace, the cross or a heart shape. In ill. 310 we feel the influence of the Italian Renaissance, knowing that Michelangelo used quite similar compositions in the Biblioteca Laurenziana.

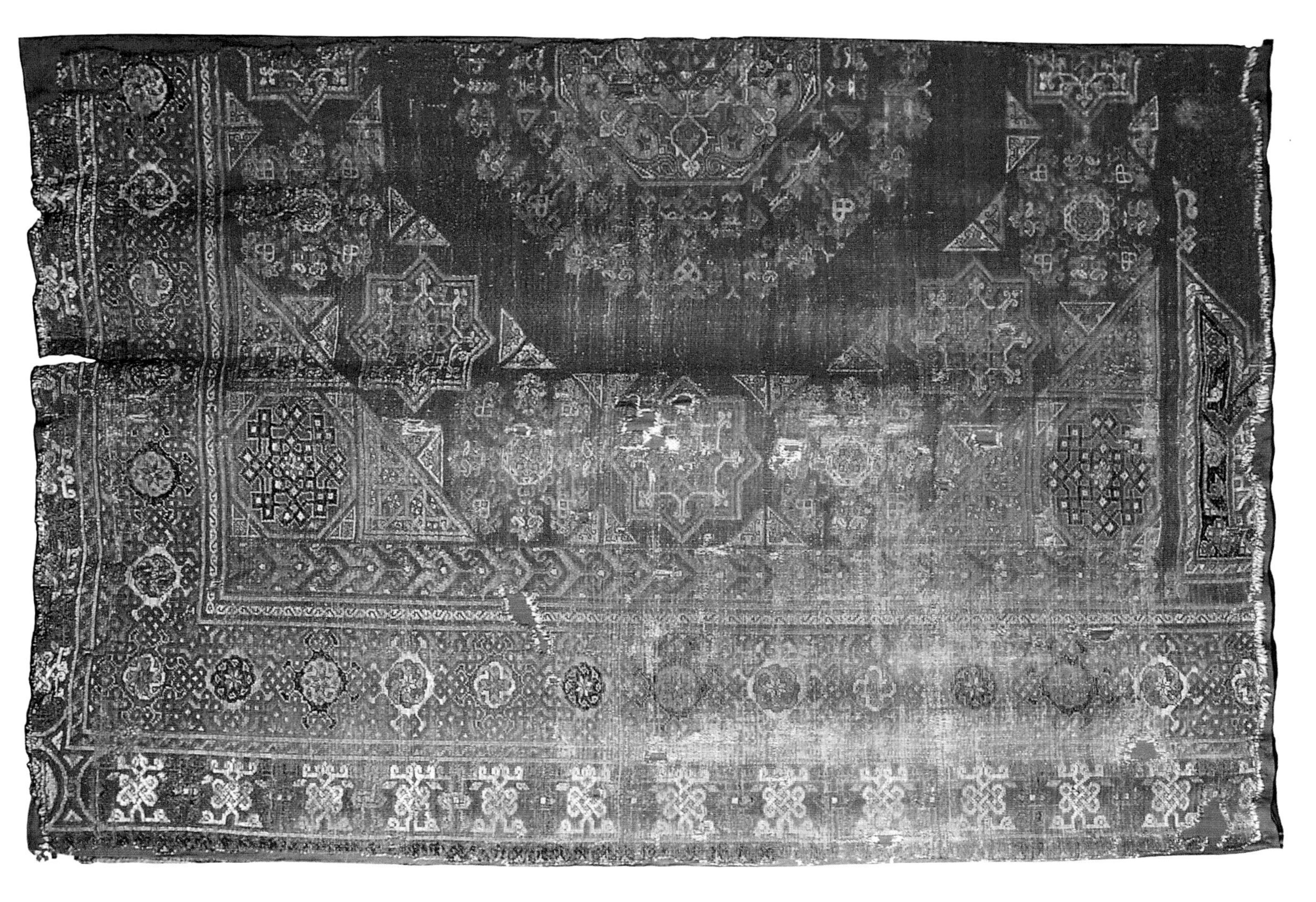

Ill. 311 (below): LV & A no. 902–1897, fragment 218 x 153 cm. Victoria and Albert Museum, London.

Ill. 312 (left): LV & A no. 902–1897: main border from ill. 311.

outside the region of West Armenian cultural influence, thus outside Cilicia as well. The yarn is S-spun as opposed to having been Z-spun, and the red colour is reported to be the result of lac dye from India rather than of madder dye or kermes. Perhaps it is the dye that can give us the most important information. We know that kermes is used as a source of red in Anatolia, the Caucasus, Persia and Egypt, but that it was not available in Syria and Mesopotamia. By the same token, most of the trade with India was carried out via the road from Hormuz to Baghdad. This reduces the geographic area of production quite considerably. From a purely stylistic standpoint, these carpets belong between the regions of Anatolia-Caucasia, that is West Armenia, and the region of north-western Persia or East Armenia. There is nothing to indicate that these carpets were not produced in western Syria, for example in Damascus, or in eastern Syria (Iraq), for example in Mossul or Baghdad. In this event the label 'Damascus carpet' as a trade name or manufacturing name would be justified. Proposing such an origin would not preclude saying that later carpets, as is the case with glass work and metal work, might have been produced in Cairo. These may be the late examples in which Whiting found 'cochineal',[184] though in all probability not that from the Mexican dactylopius coccus, but from the indigenous kermococcus vermilio instead.

Ill. 313 (left): LV & A no. 902–1897: secondary border from ill. 311.

Group B IV: Paramamluk Carpets/Chessboard Carpets

The so-called 'Mamluk carpets' cannot be discussed without dealing at the same time with the question of what are called 'Paramamluk carpets' and the 'Chessboard carpets'.

Group B IV includes these. This group is more similar to Group B III than to the preceding ones, for it makes use of the asymmetrical knot. The carpets which comprise the group, however, have Z-spun yarn, something they share with Groups B I and B II, but which is not true of carpets in Group B III. Their red colouring is achieved by the use of madder dye. Because the 'chessboard carpets' really should be seen as belonging to both groups, the author has decided to combine the two, despite the fact that the 'chessboard carpets' at first sight display a high degree of similarity. But there are differences: For one thing, whether wool or goat hair is used; and for another, the borders. The author chose not to separate these, however, since such differences are regional rather than principle.

The construction of the 'chessboard carpets' is familiar, in terms of their composition, and corresponds to Vakf. E 344 (ill. 108), which must be viewed as the prototype for the group.

A carpet in the Islamic Museum in Cairo (ill. 314) comes closest in appearance to this model or prototype, although between the two one suspects a relatively large

Ill. 314 (below): Cairo no. 15829, 283 x 203 cm. Islamic Museum, Cairo.

Ill. 315 (above left): Vakf. no. E 344: field design from ill. 108.

Ill. 316 (above right): Cairo no. 15829: field design from ill. 314.

The coupled comparisons show quite well the evolution of designs as well as the close relationship in detail between both carpets.

time gap. The cross-stars filling the ground are, as a result of their interlace designs, more ornate; they fill a space in the shape of a templar or Maltese cross in the inner part of the carpet. This has given rise to some speculation, which we will consider later. These cross-stars are connected about their axes, as is the case with Vakf. E 344, by designs (ill. 305) that are generally interpreted as cypresses but could just as well be read as fish – which is actually even more likely, considering their outward shape. In the negative areas between the crosses, the pomegranate-shaped cross-rosettes have given way to a new cross design, formed from the 'tree of Jesse'. In the border as well we find this motif again, alternating with cross-rosettes.

A fragment, today in a private collection in California,[185] (ill. 322) takes us another step in our development. The construction of the field is the same in all these examples (ills. 315, 316). It is only the negative area between the cross-stars which changes, though even these are already represented in the spectrum of variations present in Vakf. E 344 (ills. 317, 318). Half of the Cross of Jerusalem, found in the triangular negative areas along the borders (ills. 319, 320), is the proto-design for the diamond-crosses now present in all the carpets.

This development is continued in BMIK no. I 14 (ill. 323), or in TMW no. R 7.10 (ill. 324), or in the piece in the Bardini Museum in Florence.

The fragment from the former Campana Collection (ill. 325) provides an interesting permutation. Here this composition, evenly filling the entire surface, is discontinued in order to make room for the enlargement of an element much like a central medallion.

Ill. 317 (above): Vakf. no. E 344: cross star from ill. 108.

Ill. 318 (above): Cairo no. 15829: cross star from ill. 314.

Ill. 319 (above): Vakf. no. E 344: cross-crosslet in the diamond achieved by pairing the motif of the border guard from ill. 315 with its mirror image.

Ill. 320 (above): Cairo no. 15829: cross in the diamond with vestiges of the cross-crosslet from ill. 314.

The carpet in the Wher Collection (formerly C.G. Ellis, ill. 326) demonstrates a continuation of this development. However, the carpet in the Philadelphia Museum of Art (ill. 327) and the arch-form-carpet in Teheran (ill. 328, the oldest remaining arch-form carpet of this region, unfortunately ignored thus far) show the Armenian-Anatolian influence much more clearly.

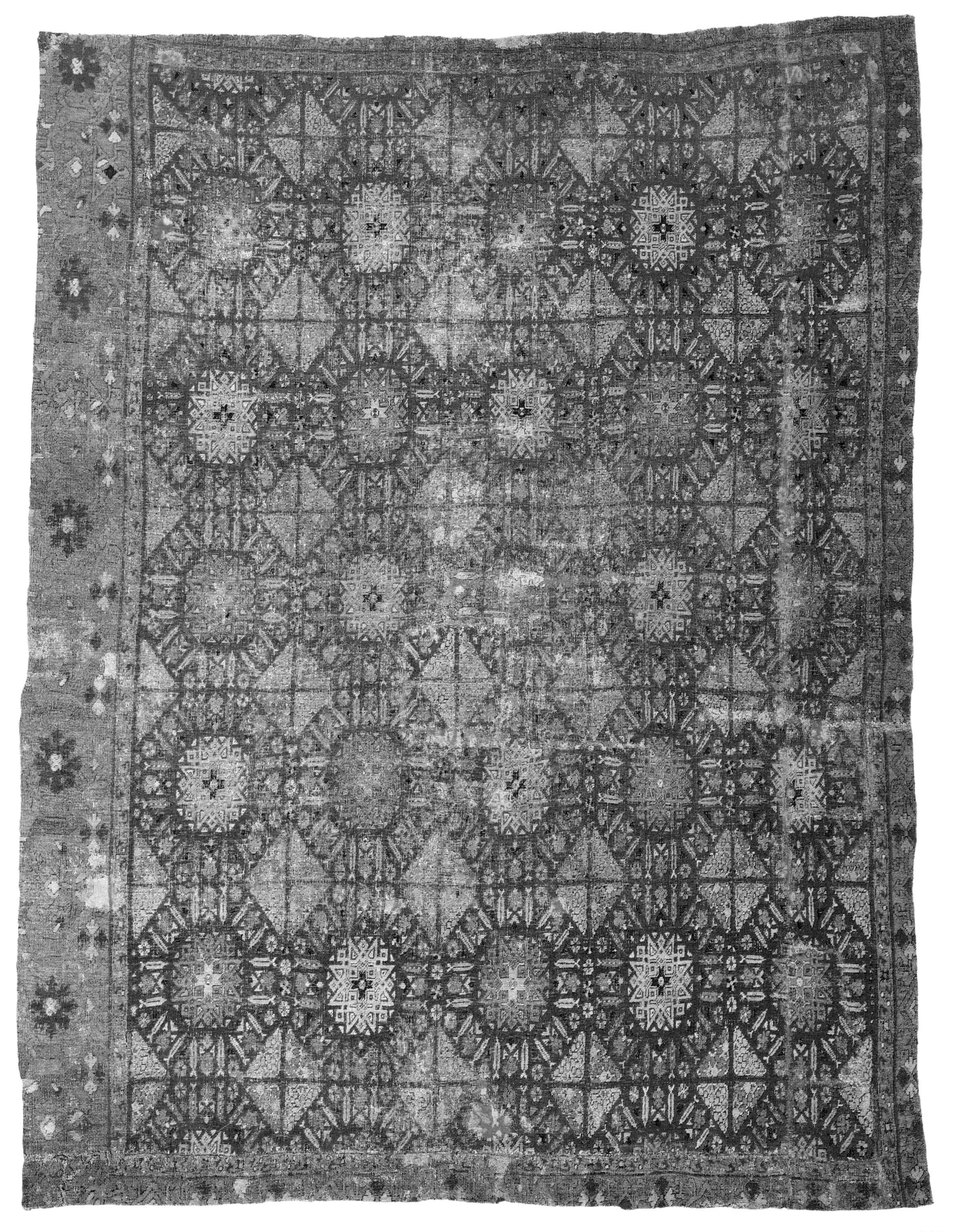

Ill. 321 (page 208): Private collection, 184 x 140 cm.

Ill. 322 (page 209): Collection of Christopher Alexander, Berkeley; 275 x 200 cm.

Ill. 323 (left): BMIK no. I.14, 396 x 208 cm. SMPK, Museum für Islamische Kunst, Berlin.

Ill. 324 (right): TMW no. R 7.10., 377 x 243 cm. Textile Museum, Washington.

The system of ornamentation filling the ground, originally of almost identical designs, is shifted somewhat, allowing the formation of more prominent guls, which here appear to be joined together much like stems.

Ill. 325 (left): Private collection, formerly Campana Collection, Milan, 305 x 230 cm.

This example shows the formation of a central design in the middle section for the first time.

Ill. 326 (right): Courtesy of the Wher Collection Switzerland, 208 x 144 cm.

In the further evolution of these compositions, they come to resemble more and more those of the LP-Holbein carpets of Group B II.

There is a sub-group which, as has already been mentioned, distinguishes itself in two ways. For one thing, goat's hair was used both in the ground and in the pile, and furthermore, the borders were constructed differently. They show cartouches in alternation with crosses or cross-rosettes. There is an interesting parallel here with a carpet[186] (ill. 708) representing the design tradition of Amida, the border of which (ill. 701) adheres to the same features in design and whose pile also consists of goat's hair. In this area there are quite obviously essential similarities in the use of material, and also the choice of design.

This gives us a place to start in determining a possible location for production. Bode-Kühnel[187] see the chessboard carpets as having been influenced by the ornamentation of the Mamluk carpets, yet also as having a definite Anatolian orientation. Erdmann[188] supposed their origin to be in southern Anatolia, placing in 'Seven Hundred Years of Oriental carpets' the caption "Anatolia (Ushak region)"[189] next to a colour photograph. Kühnel[190] thought it possible that they were produced on Rhodes, pointing out that the crosses contained in the cross-stars might possibly be those of the Knights of Malta, who lived on Rhodes until 1523. Mention is made in different archives of their carpets as 'tapedi rodioti'. This viewpoint is in itself interesting, since it is the first time that carpets were attributed to a Christian oriental institution. Even more interesting than this is Kühnel's conjecture that these carpets might have originated in Armenia Minor, in order thus "to combine Egyptian designs and knots with Anatolian material and their method of spinning." These considerations, if nothing else, should have resulted in research into the Christian origin of related designs. Robert Pinner and Michael Franses[191] finally argue in favour of production in Damascus because here, too, we find references to carpets in the inventory records.

Let us take a moment to summarize: the asymmetrical knot makes it likely that these carpets originated outside of the sphere of influence of West Armenian culture. And yet, the method of spinning as well as the material are Anatolian, that is to say: they correspond to the standards common to Asia Minor. The use of goat's hair and the border of sub-group IV a suggest their production in Jazira Province.[192] For centuries the region of Amida (Diyarbakir), Mardin and Maiyafarikin had been a centre for the use of goat's hair. Placing the entire group geographically is more difficult. The present author is inclined to think that production took place farther to the east or north-east, in the region of East Armenia. This is in no small way due to the rediscovery of a carpet, the supposed throne carpet of Kara Koyunlu, that was missing until 1984, when it was successfully relocated in Chicago.

Illustration 329 shows this carpet, which first appeared in publication in 1909 under the authorship of F. R. Martin.[193] As is shown here in detailed illustrations, this carpet features all the design characteristics of Groups B III and B IV, as well as a few others in addition (ill. 332). Martin felt he had no choice but to assume its origin to be in the area around Shiraz, believing as he did that only the wool from the Niris Sea possessed this silken lustre and softness. Martin's assignment of date is in accordance with the views of the present author. As justification he noted that he had found nothing in the carpet to suggest a date after 1450. Indubitably the most striking things about this carpet are the animal representations in the corners (ill. 330), which quite clearly are heraldic in character. In fact, through the heraldry we are able to identify this carpet more closely in a way remarkably similar to the 'Amida carpet'. By combining the four animals, we arrive at what is, aside from small differences, the coat-of-arms of the Shirvan Shahs, as preserved in Baku on the minaret of the Dzhuma Mosque (ill. 331). The carpet, however, does show one very important difference the two animals in the lower part are chained. This very clearly symbolizes the subjugation of the Shirvan Shahs at the hands of a conqueror, who in this case

Ill. 327 (page 214): PHAM no. 1955–65–2, 178 x 125 cm. Philadelphia Museum of Art, The Joseph Lees Williams Memorial Collection, Philadelphia.

Ill. 328 (page 215): Teheran, 141 x 105 cm. Carpet Museum, Teheran.

This carpet, unique in its own right, exhibits, in the upper part of the arch panel, a cross-star between two ambos and flanked on each side by a tree of life. In the lower part we see a variant of the world cosmogram. The Arabian inscription is a call for repentance and fasting.

Ill. 329 (right): Chicago no. 1926.1617, 676 x 302 cm. The Art Institute of Chicago, Chicago. Gift of Mrs. E. Crane Chadbourne, no. 817.

A carpet which, in its beauty and resplendent colours, the luxuriance of its wool and its inventiveness, is surpassed by only a handful of carpets surviving today. One is struck by the heraldic lions in the upper corners and also by their chained counterparts in the corners below. This might presumably have been an audience carpet of the Kara-Koyunlu.

Ill. 330 (above): Chicago no. 26.1617: animal depictions in the corners, photographic montage. Details from ill. 329.

could have been none other than Kara Yusuf of the Kara-Koyunlu tribe. During the time from 1405 to 1410 he succeeded in increasing his power at the expense of the Ak-Koyunlu, despite interference from the Timurs. This sort of political statement in a carpet would have been most effective at the very place where this had happened, thus making its production in the Province of Shirvan probable. Here, or in the immediate vicinity, perhaps of Tabriz, we also find mountain wool of the same fantastically soft and silken texture with the lustre mentioned above. This non-Christian carpet provides us with a way of delineating the northeastern boundary as far as design dispersal is concerned and at the same time serves as a help in dating.

Ill. 331 (right): Minaret of the Dzhuma Mosque, Baku: coat-of-arms of the Shirvan Shahs.

Ill. 332 (page 219): Chicago no. 26.1617: cruciforms, details from ill. 329.

The question as to the dating of the carpets in Group IV remains open. The same applies as has been said earlier: until scientific data have been made available, dating the oldest pieces to the 14th century must for the moment be based largely on guesswork. The fact that these carpets did not find their way into European painting until the 16th century is due to the relatively late conquest of this area by the Ottomans, with whose help trade first became possible – unless, that is, it was a matter of the sale of war booty.

As has been stated before, the carpets of Group IV a, the so-called 'chessboard carpets', are unified by the combined use of characteristic methods of production common to both East and West Armenia. It follows then that the area of production would have to be in a region bordering on both areas. The use of goat's hair leads us to consider their origin as the area east of what was once Amida (Diyarbakir). Design notwithstanding, the carpets of Group IV b, the so-called 'Para-Mamluk' carpets, suggest an East Armenian-Persian production.

In now adding Group B III, for which the same question concerning origins remains unanswered as well, the present author considers the areas of production indicated in ill. 333 to be possible. It is a known fact that artisans from all the nations under their rule were brought to the courts of the Il-Khans and the caliphs in Baghdad,[194] and this most certainly included (East) Armenians as well.

The Il-Khans ruled from Baghdad. In the middle of the 13th century Christians expanded their area of mission more than before under the Mongols. They were to be found throughout the Mongol Empire: in China as well as in Karakoram, in Baghdad as well as in Aksaray. Perhaps this is the answer to the question why the carpets represented in the Chinese scrolls can resemble the 'Mamluk carpets' so closely and yet have been 'Aksaray carpets' instead.

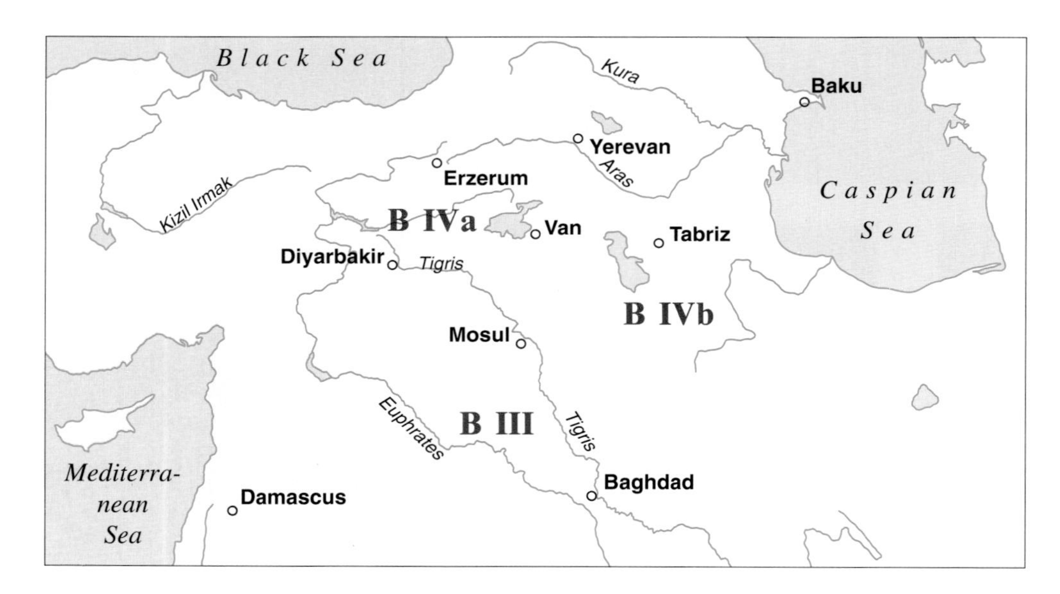

Ill. 333: presumed regions of carpet production for Groups B III and B IV.

Group B V: Spanish Carpets

Let us briefly review something discussed in the introduction (cf. p. 19): as early as the 10th century Ibn Haukal reports that knotted carpets (mahfur) were being produced in Andalusia, carpets similar to the best of the more costly Armenian products.[195]

After examining the material collected by Serjeant, we were able to conclude that in the 10th century carpets were produced only in Armenia and Andalusia.

Spanish carpets have raised quite a number of problematic questions. To begin with, one wonders how these carpets are to be viewed in connection with 'oriental' carpets, for, after all, they did – as the name implies – originate in the 'occident'. Spanish carpets, it is true, must be distinguished technically from those which originated in the Near East. However, the author feels the term 'Spanish knot' to be as misleading a term as it is meaningless. This is also the case with the terms 'Turkish' or 'Persian' knot. The knot in question is a symmetrical knot tied around only one warp string (ill. 52). Although this type of knot may be quite unusual, it is not only restricted to Spain. We find it in the Turfan fragments as well as in the fragments from Fostat. Interestingly, the oldest surviving carpet produced in central Europe incorporating figural representations[196] was also done using this technique.

Erdmann hypothesized that this might represent a parallel development in the history of carpets which in effect constitutes an imitation of Coptic cut-loop weaving.[197] For the sake of comparison, he illustrates what is obviously an example of Christian cut-loop weaving, which C.J. Lamm is said to have called an 'Abbasiden carpet'. Even more interesting is Jan Bennet's statement, "it is well known that Coptic weavers were also producing carpets in Spain during the 10th century."[198] Unfortunately his source for this is not given, thus making it impossible to consider other similar statements relevant to the issue.

As Erdmann's nomadic hypothesis was found to be unsupported due to contradictory argumentation and insufficient evidence, the author, at the beginning of this study, put forward his own hypothesis as to the emergence of the technique of weaving (pp. 51 ff.). Because the design origins were determined to be Phrygian-Urartian, it seemed to him to make much more sense to examine other related techniques in an effort to arrive at the origin of the weaving technique. The Soumak technique seemed to lend itself to this, because a Soumak exhibiting extreme changes in colour is composed of loops of wool identical to the jufti knot. All evidence indicates that by refining designs while at the same time leaving the ends of the pile to show, making the interplay of colour all the more intense, weavers facilitated the emergence of the technique of weaving. Carpets which have survived from that time confirm the fact that they did not emerge from the imitation of animal hides, but were instead the result of an already existing technique refined in town or court manufactories. What is sometimes referred to as the 'Spanish knot' is symmetrically wrapped around one warp string. If the assumption is correct that the knots were reduced in size mainly so as to be able to adapt the technique of weaving to more intricate patterns, then we can also say that the symmetrical knot tied around only the one warp string offers the possibility of very high accuracy in rendering patterns – something that cannot be claimed for other known types of knots. At the same time this knot, being symmetrical, has an advantage in that it is firmer. The present author interprets the formation of this variety of knot as an attempt to refine the already existing symmetrical knot involving two warp strings – something which was presumably experimented with elsewhere as well. If we are to accept that there

Ill. 334 (left): Private collection, 259 x 163 cm.

were imitations at all, then it can only have been Armenian carpets that were imitated, carpets which, at that time, had a legendary reputation and which for centuries set standards for subsequent production.

The author was unable to find any convincing evidence in support of the practice, followed by most authors, of dating the oldest remaining Spanish carpets to the 15th century and no earlier, despite the fact that documentation of their production during the five centuries prior to this was known to exist.

Upon closer examination of the existing material, again unfortunately without the benefit of exact scientific analyses, there appears to be reasonable doubt about the dating described above. The reason for this is that these carpets, ascribed to the 15th century, are stylistically so very different, despite the fact that their development must be seen as having been simultaneous.

If, however, we disregard our doubts as to whether all the carpets done in the aforementioned technique were in fact all produced in Spain, then we can turn our attention to what these carpets depict. We find that some exhibit designs which not only correspond to those of our chain of traditional designs in their overall concept, but also contain familiar motifs even in their details.

Erdmann writes "in accordance with an Anatolian model of the type in ills. 35/36"[199] [these are carpets of Group B II], and thus establishes, without actually checking, this influence from the east. That is presumably how he arrives at the late attribution. And here again, then, we touch upon a basic question: that of how designs are influenced. To assume, without further examination, that this influence was from the east, Asia Minor or the Orient, does not do justice to the significance of the question. There must certainly always have been influences from the east, but what is there to preclude the migration of designs in the opposite direction? This is actually very likely. The obvious compositional agreement between some early carpets and others of Armenian-Anatolian origin, or on the other hand, those of Caucasian origin, is striking. However, answers to questions such as these would take us beyond the scope of this book.

In the author's view, the oldest example of a carpet done in the technique involving a symmetrical knot around just a single warp string, the origin of which could have been Spain, is preserved in three fragments of two different colours, all three of which are identical in design. These are to be found in Frankfurt, and in private collections in Europe and America.[200] Illustration 334 shows the European fragment. The details of the design are Armenian and attributable to the 11th century.[201] Although this may come as a surprise, there are a number of possible explanations, all of which must remain hypothetical. Were designs passed on by Armenian emigrants who left their home country before the invasion of the Seljuks? Or, similarly, how close were the ties to Armenia of those who had earlier emigrated to Spain? Some Basque words still betray links with the Armenian language, without it being possible to prove a direct relationship. Or finally, and this possiblity must be considered as well: did this carpet really originate in Spain, and, if not, then where? Could it have been produced in Europe or Asia Minor?

These same questions apply to other carpets, or their fragments, that have survived from the High Middle Ages. Such carpets contain rows of coffers in which there are ponderous cross-stars. We should recognize these from Templar buildings, on which they appear as decorative ornaments. As a result of the systematic eradication of the Templars in France by Phillip II, undertaken for political reasons, no textiles are to be expected, whereas in Spain we would most certainly expect to find some. The Templars were not persecuted in Spain, but were actually able to disband and form

Ill. 335 (page 224): KGM no. 90.90., 293 x 165 cm. Formerly Kunstgewerbemuseum, Berlin. Lost in the Second World War.

There is, unfortunately, no colour photograph of this carpet. And yet even here the composition, recreated from early fabric designs and the carpet in ill. 135, is clear.

Ill. 336 (page 225): MMA no. 13.193.2., 282 x 168 cm. Metropolitan Museum of Art, New York. The Rogers Fund.

Here the circular composition gave way to the use of compartments. The fragment is the earliest surviving example of this group.

Ill. 338 (above): TMW no. R 44.2.7., 231 x 209 cm. Textile Museum, Washington.

Ill. 337 (left): LV & A no. 784–1905, 203 x 123 cm. Victoria and Albert Museum, London.

the Order of Christ or the Order of the Knights of Malta, which then continued in existence for hundreds of years.

In addition to the carpets in New York, Washington and London – MMA no. 13.193.2 (ill. 336), TMW no. R 44.2.7. (ill. 338), LV & A no. 784–1905 (ill. 337) and TMW R 44.00.5 (ill. 339) – which are certain to have originated during the 12th or 13th century, there was another carpet of which only a black and white photograph remains, the original piece having been destroyed by fire in Berlin in 1945.[202] Kurt Erdmann writes of Inv. no. KGM 90.90 (ill. 335) that it was not among the best of its group. And yet its loss is distressing in view of the fact that it was presumably the oldest of the group. Though it is true that at first the elements of its design seem to resemble those of the London carpet LV & A no. 784–1905 (considerably smaller in size), in terms of structure they exhibit more similarity to compositions such as that in ill. 135. The frames, made up of small crosses, are almost circular and yet not quite octagonal. The fact that in spite of this the carpet gives the impression of being composed of coffers is not due to these frames, but rather to the fact that the imposing crosses are placed in rows. In the case of the other examples, the large octagons are in square, or later, rectangular fields, of which three, placed one after the other, form 'runners'. In the case of the New York carpet, two such rows placed next to each other form a single, large carpet. Stripes of varying widths are used to isolate the coffers and are filled with contiguous rows of cross-stars or crosses. However, there are differences in design, based on which the sequence KGM 90.90, MMA no. 13.193.2., LV & A no. 784–1905, TMW no. R 44.2.7. might possibly enable us to derive a development. Even the cross-stars contained in the octagons are different from one another in detail. In each example the cross-star is in the centre in order to form the light-symbol cross with extensions. MMA no. 13.193.2., still without a guard stripe and particularly clear in its cross and cross-star designs, provides a transition to TMW no. R 44.2.7. and LV & A no. 784–1905. In this latter carpet cross-stars, arranged along the diagonal and exhibiting changes in colour and structure, emerge from the central cross-star and form a cross-rosette. TMW no. R 44.00.5 constitutes a special design with its motifs of interlacing. The centre, compositionally related to the gul from BOIM no. 88.29 (ills. 347, 349) as well as to the border from MBN no. 10/294 (ills. 253, 255, 257), is noteworthy. All these represent prototypes of the Holbein gul (ill. 351).

During the 14th and possibly even during the 15th century this development was continued, analogous to a certain degree with Group B II, and in part demonstrating a surprising correspondence in details. TMW no. R 44.2.2. (ill. 332), SLAM no. 122.1929 (ill. 333) and CAM no. 52.511 (ill. 334) give some idea of what is possible for the entire composition, which, in comparison to those of Group B II, is clearer and more obvious.

In concluding, let us consider two carpets which stem from the 15th century and very clearly show the sign of the design-historical evolution: LV & A no. T 104–1912 (ill. 335) and BMFA no. 39.614. (ill. 336). The first can still be regarded as a coffered-form carpet, even though the coffers are quite small; the second one corresponds to the early SP Holbein carpets of Anatolia.

A comparison of these two carpets makes the evolution of designs clear in a way that Anatolian carpets show only in detail. This, of course, raises the same questions once more: who influenced whom? Louise W. Mackie comments[203] on this as follows:

"To summarize this group, it is clear that one of the Mudejar 'wheel' carpet patterns was copied from a Turkish model and two others were strongly influenced by, if not also copied from, Turkish carpets which have not survived. Owing to the extensive use of star patterns in Moorish art, it seems surprising that the star patterns in Mudejar carpets were based on foreign models. However, the star patterns in carpets are isolated and self-contained unlike most Moorish star patterns which are continuous. Perhaps the Moorish stars were considered to be too complex and not easily adaptable for carpet patterns or perhaps the foreign models were viewed as more exotic and desirable."

These remarks are noteworthy in two respects: first of all, there is the missing correspondence to Moorish art, and secondly, the close connection to Turkish art – though here by 'Turkish' art we mean Armenian art , whether it be copied from it or 'simply' influenced by it.

During the 10th century carpets were produced in the district of Murcia, in the town of Murcia itself, in Tantala and in Alsh. Since the Province of Todmir was able to maintain independence as well as a bishopric under the Umayyads and their successors, which could actually mean that Monophysites were present, we must assume that production was continued until the conquest and then possibly destroyed at the hands of the Spanish *reconquista* in the 15th century.

Ill. 339 (inside right): TMW no. R 44.00.5., 181 x 96 cm. Textile Museum, Washington.

Ill. 340 (outside right): TMW no. R 44.2.2., 349 x 97 cm. Textile Museum, Washington.

In this group of carpets, too, there are, in terms of design evolution, an increasing number of correspondences in detail with those of Group B II.

Ill. 341 (page 230): SLAM no. 122.1929, 274 x 154 cm. The St. Louis Art Museum, St. Louis. Gift of James F. Ballard.

Ill. 342 (page 231): Cleveland no. 52.511, 419 x 236 cm. Cleveland Museum of Art, Cleveland.

Ill. 343 (left): LV & A no. T 104–1912, 442 x 182 cm. Victoria and Albert Museum, London.

This is a carpet that helps us to see a possible evolution from the use of compartments to the field design of the SP-Holbein carpets of Group C II.

Ill. 344 (right): BMFA no. 39.614, 463 x 106 cm. Courtesy of The Museum of Fine Arts, Boston. The Elisabeth H. Flint Fund, in memory of Sarah Gore Flint Townsend.

This is an example of an SP-Holbein carpet knotted with a symmetrical knot over one warp; its composition corresponds to examples from Group C II.

Part Two: From the Late Middle Ages to Modern Times

The Historical Situation

Let us pause for a moment in order to reconsider a number of important facts concerning the migration, geographically, of Armenians over the centuries. That portion of the Armenian population which was of considerable importance for the development of the Christian oriental carpet defined for itself a sphere of cultural influence, until the 11th century, that extended from north-western Persia to central Anatolia and from the Caucasus to Syria. Waves of emigration brought Armenians to western Anatolia, Syria, Egypt, to the coastal cities along the Mediterranean, Spain, France, the Netherlands, Ireland, Persia, India, China and to the Sunda Islands; they were deported primarily to northern Greece, but also to central and southern Persia, Mazanderan, Khorasan and Seistan. Fleeing from the advancing Seljuks, large numbers of Armenians emigrated to western and central Anatolia and to Cilicia. At the instigation of the Byzantine government, the Province of Waspuracan was exchanged for Wilayet Sivas, the Kingdom of Ani for regions in Cappadocia and the district of Lycandus with the city of Bizu – all these regions thus becoming the new home of more than half of the Armenian population.

The Mamluk conquest of Cilicia caused many to return to what constituted the core regions of Armenia, but also to western and central Anatolia. The Armenian patriarchate, which had relocated its seat to Sis, moved back to Echmiadzin, at the same time, however, keeping its seat in Sis.

During the 16th and 17th centuries the region under the influence of Armenian culture once again became the object of contention between east and west, that is, between the Safavids and the Ottomans. Thus borders were shifted constantly and both contenders availed themselves of Armenian artisans. Sultan Mehmed II encour-

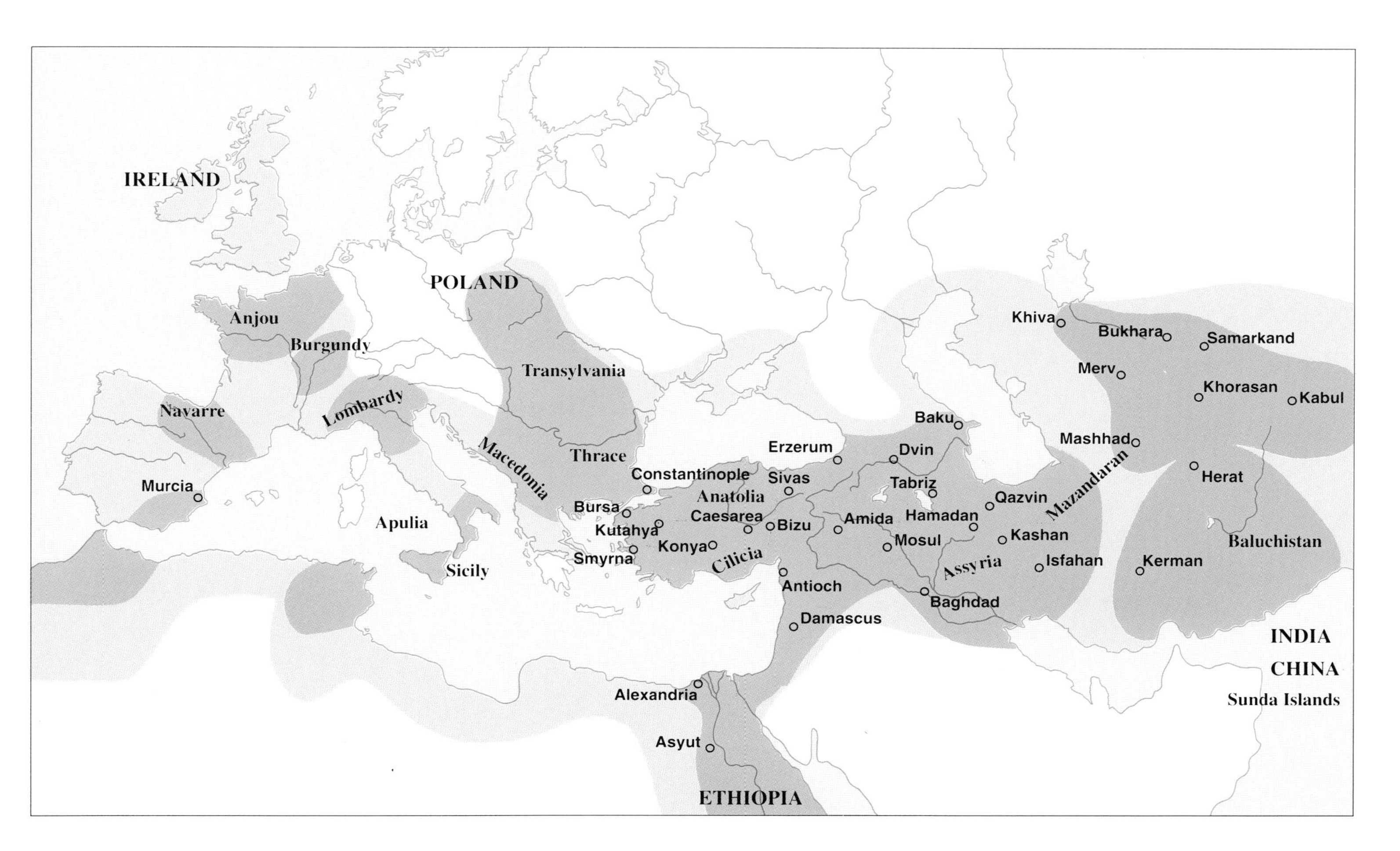

Ill. 345: Distribution of the Armenian population up to the middle of the 17th century.

The map is the outcome of many years' research carried out by the author, based on the material pertinent to Armenian history he has thus far been granted access to.

aged Armenians to settle in Istanbul, designating six large districts around Topaki Palace for them. He summoned the Armenian bishop from Bursa to Istanbul and raised him to the office of patriarch, the legal representative of all Christians who were not members of the Greek Orthodox Church.

Selim I contested the Safavids' right to Armenia, took possession of the eastern part and saw to it himself that craftsmen were brought from Tabriz to Istanbul. In their place he resettled in regions of Armenia Islamic Kurds, who, over the course of time, made life difficult for the Armenians. As a result of these and other unpopular measures public sentiment was on the side of the Safavids. Thus in 1603 Shah Abbas I tried to reclaim Armenia. Forced to retreat, Abbas I devastated the Armenian regions in order to make them of less use to the Ottomans. 23,000 families were deported to regions in Persia from West Armenia, and well over 100,000 from central Armenia. These Armenians were resettled not only in the areas around Hamadan, Kashan, Isfahan, Kazvin, and Mazanderan, but also in central Persia in the area of Meshed, in the barren regions of Qashqai, Baktiari and Afshari, as well as in the region of Kabul and Baluchistan in Afghanistan. In Persia the best-known Armenian centre was New Julfa near Isfahan, which under the protection of Shah Abbas I became one of the most prosperous commercial cities – from which the Shah's court made a very considerable profit. And finally, it was the unusually high number of Armenians working there that accounted for the fact that this region achieved its cultural heyday during this period.

The map in ill. 345 clearly shows all the places Armenians were to be found up to the beginning of the 17th century. Over the course of the centuries, many of these regions developed into carpet centres, which the various nationalities then claimed for themselves.

The Christian Oriental Carpet II

C: From the Late Middle Ages up to the 18th Century

The C Groups encompass the majority of the Christian carpets from the 15th up to the 18th century and in part even beyond this. To have considered all these groups would have taken the author well beyond the scope of this book.

Having been able to follow the evolution in traditional designs through the centuries, we realize that in spite of an ever-growing variety in design, nothing has changed in terms of their actual structure. This is confirmed time and again in comparisons drawn between the traditional designs in the early Christian mosaics (ills. 67–80) and the carpets dating from the second millenium. One could go so far as to say that all the designs found in the Christian carpet can be traced back to the prototypes of ills. 72 and 73, which the author refers to as cross-star carpets in textile form. This structural scheme unifies in an ideal way the inexhaustible variety of possibilities that can be achieved by a mere change in emphasis, colour, or connective lines. The placement and use of coffers, diamonds and diagonal stripes is predetermined in the same way, as is the possibility of incorporating subparts into large designs. Depending on the size of the carpet and its intended purpose, use was made of all these options. We see that the most common design was that involving the 'endless repeat', from which one part was isolated and used. This is the case for all the carpets in Group C. As things continued to evolve, such an isolated element, as with all design details, can undergo a completely independent development. This is what results in the individual differences among the separate groups. The existence of original carpets that have survived varies greatly from group to group, there being several hundred of one type, but only single examples of another. As far as possible, the author has attempted to order the groups chronologically. This was not always possible, due to frequent parallels in origin. Large groups such as the Holbein and Lotto carpets (Groups C II and C III), which were produced over longer periods of time, do show, in accordance with the development, differences in their fields. Yet, it is their border development that is much more interesting, since it provides a way of connecting the different groups. For this reason this development is given greater attention here. Precisely the fact that the same borders appear on carpets of different groups makes clear their temporal connectedness, as well as the correspondence in the origin of these groups. This is apparent with the carpets discussed above. The same can be said for the gul development of Group C X, which is of the utmost importance for the overall picture insofar as the parallel existence of intermediate steps in their development, and their attribution to different tribes, made it seem very nearly impossible to show the evolution of one single design.

Group C I: Cross-Star Carpets – Eastern Design Groups

This design tradition and ills. 72, 73, 74 and 79 may be recalled. We encountered the representation of a carpet with such a design in ill. 173 – Jan van Eyck's painting from 1436 – where it is depicted at the Virgin Mary's feet (detail in ill. 346). But, in the case of such carpets filled with fields of endless cross-star repeats, there is a time gap extending to the 18th/19th century. Even if we assume that a majority of such carpets were lost or have not yet been rediscovered, it is surprising that a design of this sort was able to survive almost unchanged for a period of over 300 years (ill. 347). Doris Eder[204] attributes such carpets, and those related in design, to the Lezghians. According to the present author's own investigations, which coincide with those carried out by Wahram Tatikian and Mania Ghazarian, such carpets belong to the Artsagh-Group and were produced by Armenian families, one of which is still living today in Chatschahar (Kirovabad).

An example of this group, dated 1815 and bearing Armenian writing, is also located in the Museum for Ethnology in Erivan (ill. 348). In this piece, which exhibits an astounding correspondence to the mosaic carpet from ill. 72 (its elder by almost 1500 years), the Christian character is almost more obvious because brightly outlined Greek crosses were incorporated into the negative areas between the large cross-stars.

In addition, the so-called 'Djidjims' in Zili-technique, the old Armenian 'Zilu' (ill. 349), flat-weaves with double rows of large cross-stars, which themselves strongly resemble the west European-Spanish carpets of Group B V, all belong to this group in terms of their design. Another fairly widely-spread variant in design in Armenia and southeastern Anatolia can be found in DIA no. 49.24 (ill. 350). Here the design filling the field was reduced to the coffered form of Group B II. Three large cross-stars take their places one above the other in square coffers. The main border is identical to that of a small group of 'Lotto carpets' (Group C III C_1). The outer secondary border is unusual. Here in heart designs of different colours we find half-crosses alternating with red carnations. Between the hearts there are red carnations on a white ground. This border has its parallel in those of the Syrian-Monophysite evangelistary of Mar-

Ill. 346 (left): Jan van Eyck: The Madonna, of the Kanonikus van der Paele Municipal Gallery, Bruges. Detail from ill. 173.

Ill. 347 (right): Cross-star carpet, 281 x 140 cm. Kunstauktionshaus Dr. Fritz Nagel, Stuttgart (315/3743).

Ill. 348 (left): Shusha, dated 1815, 245 x 131 cm. Armenian State Museum for Ethnology, Erivan.

The extent to which the cross-star design of the 5th century (ills. 72, 73) was able to survive almost completely unchanged through the 15th (ill. 346) and on into the 19th century is astounding.

Ill. 349 (above right): 'Zili', 456 x 187 cm. Privat collection.

Again the cross-star design is continually present throughout the development of all the other individual designs, including the coffer or the layout in rows.

Ill. 350 (below right): DIA no. 49.24, 284 x 183 cm. Detroit Institute of Arts, Detroit. Gift of an anonymous donor.

Ill. 351 (left): 'Crivelli' carpet, BUIM no. 14940, 164 x 60 cm; fragment. Iparmüvészeti Muzeum, Budapest. On the left the original, on the right its mirror image for the sake of completion.

This double-medallion type originated during the 15th century. It is this type that Crivelli depicted in his painting of the annunciation.

Ill. 352 (right): 'Crivelli' carpet from a mosque in Sivrihisar (Eskisehir).

The details of this fragment appear to date from an earlier time than do those in the Budapest specimen. The instances of correspondence in structure with several carpets of Group B V attract our attention.

din,[205] and might therefore serve to indicate that this carpet could have been produced in Tur Abdin, which is to say in south-eastern Anatolia.

Carpets exhibit every conceivable permutation and possibility of combination, starting from the filling of the field to the use of a single motif with medallion character.

The author has already pointed out the close relationship between Group C I and Group B V. This also applies to several carpets which used the compositional scheme of Group B II, coffers arranged in rows. The best-known of these individual carpets, and we cannot as yet use the term sub-group here, is what is referred to in the literature as the 'Crivelli Carpet', belonging to the Budapest Iparmüvészeti-Museum, BUIM no. 14940 (ill. 351). The name comes from a painting by Carlo Crivelli from the latter part of the 15th century, in which the Annunciation is depicted, showing a carpet from Group C I next to one from Group B II.[206]

Although the Budapest carpet is now exactly half of what was its actual size, there is no difficulty in reconstructing the entire piece. The field is filled by two large cross-star medallions. If we compare this carpet with earlier examples from Group B V, we see signs of pattern disintegration. The fact that this piece is filled with disparate motifs including even birds, in this respect analogous to the Crivelli painting, indicates that it stems from a relatively late phase in the type development. The dating of this to the 15th century, made possible by comparison with other paintings, seems reasonable, provided that the second carpet from Group B II represented here be dated earlier. The leaf-form cross border of the Budapest fragment is later in its development than, for example, the comparable border shown on the carpet from Group B II in the Crivelli painting.

Ill. 353 (right): TIEM no. 378. Türk ve Islam Eserleri Müzesi, Istanbul.

At the First International Congress on Turkish Carpets, Istanbul 1984, Nejat Diyarbekirli presented another 'Crivelli carpet' (ill. 352) which, in terms of design development, should be dated much earlier. In contrast to the Budapest fragment, this is an arch-form carpet, the field of which is filled by a single cross-star. And whereas this seems to resemble the cross-star in the Crivelli painting more closely – the central cross-star is itself complimented by cross-stars on its cross arms, the cross arms being set apart by different colours – it is, on the other hand, even clearer in the design development. The cross-(knot-) border, too, indicates a carpet much older in age. Due to a multitude of similarities in colour, structure and ornamentation, we can assume a closeness in space (i.e. geographic origin) and time between this and PHAM 43.40.67 (ill. 271), which is attributed to the first part of the 15th century.

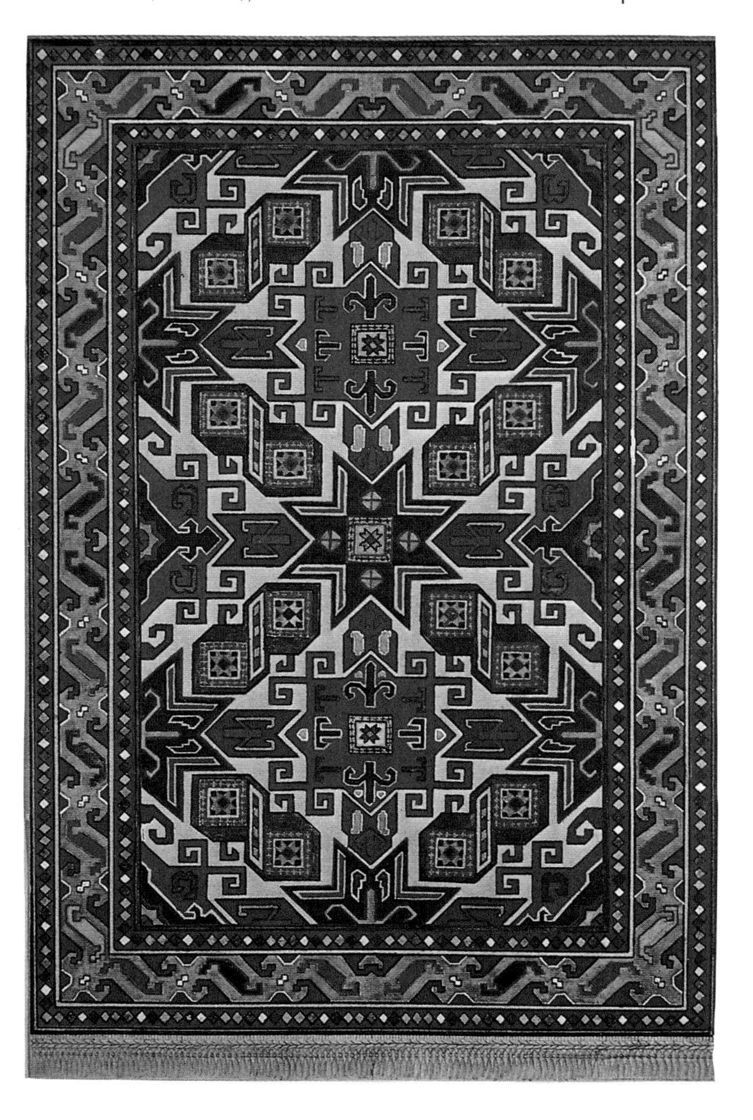

Ill. 354 (right): So-called star kazak, 205 x 130 cm.

Various developments in design make their mark on the star kazaks of the 18th/19th centuries, some being traceable back to the cross-stars.

Yet another carpet with large cross-stars is TIEM no. 378 (ill. 353), structurally related to the one in Budapest, though much clearer in its details. Here we clearly see a stage in the design development: the purely ornamental filling of the triangular shapes, which we still have here, gives way to lively forms in the development to follow. The main border resembles in its structure those we find among some early carpets attributed to the Turkmen (Salor and Saryk) with an arrangement of the basic cross form types C_1 or C_2. The so-called 'Star-Kazaks' from the late 18th and 19th centuries are also part of what was to succeed the 'Crivelli carpet'. As a result of the isolation of the medallion, the interconnectedness within the field was not as clear as we can assume it must have been in the case of some 'Star-Kazaks'. The present author cannot, however, concur with the group division presented in HALI[207], because this gives prime attention to suspected connections between isolated details while not paying heed to the design-historical developments. Of the illustrated pieces, no. 13 is by far the earliest example (ill. 354).

Group C II: Small-Pattern (SP) Holbein Carpets

In our treatment of Group B V we touched upon how problematic it is to establish the design-historical connections, in particular with regard to the SP-Holbein carpets. Whether Spanish weavers were influenced by those in Asia Minor; or whether the 'recirculation' of designs from Spain might not in fact have contributed to the formation of patterns typical of Asia Minor, or, finally, whether both were not part of a shared development – are all questions which for the present cannot be answered.

Early prototypes exist in both the east and the west. All are based on comparable basic designs from our traditional chain of designs that originated within the sphere of Armenian-Syrian cultural influence. And actually if we simplify things, even SP-Holbein carpets are nothing more than a special form of the cross-star carpet.

Two carpets, Vakf. no. A 305 (ill. 240) as well as Mevl. no. 860/861/1033 (ills. 246, 249), have already been cited above. BOIM no. 88.29 (ill. 355) represents a further prototype and may be examined now before the rest of the group.

The golden yellow ground of this unusual carpet is filled by guls, which are again based on the ever-present motif of the cross-star. Kurt Erdmann gave this gul the name 'free paraphrase of the Holbein-gul'[208] and dated the carpet to the 17th century. When we set out to analyze this gul, we discover it to be a combination of the basic form types C_1 and F, the entire form being enclosed by interlacing. In this new design we recognize an older one: the star-tile. This gul is not a 'paraphrase' of the Holbein gul, but rather its prototype. It is a further development or special form of the gul in Vakf. A 305 (ill. 356). We find it in a number of early carpets, the origins of which are quite varied, as for example in the Group B III. Its border belongs to the basic form types B, which, when doubled, was likewise used as a border detail or field gul (ills. 273, 274).

The carpet is to be dated to the latter part of the 14th century. Its closeness in design to Group B IV gives us reason to assume that it was produced in south-eastern Anatolia.

The structure of the inner panel is the same for all carpets in Group C II: in diagonal alternation there are arabesque crosses and Holbein guls, which are expanded to crosses by the use of cross-star rosettes. The only differences concern the choice of colour and how the Holbein guls are filled. Generalizing, one can say that early examples have an astounding range of colour, with a true exuberance in their interplay, whereas the most recent carpets tend to create a more stereotyped and monotonous impression.

Of greater interest are the borders, as was already mentioned in the introduction to Group C. They show what it is that unifies the different groups and provides points of reference for their dating. It would appear reasonable then, with the help of these borders, to demonstrate their development, and to order the carpets within this group according to border types. To begin with, the author will examine the borders of the carpets in Stuttgart, Sibiu (Hermannstadt), Washington and of the fragment in Istanbul, which, strangely enough, Robert Pinner and Jackie Stanger left out of their study.[209] This is without a doubt a very archaic design with a long tradition – ills. 95, 97 and 98 clearly showed how it was to be seen in relation to others. The half-cross within the border had its parallel in the continuation of this design within the devel-

Ill. 355 (left): BOIM no. 88.29, 158 x 114 cm. Staatliche Museen zu Berlin, Islamisches Museum, Berlin.

A very important carpet in that it connects Groups B III/IV with Group C II.

Ill. 356: Vakf. no. A 305: Main gul of the field design; detail from ill. 240.

Ill. 357: BOIM no. 88.29.: Main gul of the field design; detail from ill. 355.

Ill. 358: Mevl. 860/861/1033: Main gul of the field design; detail from ill. 249.

Ill. 359: 'Holbein' gul; detail from ill. 360.

Ill. 360 (page 251): 'Stuttgart Holbein carpet', 279 x 190 cm. Owned privately.

Despite the fact that the carbon dating analysis indicates the 14th/15th century as a date of production, the carpet seems to be a copy of an unknown model from this time period. It contains design details that the author has found only in paintings of the 16th/17th century in which such carpets are depicted.

opment of the so-called Kufic borders already discussed (ills. 102, 103, 109 and 110). The group-type C II a merges in its further development with group-type C II b, which can be traced back to TIEM no. 685 (ill. 99) and thus related to the same basic form type B (ill. 24).

In summing up, we can say that as carpets decrease in age, the distance separating them visually from their basic design increases until, in the end, lacking any semblance, they become completely debased. What began with recombinations at the level of motif halves and quarters became increasingly freer, involving only smaller parts; however, this was always done so that the Christian symbolism remained largely recognizable.

Border Type C II a

To begin with, let us consider the 'Stuttgart Holbein carpet' (ills. 360, 361). Despite the fact that the carbon-dating analysis[210] showed this carpet to have originated either between 1330 and 1345, or between 1390 and 1430, the presence of congo red, which, according to the present author's information was not discovered until after 1884, indicates that it was produced in the 1880s. Although there are very significant differences with regard to the Anatolian Holbein carpets – its use of cotton for the ground weave, for example – the carpet is a very interesting copy of a model yet unknown, in which all the known Holbein-carpet variants in the history of design are united. Moreover, it contains details with which we are familiar only from paintings from the 16th/17th century. This fact alone argues against this carpet being a 'recreation' of the Hermannstadt carpet, for example, since this knowledge cannot have been available in any of the possible weaving centres of that area. The present author argues in favour of the Caucasus as the location for the production of this carpet, not only because of the unusually high quality of the wool there. In contrast to all the Holbein carpets, which are characterized by a plain ground, the ground here is reddish-dark brown with a purple-like effect. Superimposed on this we find, in comparison with Anatolian pieces, much larger arabesque crosses (41 x 39 cm, ill. 248) alternating diagonally with Holbein guls (24 x 27cm, ill. 359). The latter are complemented by cross-star rosettes along the horizontal or vertical axis, such that they become crosses. The centre of the diamond-form composition is dominated by a particularly striking arabesque cross. Nowhere throughout the whole of the inner panel do we find a design executed twice in the same way. Each design is distin-

Ill. 361 (right): Main and secondary border from ill. 360.

Ill. 362: Variants of the 'Holbein' gul from ill. 360.

guished from the others by means of sophisticated and inventive changes in colour. Beyond this, the eight cross variants in the Holbein guls form a kaleidoscope of prototypes (ill. 362) that demonstrate the entire breadth of design development in Anatolia. The carpet is enclosed by the wide border already discussed above, consisting of alternating half-crosses and the archaic secondary border of scrolled vines, with which we are also familiar.

A nearly identical combination of designs can be found in the carpet from Hermannstadt (Sibiu)[211/212] (ills. 365, 363), which, however, both structurally and materially, belongs to the Anatolian Holbein carpets, as do those that are to follow. The guls are significantly smaller, their range of variation more limited, though still richer than in the other known examples of this group. Instead of the eight cross variants present in the Holbein guls, there are only four here. The outside border of scrolled vines, too, consisting of three colours in the Holbein guls, is done in only two colours here. What does remain, with some restrictions, is the striking change of colour in the details of the arabesque guls.

Ill. 363: Borders from ill. 365.

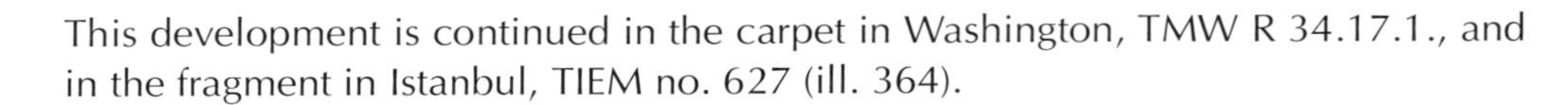

This development is continued in the carpet in Washington, TMW R 34.17.1., and in the fragment in Istanbul, TIEM no. 627 (ill. 364).

Ill. 364: TIEM no. 627, 200 x 155 cm, fragment: borders.

Common to both is that the Holbein guls now contain only one cross-variant – different, however, in each case – and that colour changes are repeated following every other diagonal row, thus enabling them to appear clearer. In the case of the Hermannstadt piece, this repetition occurs after every third row. Whereas rudiments of the scrolled vine border are preserved in sections in TMW R 34.17.1., this has been replaced in TIEM no. 627 by S-secondary borders on either side.

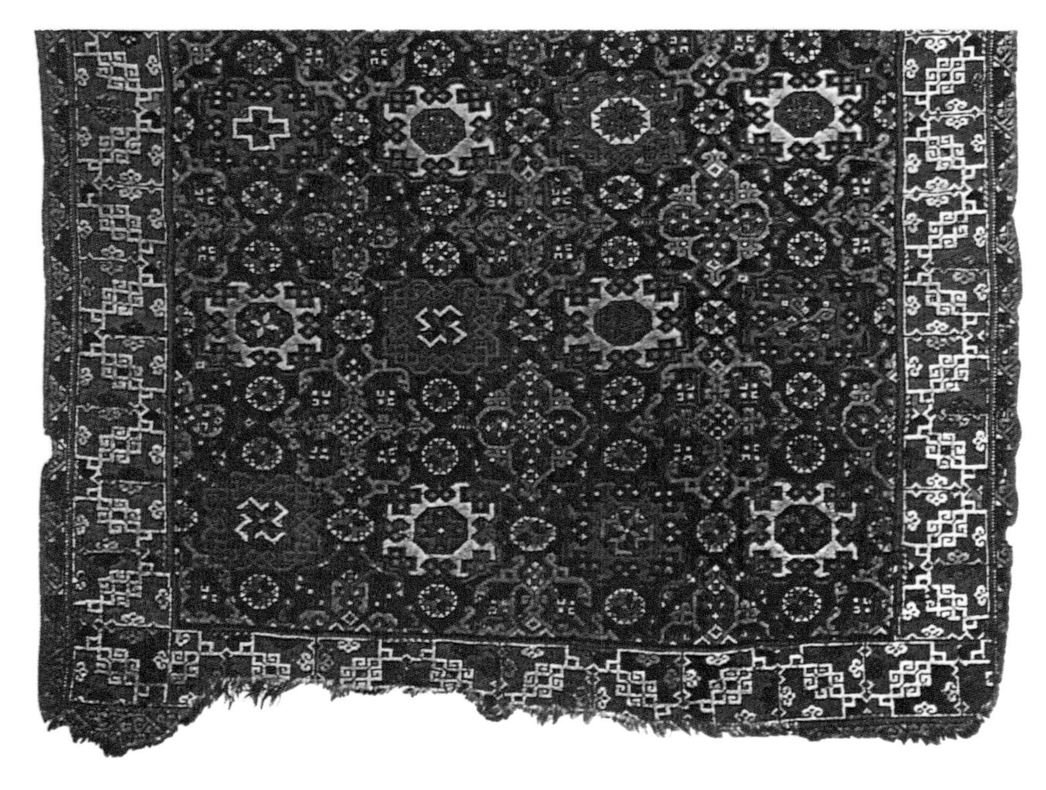

Ill. 365: 388 x 180 cm. Restored fragment. Bruckenthal Museum, Hermannstadt (Sibiu).

Border-Type C II b_1

We have to assume that carpets exhibiting this border-type were already made alongside those of type C II a. The oldest of these, the carpet in the Wher Collection (ill. 367, 366), might well prove to be more recent than the Hermannstadt carpet if we draw on the field pattern for our comparison, though it is probably earlier than the aforementioned TMW R 34.17.1. or the fragment TIEM no. 627. However, a fragment with the same border, TIEM no. 303, ought to be approximately from the same period as those named above.

Ill. 366 (right): Wher Collection: border from ill. 367 with diagram.

Ill. 367 (page 257): 264 x 155 cm. Courtesy of the Wher Collection, Switzerland.

Border-Type C II b_2

What has already been said applies generally to the two fragments of this type. Keir no. 5 is, as a result of its greater richness in colour and range of variation, obviously the earlier example. BOIM no. I. 6737 (ill. 368) exhibits no colour change in its red ground nor any design variants. Despite the expressiveness of this piece, a certain impoverishment is evident.

Ill. 368 (right): BOIM no. I.6737, 159 x 89 cm, fragment: border with diagram.

Border-Type C II c_1

Similar to type C II b_2, this border-type is not restricted to Group C II. The author is familiar with the original design of this group type as it relates to Group C II only in

fragment no. 6 of the Keir Collection (ill. 369). It shows half-crosses joined together in rows.

Ill. 369 (right): The Keir Collection, 89 x 42 cm, fragment: border with diagram.

Border-Type C II c_2

Even this unusual reduction of the original design presented above appears to have survived in one example from Group C II, whereas it is still represented in a number of examples from Group C III. Nonetheless, the carpet in the parish church of Medias[213] (ill. 370, 371) is especially noteworthy for its richness of design and breadth of variation, comparable in this to the example in Hermannstadt (Sibiu).

Ill. 371 (right): Medias: border from ill. 370 with diagram.

Border-Type C II d_1

This type can be traced back to C II b_1. The hook-forms in the upper part were changed into interlace, as had already been done in the lower half. In the process, however, what remained of the cross design was lost. In order to compensate for this loss, both what was once the centre as well as the side connection were changed into an interlace cross. Among the classic Holbein carpets, this border-type is the most common and the one to have been used most frequently over a longer period of time. Whereas most of these examples, when compared to those discussed above, are lacking in richness of design and variation, there are exceptions, one being the example in Philadelphia, PHAM no. 55–65–5 (ill. 383). There are changes of colour in the ground as shown in ills. 377, 375 or in the fragment in East Berlin, BOIM I.37 (ill. 372). This is less striking in BMIK no. 82.894 from Berlin. Yet, on the other hand, there are also extremely monotonous examples as in the case of MMA no. 61.65 from the McMullan Collection.

Ill. 370 (page 259): Medias, Protestant church, 270 x 148 cm (according to Schmutzler).

Ill. 372 (right): BOIM no. I.37, fragment. Staatliche Museen zu Berlin, Islamisches Museum, Berlin. Border with diagram.

Ill. 373 (right): BOIM nr. 1.38, 150 x 62 cm, fragment. Staatliche Museen zu Berlin, Islamisches Museum, Berlin; border.

Ill. 374 (right): Private collection: border from ill. 376.

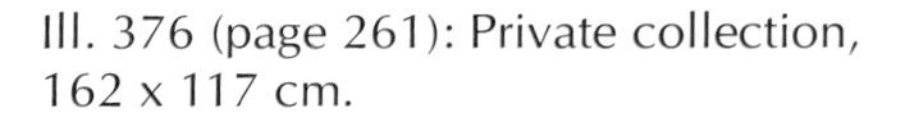

Ill. 376 (page 261): Private collection, 162 x 117 cm.

Border-Type C II d_2

Here we encounter a reduction in the design of C II d_1 in which the original design, though still visible, has undergone further change. In place of the interlace crosses, bars have been added which in turn cover the S-symbols in the middle, signifying 'God'. In the fragments BMIK no. 76.1148 (ill. 375) and BMIK no. 79.111 this type already possesses the character of a secondary border.

Ill. 375 (right): BMIK no. 76.1148, 152 x 76 cm, fragment. SMPK, Museum für Islamische Kunst, Berlin. Border with diagram.

Border-Type C II d_3

The border of the carpet BOIM no. 1.26 (ill. 377, 378) likewise belongs to the type-sequence C II d. Here, in comparison to type C II d_2, the inner stripe was exchanged in favor of a design more easily understood. In the segment shown here, we see cross-rosettes of endless repeat set in a single line of diamonds.

Ill. 377 (right): BOIM no. I.26: border from ill. 378.

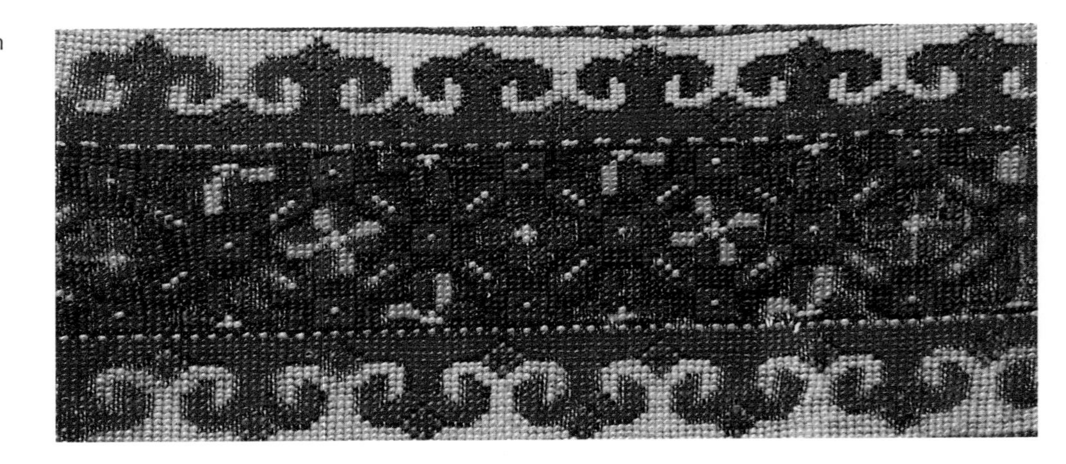

Ill. 378 (page 263): BOIM no. I.26, 220 x 166 cm. Staatliche Museen zu Berlin, Islamisches Museum, Berlin.

A further reduction of C II d_2 and d_3 is possible such that the inner stripe is left out. Although examples of this are known to exist, the present author has, to date, not found any in Group C II.

Border-Type C II e_1

This border-type can be counted as one of the oldest designs within the Christian tradition of oriental carpets. Here, too, a stripe from the familiar composition consisting of leaf-form crosses within diamonds (ill. 145, 147) was used for the border. The border grew out of the fusion or combination of several adjacent elements of the basic form type B. Up to now only one privately-owned fragment has yet appeared in publication[214] (ill. 382, 379).

Ill. 379 (right): Private collection: border from ill. 382 with diagram.

Border-Type C II e_2

This border is also made up of leaf-form crosses in a diamond-form composition, which, at first glance, have a completely different effect. Portions of the basic form type H_1 have been put in rows in the shape of leaves. This has been done in such a way as to make the formation of a diamond-cross from the negative shapes possible. This border represents one of the designs already in use in the mid 1400s. As an example of this PHAM no. 55–65–5 (ill. 380) may be consulted.

Ill. 380 (right): PHAM no. 55.65.5: border from ill. 383.

Border-Type C II f

This type can be seen in conjunction with both C II a as well as with C II e. Old elements are revived by being put together in a new combination. In the final analysis it is of no consequence whether one decides that the cross-star is to be surrounded by diamond crosses or the diamond cross by cross-stars. Again, a stripe of endless repeat was used for the border. Whereas with BUIM no. 14785 (ill. 548) in Budapest the complete carpet is preserved, in East Berlin the border was used only for the purpose of mending (BOIM no. 1.37).

Ill. 381 (right): BOIM no. I.37: border.

'Kotshanak' Secondary Borders

As this border played an essential part not only in Group C II, but also in early carpets produced in central Asia, it will be analyzed as well. One problem consists in the fact that the precursor, as it appears in the carpet in the Wher Collection (ill. 384), is only rarely found, and also that the encoding is achieved by the use of different colours. Thus the negative elements appear much more prominent in their colour

Ill. 382 (right): Private collection: fragment.

Ill. 383 (page 267): PHAM no. 55.65.5, 165 x 110 cm. Philadelphia Museum of Art, Philadelphia. The Joseph Lees Williams Memorial Collection.

than the actual design, hence the name 'kotshanak' (Turkmenian 'kotshak' = scroll, curlicue).

Ill. 384 (right): 'Kotshanak' border from ill. 367 with diagram.

If, however, we examine this design more closely, we discover that the border was constructed from two elements: the 'Kotshak cross' (cf. Group C V a, p. 318) of the basic form type E (ill. 23) and the cross-rosettes placed between. The combination of these two is one of the oldest designs to have originated within the sphere of Armenian cultural influence. It has its roots in identical Urartian models (ill. 385). The coloured 'kotshak' scrolls gain prominence only as colour-negative designs, having nothing to do with the actual pattern. As with so many Turkmenian expressions, such terms reflect the fact that, on the part of this population group, an appreciation for the actual meaning of such designs was altogether lacking, and hence their understandable desire for answers. Later, in our discussion of 'Turkmenian' carpets, we will return to this problem.

The Kotshanak border is an Armenian border with a tradition going back over 2,500 years. We encounter it in all the old weaving regions, both those in the east and those in the west.

Ill. 385 (right): Prototype of the 'Kotshanak' border from an Urartian bronze belt fragment from Kamir-Blur, 8th century B.C., Historical Museum, Erivan.

A further question remains to be answered: where were these carpets produced? Every author concerned with this subject has identified Ushak as their place of production – most likely under the influence of Bode's comments, cited below:[215]

"One wishes to place the older design models, which concern us here, in Smyrna as well, on account of their correspondence in design. This might come close to being correct, provided we are not too rigid about which location we choose. We must keep in mind the vast hinterland, for which Smyrna served as a port of export, instead of restricting ourselves to the city itself. Since, however, we know a production centre in this region still in operation today, namely Ushak, of which mention is made as early as the 16th century, and whose more recent products can most easily be seen as consistent with the older genre of that time, we therefore have good reason to generalize the description 'Ushak carpets' from the later group to the earlier one."

This legend receives further elaboration by Erdmann as follows:[216]

"These later Smyrna carpets owe their existence to the manufactories which existed either in Ushak itself or its vicinity and which, at the end of the 16th century, were so famous that they were receiving orders from the west – as is demonstrated by carpets bearing European coats-of-arms. We have in our possession originals dated 1584 and 1585. Representations of carpets in paintings date as far back as the mid-1500s. We can thus assume that this genre originated during the first part of that same century, which is the same time as the Ottoman carpets. As was the case with this latter group, this genre concerned itself with renewing the designs characteristic of the Persian carpet; however, due to its having a different point of departure, the results are also different. Just as the production of the Ottoman carpets was assigned to the manufactories of Cairo, the production of the new Ushak patterns was apparently entrusted to the older manufactories still in operation within the city. For it was here that the first two types of small-patterned, geometric carpets with their offset rows of alternating figures were made. This is confirmed by the close, technical connections present between these and the more recent 'Ushak carpets'."

This is the extent of the 'evidence' for proposing Ushak as a place of production. In 1630 (!) Ushak is mentioned for the first time as a location for the production of carpets: Ewliya Celebi reports that carpet dealers in Constantinople stocked "carpets from Smyrna, Salonica, Cairo, Isfahan, Ushak and Kavala".[217]

Actually the entire quotation, which Bode and Erdmann ultimately refer to, destroys the Ushak legend. The carpets made to order for Sir Edward Montagu of Boughton from 1584 and 1585, cited by Erdmann, are doubtless European and very possibly English products.[218] Those truly knowledgeable in this matter have long since recognized that the profusion of carpets of the most disparate sort, but attributed to Ushak, can certainly not all have been produced there. In addition one must consider that Ushak, a city with a large proportion of Armenian and Greek inhabitants, had probably accommodated an Ottoman manufactory since the beginning of the 17th century. And, although it is likely to be the existence of this manufactory that most authors would like to cite, it is, for purely temporal reasons, simply not possible for the Christian carpets now being discussed to have been produced there. They originated earlier. The passage quoted above reports carpets from Smyrna, Saloniki and Kavala in addition to Ushak. For centuries all these cities had been centres with a high proportion of Armenian inhabitants, making them very likely candidates for the production of Christian carpets. Moreover, since we know that carpets were produced in England, Poland, the Netherlands and Scandinavia, we have to be able to assume the possibility of their production in the Armenian centres of Italy, for example in Venice or Florence. We can hypothesize, with a certain degree of justification, that the majority of the carpets discussed here originated in western Anatolia, perhaps even in Smyrna and Ushak. The fact remains that, until the genocide of the Armenians in this part of the country, a majority of the carpets had always been described as Smyrna carpets. It was not until after 1915 that they began to be attributed to Ushak.

Group C III: Lotto Carpets

The structure of the field pattern of this group constitutes a variant of the cross-star composition, comparable to that of the preceding groups. Again, it can be traced back to TIEM no. 685 (ill. 96) and Mevl. no. 860/861/1033 (ill. 249). A painting of the Virgin Mary by Hans Memling dating from the last quarter of the 15th century (ill. 388) shows another proto-design in an Armenian carpet: a development parallel to the arabesque gul of the SP-Holbein carpets from Group C II (ill. 386). It appears that 'Lotto carpets' were the weavers' answer to the call to produce more reddish-yellow pile fabrics, brocades or appliqué-work for church decoration, a fashion that from the 15th to the 17th century was prevalent everywhere in Europe. An increased emphasis on floral patterns had become the standard in Europe as well, and the design potential of the carpet fulfilled these expectations. Both the arabesque cross as well as the cross shapes in between were reworked into the more floral designs

Ill. 386 (left): 'Arabesque cross' from ill. 367.

Ill. 388 (page 270): Hans Memling: Madonna Enthroned. Before 1494. Galleria degli Uffizi, Florence.

The carpet depicted here demonstrates nicely the intermediate stage between the carpet in ill. 249 (detail ill. 358) and the so-called 'Lotto' carpets.

of leaf-form crosses, the intricacies of which are seldom as clear as in the carpet in Detroit, for example. Here the cross shape, set apart by means of different colours, clearly shows the development from the basic form type B (ill. 387). The development of the field design is very unobtrusive and can only be followed by examining the piece in detail.

Ill. 387 (page 271): DIA no. 70.926; 171 x 117 cm, Detroit Institute of Arts, Detroit. Gift of Mr. and Mrs. Harold J. Quilhot.

Early examples still show cross-stars in the centres of the leaf-form crosses. In the beginning these were medallion-like, as for example in MMA no. 22.100.112 (ill. 389), then diamond (ill. 390), only to disappear completely in the end. Ellis[219] tried to group the 'Lotto carpets' into three different styles: the first being 'Anatolian', the second 'Kilim' and the third 'ornamental'. At the same time he suspected that only those carpets 'Anatolian' in style were produced in Anatolia, that is, in the vicinity of Konya, Ushak or the general area. He suspected the other two groups to contain copies from south-eastern Europe and Italy. In essence this view accords well with that of the present author, with the exception, that is, of how the groups are divided. It is questionable whether, in fact, the carpets in Group C III can be divided into groups of this sort at all. Only a very negligible development can be determined, and it is restricted to the formation of details. Simply dividing these carpets in this manner and attributing their production to certain regions – 'Anatolian style'/Anatolia – presupposes that Group C III represents the generation of carpets next in line after Group C II and that there is no doubt about its having been produced in Anatolia, which is not the case.

As in the case of the 'Holbein carpets' from Group C II, the border development is also of great importance in the case of the 'Lotto carpets'. It is the author's opinion that questions as to origin and production dates can be answered more easily by taking this into consideration. For this reason Group C III will likewise be ordered according to border-types. This shows that there is a time overlap with Group C II. We will also discover that some borders were used simultaneously, rather than one after the other, which would support the assumption that different centres of production were involved.

It is true that those carpets with a border corresponding to the border-type C II c_2 are always considered to be the oldest. This would require that such carpets follow directly after the SP-Holbein carpets. There does, however, seem to have been a development which must have occurred at the same time as that which led to the SP-Holbein carpets. Moreover, the 'Lotto carpet' can be traced back to prototypes that have no direct connection with Group C II. With respect to the development of borders, the author proposes subdividing the group as follows:

Border-Type C III a

This is a cartouche border which presents, in adjacent rows, what are almost diamond-cross medallions of alternating colours. It grew out of the proto-designs of the arabesque crosses discussed above. The best example of this type is to be found in the carpet MMA no. 22.100.112 (ills. 395, 393), in which the design is perfectly preserved. We find the border slightly reduced in form in the Stuttgart 'Calwer-Lotto' (ills. 396, 394); in Florence (Bargello); in an example in the Wher Collection; in Varese (Poliaghi); in Bausback 78, or in TIEM no. 958. Later reductions can for example be seen in CHAM no. 47.389; Bausback 75/49; in Vienna; with a reduction by half in Florence (Bardini); or, finally, in the example of Boughton no. 4, which shows an utter lack of appreciation for the original design.

Ill. 389: MMA no. 22.100.112: 'Lotto' gul from ill. 395.

Ill. 390: TIEM no. 702, 518 x 275 cm: 'Lotto' gul.

Ill. 391: 'Calwer-Lotto': 'Lotto' gul from ill. 396.

Ill. 392: DIA no. 25.42: 'Lotto' gul from ill. 387.

Ill. 393 (left): MMA no. 22.100.112: border from ill. 395.

Ill. 394 (left): 'Calwer-Lotto': border from ill. 396.

Border-Type C III b

This type is identical to C II f. Examples of this border are rare, one being on a white ground in Dörling 113/408 and in the Museum für Kunst und Gewerbe in Hamburg (ill. 397, not numbered), another on a blue ground in Bausback 77/6.

Ill. 397 (left): Hamburg no., 183 x 125 cm, Museum für Kunst und Gewerbe, Hamburg. Border.

Border-Type C III c_1

This type is likewise rare. Square cartouches or coffers, in the middle of which are located cross-rosette-like eight-pointed stars, appear in adjacent rows. The genesis of this border can be reconstructed in the following manner: Basic form type B

Ill. 395 (right): MMA no. 22.100.112, 173 x 120 cm, Metropolitan Museum of Art, New York. The James F. Ballard Collection. Gift of James F. Ballard, 1922.

becomes enclosed in a square, making the hook-forms superfluous. The cross arms are preserved, but are worked into lilies facing inward. The tips of the lilies are simultaneously the tips of the cross inscribed in the eight-pointed star. We find examples in Eskenazi (ill. 398), in a private collection (ill. 399), in the Bavarian Nationalmuseum in Munich and in the TIEM.

Ill. 399 (right): Private collection, 214 x 120 cm. Border.

Border-Type C III c_2

This border-type and the next one, as well as other variants, appear to have evolved from C III c_1. The cross-rosettes, filled with eight-pointed stars, have been given lobed extensions. Of the elements connecting these cross-rosettes only two independent swastika arms have been preserved, between which the 'S'-symbol for God has been placed. It is only from example no. 20 (ill. 400) of the Keir Collection that we know this type.

Ill. 400 (right): Keir Collection no. 20, 153 x 115 cm. The Keir Collection. Border.

Border-Type C III c_3

Here we observe what is presumably a parallel development, in which the cross-rosettes take up in a meandering pattern, thus becoming linked with the older undulating scroll border. An example of this is the Detroit carpet DIA no. 70.926 (ills. 387, 401) cited above. Here we can also add a piece from a private collection (ill. 402). Presumably, at the end of this series we find the carpet in Berlin, BMIK 82.707 (ills. 420, 421) with its unusual combination of colours, the border of which is reduced to a double undulating scroll which crosses back over itself.

Ill. 396 (page 277): 'Calwer-Lctto', 355 x 190 cm. Staatsgalerie, Stuttgart. Gift of Hans Calwer, Stuttgart, 1969(?).

Ill. 401 (left): DIA no. 70.926.: border from ill. 387.

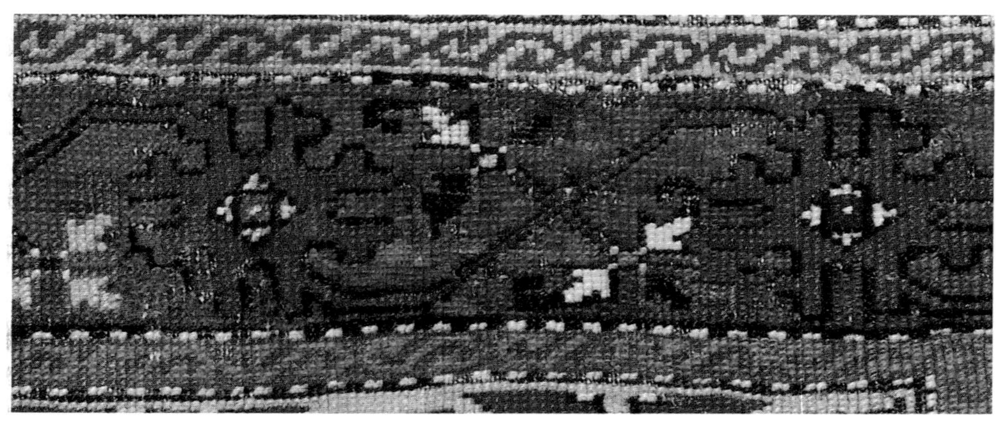

Ill. 402 (left): Private collection, 176 x 107 cm: border.

Ill. 403 (left): Beshir, N.Y.: border from ill. 405.

Border-Type C III c_4

Ill. 404 (left): Private collection: border from ill. 422.

Ill. 398 (right): Eskenazi, Milan. 158 x 110 cm.

We find a design in four nearly identical carpets (McMullan Collection, MMA no. 62.231, Museum für Kunst und Gewerbe, Hamburg, no. 1949.16, private collection [ills. 404, 422]) which, though somewhat out of the ordinary, is to be placed at the end of this type. Each of these carpets bears the alliance coat-of-arms of the Genoese Doria and Centurione families. They were, in all probability, made on the occasion of the union of both families around 1600. The border displays cross-rosettes on a blue ground, as we saw in the previous groups. However, in the sections containing meandering patterns we find, within a white-dotted border, brown ellipses joined to give the impression of leaves. The connection to the border of the carpet of Beshir, New York (ills. 403, 405), is clear. M. Beattie and Ellis view these carpets as products of the 19th century,[220] a conclusion which remains unsubstantiated to this day.

Border-Type C III d_1 and d_2

C III d_1 is identical to C III c_1, and C III d_2 identical to C II c_2. This is again the pseudo-Kufic half-cross from the basic form type B which has been discussed in detail and which here in this group also survived only as a small fragment in the McMullan Collection, MMA no. 1972.80.6., in conjunction with C III d_2 (ill. 406). The border shows both of them next to each other. C III d_2 exists as a quarter design in several examples: in STLCAM no. 104.1929, in PHAM no. 67–30–308 (ill. 407), in MMA no. 08.167.1. (ill. 408), in the piece from the Wher Collection, in the beautiful Eskenazi carpet 82/7 (ill. 409) and in the Cittone carpet. In our discussion of C III c_1 reference was made to the origin of the connecting links of the quarter designs. The emergence of C III d_1 marks the beginning of a parallel development which starts during the latter part of the 15th century.

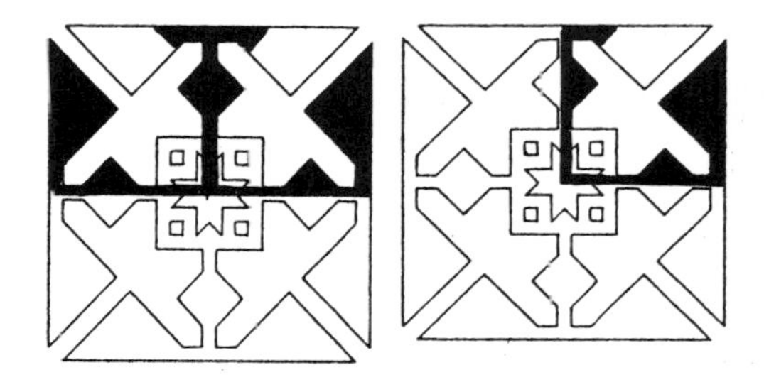

Ill. 406 (right): MMA no. 1972.80.6, 33 x 64 cm, fragment: border with diagram. Metropolitan Museum of Art, New York. Joseph V. McMullan Collection.

Ill. 407 (right): PHAM no. 67-30-308, 162 x 190 cm. Philadelphia Museum of Art, Philadelphia. The Samuel S. White III and Vera White Collection. Border.

Ill. 405: Beshir, New York, 152 x 129 cm.

Ill. 408 (left): MMA no. 08.167.1; Metropolitan Museum of Art, New York. Border.

Border-Type C III d_3

This type is identical to C II d_1. An example is located in the Cincinnati Art Museum – no. 1957.327 (ill. 410).

Ill. 410 (left): CAM no. 1957.327, Cincinnati Art Museum, Cincinnati. Border.

Border-Type C III e

We are already familiar with this border from Group B II (cf. ills. 270, 272 and 273). The difference lies in the use of the later 'acorn-shaped' formation of what was formerly an 'E-design' (cf. figs. p. 38). This border is related both to Group C III c, with the cross from that group being replaced with the 'tree of Jesse' (cf. ills. 305–310) and to Group C III f. Thus far there is only one example from a private collection (ill. 411) known to the present author.

Ill. 411 (left): Owned privately, 136 x 115 cm; border.

Ill. 409: Eskenazi, Milan; 228 x 226 cm.

Border-Type C III f_1

For this group, as for so many others, the splitting in half of the cross from the basic form types B or E serves as the point of departure, even though this may not be apparent at first sight (in C III f_4 the whole cross is still preserved). In the Harman carpet[221] (ill. 412) this can still be discerned, whereas in the Medias example[222] this is no longer the case.

Ill. 412: (right): Protestant church, Harman; 182 x 145 cm; (according to Schmutzler), border with diagram.

It is relatively easy to determine that, again, this border is simply half of a cross composition.

Border-Type C III f_2

What was said above can also be applied to this type. In the literature it has come to bear the unfortunate and misleading name 'cloud-band border' probably because one author or the other believed it to bear a resemblance to cloud-bands. TIEM no. 698 (ill. 417) clearly shows this connection in its field pattern. Here, too, the half-cross constitutes the basic design. Whether or not there was a direct or indirect connection between this design and the coat-of-arms of Florence, in which – precisely during the 16th century – the lily exhibited a very similar design, cannot be proven at this time. The probability does, however, exist. There are numerous privately owned examples (ill. 413), such as those in the former Schmutzler Collection, in Sighisoara[223] and in Detroit (no. 25.42, ill. 414).

Ill. 414 (right): DIA no. 25.42. Detroit Institute of Arts, Detroit. Border with diagram.

Ill. 415 (right): Owned privately, 193 x 128 cm; border from ill. 413.

This border has come to be known as a 'cloud-band' border in the literature. It is certainly correct to deduce a Chinese influence regarding the design of certain details, and yet this design, similar in structure to that of ill. 412, is based on a cruciform.

Ill. 413 (right): Owned privately, 193 x 128 cm.

Ill. 416 (left): Owned privately, 'cloud-band' cross medallion from ill. 466.

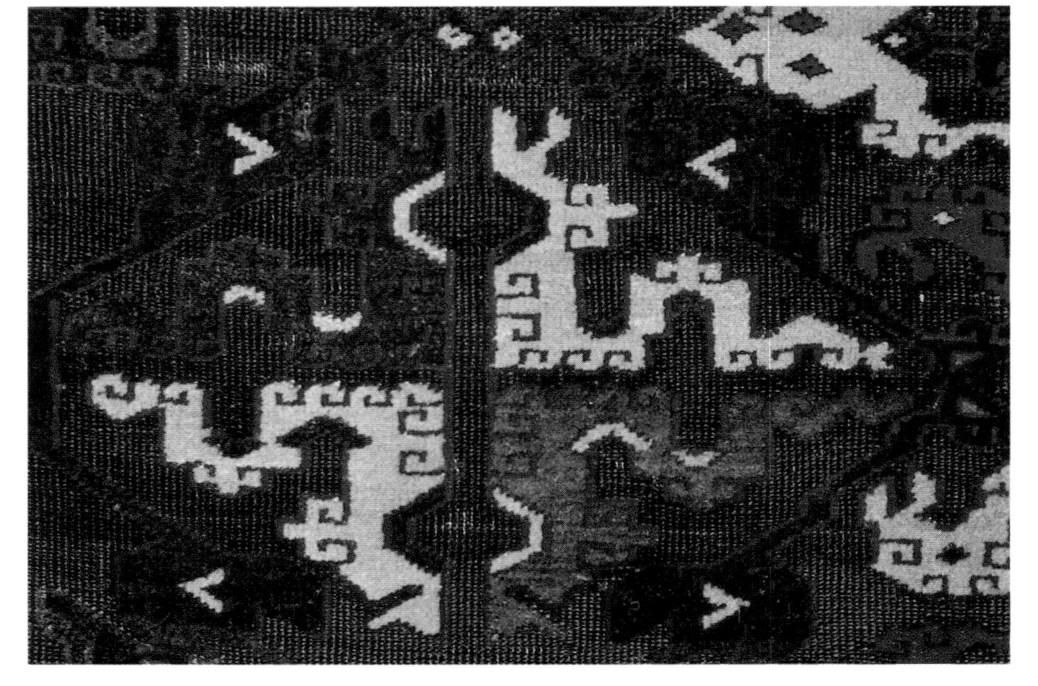

Ill. 417 (left): TIEM no. 698: 'cloud-band' cross medallion. Türk ve Islam Eserleri Müzesi, Istanbul.

Ill. 421 (right): BMIK no. 82.707, 362 x 211 cm. SMPK, Museum für Islamische Kunst, Berlin.

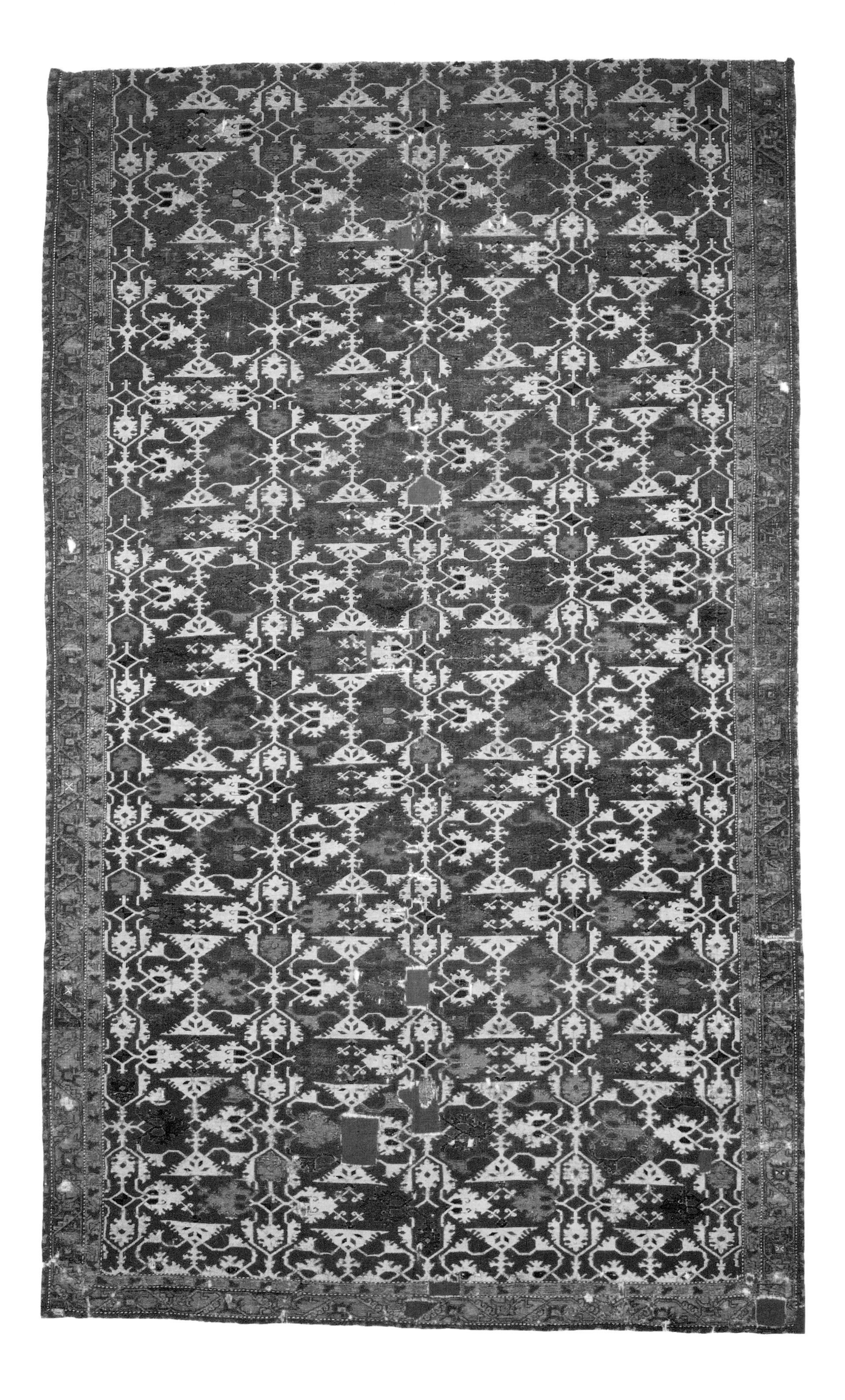

Border-Type C III f_3

Again we find half of a diamond-cross, formed from four late designs of 'the tree of Jesse' facing one another, used here for the border. The complete diamond-cross is preserved in the McMullan carpet no. 75. We find the border in TIEM no. 709 (ill. 418).

Ill. 418 (right): TIEM no. 709: border. Türk ve Islam Eserleri Müzesi, Istanbul.

Border-Type C III f_4

Ill. 422 (page 289): Owned privately. Italian 'Lotto carpet' with the alliance coat-of-arms of the Genoese Doria and Centurione families, c. 1600.

It has as yet not been possible to prove that the majority of carpets of Group C III were produced in Italy. Those exhibiting a coat-of-arms constitute an exception to this. It can be assumed that they originated in one of the many Armenian settlements.

The last type in this series shows us the complete diamond-cross in a section from a pattern of endless repeat.

One might suspect that here we are dealing with a modification of the Type C II e_1 (ill. 373). The basic design is a leaf-form cross very similar to the one cited here, yet reduced. In its middle there is a 'Kotshak cross' with extended axes. All in all, it represents no more than a refinement of this old motif. The only known example was located in the McMullan Collection (no. 74), now MMA no. 1972.80.8 (ill. 419).

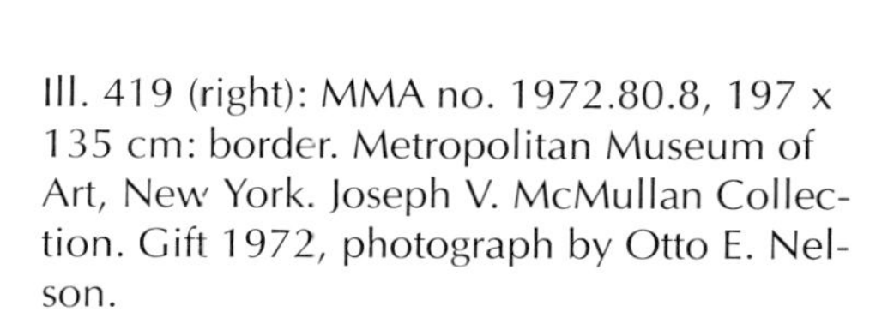

Ill. 419 (right): MMA no. 1972.80.8, 197 x 135 cm: border. Metropolitan Museum of Art, New York. Joseph V. McMullan Collection. Gift 1972, photograph by Otto E. Nelson.

There are very few borders that contain the entire design. It is usually cut in half or in fourths.

At their present state our investigations do not permit us to make any final pronouncements as to which centres of production this entire group might have originated from. We must remember that beginning with the exodus of emigrants during the 11th and 12th centuries, and even more so during the 13th and 14th centuries, carpets were produced at different locations in Europe in a manner completely in keeping with the traditions of the home country. Furthermore, we must consider that designs did not move in only one direction, but instead, that a lively exchange of these in both directions was the case. Against this background it is possible only to isolate tendencies within the limits presented here which might provide clues as to their origin. At the same time, the ordering of them here takes into account the geographic movement from east to west. In the view of the author, at the present point in his investigations, the groups below are to be attributed as follows: C III a-c_1 to central Anatolia, C III c_2-c_3 and e to western Anatolia, C III c_4 and f_2 to Italy, C III d_1-d_3 to Greece, C III f_1 and f_3 to eastern Europe, whereas C III f_4 probably belongs to the southeastern region of central Anatolia. In terms of time, the oldest examples probably date back to the late 15th century, with the majority going only as far back as the 16th and only a handful of very debased types datable to the 17th century. There are two reasons for this reduction in the production of carpets in general, and for the termination of the production of the 'Lotto carpet' in particular. For one thing there were the reform movements in the churches of Europe, calling for the renewal of its commitment to the poor and thus a break with the pomp and splendour then characteristic of churches. The Reformation and ensuing secularization of the 16th century resulted in these churches being emptied of ornamental objects, from which time carpets became associated only with the worldly decoration of the distinguished homes of the gentry. This was a significant turning point in the history of carpets. The second reason has to do with the fact that, as a consequence of the subsequent Inquisition, that portion of the population that was inclined to follow heretical religious teachings was subjected to great suffering. This was particularly the case, as it had been in the preceding centuries, of the Armenians.

This turning point also marked the end of the Renaissance. The burgeoning countermovement, which we know as the Baroque, was to a large extent forced to look to markets outside of the European sphere of influence. As a result of the shift in potential customers, the carpet underwent a very significant change stylistically, adopting a more secular character.

Ill. 420 (left): BMIK no. 82.707.: field detail from ill. 421.

Group C IV: Cross-Star Carpets – Western Design Groups

As the previous groups have repeatedly shown, the cross-star is a central motif of the Christian oriental carpet. We encountered the most obvious cross-star designs in the early western European carpets from Group B V and their counterparts in Group C I from the eastern regions. Among the products of the weaving centres in the western region of central Anatolia the cross-star carpet is common as well. The cross-star carpets of Group C IV have their roots in the cross-star tile patterns of the 12th/13th century (ills. 150, 151). The cross-stars which occur now succeed the star-tiles. Carpets of this kind are known as 'Star-Ushaks' in the literature. Similarities in the formation of the light-symbol cross led scholars to separate them into groups, and their border developments, in turn, led them in some cases, to attempt to place these in a certain chronological order. Since the groups, however, partially originated at the same time it is difficult to keep a strict chronological sequence.

Group C IV a: Star-Ushak Carpets I

The structural scheme of the entire group can best be demonstrated by referring to the carpet in the Meyer-Müller Collection, Zurich (ill. 423). In comparing the segment of endless repeat found here with the Genevan example from Group B II (ill. 250), we find first of all that the entire composition has been rotated by about 45 degrees and secondly that the world-picture has been replaced by a light-symbol cross of the basic form type H. The star-tiles have been completely preserved. The cross-stars have been widened and no longer appear in their original form, but instead, during the subsequent period, make up the ground which is covered by light-symbol crosses, here still contained within the star-tiles.

Both of our next two examples make the developmental progression up to our last group, Group C IV d, clear. We will see how the well-defined star-tile design becomes progressively more round.

The carpet at the Philadelphia Museum of Art (ill. 424) substitutes a dulled leaf-like design for the sharp, eight-pointed forms in every other row.

In the Eskenazi example (ill. 425), what was once a star-tile is still recognizable as such, though here it has almost completely taken on the rounded shape of a medallion. It is important to note the changes in the interior, where there is evidence of a division into three parts: a second star-tile, red in its ground, has been worked into the blue ground of the outer star-tile and in it we find a blue cross-star of the basic form type G_2. The centre of this cross-star is made up of a light-symbol cross, floral in its execution, of the basic form type H_1.

BMIK no. 85.981[224], in its structure and detail, is very much like the Eskenazi example. The colours have been exchanged, with the ground becoming blue, the star-tile red, and so on. However, what does strike us is the completely different arrangement of the inner light-symbol crosses (ill. 430), which here bears a close resemblance to that of the Philadelphia carpet and which, furthermore, shows the connection to Groups C IV b and C IV c.

Ill. 423 (left): Meyer-Müller Collection, Zurich; 440 x 200 cm.

This carpet stands at the beginning of a line of development that opens with a simple cross-star tile design and closes with complex medallion compositions.

Ill. 424 (right): PHAM no. 55.65.13., 273 x 200 cm. Philadelphia Museum of Art, Philadelphia. The Joseph Lees Williams Memorial Collection.

Ill. 425 (left): Eskenazi, Milan;
428 x 203 cm.

The example illustrated by Lefevre in the auction catalogue of 21 March, 1975 (ill. 426) represents a later stage in development of the designs in the Eskenazi carpet. Here the blue elements of what was once the outer star-tile of the Eskenazi carpet, have 'drifted apart', the red star-tile has become the background, the blue one on the inside taking on the form of a diamond leaf-form cross. In this leaf-form cross a light-symbol cross, made up of palmettes, is to be found. BOIM no. I.9[225] also belongs here. These blue leaf-form crosses can also become completely independent elements in their own right, as is shown in the beautiful example from the Ballard Collection in the St. Louis Art Museum (SLAM no. 98.1929, ill. 427).

The borders of this group are for the most part delicate, floral, meandering scrolls, with the borders in BOIM no. I.9 and SLAM no. 98.1929 returning back to MMA no. 58.63 (ill. 435) in their development.

Ill. 426 (right): Lefevre Auction from 21.3.1975, London; 436 x 233 cm. Detail.

Group C IV b: Star-Ushak Carpets II

This group, as with the previous group, takes its compositional bearings from the star-cross-tile. Illustration 428 provides us with an example of this tendency. In place of what should actually be a cross-tile, we find in this case a diamond leaf-form cross as a result of the 'drifting apart' mentioned before. In contrast to Group C IV a, an outline of the star-tile is retained, although in its make-up it represents an extreme combination of the light-symbol crosses of the basic form types H_1 and H_2 which we already encountered in BMIK no. 85.981 from Group C IV a (ill. 430). In this form it is found in the art of the Italian Renaissance, one of the main import markets of this period. A detail from a fresco by Carpaccio (ill. 429) demonstrates what was common to the structures of these. There are large-format examples with patterns of infinite repeat, and again others that isolate the light-symbol cross in the shape of a medallion in the fashion of Group B II. A few of these have been able to retain the earliest designs from the chain of evolution described here. Since the border development can be followed quite well in these examples, they will also be treated here.

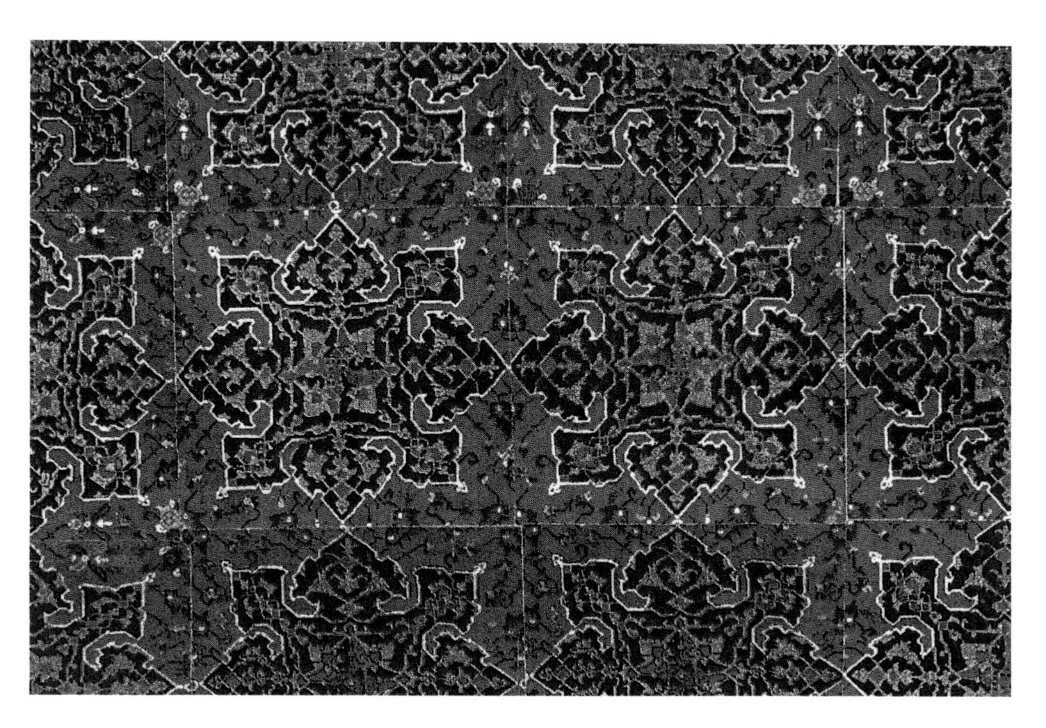

Ill. 428 (left): cross star tile design, photographic montage.

The composition of this montage now corresponds to ill. 423, the difference simply being that it has been rotated about its axis by 45 degrees.

To begin with, let us consider Vakf. no. E 26, a carpet fragment which continues the double-medallion composition of Group B II. The ground shows a somewhat staggered and trimmed segment from a larger drawing, as was typical of work done to order according to certain size specifications. In contrast to all the other representatives of this group, here the basic colour of the field is blue. In ill. 431 we see the upper cross-star, which – though somewhat damaged – is still better preserved. We recognize the cross arms which are set apart in colour and also in the centre the cross-star within a cross-star. The undulating scroll border suggests an early design.

TIEM no. 763 (ill. 432) corresponds in its double-medallion composition to Vakf. no. E 26; the use of red as the basic colour for the field distinguishes both. The central cross-star, set apart in colour, is clearly discernable in its octagon, and yet already at this stage the designs surrounding it begin to encroach upon it. The border consists of an undulating line which, in alternating fashion, encloses trapezoidal areas

Ill. 427 (page 296): SLAM no. 98.1929., 315 x 229 cm. The St. Louis Art Museum, St. Louis. Gift of James F. Ballard.

Ill. 429 (above): Vittore Carpaccio: Legend of St. Ursula, The Reception of the English Envoy. 1490/95. Accademia, Venice.

Carpaccio's fresco shows what is a typical composition for the time: two cross systems, one clearly superimposed on the other; this served as a model for carpets in Group C IV.

Ill. 430 (right): BMIK no. 85.981, 276 x 187 cm. Two star-tiles. SMPK, Museum für Islamische Kunst, Berlin.

These two close-ups demonstrate quite nicely the two possible ways of giving more emphasis to either of the two cross systems.

Ill. 431 (above left): Vakf. no. E 26, 237 x 147 cm; upper light-symbol cross star tile. Vakiflar Carpet Museum, Istanbul.

Ill. 432 (below left): TIEM no. 763; light-symbol cross star tile. Türk ve Islam Eserleri Müzesi, Istanbul.

wherein we find cross-stars framed in floral designs (ill. 434). This is the early form of a border combining two developmental systems – inclusion on an alternating basis, and arrangement in rows.

TIEM no. 763[226] demonstrates a continued development in its border, in as much as the reduced, debased cross-stars here begin to show signs of what will later be characterized as floral.

The half-stars in the upper and lower halves of Vakf. no. E 29 have been reduced to such an extent that what remains can already be regarded as corner designs for the later medallion of double-niche carpets. It may be that this carpet served as a prototype for these.

WÖMAK no. T 8384 (ill. 434) and, among others, the carpet in the Hubel Collection[227] provide a direct connection to TIEM no. 763 in the evolution of borders. A somewhat wider and a very narrow floral figure alternate with one another, with only the former containing the rudiments of a cross-star, but here completely devoid of any meaning.

Ill. 433 (right): TIEM no. 763: border to Ill. 432.

The series of borders shows the various stages of transformation in moving from the cross star design to the 'tree of Jesse'.

Ill. 434 (right): WÖMAK no. 8384, 403 x 200 cm; border.

Ill. 435 (right): MMA no. 58.63, 426 x 231 cm: border. Metropolitan Museum of Art, New York. Gift of Joseph V. McMullan.

Ill. 436 (page 302): Owned privately, 350 x 185 cm.

Carpets of this kind are termed 'Star Ushaks'.

Ill. 437 (page 303): Owned privately, 232 x 135 cm.

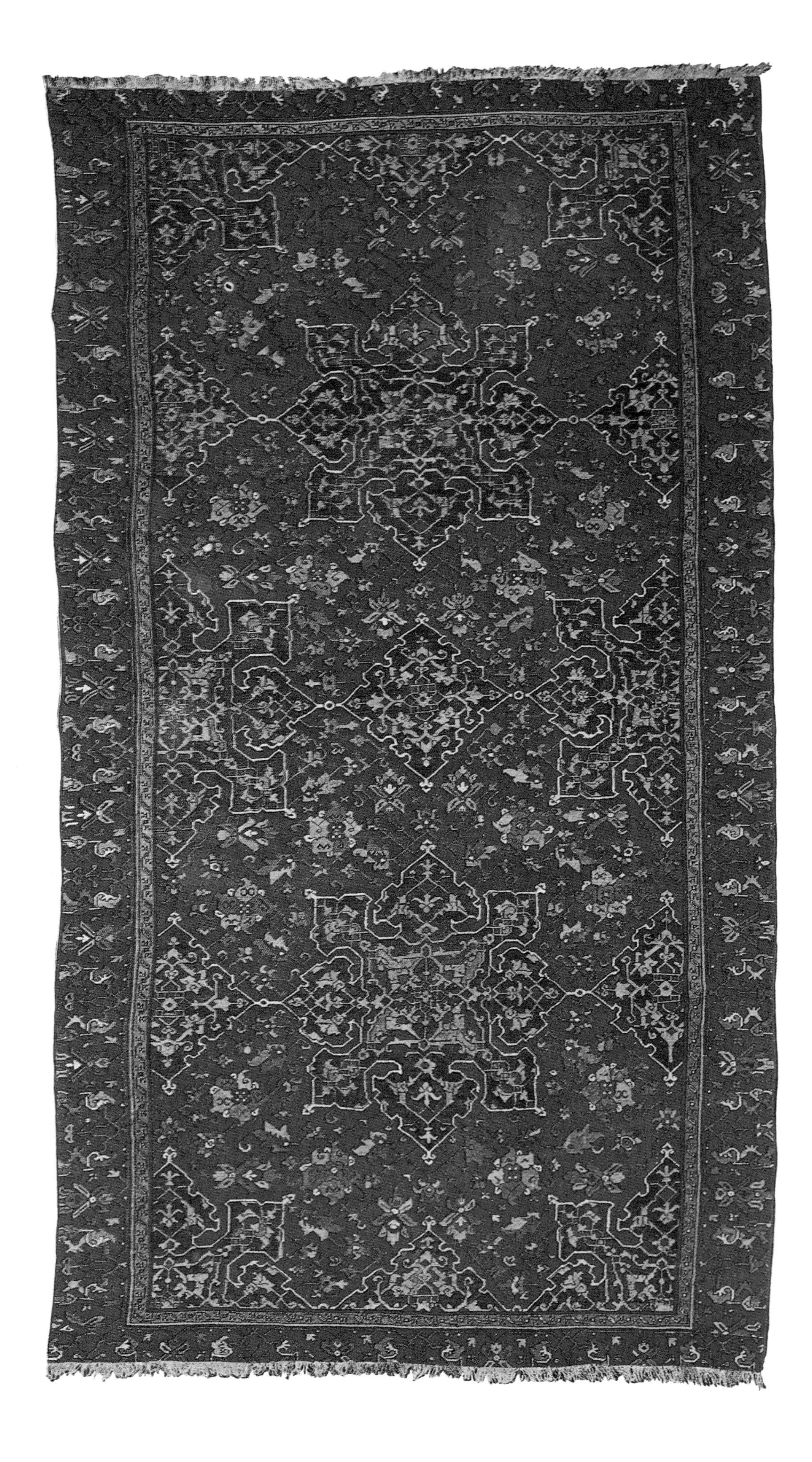

As designs continued to develop, we find what is left of the cross-star being replaced by the 'tree of Jesse' (ill. 435) in subsequent carpets. The question as to why these designs were replaced at all remains unanswered. It appears that this development coincided with the reign of Selim I (1512–1520), whose rule was not characterized by the same highly tolerant attitude shared by his predecessors, who had taken their bearings from the West. Thus this design would suggest a form of encodement – something which we have been able to observe and point out in our previous discussion and which we will again encounter in things to come. The most beautiful and best-known example of this is also one of the largest: the carpet, once part of the McMullan Collection, now in the MMA under the number 58.63 (ill. 415).[228] A comparable piece, though smaller, is in private ownership[229] (ill. 436).

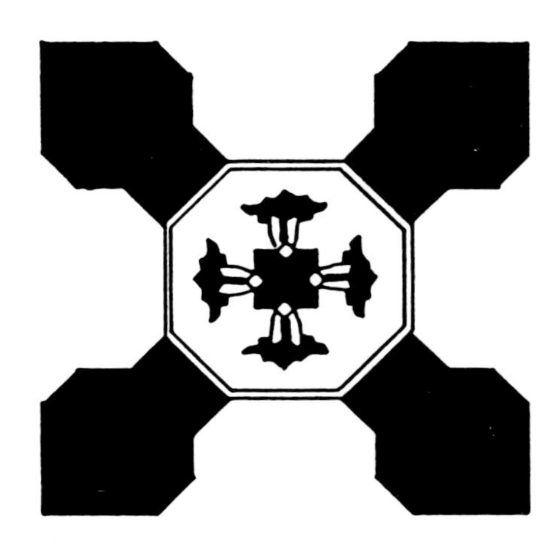

Group C IV c: Star-Ushak Carpets III

There is a third group which can perhaps be assigned to the same time period as those just cited, or even earlier. It can be assigned to the last quarter of the 15th century. Already in Group C IV a our attention was drawn to the two possible types of light-symbol crosses, H_1 and H_2, present in BMIK no. 85.981 (ill. 430). What we find here in Group C IV c is that the positive design of the cross arms has lost its own individual colour, thus becoming more similar to the background. What remains is the floral decoration within, which in its appearance, however, cannot substitute as a cross. The diagonal beams of the light-symbol cross likewise retain their basic form type H_2 (ill. 23). Yet in place of this, the central octagon has been filled by a cross of remarkable appearance. What makes up the centre of the eight-pointed star contained within this varies throughout all the carpets known to the author, whereas outwardly one has the impression that the crosses change very little.

The variants Vakf. no. A 98 (ill. 438) and Vakf. no. A 222[230] appear to be the most interesting. Here the eight-pointed stars have undergone an eight-fold division in colour and have been decorated with a cross-star rosette, reminiscent of the late central designs of Group B II. MMA no. 1972.80.4,[231] from the former McMullan Collection, contains, instead of this, the eight-pointed cross-star by itself or together with lily-crosses. Bernheimer no. 55940 and PHAM no. 55.65.1[232] (ill. 442) also have an eight- or six-fold colour change; in the centre, however, the former features a 'Kotshak'-cross-rosette and the latter a cross formed from four lilies facing toward one another. BOIM no. I.6932 (ill. 439) and LV & A no. 278–1906 and Halevim (ill. 443) all have only the opposed leaf-form cross in the centre of the octagon as just described.

The New York, Munich and London examples no longer have borders. The piece from East Berlin (ill. 440) possesses a combination of a leaf-scroll border, seen in Vakf. no. E 26 (Group C IV b), or even better in the Stuttgart Holbein carpet (ill. 361, upper half), and eight-lobed leaf-designs, almost square in appearance, in which there are leaf-form crosses of two colours. An Armenian S-border separates the main border from the field. The same border as the one described above is to be found in each of the two examples in the Vakiflar Museum in Istanbul (ill. 441), with the exception that in these the S-border has been replaced by an early form of the so-called 'cloud-band border' (cf. p. 135), here functioning as the main border. The border of PHAM no. 55.65.1 on the whole corresponds to that of MMA no. 58.63[233] from Group C IV b (ill. 435), the one difference being that an additional change in colour occurs within the pointed, trapezoidal areas along either side of the vertical axis.

Ill. 438 (right): Vakf. no. A 98, 395 x 250 cm: light-symbol cross. Vakiflar Carpet Museum, Istanbul.

Ill. 439 (right): BOIM no. I.6932, 232 x 137 cm: light-symbol cross. Staatliche Museen zu Berlin, Islamisches Museum, Berlin.

Ill. 442 (left): PHAM no. 55.65.1, 474 x 201 cm. Philadelphia Museum of Art, Philadelphia. The Joseph Lees Williams Memorial Collection.

Ill. 443 (right): Halevim, 205 x 120 cm. Davide Halevim, Milan.

Ill. 440 (right): BOIM no. I.6932: border to ill. 439.

Ill. 441 (right): Vakf. no. A 222, 319 x 194 cm: border. Vakiflar Carpet Museum, Istanbul.

Group C IV d: Medallion Ushak Carpets

At the end of our design evolution discussed here we find the so-called 'medallion Ushaks'. In our treatment of Group C IV a we have looked at the development of these. Over the course of time the star-tiles had lost more and more of their sharp-edged, octagonal shape in favor of one more medallion-like in its roundness. In this medallion shape Erdmann[234] saw 'an Ottoman response to the design revolution in the Persian carpet.' The evolution of designs discussed thus far, however, clearly shows that it may, in fact, even be necessary to assume the contrary. What is more, this development is by no means new, nor does it originate in Persia; instead, it was for centuries a feature of the designs traditionally belonging to the region of Armenian cultural influence. Reference was made to this fact on page 62.

The compositional design of Group C IV c was provided by Group C IV a: diagonally staggered circular shapes in a segment of endless repeat. This segment shows a central medallion accompanied on either side by two halved cross-stars. Depending on the size of the carpet, this pattern can be repeated completely or in part. The medallions are filled with leaf-form crosses. The halved cross-stars, on the other hand, still contain the light-symbol cross halves. There are a few odd carpets dark blue in their ground with light blue half-stars and red central medallions, as well as numerous carpets red in ground and likewise with light blue half-stars but dark blue

Ill. 444 (right): Thyssen, 544 x 261 cm. Thyssen-Bornemisza Collection, Lugano.

The carpet represents one of the few so-called 'Medallion Ushaks' on a blue ground.

Ill. 445 (page 310): Bausback, 400 x 250 cm. Franz Bausback, Mannheim.

Ill. 446 (page 311): Nagel, 272 x 170 cm. Kunstauktionshaus Dr. Fritz Nagel, Stuttgart (294/367).

central medallions. It is commonly thought that those blue in their ground are the older ones. It is indisputable that some with blue grounds are obviously more exact in their initial design and execution. This is particulary true of the half-stars. Yet among these there are also late forms and even quite debased examples. The present author is of the impression that those done in different colours also stem from different manufactories, in which case the red ground carpets do not by definition have to be copies of pieces on blue ground. What does strike us is that among the red ground examples there are a greater number that have a distinct, unmistakable cross in the centre, whereas this cannot be said of those on blue ground. With the existence of the Berlin example BMIK no. I.4928,[235] which shows the coat-of-arms and initials of the Grand Marshal of Lithuania, Krystof Wiesiolowski, we can be certain that production was carried out in eastern Europe or at least in Poland and most likely in other countries such as Italy.

Early examples on blue ground are to be found, among other places, in the National Museum of Kuwait, the Thyssen Collection (ill. 444), the Museum für Kunst und Gewerbe in Hamburg, and the TIEM in Istanbul. Red ground examples exist in the Iten-Maritz and Bausback Collections (ill. 445), the TIEM and the Vakiflar Museum, as well as in the Islamic Museum in Berlin. Other examples have been shown by Christie's in New York (19.12.1979), Sotheby's in New York (1.11.1980 and 22.3.1980), and by Lefevre in London (6.10.1978).

Here mention should be made of an early example (ill. 446) that does not seem to belong to any of the known groups; it was displayed at the 294th auction at Nagel's and presumably has its origin in the Armenian regions of eastern Anatolia.

Later examples no longer show the exact markings of the early pieces. More than anything this applies to the cross in the medallion, yet often also to its outer shape. In the case of the carpets on a blue ground, as for example in the one in Vienna[236] (WÖMAK no. Or. 298), the otherwise circular medallions are compressed into rhomboid-like ellipses, or, as in the Sotheby piece (New York, 14.2.1981), the horizontal cross arms are left out of what is already a somewhat deformed circular medallion. This is also the case with the red ground carpet of Bernheimer's or in TIEM no. 1599. Bernheimer showed a number of other late examples as well, in which both the external design and the content of the central medallions had changed. As in TIEM no. 4, the content of one of the medallions shows, aside from a flowering cross, nothing more than a flower-strewn field; and in another with a blue ground we find a completely haphazard filling, showing leafwork elements that are otherwise common.

We have frequently touched on the question of origin. Here we must distinguish between the origin of the designs and the place where production actually took place. The designs of Group C IV b make up an integral part in the Armenian tradition of manuscript illumination. This we saw on the opening page of the manuscript no. 6305 in the Matendaran in Erivan, dating from the beginning of the 14th century (ill. 447). Such designs have their counterparts in the art of the Italian Renaissance. We can be sure that the examples of Group C IV d appealed to the Ottomans, which does not preclude, however, the possibility that these were produced for the Christian faith. On page 268ff the Ushak-legend was discussed at length. The old trade name 'Smyrna' for the carpets of this group may be a generic term which might also have been used to stand for Ushak. In the absence of any conclusive evidence, the attempt to attribute such carpets exclusively to Ushak is utterly unfounded. Precisely here, in this group, there is substantial evidence to indicate their production in Europe: carpets from Group C IV b can be traced to England, and those from Group C IV d to Poland. This, in view of the fact that until quite recently all such carpets were attributed to Ushak, should make us think.

Ill. 447 (right): Evangelistary, Siwnik', 14th century: opening page of the Gospel according to Luke. Matenadaran, Erivan, codex 6305, F. 128r.

This early page contains prototypes not only for Group C IV, but for the carpets presented in Group IX b (ills. 535–542) as well.

The earliest examples go as far back as the last quarter of the 15th century, at least some of the carpets from Group C IV a-c. The earliest representation of a carpet from Group C IV b in a painting dates back to 1534. Paris Bordone shows the carpet lying on the floor before the throne of the Doge of Venice. Examples of this group produced in England are dated 1584 and 1585[237]. This shows that the transfer of designs from the region of the Mediterranean went largely unnoticed in England until quite late. On the other hand, however, from as early as 1570 we find a painting of the English royal family, in which a carpet from the latest group, C IV d, is represented.[238] This means that the evolution of designs for the entire group was already complete by this time. Late developments, and particularly production in Europe (there is record of carpets having been produced in Spain), will not be included here. They may well have continued on into the first half of the 17th century.

Group C V: Diamond-Form Cross Carpets and Step-Form Cross Carpets

The diamond-cross and step-form cross compositions are amongst the oldest of the traditional designs to originate within the sphere of Armenian cultural influence since the empires of the Urartu and Phrygians. This traditional set of designs was continued in the mosaics of the Hellenistic, Roman and early Christian periods. In the manuscript illumination of Armenia and Syria (cf. pp. 125 ff.) during the High Middle Ages, representations of carpets with diamond-cross and step-form cross compositions document their existence in the area of other textiles as well.

Group C V a: Memling Gul Carpets

Characteristic of the carpets represented in this group is the hooked step-form cross, referred to in the literature as the 'Memling gul' after Hans Memling, who often included depictions of this carpet type in his paintings of the Virgin Mary. The earliest depiction of this type of carpet is to be found somewhat earlier in the book of hours of an unknown French master from around 1460.[239] In a scene from King René of Anjou's novel 'Cuer d'Amour Epris', we find a 'Memling gul carpet' depicted beside a cross-block carpet. Judging from this picture, it is a long, narrow runner, containing two sets of five 'Memling guls', each in turn filled with cross-stars. In the negative area between the guls we find diamonds filled with crosses, the diamonds being joined together along the central vertical axis by cross pieces which form stems. The border contains the familiar opposed cross-leaf halves. Memling himself does not reserve this carpet exclusively for his paintings of the Virgin Mary, but also uses it as a table cloth in a still life[240] (ill. 448). In this example we discover three rows of guls, containing differently shaped crosses and separated by diamond-stems.

Ill. 448 (page 315): Hans Memling: The Flower Vase. Before 1494. Thyssen-Bornemisza Collection, Lugano.

The still life has on its reverse side the portrait of a man and is at the same time the recto of a 'closed' diptych, most likely for the adoration of the Virgin Mary. In reading this still life, the Christian symbolism is not to be overlooked. In the pilgrim's vase we find together several floral symbols for the Virgin Mary: lilies, iris and columbines (divine grace, innocence, forgiveness of sins, and yearning to be with God). These symbols make up an essential part of the border of a number of paradise-gate carpets (Group C XII b).

The Memling gul is doubtless a special form of the step-form cross, and one we already know from Armenian manuscripts of the 12th century. It constitutes one of the principal designs within the Armenian tradition of carpet designs. It has remained, on into the present century, the most wide-spread, crossing the borders within the region of Armenian cultural influence and reaching into most parts of central and western Anatolia, where, however, it did not survive the Holocaust.

Ill. 449: Mevl. 859; Mevlana Museum, Konya.

Whether the 'hook formation' was added during the 13th or 14th century, and why it was added, are questions which still remain unanswered. Of all the carpets of this type to have survived, Mevl. no. 859 (ill. 449) appears to be the oldest, purer and clearer in its execution than those represented in paintings from the 15th century cited above. Despite its reduction, the border is reminiscent of that from TIEM no. 685 (ill. 96) and bears a similarity to the reduced form in the 'Zili', which the author referred to in explaining the development of the 'Kufi border' (ill. 110). For these reasons it seems possible that this carpet may have originated during the 14th century, if not earlier, whereas the Budapest example BUIM no. 14427 (ill. 450) probably stems from the latter part of the 15th century.

Although throughout the centuries the outline of the hooked step-form cross remained quite constant, the inner pattern changed frequently. We can regard the use of cross-stars as being one of the oldest ways of completing this inner design, although it is not only the existence of these (from the middle of the 15th century on) that indicates it. This use of the cross-star has survived in various weaving areas on into the 20th century. The Memling still life (before 1494, ill. 448) already showed us that the central cross-star can be replaced by crosses of various types. This suggests the possibility of looking at the development of the cross shapes for help in dating, whereas the borders had been our only avenue previously.

Ill. 450: BUIM no. 14427, 62 x 93 cm and 107.5 x 93 cm, fragments. Iparmüvészeti Muzeum, Budapest.

In its centre, Mevl. no. 859 (ills. 449, 40) has a cross, the likes of which we find in the Armenian-Cilician Tübingen evangelistary from 1193 (ill. 184). This may provide us with a point of reference.

The carpet in the Memling still life discussed above (ill. 448) shows two later cross designs, both of which are further developments of the basic form type E: one we find in the two outer rows with their cross-star centres, the second is represented in those crosses with more clearly defined cross arms. We can be fairly sure that both developed from the carpet from Mevl. no. 859.

Eder presents illustrations of Memling gul carpets,[241] which she then assigns to the Kasak or the Moghan carpets. A particularly beautiful and early example is a carpet from the Victoria & Albert Museum in London, LV & A no. 397–1880 (ill. 454), which shows Memling guls in double rows separated by diamond-stems. Most of these examples contain a cruciform of the basic form type E (ill. 23) in their centre, a cross referred to as the 'Kotshak cross'. Kotshak, Gotshak or Kotshanak are Turkoman terms meaning curlicue or (little) horn. Translated, 'Kotshak cross' thus means horned cross. Brüggemann describes it as an 'Old Turkish motif'[242] and, referring to Bidder, suspects it to have originated in China during the Han period (206 BC – AD220). We have already shown on page 266 that ever since the first millennium B.C. the 'Kotshak cross' had been an element of Urartian design.

The oldest depiction of the 'Kotshak cross' known to the present author to date is Urartian and shows the symbol of the sun flanked by two eagles. This is suspended above the depiction of the Chaldi deity and is part of a relief on the base of a column from Adiljevaz (Van Province). The relief (ill. 451) is dated to the 8th century BC[243] There are identical designs on belt buckles from the same time period[244] (ill. 385), as well as examples from Phrygian art of this period, such as that found in the

Ill. 451 (left): Relief from Adiljevaz; Urartu, 8th century B.C.; upper section. Museum for Anatolian Civilizations, Ankara.

We are presented here with a Kotshak cross-tree of life composition (the life-giving sun symbol could even be seen as the original design behind the idea of the 'tree of Jesse'), flanked by two eagles carrying hares. It is here that we find the origin of the hare symbol, a symbol for the 'believer'. See also ill. 166.

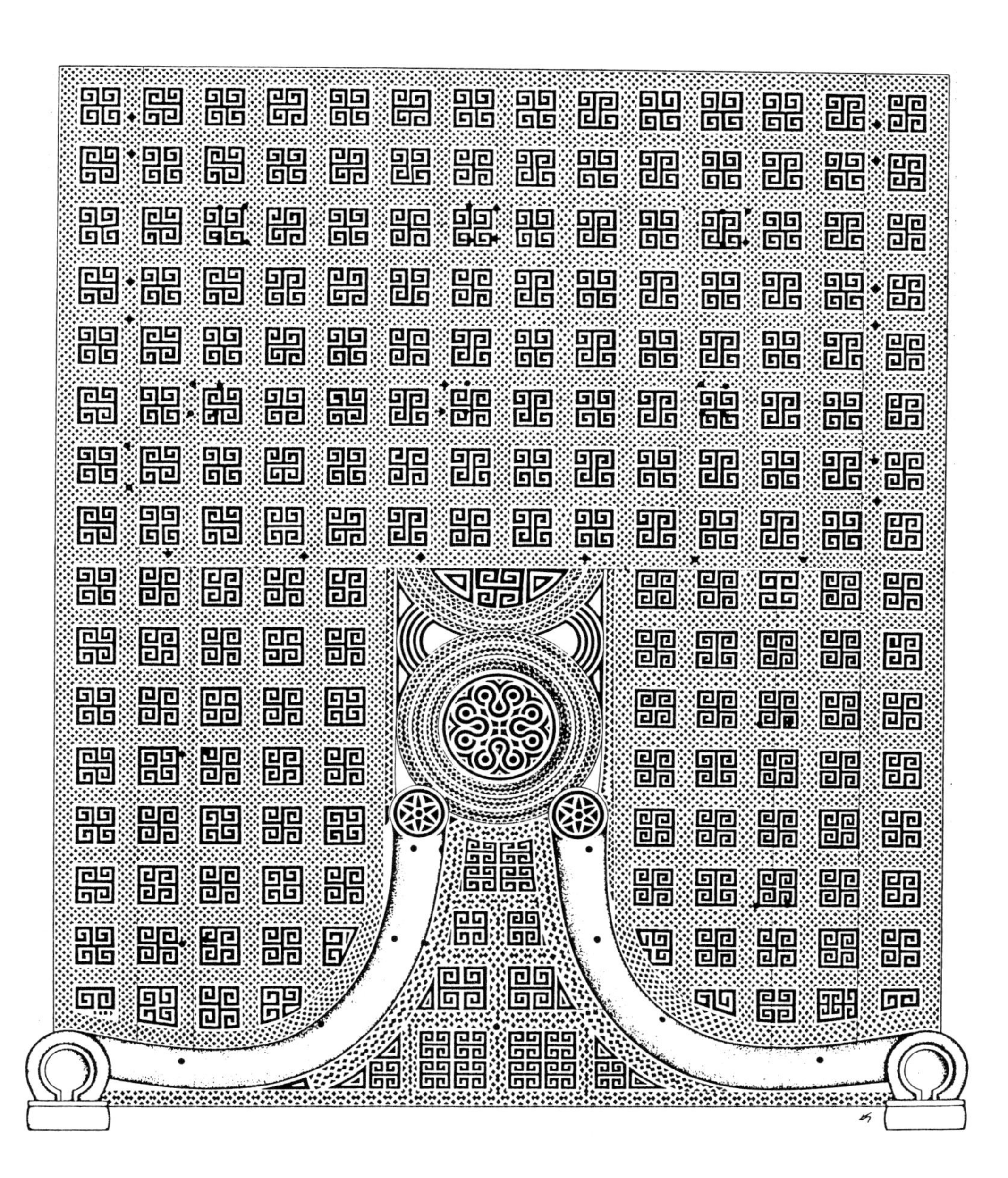

Ill. 452 (right): Furniture fragment from Gordion; Phrygian, 8th century B.C. (according to Young).

In addition to the swastika motifs, the medallion-like Kotshak cross is worthy of special note.

medallion of the decorative inlay work on the furniture fragment from Gordion[245] (ill. 452). From the Urartians and Phrygians the chain of traditional designs leads directly to the collection of designs of the Christian Oriental Church (ills. 55, 56). No evidence has yet been found to suggest a transfer of designs to the region of central Asia at a time before Christ. It is, in fact, not likely to have happened.

Cross shapes in general, and those of the basic form type E in particular, emerge for the first time in central Asia in connection with Christianization. Thus they justify the assumption that such cruciforms were, in the case of the Mongols, only of Christian, or, more usually, Nestorian origin. In fact, this is all the more likely considering that during the 13th century the majority of the tribes were adherents of the Christian-Nestorian faith (cf. pp. 152 ff.). This is especially the case of the crosses depicted on shields (ill. 453), in which Brüggemann detects 'tribal symbols of some Oghuz tribes.' We must remember that the Nestorians knew only the 'cross of victory', and that it was with the support of Armenians that the Nestorian General Ketboga of the Mongols conquered Baghdad![246]

Carpets containing the 'Memling gul' come from the Armenian weaving centres throughout the Caucasus and from central and western Anatolia as well. What is

وتوغل من هناك الى بلاد الهند حتى انتهى الى بلدة قنوج وارض القندهار وحدود كشمير وعاد على تلك الجهة وهادن ملوك الهند وصالحهم ورضي منهم بذلك ومن بعده لم يتجاوز احد من المجاهدين والغزاة حدود كابل الى حين ظهور دولة الترك واستيلائهم على غزنة واهتمام ناصر الدين سبكتكين بسياساتهم وتجريد همته وحميته لغزو الهند ومن بعده يمين الدولة محمود فانه جد واجتهد واهتم لمحاربتهم واحتشد وتجرد لقتالهم وغزواتهم وفتوحه مشهورة ونكاياته فيهم مدونة مسطورة ودهلي من بلاد الهند هي في الشرف وعلو المكانة بمثابة القلب من الجسد والمواضع الباقية بمنزلة الاعضاء والان فجميع سكانها مسلمون ذووا عتقاد صحيح وقد اعتادوا الغزو والجهاد وهواؤها وماؤها وارضها في غاية الصحة والموافقة للابدان وعسكرها المجاهد والمرابط زيادة على ثلثمائة الف وعرضها فسيحة جدا وهي من اشهر البلدان بحسب ما قرر المشاهدون لها وما ذكره الشيخ ابو الريحان في كتابه ان الشخص اذا تجاوز الطرف الفاصل بين خراسان والهند وعبر هذه المياه الخمس الكبار اعني ماء السند . وماء جيلم وماء الهاوور . وماء سلوب . وماء ساج . على هذا الموجب . بسان . جبل جود . بلاهور . كوجه . سودره . لوهاوور . جالندر . حدكوكر جوب مولتان . احه حاسى . سرستى كيل . سنام بتربده . سامانه . محنير . كهران . الوور . فاذا توغل السائر من طرف دهلي الى نواحي الهند على هذا المنوال عوص بدرون كره منكبور بهار ستركك سلحت لكنوت وكل واحد من هذه البلاد مشتمل على ضياع كثيرة وقرى متعددة وقلاع حصينة وقصبات متنوعة ونواحي معمورة تجاوز الحد والحصر والعدد

ذكر

ولادة سديو وتعديد ملوك الذين كانوا قبل السلطان محمود

زعم عباد الاصنام من الهندان باسديو في مجيه الادنى جاء بصورة الانسان في وقت كثرة الجبابرة في الارض وامتلاء العالم بالظلم والجور والعدوان واستخرابه بالبغي والظلم وكثرة الجور وظهر باسديو ببلدة ماهورة من اخت كنش الذي كان حاكما بذلك المقام وهم كانوا من جنس جاث اصحاب المواشي وطبقة شودر وكنش من طريق التنجيم والتقويم هو الذي هلاكه يكون على يد باسديو وفي وقت وضع الحمل وكل القابلة على اخته حتى يحمل المولود حال ما يولد الى كنش فيقتله ذكرا كان او انثى الى ان ولد بينهند رفسلمه الى شخص وامر باخفائه ثم من بطنه السادس وجد باسديو في ليلة مطيرة والقمر في منزلة او هي كان على درجة الطالع ثم ان باسديو سرقه ابوه من الجماعة بسبب نوم ثقيل غلب عليهم حتى ابطل حواسهم ثم اخفاه في موضع هو اصطبل البقر وهو قريب من ماهورة وبينهما نهر جون ثم بدله ابوه بنت كندلان ولادتها اتفقت في تلك الساعة فسلمها ابوه اليهم عوضا عن باسديو فتسلمها الوالي فلما اخرجت البنت اخته وطارت في الهواء وسلم باسديو الى دايته خونتا طلع كنش على هذه الحال وما زال يفكر في الكيد والمكر لبلوغ غرضه وكان ينعكس عليه ويعود اليه مكره الردي الى ان بلغ باسديو حد البلوغ فطلبه كنش من ابيه وامه حتى يصارعه وانف كنش من مصارعته في الملا بين الناس فطلب الحلوة واراد ان يهلكه بالسم او بلسع الافاعي والحيات فعاد البلاء الى كنش وهلك واجلس باسديو بعده على تخت مملكته لكنش ليكون من اجله قائما مقامه وفي كل شهر كانوا يسمونه باسم جميل وافتتحوا الشهر منكهر وفي الحادي عشر من كل شهر من اجل خروجه في ذلك اليوم جمو ساهوده واستولى على ملك باسديو واخرجه منه فمضى الى باسديو الى البحر وتحصن بقلعة باروى دهبية بقرب الساحل وسكن هناك وعمل الاولاد عمه الذي كان سلطان قنوج وكان بينهم حديث راجا جيد ستر وهو اشجعهم . وشهادبوه وبهيمسين . ونكل . وكان معهم سبعة من الشوهني وكانت الخصوم قوية وحاربوا حرباً باسديكا

جنگ باندوان و کیرو

Ill. 454 (right): LV & A no. 397–1880; 267 x 109 cm. Victoria and Albert Museum, London.

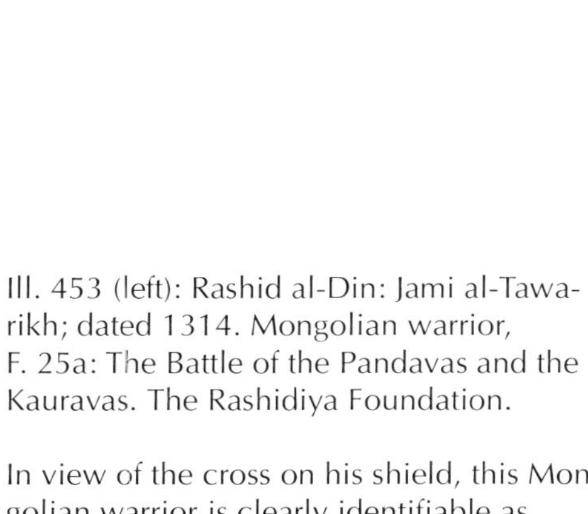

Ill. 453 (left): Rashid al-Din: Jami al-Tawarikh; dated 1314. Mongolian warrior, F. 25a: The Battle of the Pandavas and the Kauravas. The Rashidiya Foundation.

In view of the cross on his shield, this Mongolian warrior is clearly identifiable as Christian. Of the tribes of Genghis Khan, the Kereit, Naiman, Ongut and portions of the Karakhitai were adherents of the Christian-Nestorian faith. In 1258 Ketboga, a Nestorian Mongol general, took Baghdad with the help of the Armenians.

Ill. 455 (page 323): North Armenia, 196 x 156 cm. Private collection.

Octagons containing majestic Kotshak crosses have been worked into exceptionally clear stepped crosses. The negative areas clearly show the arrangement of the tiles.

Ill. 456 (page 324): Anatolia, 191 x 128 cm. Reiner Grünzner, Schloss Ehningen.

Ill. 457 (page 325): Anatolia, 211 x 147 cm. Private collection.

Ill. 456: Here the double-medallion coffer type from the 17th through the 19th centuries is represented, whereas in ill. 457 – despite the similarity in the layout – we have a segment from a Greek cross-stepped cross composition.

Ill. 458 (page 326): South-western Persia, 168 x 116 cm. Auktionshaus Dr. Fritz Nagel, Stuttgart (296/3175).

Ill. 459 (page 327): South-western Persia, 181 x 136 cm. Auktionshaus Dr. Fritz Nagel, Stuttgart (306/3425).

Often in the Persian examples the stepped cross takes on the role of a central medallion.

astounding is that until the latter part of the 19th century these carpets demonstrate a constancy of design that corresponds, quite accurately, to the models in the paintings of the 15th century. The trade name for late Caucasian examples is 'Kasak' or 'Gendje', for those from central Anatolia 'Konya', and examples from western Anatolia are bought and sold under the name 'Manyas'.

Iten-Maritz[247] associated the carpets he classified as Manyas with the Circassians, who were Christian until the end of the 18th century. They come from the north-eastern slope of the Great Caucasus and were persistent in offering resistance to the Russian conquest. Large segments of the population emigrated to Anatolia, settling in particular in the regions of Bergama, Cannakkale, Sindirgi, Manyas and Kars. Unfortunately, it has not yet been possible to ascribe carpets to the Circassians which were produced prior to the Armenian massacres. In actual fact, the author was told with overwhelming consistency that, while the Circassians had always produced embroidered goods, they had not, even during earlier periods, knotted carpets. These, it was explained, had been acquired from the Armenians from time immemorial.

Group C V b: Step-Form Cross Carpets

There are a number of carpets which are not, unlike the Memling guls, complemented by hooks. Most of them are of more recent date. An especially archaic example can be seen in ill. 455: a carpet with a composition analogous to Group B II. Within the diamond-crosses there are unusually clear and expressive 'Kotshak crosses' such as were discussed in the preceding section. In the opinion of Professor Wahram Tatikian, this carpet originated in Gugark, in the northern part of Armenia, north-west of Lake Sevan. In its conservative use of colour, it functions as a link to carpets produced in the provinces of Turkmenia.

Single step-form crosses likewise adorn examples that have taken their place in the literature as 'cross medallion Konagkend', Bergama, Qashqai or Afshar carpets. All of these grew out of the Armenian tradition which the emigrants transposed into their new areas of settlement. Illustrations 456–459 present carpets from different centres of production without commentary.

Step-form crosses occur in a grid-like surface pattern in carpets which Eder refers to as 'Baku'. For her the step-form cross is a 'stepped diamond', which, however, in its cruciform has hardly anything in common with a diamond[248] (ill. 460 shows step-form crosses in the ground enclosing a panel of 'Memling-gul diamonds'). According to Professor Tatikian in Erivan, these carpets do not come from Baku, but rather from the Armenian province of Sisian. We also find step-form crosses in carpets referred to as 'Beluch', particularly among those using the symmetrical knot (ills. 462–464). Although this group of carpets was until recently still being knotted by Christians in south-western Anatolia and south-western Persia, there is also a connection to those produced in southern Persia and in the border region between Persia and Afghanistan. A number of weavers who show the ethnic mix we call Beluch see their home in what today is northwestern Syria and the southern region of the Taurus. The question as to whether in this group we are dealing with those who, at the end of the 14th century, fled to southern Persia, in the region of Shiraz, in the face of the advancing Timurid armies – some being forced into eastern Persia (Meshed) and Afghanistan (south of Herat) along the way – or with those who were forced by Shah Abbas to settle in the region of Kabul, cannot presently be answered. In any case, this constitutes an important part of what we refer to as the 'southern route' in the migration of designs.

Ill. 460 (page 328): Eastern Caucasus, 147 x 118 cm. Auktionshaus Dr. Fritz Nagel, Stuttgart (273/141).

This specimen, much like examples from early Irish illuminated manuscripts, shows a carpet within a carpet. Though a special form of Memling gul, filled with diamond-form crosses, in the central field it is framed by a stepped (light) cross border.

Ill. 461 (page 329): Eastern Persia/Baluchistan, 145 x 93 cm. Private collection.

Carpets from Baluchistan are rarely as well defined as this one, which shows a diamond-form cross on a white ground decorating the middle.

Ill. 463 (above): Eastern Persia/Baluchistan, 130 x 96 cm. Private collection.

This carpet uses the cross from its border to fill the field, the white dots in each case marking the centres of the crosses.

Ill. 462 (left): Eastern Persia/Baluchistan, 167 x 78 cm (symmetrical knots). Private collection.

The three carpets illustrated here belong to the most important group of this region. Common to each of them is the strongly expressive cross border. The archaic step-form cross design of ill. 462 calls to mind the depictions in examples from the illustrated manuscripts of the 12th to the 14th centuries. Illustrations 463 and 464, on the other hand, still show the connection to Groups B II, C III and C V d.

Ill. 464 (above): Eastern Persia/Baluchistan, 180 x 113 cm. Private collection.

The 'Mushwani' design is formed here by three diamond-form crosses. A comparison with ills. 474 and 480 clearly demonstrates their virtual concurrence in development and their close relationship to the carpets of Group C V d.

Ill. 465 (right): Eastern Persia/Baluchistan, private collection.

The archaic example, too, is referred to as 'Mushwani'. Its composition as well as the cross stars in the octagons are still visible enough to make the connection to Group B II and also to Group C V d quite obvious.

Group C V c: Dragon Carpets

The best-known group of diamond or step-form cross carpets are without a doubt the dragon carpets. In approaching these from examples based on the latest stage of development – and strangely enough these are always referred to as the earliest – we would hardly suspect their origin within Group C V.[249]

Here, at the beginning of this development, we can again place the frequently-cited Mevl. no. 860/861/1033 (ill. 249), which we discussed in Group B I. It stands alongside carpets from the 13th through the 15th centuries which we are familiar with from depictions such as those in ills. 143/147, 170 and 172. Within a latticework of diamonds we find diamonds or step-form crosses of varying designs. Although the immediate forerunner of the dragon carpet has as yet not been found, we can arrive at a hypothetical approximation of it by freely combining the sum of the possibilities we have thus far seen. Few examples have survived, the largest of which is certainly that said to be located in the Art Museum of Chicago.[250/251] A smaller, perhaps even somewhat earlier example – a segment from the endless repeat – is to be found in a private collection[252] (ill. 466). A row of diamonds determines the structure, such that at each narrow end two half-diamonds complement the surface. The designs used to fill the central diamonds are complex. A look at the Van Eyck carpet from ills. 171 and 172 should serve to facilitate our understanding. What was there first strictly geometrical in design has in the Chicago carpet become floral, and this in the same way that the cross was made equal to or exchanged for the 'tree of Jesse'. This is especially the case for the centre. In the upper and lower halves of the diamonds there are green step-form cross halves on a red ground; 'palmette' half-crosses are inscribed in these. The shape of this 'palmette' is worthy of note because its design is only to be found during the time span from just before the end of the 15th to the beginning of the 16th century. The main border contains the very same design of the 'tree of Jesse' that we have already seen in MBN no. 10/294 from Group B II (ills. 250/251, 308), the added difference here being that this appears mirrored (ill. 310) so that a cross is formed in the middle. Even the secondary borders are rare, early forms of those repeatedly encountered in Group C IV. The outer secondary border contains one of the frame ornaments typical of Armenian illumination, and the one most frequently used. It has been part of the Armenian basic collection of designs since the 12th century. Out of this design grew the later 'crenellated borders'. It should not be left unmentioned that the diamond repeat of the large diamond on a yellow ground now visible was developed by consolidating into one what were once four diamonds, and furthermore, that the two rows with cross-stars now present were once the points of intersection of a latticework of diamonds as is shown in the carpet representation in the Van Eyck painting (ill. 172). This will be important in the context of the crossflower carpets yet to be discussed (ill. 466 ff.). At this juncture, suffice it to say that this compositional scheme is, in turn, identical with that of the SP-Holbein carpets (ill. 360 ff.), in which all of the cross-stars form the points of intersection.

Although MMA no. 56.217, the 'Nigde carpet'(ill. 467), came later in this evolution, it also shows, presumably as a consequence of its size, other cross-stars in the remaining rows. The palmettes in the green step-form crosses are important for our comparison. They have become harsher, stiffer, more strictly geometric. The centres of the differently coloured diamonds, their grounds being red, white, yellow and blue, have been dissolved, such that two 'cloud-band' half-crosses surround a palmette cross. This composition is to some extent related to the arabesque crosses of the SP-Holbein carpets (ill. 386).

Ill. 466 (page 333): Private collection, 197 x 145 cm.

This carpet shows no more than a very small segment from a larger composition, to be found in a nearly identical fashion in the larger carpet (785 x 275 cm) of the former Prince-Roman-Sanguszko-Collection, and later in the Art Institute of Chicago (now missing).

Ill. 467 (left): MMA no. 56.217, the 'Nigde carpet', 752 x 305 cm. Metropolitan Museum of Art, New York. Gift of J.V. McMullan.

Ill. 468 (left): The Keir Collection, 469 x 223 cm.

This, the earliest of the classic 'dragon carpets', is also one of the most beautiful.

Ill. 469 (left): Private collection,
438 x 213 cm.

The white ground lends even more clarity to the compositional scheme.

Ill. 470 (right): Dumbarton Oaks Collection, no. 8, 472 x 226 cm.

The carpet is dominated by depictions in the diamonds of the 'tree of Jesse', these having completely replaced the cruciforms.

There is little separating the Nigde carpet from the so-called dragon carpet. The earliest of this latter type known to the present author is quite possibly that of the Keir Collection[253] (ill. 468). Like almost all of the early carpets of this genre, it resorts to the old diamond system mentioned above with the four-part division of the central diamond of its predecessors. The large diamonds are distinguished by what were once differently coloured connecting cross pieces in the sense of the Van Eyck carpet depictions. As a result of the overlap of the two colour systems, greenish blue and white in the Keir carpet, the old, more intricate diamond system is recreated. In the oldest examples, the well-known cross-stars of the forerunners are replaced, with the exception of (at the most) five stars which remain, by the symbol of the 'tree of Jesse' (ill. 309). This applies to carpets in the private collections of Keir, Wher, Burrell, H.T. Hallowell III., and to those in the Vienna Museum, the Textile Museum in Washington and the TIEM. More recent examples, however, do not even exhibit these cross-stars. This can even be the case with carpets that have in fact kept the colour system of the Keir piece, such as the beautiful example on a white ground found in private ownership[254] (ill. 469).

The next obvious question concerns the origin of the 'dragon' designs. If we consider what is without a doubt the oldest example, the Keir carpet, comparing it with the Nigde piece, it would appear that the 'dragons' have been achieved simply by rotating the so-called 'cloud-bands' by 180 degrees. The dragons do bear a strong resemblance to these. The author assumes this to mean that from the cloud-band-like half-crosses, S-shaped symbols developed. The question is whether, then, with reference to these S-shaped symbols, we are really dealing with 'dragons'. It was probably F. R. Martin who initiated the term 'dragon carpet', although he did not use it himself.[255] On the one hand he recognized that he was looking at Armenian products, yet in the 'dragons' he saw only Chinese models.

During the period from 1895 to 1908, however, Martin was able to settle the question as to the origin of the 'dragon carpets'. He determined that they had not come from Kuba, but rather from the districts of Van and Sivas, and he arrived at this conclusion before 1908.[255] The special significance of this date is that it is prior to 1915, the year of the great Armenians massacre. In 1922 both Kendrick and Tattersall concurred with Martin. What must ultimately be considered unfounded doubts about the results of Martin's research were voiced by the carpet dealer Heinrich Jacoby and go back to the year 1923.[256] His doubts were presumably based on the new situation created in Turkey by the genocide visited upon the Armenians in 1915, as well as on what was largely ignorance of the historical facts. Jacoby's statements, however, provided the basis for the article by Arthur Upham Pope on 'The Myth of the Armenian Dragon Carpets,'[257] which appeared in 1925. Pope was very much the victim of Yule's confusing translation of the Marco Polo text, a translation which Erdmann later accepted, thus arriving at the completely erroneous conclusion (cf. discussion pp. 14 ff.) that the 'dragon carpets' were not produced in Armenia. It appears, then, that Pope was also responsible for the expression 'dragon carpet', intending, as he did, to rule out its production in Christian Armenia. After all, the European view of the dragon as evil would not consort well with a dragon of Christian origin. The placement of the 'dragon carpets' in the Armenian regions of the Van and Sivas districts concurs with the results of the present author's investigations from 1978 to 1985. It was only thereafter, beginning in December 1985, that the author had access to Martin's book confirming his opinion.

The issue of the dragon and its S-shapes as symbols for God in Armenian art was discussed on page 37 ff. The 'S' was often used interchangeably with the cross. It appears that its use increased at those times when pressure from outside did not permit the depiction of the cross. 'Dragon carpets' were seemingly produced during those times when the practice of enforced Islamization was intensified. It is for this

Ill. 471: BMIK no. I.2, 523 x 224 cm. SMPK, Museum für Islamische Kunst, Berlin.

The weavers involved in making this carpet drew on older models. The composition was preserved, as were the hares facing the tree of life within the hexagons – certainly relics of a much older tradition.

reason that only the early examples contain depictions of the cross, which were only subsequently replaced by the S-shapes – described as 'dragons' – and by the Armenian design of the 'tree of Jesse'.

In the evolution of these carpets one criterion has already been mentioned: the existence, in the early examples, of cross-stars, and the uniform use of colour in the frames surrounding the large diamonds. The composition of early examples always presents a segment of 'endless repeat' much like that found in the 'Nigde carpet' or its forerunners. The next step is the partial or complete loss of the cross-stars and a colour change in the surrounding lanceolate leaves independent of the large diamond-form composition. In this context, examples in the following collections must be mentioned: Cittone,[258] Thyssen,[259] Dumbarton Oaks[260] (ill. 470) and also the Washington Textile Museum.[261] Finally, the segment is reduced in size, such that what was formerly a large diamond now extends across the width of the panel. Examples of this are found in the Rietberg Museum of Zurich[262] and the Washington Textile Museum.[263] Concurrent with this, the other individual details degenerate beyond all recognition.

This can also happen with carpets that have kept the early compositional scheme, as for example the 'Graf carpet'[264] (ill. 472). This carpet is attributed to the 15th century by most authors. Karabacek even argued for the 13th(!)[265]. Though it may be an important carpet in terms of the thickness of its weave, the quality of its yarn and its former colourfulness, it is a very late variant in the historical development of Group C V c. Moreover, it stands outside the main group along with a few other carpets, an older one of which is located in West Berlin[266] (ill. 471), and a more recent one in the Washington Textile Museum.[267] What makes the carpet in Berlin interesting are the hexagons inlaid in the small diamonds, one or two in each row. In each of these we find two differently coloured hares, turned inward, facing a tree of life.[268]

The carpet in Washington is stranger. It has been enlivened with 'domestic animals', making its use as a sacred object unlikely. Seeing horses, goats, dogs, geese, cocks and doves (?), one might be tempted to think of Noah's Ark; and yet in this case it is more likely that by this time the passage of the old meaning from one generation to the next had already ceased. The carpet bears an inscription of the date, which has been read variously – as shown in the following: AH 1001 (AD 1592), AH 1101 (AD 1689) or AH 1201 (AD 1786). Charles Grant Ellis dates this carpet, along with the 'Graf' piece, to the 19th century.[269] This last date accords well with the evolution over time of both designs and borders. For these same reasons the present author proposes the late 17th or early 18th century for the Berlin carpet, and the end of the 18th century for the 'Graf' example.

The carpets just mentioned come at the end of an evolution, which is to say, most carpets within the group are to be dated earlier. Both the borders, as well as the details of the panel design, would suggest that the forerunners (private collection [ill. 466] and Chicago [??]) should be assigned to the late 15th or the early 16th century.[270] Accordingly, the Nigde carpet would be datable to the middle or latter part of the 16th century, and examples similar to the Keir carpet to the end of the 16th century. The majority of the classic examples probably originated during the 17th century, and those that underwent simplification toward the end of this period. The degeneration in composition and detail is not likely to have begun before the 18th century.

Without exception, the carpets represented in Group C V c originated in the northern settlements of West Armenia, located between the districts of Van and Sivas. This was once the most extensive region of the Ottoman Empire.

Ill. 472 (right): BOIM no. I.3, the 'Graf' dragon carpet; originally 678 x 230 cm, largely destroyed by fire during the War. Shown here is a section 320 x 230 cm. What is left is located in the Islamisches Museum der Staatlichen Museen zu Berlin (according to Sarre/Trenkwald).

For many the 'Graf' dragon carpet was the most beautiful and the earliest of its kind. From the perspective of our evolution of designs it is a very late and degenerate specimen, making it next to impossible to divine its actual layout.

Group C V d: Flowering-Cross Carpets – Sunburst Carpets

The origins of the entire group of flowering-cross carpets must be found in the 1500s, yet to date the author has not seen one from this time. Hypothetically, we could see their forerunners as a mixture of the Nigde carpet and the SP-Holbein carpet. There are only very few examples from the 1600s or earlier that seem to shed light on the original designs and their interrelatedness. One is shown in ill. 473.[271] The former composition is still quite easy to make out on the red ground. With reference to the Nigde carpet (ill. 467) or the Stuttgart Holbein carpet (ill. 360), the cross-stars and Holbein guls, respectively, have here been changed into flowering crosses on a white ground, and the large diamond or arabesque crosses have found their equivalents in the floral diamond-shaped flowery light-symbol crosses.

The grid of diamonds which makes up the overall composition in the slightly later example from the Washington Textile Museum TMW R 36.2.3[272] (ill. 474) is even clearer. This carpet has already taken on the format of the dragon carpets and has worked the particularly beautiful central flower light-symbol cross on white ground into something like a central medallion. Similar to this is the fragment TIEM no. 28, which further restricts the vertical segment of the composition in a way analogous to the development of the dragon carpets.[273] Similarly, there are other carpets and fragments that are generally restricted in the number of large diamonds they employ. Thus, depending on their length, there may be one or two or more diamonds with two halves at the top and the bottom. Each of these will be filled with different cruciform flower designs. The large diamonds have been compressed into the shape of octagons and framed, as in the case of the dragon carpets – not, however, by elegant lanceolar leaves, but instead by strips curved at the ends, in which we see the veins of leaves, herring-bone-like in appearance. We find early examples in Boston,[274] and with Sailer,[275] both consisting of elements from TMW R 36.2.3 (ill. 474), though composed differently. A continuation of this development can be observed in one of private ownership[276] (ill. 479 a, b). Here the centre is made up of an extraordinarily powerful and clear flowery light-symbol cross, which can be considered the prototype of the later 'Eagle Kasaks'. In the TIEM there are numerous fragments that should be mentioned at this point[277], as for example, TIEM no. 896, 897, 898, 55, 944 and 726.

The breadth of variation found in the flowering-cross carpets of the 17th and 18th centuries is virtually limitless. If we compare TMW R. 36.2.1[278] (ill. 475) with ills. 473 and 474, we clearly see the potential. The large, diamond-shaped flowery, light-symbol crosses have changed their shape to such an extent that we literally have to look for them in the new composition, whereas the small cruciform flowers on white ground have increased in size, becoming more important for these carpets. The border as well shows a further development of the one found above. Again, it is the geometric leaves of the palmette which indicate the later date of production. The early dragon carpet from the Museum of Fine Arts in Boston demonstrates an interesting intermediate version of this border.[279]

Ill. 473 (page 343): Private collection, 347 x 261 cm.

A very unusual example that makes it possible to reconstruct how it relates, in terms of development to Groups B I, C I and C II.

What Ellis has referred to as the 'Vase Carpet' of the Keshishian Collection[280] (ill. 477) also belongs in the series of carpets from the 17th century outlined here, despite the fact that its overall impression seems quite different. Other carpets to be included here are also TMW R 36.2.2, TMW R 36.2.5, TMW R 36.2.13/14, TIEM no. 831, TIEM no. 126, TIEM no. 724 or TIEM no. 174. A carpet from the 16th/17th century in the Ethnographic Museum of Armenia in Sardarabad/Hoktemberian conveys a

Ill. 474 (left): TMW no. R 36.2.3, 565 x 237 cm. Textile Museum, Washington.

Ill. 475 (right): TMW no. R 36.2.1, 458 x 239 cm. Textile Museum, Washington.

By comparing ill. 474 with ill. 475, it becomes quite apparent to what extent designs can change once the composition they were based on is no longer intelligible.

Ill. 476 (left): Sardarabad-Hoktemberian, Ethnographic Museum of Armenia, 283 x 108, from Van.

The tone of this carpet is set by three large, vivid crosses. In the illustrations to follow, this same motif will undergo variation, appearing finally as a field design. The outer secondary border is not visible, having either been left off or sewn over.

Ill. 477 (right): Harold M. Keshishian Collection, 640 x 244 cm.

completely different impression[281] (ill. 476). Here, in this carpet we see what may well be the most beautiful and most striking of flowering crosses. From here the development continues to the flowering-cross carpets of the southeastern region of Anatolia. These are floral carpets with 'Afshan' designs, as seen in examples in the Historical Museum in Erivan,[282] in St. Louis,[283] in Washington[284] and in Sardarabad[285] (ill. 478, from Aintap). The carpet in Vienna[286] represents a transitional design linking it to the Armenian provinces more to the north.

Ill. 478 (page 348): Sardarabad-Hoktemberian, Ethnographic Museum of Armenia, 650 x 250 cm, from Aintap (Gaziantep), detail.

This variant, which fills the entire surface area, is referred to as the Awshan design.

The carpet in ill. 105[287] (ill. 479 b), shown by Erdmann as from the latter part of the 17th century, joins several variants of the flowering-cross carpet, that is to say those framed with those not framed. The latter in this combination were to become typical of the 18th century. In this connection we must mention the truly great examples from the McMullan[288] (ill. 481), the Wher,[289] and the Vakiflar[290] Collections, and from the collection of the Museum of Fine Arts in Boston[291], as well as the fragments from the TIEM[292] and many, many others.

Ill. 479 a (above left): Private collection, 372 x 178 cm.

Ill. 479 b (above right): Private collection, 355 x 200 cm.

Ill. 480 a (above left): 'Gohar carpet', 351 x 178 cm. Owned privately.

In view of its Armenian inscription, we can conclude that this carpet, dated 1680, was a votive gift to a church.

Ill. 480 b (above right): Privately owned, 266 x 155 cm. Reiner Grünzner, Schloss Ehningen.

Of special significance in this context is the 'Gohar carpet' (ill. 480 a), dated 1680 and bearing an Armenian inscription. Thus, on the one hand, this carpet offers a valuable reference for dating as well as a clue as to it purpose:[293]

"I, Gohar, sinful and sick in my soul, made this carpet with my own hands. Let anyone who reads this pray for me that I might be forgiven. 1129 (AD 1680)"

The carpet is obviously a votive gift, as was customary in this time throughout the Christian world, the only difference here being that it is a carpet. Carpets in the Transylvanian churches were also frequently votive gifts,[294] which gives us reason to assume that the 'Gohar carpet' is not the only one of its kind (cf. also ill. 553).

Ill. 481 (right): MMA no. 1970.302.10, 653 x 183 cm. Metropolitan Museum of Art, New York. Gift of J .V. McMullan, 1970.

The carpets shown in ills. 479a-481 demonstrate the development from more rigidly defined diamonds at the beginning of the 17th century to their dissolution during the 18th century. The so-called 'eagle-Kasaks' come at the close of this group's development; they generally contain only between one and three large light-symbol crosses in the ground.

Flowering-cross carpets are presumed to come from the Dukedom of Artzakh in the region of Karabagh, which is in central Armenia. It does appear, however, that in addition to the Armenian centres around Aintep and Mardin in southeastern Anatolia, carpets with related compositional features were also produced, both in the West Armenian areas of settlement of central and western Anatolia as well as in the Persian areas of East Armenia around Isfahan/New Julfa, Herat and the Fars region (the area of Qashqai and Afshari). In Persia this has certainly been the case since the beginning of the 17th century.

Group C V e: Ghirlandaio Carpets

Although we can assume that all the cross diamond or flowering-cross carpets can be traced back to related basic designs within the same chain of traditional designs, they begin to take on a wide range of different appearances from as early as the 15th century . One of these, already published by Lessing in 1877,[295] is the carpet which Domenico Ghirlandaio, in 1480, depicts spread at the feet of the Virgin Mary in his painting 'Enthroned Madonna' (ill. 482). The field of the carpet contains two complete diamonds, placed one after the other, into each of which has been worked a complicated cross-star composition. We recognize the main border from our discussion of the SP-Holbein carpets of Group C II and see its correspondence to Type C II b_1 (ill. 366). Another feature worthy of attention is the clearly recognizable inner secondary border of the Armenian 'S'-designs. Though they are not relevant to this context, we should also take note of the flowers in the vase intended for the Virgin Mary: lilies, roses, carnations and hyacinths. These will be of importance later when we discuss the 'arch-form carpets' of Group C XII.

A carpet of the kind depicted by Ghirlandaio has, to this day, not been found. There are, however, a number of closely related carpets. The earliest, and very likely the most beautiful as well, is owned privately[296] (ill. 483). Here too, as in the case of the Ghirlandaio carpet, two diamonds fill the field like a segment from an endless repeat. The dark bluish-green ground, on which we find red and white cross-star rosettes, brings to mind the 'system of cross pieces' found in the 'Van Eyck carpets' (ills. 170, 172), the only difference being that here it is in negative. We are also reminded of the composition of the somewhat later dragon carpets, and there are doubtless also parallels to be found with the examples of Group B II. The diamond motif here can also be interpreted as a cosmogram. Around the centre, a cross-rosette in two colours, also known as 'Talish rose' and part of the Armenian collection of designs since Urartian times, there are octagonal stripes of varying colours and widths. These depict the heavenly spheres inset in the quadrant of the earth. This square is then complimented and extended on each of its sides, the four cardinal points, through the use of the complicated cross arms of the Ghirlandaio composition, each becoming finally a diamond-cross. The same half or quarter crosses fill the step-form cross halves in the negative areas of the diamonds. The carpet is enclosed by the border type C II e_1 (ill. 380), the leaf-form cross border, which, as described before, grew out of a combination of two contiguous parts of the basic form type B (ill. 22). This carpet may well have originated during the 15th century. No decision can yet be made as to whether it is or is not older than the one depicted in the Ghirlandaio painting.

This carpet is followed by a series of carpets that can be distinguished by how the central octagons are filled and by the borders. Brüggemann[297] illustrates a carpet which was displayed in Frankfurt and Essen, and in which a beautiful, clear Greek

Ill. 482: Domenico Ghirlandaio: Enthroned Madonna; middle of the 15th century. Galleria degli Uffizi, Florence.

Here, as in ill. 448, we see a vase with the floral symbols of the Virgin Mary placed on the carpet which lies at her feet.

cross fills the octagons. The border is made up of a combination of Greek crosses and halved knotted-crosses[298] which, like the Kotshanak border' (ill. 384), has an unusual appearance as a result of the colour change in its negative areas.

A further example is a carpet illustrated by L. Coen,[299] the border of which certainly does not permit assignment to the 19th, but rather to the 16th century. In this case the quadrants of the earth are filled with a late form of the 'Gloria Crucis' (Group B II).

Whereas the carpets cited in the preceding section exhibited two diamonds, there are examples such as those in the McMullan Collection,[300] in which one diamond virtually incorporates the function of a central medallion. While MMA no. 1972.80.12, despite the green colour of its ground and the position in Group C I of

Ill. 483 (left): Owned privately, 250 x 146 cm.

The border recalls the early field designs in ills. 147 and 175.

Ill. 484: Owned privately: world cosmogram from ill. 483.

Ill. 485: MMA no. 1974.149.23: world cosmogram from ill. 488.

Ill. 486: MMA no. 1972.80.12., 171 x 147 cm. Detail world cosmogram. Metropolitan Museum of Art, New York. Gift of J.V. McMullan.

Ill. 487: BMIK no. 85.819, light-symbol cross variants from ill. 490.

Ill. 488: MMA no. 1974.149.23., 159 x 132 cm. Metropolitan Museum of Art, New York. Gift of J.V. McMullan.

Ill. 489: Cathedral of St. Catherine, Sion, 227 x 138 cm.

Ill. 490 (left): BMIK no. 85.819, 327 x 185 cm. SMPK, Museum für Islamische Kunst, Berlin.

Whereas all other known examples make use of the 1-2-3 medallion type, here Ghirlandaio diamond-form crosses fill the ground in a tile-like manner.

Ill. 491 (right): Owned privately; 226 x 150 cm.

These are Ghirlandaio diamond-form crosses as well, though of a later design from the 17th/18th century.

Ill. 492 (left): Owned privately; 175 x 129 cm.

The time difference, in comparison to this example from the second part of the 19th century, is even clearer.

Ill. 493 (left): The former Pohlmann Collection, Berlin; 250 x 160 cm.

The 'Pohlmann carpet' is reminiscent of the central Armenian triple-medallion soumaks and must have originated at the beginning of the 16th century.

Ill. 494 (right): Auction, Galerie Koller, on 2.4.1985 in Zurich, no. 1320, 228 x 130 cm.

Despite the fact that the patterning in this carpet is somewhat less definite, its origin is only slightly later. The border here is also common to the 'SP-Holbein carpets' of Group C II.

its border, retains the field composition, showing only half of it, MMA no. 1974.149.23 (ill. 488) adopts structural elements from Group B II. This means that its spandrels are now no longer filled with four-part diamond-crosses, but rather with cross-star octagons which are closely related to several guls from Group C X such as C X HG a_2 (ill. 549). In the afore-mentioned carpet, MMA no. 1974.149.23, the Greek cross, found in the central octagon of its forerunners (ills. 484, 486), has been supplanted by the hooked 'Memling gul', the colours of which, however, allow only the step-form cross contained within it to be visually effective.

The carpet in ill. 489, discovered in 1980 in Sion,[301] offers a very interesting combination of different group elements. The middle of the inner panel consists of a Ghirlandaio diamond, while at each end cross-star octagons set into rectangles are framed in such a way that their border, together with that surrounding the rest of the design, forms the so-called 'keyhole' design. In this case, the carpet itself makes it perfectly clear that what we have is merely a design variation in the framing, to which no significance need necessarily be attached. The border corresponds to that of several carpets within Group B II. Similarities in detail can be found in the Ghirlandaio painting, thus making it possible to assume its production during the middle or latter part of the 15th century.

A carpet from the former Königliches Kunstgewerbemuseum in Berlin, now in the Museum für Islamische Kunst – no. 85.819 – should not be left unmentioned. As its field pattern it exhibits the Ghirlandaio diamond-crosses (ill. 487) ordered diagonally just like that found in small-pattern diamond-form compositions. Here the central squares have been filled with leaf light-symbol crosses similar to those in certain cross-star carpets from Group C IV (e.g. ill. 423). The border corresponds to the C III f_3-type (ill. 418). The tradition of the 'Ghirlandaio carpets', sometimes referred to as 'Bergama' or 'Cannakkale', extends all the way up to the beginning of this century. The examples mentioned above may well date from the 16th century or even earlier. One from the 17th century was exhibited in 1983 in the Sailer Gallery at Eggenberg Castle near Graz[302] (ill. 491) and a carpet from the 19th century, now owned privately (ill. 492), completes this series of development.

There are several other closely related carpets which do not actually fit in this series. The first of these, formerly part of the Pohlmann Collection in Berlin[303] (ill. 493), also contains the Ghirlandaio diamond-crosses in its centres. The composition, too, is identical to that of the early carpets from Group C V e. Yet, the layout of the diamonds strikes one as quite unusual. Crosses and the symbols of lilies extend into the diamonds from the negative area and provide the diamond with a light dental-band outline reminiscent of the central Armenian three medallion-soumaks. The colours of the Pohlmann example are unknown, but the carpet itself, judging from the black and white illustration, might have originated around 1500, despite certain weaknesses in its execution.

A carpet recently sold at an auction at the Koller Gallery[304] (ill. 494) is very closely related. It is quite similar to the one just discussed, though probably produced later, perhaps in the middle of the 16th century. The centre in each case is formed by a cross-star within an octagon cut apart by a band with three crosses. The border is of the C II d_3 type.

A later example in the TIEM,[305] which has been reduced even more, has the same border. What we may possibly be seeing here is a late form of the Ghirlandaio diamond-cross. These examples show smooth transitions to the late carpets of Group B II and subsequently to Group C VI.

The question remains as to where these carpets came from. Although it is difficult to propose western Anatolia as the origin of the first carpet from the above discussion, it is more than likely that the group originated in this area, perhaps even in the region of Cannakkale. The carpet depicted by Ghirlandaio, as well as a number of other examples dating from the 19th century, have S-secondary borders, indicating Armenian production. In fact, most of the design elements and symbols found in these carpets are part of what we have elsewhere referred to as the basic set of designs traditionally available to Armenian artisans. As we have already established, the number of Armenians living in the regions of western Anatolia was quite high. We must also remember that only as a result of the Ottoman presence in this part of the country did it first become possible for Armenians to settle and develop here. Bursa was the Armenian bishopric. It was in 1454 that the Armenian bishop, named patriarch of all Monophysites in Istanbul by Mehmed II, moved to Istanbul at Mehmed's wish.

Group C VI: Bergama Coffered-Form Carpets

To start with, let us examine a fragment, already discussed in the context of Group B II, from the Alanya Museum (ill. 495), which dates from the 15th century. The composition, identical to the centre of a piece yet to be discussed, the Viennese silk carpet (ill. 224) from Group C VII, presents an imposing Greek cross filled with the world-picture. This in turn is connected to the Holbein guls and cross-stars located in the cross beams by means of cross pieces such that within this cross yet another cross emerges.

This doubling up of crosses, a cross within a cross, makes one of these almost by necessity superfluous. As a consequence, the Greek cross is lost; the cross-star octagons in the corners move toward the centre of the field, as was the case with the carpet in the Istanbul exhibition of October 1984 (ill. 496), in which the old composition is still visible as a result of the space left between them. Then, however, both pairs of octagons move together to form panels above and below, something we saw with respect to a few of the later examples from Group B II. As other examples of this, let us here offer DIA no. 22.225 (ill. 497), TIEM no. 694 and no. 329 (ill. 498) – but also the carpet in the MMA from the McMullan Collection.[306] They must all date from the 16th century. The Kotshanak border, already discussed in connection with the SP-Holbein carpets of Group C II (ill. 384), is typical of the examples from the 17th and 18th centuries. We have also seen it in TIEM no. 329 (ill. 498). Illustrations 493, 494, 495 exhibit different designs of this border, all of which still quite clearly show, especially in the early examples, the original connection between the Kotshak cross and the cross-rosette, which harks back to the Urartian design tradition. (cf. ills. 384, 385).

During the 16th century there was a very strong tendency to produce medallion carpets; the carpets of this group (C VI) provide ideal conditions to satisfy this need. Consequently, if we simply dispense with these two panels – the one above, the other below, we create a central medallion carpet like Vakf. no. E 3 (ill. 503), the middle of which is filled by a slightly degenerate variant of the 'Lotto' gul (ills. 389, 390, 391).

This again raises the question as to the area of production. And although we cannot yet offer a definitive answer, there is nothing to be said against the area of western Anatolia as their place of origin, Bergama included.

Ill. 495 (right): Alanya no. 411,150 x 196 cm. Museum, Alanya.

A fragment made of exceptionally luxuriant wool and in its structure quite similar to the following Group C VII. There are also ties to the Amsterdam carpet in ill. 293.

Ill. 496 (below): Owned privately.

Here the composition is restricted to a central cross motif, in the corners of which we find S-symbols, with very distinct crosses filling the four corners of the field.

Ill. 497 (page 364): DIA no. 22.225; 182 x 141 cm. Detroit Institute of Arts, Detroit. A purchase of the city of Detroit.

This fragment could take its place at the end of the development of the LP-Holbein carpets in Group B II, with which it shares a common central medallion.

Ill. 498 (page 365): TIEM no. 329. Türk ve Islam Eserleri Müzesi, Istanbul.

The Kotshanak border and the gul designs in the narrow panels betray the closeness in time to Group C II.

Ill. 499: Private collection, 171 x 155 cm.

The structure of the preceding examples is kept, though it appears stiffer. In the central square it is still possible, despite the abundance of filler motifs, to discern the cross star.

Ill. 500 (right): TIEM no. 303, fragment 196 x 100 cm: Kotshanak border from a carpet in Group C II. Türk ve Islam Eserleri Müzesi, Istanbul.

Ill. 501 (right): Vakf. no. E 97: Kotshanak border.

Ill. 502 (right): LV & A no. 31–1956: Kotshanak border.

These three borders demonstrate very well one of the possible developments: the diamond-form cross from ill. 500 appears in ill. 501 still unchanged, though in ill. 502 it has been modified on one side. On the other hand, the former Urartian cross rosette in the later examples has been replaced by the cross-star throughout.

Ill. 503: Vakf. no. E 3, 165 x 136 cm. Vakiflar Carpet Museum, Istanbul.

Here, at the conclusion of this group, we have an example which has been reduced to a central medallion carpet. Its centre is decorated by a cruciform which, in turn, connects the arabesque cross to the Lotto gul.

Group C VII: Damascus/Mamluk Carpets II

In our treatment of Group B III we already referred to the earliest carpets of this group and the difficulty of classifying them geographically. Despite the results of Erdmann's research, the present author firmly believes in his own research and interpretation – that some of the early examples originated in East Armenia. The presence of S-borders are but one proof that the production centres were to be found in the Armenian settlements of Syria or Iraq. It has also been pointed out that ascribing production to this region by no means precludes the possibility that carpets of this sort might also have been made in Cairo. This is actually even probable for some of the more recent examples that have been dyed with cochineal.

Ill. 504 (page 369): TMW no. 1965.49.1, 210 x 220 cm; fragment. Textile Museum, Washington.
The border exhibits the coat-of-arms of Mamluk Sultan Qaitbay. In view of the fact that all the details are Christian, the carpet must have been a gift to the Sultan.

We must assume that the Mamluks had not only subsumed Palestine, Lebanon, Syria and the regions of Cilicia and Armenia Minor under their control, but also most of Mesopotamia. Just as Syrian glassmakers and metalworkers were brought from Mossul, weavers must also have been relocated from the invaded regions to the capital of Cairo – a practice which had been followed continually during the preceding centuries. And for this reason, we should not be surprised to find the fragment at the Textile Museum of Washington[307] (ill. 504), which contains the coat-of-arms of the Mamluk Sultan Qaitbay in its field. Strange as it may sound, the caliphs and sultans, whether Mamluk or Ottoman, were the guarantors for the existence of Monophystic minorities such as the Armenians. The Prophet Mohammed had already guaranteed the Armenians freedom of religion and rights at the holy places of Jerusalem, privileges that the Caliphs, Saladin and even the Mamluks confirmed.[308] In return, the Armenians showed them loyalty – something that the Ottomans in particular would greatly appreciate later.

The Mamluk Sultan Qaitbay was the temporal ruler of the Armenians living in this region. For this reason it is not unusual to find his coat-of-arms represented in this carpet. The most likely explanation for this is that the carpet was a gift. The decoration, in its entirety, is so Christian that even the possibility of its having been made to order seems remote.

The majority of the carpets in this group originated during the 15th century and most likely not in Egypt. Many of them are based on cross compositions, which include complex world-pictures. This is true of both BOIM no. 91.26[309] (ill. 506) as well as of the Viennese silk carpet (ill. 224), without question the most beautiful carpet of this group. Unfortunately, most of the illustrations found in the literature on this carpet only show segments, in which case the powerful central cross is not recognized for what it is. Despite the confusing variety of detail, this is resolved so that a surprisingly clear Greek cross emerges from the composition. An S-secondary inner border distinguishes even this carpet as an Armenian product.

Due to the unity achieved by its colourful appearance, its wide range of variation is less striking. With the exception of later carpets, probably produced in Egypt, like the one from the Palazzo Pitti,[310] the centre of the world-picture is a cross. Outwardly it can have a variety of different shapes: that of a Greek cross, as is the case in East Berlin or Boston;[311] a cross-star within a cross, as with the silk carpet, or with the example from the MMA (ill. 507); a cross-star by itself, as in Vienna[312] or with Cittone or, however, an unusual cross shape, as is found in the Poliaghi Collection[313] in Varese; or in the TMW (ill. 508), which combines all of these possibilities.

Perhaps we can also apply a principle to the carpets of Group C VII which can certainly be applied to many other carpet groups: the clearer the shape of the cross, the more likely it is that we are looking at an older Christian design. By contrast, the absence of the cruciform altogether, as well as of other Armenian design elements, may indicate that we are dealing with either a commissioned piece or works of imitation by non-Christian weavers.

Ill. 505 (left): MMA no. 1970.105, 878 x 224 cm. The Simonetti-Mamluk carpet. Metropolitan Museum of Art, New York. The Fletcher Fund 1970.

The detail (right) is a very nice example of the world cosmogram with the cross-star in the star tile.

Ill. 506 (left): BOIM no. 91.26, 196 x 130 cm. Staatliche Museen zu Berlin, Islamisches Museum, Berlin.

Whereas the cosmogram within the cross stands out more vividly in the example here from Berlin, the Greek cross design is more distinct in the New York example (ill. 505).

Ill. 507 (above): MMA 41.190.262, 250 x 218 cm. Metropolitan Museum of Art, New York. Bequest of George Blumenthal, 1941.

Group C VIII: North-west Persian Medallion Carpets Cross-Star Carpets – East Armenian Design Groups

The author presented part of what is at issue here in a paper given at the First International Congress on Turkish Carpets[314] in Istanbul in 1984.
For the moment we are primarily concerned with the development of this carpet group, which distinguishes itself from the preceding ones in that here the carpets were produced using the asymmetrical knot. The majority of these carpets have borders of the same type, for which there is an important link in the evolution of design to the prototypes for the 'dragon carpets'. Two fragments[315] of perhaps the same carpet, closely related to the 'Nigde carpet', show the early designs of the border development from the end of the 15th or the beginning of the 16th century (ill. 510). We see alternating white and black cruciform flowers inscribed in red Greek crosses, with light-symbol cross rosettes located within the former. The use of blue and yellow dye helps in the creation of the Old Armenian E design. The ‹E›s form, alternatingly, the border both in the fragments here as well as in the carpets ascribed to north-western Persia. Either as a result of colour changes, or due to the combination with a continuous scroll vine, or to the formation of what were once negative shapes into heart shapes, the border takes on a new form. Again we can conclude, as we did with regard to the flowering-cross carpets, that the age can be determined by observing the degree to which the blossom leaves become stiff or more geometrical. Since, moreover, there are two examples within the group which already bear a date, we can date those remaining in terms of how they relate to these. This is especially the case with examples which, because of their subject matter, cannot be included in a history of the Christian oriental carpet. Though they were almost certainly produced by Christian weavers, they were not intended for use in the Christian faith. We will return to these.

Let us place two carpets at the beginning of our discussion of this development. One of these, in a private collection in California[316] (ills. 512, 511, 513, 514), is virtually unknown, whereas the other, in the possession of the Gulbenkian-Foundation[317] (ill. 515), is quite well-known through its many reproductions. Despite the fact that there is a slight difference in age as well as certain differences in detail, both share a multitude of features, the central medallion (ill. 513) being the first. In the case of the carpet first mentioned, our first impression is of its similarity here to the cross-star carpets of the western design group (Group C IV), the eastern part of which, at least, formed the early pieces. Being lighter in colour, the eight-armed light-symbol cross stands out against the dark blue background. In the centre we find the light-symbol cross – extending from the star tile – on the red ground of the octagon. And here it is even closer to its original design than in the examples from Group C IV, the so-called 'star Ushaks'. We are reminded of analogous designs from Group B II. The octagon, for its own part, is set onto the blue ground of an octangular star, whose segments are notched in to resemble leaves. Here, in the extension of the cross arms, we find yellow blossoms as well as blue ones in the extensions of the beams. These blossoms are vivid reminders of the 'tree of Jesse' design which was discussed earlier. In the case of the Lisbon carpet, we see the cruciform flower in the medallion clearly accentuated in its colour within the octagonal star. In the middle there is a cross-star decorating the octagon. Yet here, despite the retention of the cruciform, the extensions do not form an eight-armed light-symbol cross, but rather a medallion rosette, set in blue with 16 leaves – something we were given an indication of in the above. Spiral-shaped scroll blossoms, rolled up, cover the blue ground of both carpets and come together frequently to form the 'E' design discussed (ill. 514). The composition of this decorative scroll pattern was conceived such that cruciform flowers, known to us from Group C V d (ills. 475, 478), or alternatively Kotshak crosses, emerge on a continuing basis. The centres of both contain, in alternation with small cruciform

Ill. 508 (page 374): TMW no. R 7.5, 420 x 273 cm. Textile Museum, Washington.

Here, too, in this Washington carpet the Greek cross is visible, though the star tile with its triangular cross arms is more prominent in its colour.

Ill. 509 (page 375): WÖMAK no. T 8382, 480 x 340 cm. Österr. Museum für angewandte Kunst, Vienna.

Here, in the centre of the octagonal we find a light-symbol cross design, though the old Greek cross composition can still be recognized as such. All of the smaller cross and star motifs are arranged around the Gloria Crucis.

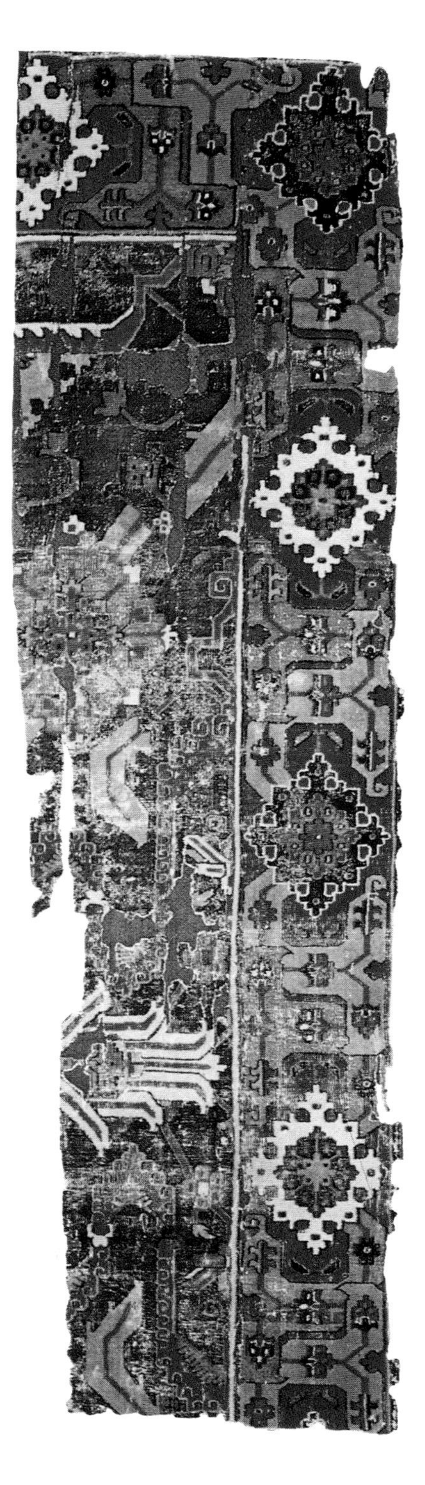

Ill. 510 (inside right): Eskenazi, Milan, 253 x 71 cm; fragment.

In contrast to all of the compositions that come later, this border shows quite distinctly its origin in red Greek crosses and yellow and blue reciprocal half-crosses.

Ill. 511 (outside right): Christopher Alexander Collection, Berkeley: border from ill. 512.

flowers, the cross-rosette or 'Talish rose', which, as we know from our previous discussion, belongs to the collection of traditional Armenian designs. Let us briefly add here that the design of the field is also to be found in a non-medallion carpet, BOIM no. I 1534 (ill. 516), which exhibits the early design of the familiar cartouche border. In this border we also have Kotshak cruciform flowers in alternation with cross-rosettes in the centres of the cartouches, which we encounter in the remaining carpets of the group as well.

Since these borders represent earlier, preliminary stages in the development of the carpet to follow, dated 1543 (ill. 521), we can consider it likely that these carpets were produced prior to this, i.e. about 1500. The development from the beginning of the 16th century proceeds, in the eyes of the present author, along a number of different tracks. First of all we have the ongoing development in the Armenian areas of settlement in northwestern Persia. Examples such as that in the former Tucher von

Ill. 512: Christopher Alexander Collection, Berkeley; 594 x 220 cm.

A very early representative of the so-called north-west Persian medallion carpet from the end of the 15th century.

Ill. 513: Christopher Alexander Collection, Berkeley: star tile within the central medallion from ill. 512.

Ill. 514: Christopher Alexander Collection, Berkeley: detail of the field design from ill. 512.

Ill. 515 (left): Gulbenkian Foundation, Lisbon; 530 x 222 cm.

This carpet, its origin being only slightly later, is very likely the most beautiful in its colour.

Ill. 516 (right): BOIM no. I. 1534, 220 x 128 cm. Staatliche Museen zu Berlin, Islamisches Museum, Berlin.

While it does not exhibit a medallion, this relatively small carpet is close to those discussed in the preceding in terms of the history of development.

Ill. 517: MMA no. 46.128, 808 x 414 cm; the 'Anhalt-medallion carpet'. Metropolitan Museum of Art, New York. Gift of Samuel H. Kress Foundation by Ruth H. Kress, 1946.

The Anhalt carpet is said to come from the Turkish booty of Vienna. It is presumed to have been finished for the young Sultan Süleyman Shah I at the beginning of the 1520s. The 'imperial' colours yellow and purple, as well as its correlation with the Tugra, support this assumption.

Ill. 518 (left): Plate, so-called 'Goldenhorn Ware', c. 1520. The C.L. David Collection, Copenhagen.

Ill. 519 (below): Tuğra Süleyman I, before 1530(?). Topkapi Palace Museum Library, Istanbul, no. 1400.

Ill. 520 (left): LV & A no. 272–1893: the 'Ardebil carpet', dated 1539. 1052 x 533 cm. Victoria and Albert Museum, London.

One of what were originally two carpets of equal dimensions, which were very probably commissioned for the Mihrimah Mosque on the occasion of the wedding of Princess Mihrimah to the Grand Vizier Rüstem Pasha in 1539.

Ill. 521 (right): So-called 'hunting carpet', dated AH 949 (AD 1543), 682 x 356 cm. Museo Poldi Pezzoli, Milan.

The figural representations are based on models from the Safavid tradition of court painting. We do not yet know whether the carpet was designed in Persia or rather by Persian artists of the Ottoman Court.

Ill. 522 (left): The Keir Collection, no. 45; 370 x 216 cm.

Ill. 523 (right): WÖMAK no. T 10.211, 746 x 294 cm. Österr. Museum für angewandte Kunst, Vienna.

Whereas the carpet from the Keir Collection can obviously be traced back to such models as that shown in ill. 515, in this example as well as the next the ground has been covered with cross-star tile designs.

Ill. 524 (page 388): MMA no. 10.61.3., 498 x 340 cm. Metropolitan Museum of Art, New York. F.C. Hewitt Foundation, 1910.

This carpet restricts itself to the star tile design, with the dragon-phoenix motif alternating with depictions of four winged lions in the centres. In this case, the dragon is in the shape of the 'E'. Shown together with the phoenix, it symbolizes Christ risen from the dead; the lions likewise serve as symbols for Christ.

Ill. 525 (page 389): So-called garden carpet, 550 x 320 cm. Private collection.

The composition of this carpet, a large Greek cross, is a model for the so-called garden carpets. The quarter sections likewise form their own crosses, with further crosses emerging in each half-section of these. This classic layout is also to be found in antependia.

Simmelsdorf Collection in Vienna, the carpets no. 64.311 and no. 22.100.75[318] in the MMA, in East Berlin (ill. 516), in the Textile Museum of Washington[319], and in the National Museum of Kuwait, belong to this sub-group. A late example in the Keir Collection (ill. 522), from the end of the 16th century, shows quite nicely the transition to the field designs of Group C IX. Here we find another sub-group, which we could ascribe to a manufactory at the Safavid court. Carpets to be included here are, for example, the AH 929 or AH 949, dated AD 1522/23 or AD 1542/43 respectively (the later date in each case appears to the author to be the more probable from a design-historical point of view), the Poldi-Pezzoli-Museum carpet in Milan (ill. 521), and also the carpet from the Parish-Watson Collection.[320]

We could refer to the third sub-group as the Anhalt-Ardabil Group. These are carpets which were probably made after 1514 by weavers from Tabriz, working for the Ottoman Court in Istanbul. In fact, the Ardabil carpets (ill. 520) are very likely to have been commissioned in 1539 for the wedding of Princess Mihrimah to the Grand Vizier, Rüstem Pasha, at the same time the Mihrimah Mosque was commissioned to be built.[314] Whereas the carpets presumed to be the products of a workshop at the Safavid Court, as well as the Ottoman examples just mentioned, cannot be seen as Christian, it is possible to regard as Christian those that originated in the East Armenian settlement areas of north-western Persia.

The Anhalt carpet (ill. 517) occupies a special position. On the one hand, it exhibits all the features of a Christian carpet – the alternating 'E' designs in the border mentioned above, as well as a cross in the centre of the medallion. Yet the decoration present here was used from 1518 on by Sultan Selim-Shah I and by his successor Sultan Süleyman-Shah I in the official tugras (ill. 519). Obviously some of the traditional Armenian designs (ill. 518) were being used by the Ottomans from the middle of the 15th century, as is shown in the tugras belonging to Mehmed II, and that belonging to Bayezid II, dating from 1457 and 1485, respectively.[321] The correspondence between carpet decoration and the designs used to fill the tugras, and also the use of yellow and purple, support the contention that the Anhalt carpet, which comes to us from the booty taken after the victory at Vienna in 1683, was the audience carpet of the young Süleyman II, and perhaps even of Selim I. This carpet could have been kept unused in the estate by the representatives of the Sultan Shah precisely because it belonged to him.

The cartouche carpets also constitute special examples of this group and can clearly be referred to as Christian. Carpets of this type can be found with and without medallions. The example in Vienna[322] (ill. 523), particularly beautiful due to its colours, contains a medallion, as does the Bernheimer example,[323] which is identical in its composition. Carpets without medallions, exhibiting instead only a design involving a union of light-symbol crosses and a diamond-form composition, are for example in Lyon, LMHT no. 25.423, and in New York[324] (ill. 524). The depictions of the 'dragon-phoenix' motif in the centres of the crosses, and their importance as an oriental symbol from the early Christian church, was already thoroughly discussed in the section dealing with Group B II (p. 194). The S-symbols, quite easy to recognize in the Viennese carpet, make out these carpets as Armenian products, probably from northwestern Persia.

The carpet referred to by Walter B. Denny[325] and King[326] as the oldest example from north-western Persia to show a medallion cannot be left out of this discussion, as the present author is unable to concur with their opinion. To be sure, the use of cross-stars in the ground in the 'chessboard' manner, or in the way done in Paramamluk carpets, strikes us as archaic at first sight. These cross-stars alternate with two different leaf-form crosses of the basic form type C_1, with the larger ones alternating against a background of either yellow or brown to make them more visible.

Superimposed on this ground is a central medallion in which what remains of two overlapping Kotshak crosses can still be discerned, though they no longer exercise any influence on the overall design. The same can be said of the flowery light-symbol cross in the centre. Of graver consequence for determining the age is the seriously degenerated and reduced border. The blossoms which we see throughout the carpet indicate a stage of development which, though it does correspond to the first part of the 16th century, is definitely not an early form. From the rounding and closing of what was once the central cruciform, we can also assume a later phase of development, which allows what might even be a regressive tendency from the Ottoman region, not to be dated before c. 1530.

In completing our treatment of this group, let us look at a carpet that must have served as a model for a group of so-called 'garden carpets' of Persian and Indian origin. The carpet presented here[327] (ill. 525) can also certainly be considered a garden carpet. A powerful Greek cross makes up the entire composition. In the middle, within the square central medallion, there is an almost octagonal area, at the centre of which is a cross-star. The negative areas between the cross beams, depicted here as tree-lined streams, also have cruciforms with cruciform flower centres. The clearly discernible beams of light of the large cross and the smaller ones have been reformed to resemble diagonally composed trees. The negative areas yet remaining were filled with light-symbol crosses in eight-pointed stars. Despite its assignment to the 18th century, the carpet probably originated during the second part of the 16th century.

Group C IX a: Carpets from New Julfa/Isfahan

We have already examined the historical situation (cf. pp. 237 ff.). Much like Mehmed II in Istanbul 150 years before, Shah Abbas I encouraged the resettlement of large segments of the Armenian population in the immediate area of his residence in Isfahan. New Julfa became a point of convergence for these Armenians who were bestowed considerable privileges and who, because of their skills and their industriousness, helped Isfahan rise to a flourishing centre for trade and intellectual thought within a very short time.

We could hardly provide better evidence of Armenian influence than to cite the fact that as early as 1618 Armenians held the monopoly in the prestigious silk trade between Persia and the rest of the world.

In a paper read in Washington,[328] Ulrich Schürmann argued in favour of considering the vase carpets to be the successors of the Armenian dragon carpets, while disputing their supposed production in Kerman. However, he assumed that this succession had already been introduced by the time Armenia was divided between the Ottomans and the Safavids in 1555. In the author's view this time would have preceded the production date of the oldest dragon carpets. Perhaps we should make some distinctions here. The dragon carpets are products of West Armenia, the flowering-cross carpets products of central Armenia, and what we know as the vase carpets were produced in Persia and East Armenia. This is also the case for the innumerable Isfahan carpets. If, for the sake of comparison, we look at the decorations on the early Armenian churches in New Julfa, we discover that the majority of the designs manifest in the carpets are present there. The basic compositional theme was preserved in each instance; only the actual execution of the details was subject to fashion or to the existing constraints in the centres of production.

We know that Armenian artisans were in the employ of the Safavid Court in Tabriz; furthermore, we know that even before the beginning of the 17th century Armenian

Ill. 526 (right): Inside the cathedral of New Julfa, looking east. First half of the 17th century.

The Armenians resettled by Shah Abbas I in New Julfa, near Isfahan, drew on their own set of designs in decorating the churches they built there. In them, we find very nearly all of the ornamentation typical of Armenian carpets produced in Persia.

Ill. 527 (below): St. Stephen's, New Julfa. Panel of pargetry, 1613/14.

We find the palmette and leaf designs also in ills. 530 and 531.

Ill. 528 (above) Cathedral, New Julfa: wall decorations from the second part of the 17th century.

These wall decorations show designs much like those we know from carpets or arch-form carpets. The paintings are separated in each case by stripes of 'border'.

Ill. 529 (below): Cathedral, New Julfa: tiled panel, 1715 /16.

The panel design here connects the carpets of ills. 523 and 524.

Ill. 530 (above): Julfa or New Julfa, c. 1600, 96 x 140 cm. Formerly the Baranovicz Collection, Paris. Franz Bausback, Mannheim.

This, the earliest example in our design evolution of the Isfahan-New Julfa carpets, bears an Armenian inscription. The carpet might have originated in the Caucasus before the deportation.

Ill. 531 (page 395): Isfahan, first half of the 17th century, 165 x 99 cm. Thyssen-Bornemisza Collection, Lugano.

Such carpets have usually been considered to be 'Indian'. Yet, this assumption overlooked the fact that at the beginning of the 17th century foreign trade was conducted entirely by Armenians. In terms of the evolution of designs, these carpets must be counted among the earliest Isfahan-New Julfa carpets.

artisans were working for the Shah[329], and that they established favorable conditions for those newly arrived. But only because of the mass colonization of New Julfa, and the construction of churches with their concomitant decoration, is it finally possible for us to compare the imported collection of designs with carpets from the same period.

In comparing the carpets, we are reminded of those from central Armenia rather than the examples from West Armenia. Let us return once again to the beautiful example in Group C V d from the museum in Sardarabad (ill. 476). Here the composition is clear. In the end, nearly all central Persian/East Armenian carpets from the 17th and 18th centuries are variants of one and the same theme, with even the so-called vase carpets being a late variant. The lovely fragment from Bausback (ill. 530) from the beginning of the 17th century, with its secondary border containing Armenian lettering, may have originated in what was still Julfa or also in New Julfa. The examples from the Thyssen Collection (ills. 531, 532), thought by Pagnano to be Indian,[330] follow here, and may be considered to be representative of the carpets from the early 17th century. The example from the Gulbenkian Foundation (ill. 533) could likewise be seen as representative of the end of the 17th century, and the Frankfurt example (ill. 534) of the beginning of the 18th century. A comparison with the above-mentioned surface patterns in the churches of New Julfa (ills. 526–529) shows an obvious correspondence in the use of designs.

Ill. 532 (left): Isfahan, early to late 1650s, 277 x 144 cm. Thyssen-Bornemisza Collection, Lugano.

What was said regarding the carpet in the previous illustration also applies to this example. In its composition it corresponds to this one.

Ill. 533 (right): Isfahan, end of the 17th century, 471 x 198 cm. Gulbenkian Foundation, Lisbon.

Ill. 534 (left): Isfahan, beginning of the 18th century, 700 x 230 cm. Museum für Kunsthandwerk, Frankfurt, no. 13297. Gift of Ulrich Schürmann.

Group C IX b: Carpets from South-western Persia: The Fars Region and the Afshari and Qashqai Territories

The enforced colonization by Shah Abbas I of entire segments of the Armenian population during the first few years of the 17th century, as indicated on page 237ff, was not restricted to Isfahan/New Julfa. The migration of large family groups led from Tabriz and Isfahan south into the Qashqai desert regions and the Afshari territories, and later from there on to Meshed, the Kabul region, and to Baluchistan. The region of south-western Persia had already once been settled, 1,000 years previous to this, by Armenian artisans at the decree of the Sassanids. They were then forced to establish a textile industry there.

The early material which has survived from this region is still less ordered and less accessible than have been the carpets from most of the other groups. This is perhaps in part due to the fact that no large collections from this special region have yet come to light. In view of the quantity of carpets from the 19th century, we can conclude that there must have been a fairly large industry there during the 17th and 18th centuries as well. In this connection it will suffice to examine but a few examples which can be considered representative of this area.

The first example (ill. 535) is directly related to the chain of traditional designs that has been cited frequently throughout this book. Illustration 174, the carpet in the Van Eyck painting, belongs here just as do ill. 250, the cross-star tile carpet; the cross-star carpets of Group C I (ills. 347–354); the Holbein carpets of Group C II (ills. 360–382); and also the cross-star carpets of Group C IV c (ills. 426, 442, 443). The first example is a highly original variant of the cross-star tile design, a segment from an endless repeat. Two rows of four guls are arranged so that the negative designs work to form new gul variants. The gul that makes up the overall pattern in ill. 536

Ill. 535 (left): Private collection; gul detail from ill. 536.

The gul which in this case determines the overall pattern is a special form of the Holbein gul; a proto-design from the 15th century was suspected in ill. 237.

Ill. 536 (page 400): Fars-Afshari region, 205 x 152 cm. Private collection.

400

Ill. 537 (page 401): Caucasus, so-called Surahani, 303 x 205 cm. Private collection.

This carpet as well as the next two exhibit common features of composition in spite of the fact that each was produced in a different region. See also the illumination from ill. 447, which as early as the 14th century served as a proto-design.

Ill. 538 (left): Caucasus, so-called Alpan-Kuba, 200 x 99 cm. Private collection.

Ill. 539 (right): Caucasus, St. Stefano Monastery, 310 x 205. Private collection.

This carpet was produced during the latter part of the 19th century in the St. Stefano Monastery in memory of Hovhan Agha and his deceased father, Khatchig, and his mother, Maryanos.

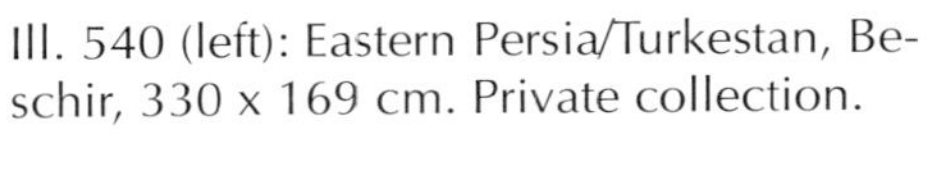

Ill. 540 (left): Eastern Persia/Turkestan, Beschir, 330 x 169 cm. Private collection.

Ill. 541 (right): Fars-Afshari region, 125 x 89 cm. Private collection.

Exchanging the colour blue of the ground for red places this carpet in the proximity of Group C X.

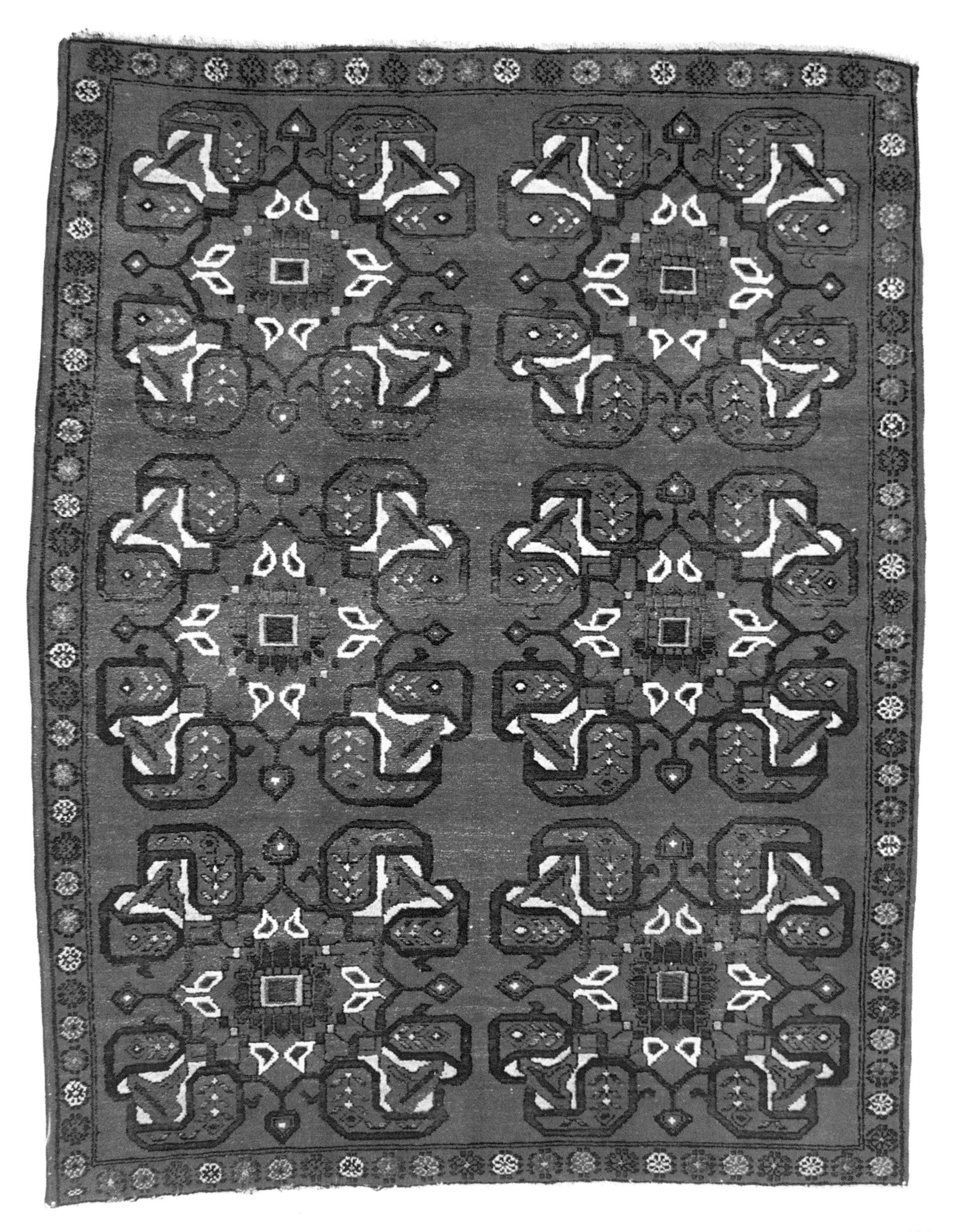

is a special form of the Holbein gul (ill. 359), from which it is derived. In the stripes of the border we find elements of the Caucasian-Armenian collection of designs from the Artsagh region. The outer cartouche border with its white ground is a late form of the same design also found in so-called 'Transylvanian' arch-form carpets (ills. 675, 679). In both these and the dragon carpets we find the outer, reciprocal crenellated border, whereas the inner scroll border consists of S-designs and the 'tree of Jesse', these being clear indications of Armenian production.

There are designs in the Caucasus which are directly related to early so-called Surahanis (ill. 537) and to Alpan-Kubas (ill. 538) as well as designs in Turkestan that are related to the Beshir carpets dating from the early 19th century (ill. 540). In each case, these related designs proceed from the same principle of construction. In ill. 541 we see a variant without a main border which, due to its red ground, clearly shows its closeness to the carpets in Group C X. These carpets are to be placed in the 17th/18th century because of their similarity in design to the groups cited above. Illustration 542, a carpet from the 19th century, shows a stage in the development of this group – carpets referred to as 'south-west Persian Holbein'. Also the votive carpet from ill. 539 is amongst those related to the Caucasus.

Ill. 542 (left): Fars-Afshari region, 116 x 99 cm. The Carpet Collector's Gallery, Cleveland Heights, Cleveland.

The use of ornamentation during the 18th/19th century to fill the negative areas brought about a fundamental change in the appearance of carpets. Toward the end of the 19th century filler motifs begin to take the place of major ornamentation.

Ill. 543 (right): Fars-Afshari region, 111 x 91 cm. Auktionshaus Dr. Fritz Nagel, Stuttgart (308/3206).

Ill. 545 (page 409): Fars region, Qashqai territory, 183 x 118 cm. Auktionshaus Dr. Fritz Nagel, Stuttgart, (286/299).

The composition of the carpet in ill. 543 can also be traced to a pattern that we can follow from the early-Christian mosaics (ill. 70) and the Van Eyck painting (ill. 170) all the way to the 18th century. Diamond-cross compositions belong to the traditional collection of designs which originated within the sphere of Armenian cultural influence. They are to be found very frequently in Group C IX b, however only up to the middle of the 18th century with this degree of clarity. In place of an all-over repeat (ill. 544) we find medallion designs, usually two or three placed one after the other, as in ill. 545, though there are also single medallion carpets such as those shown in ills. 546 or 547.

Ill. 544 (below): Fars-Afshari region, 125 x 106 cm. Auktionshaus Dr. Fritz Nagel, Stuttgart (297/3266).

In discussing the step-form cross carpets from Group C V b, two other possibilities for structuring the single medallions were presented (ills. 458 and 459) which should also be included in this context.

Ill. 546 (left): Fars region, Qashqai territory, 171 x 136 cm. Auktionshaus Dr. Fritz Nagel, Stuttgart (286/285).

Ill. 547 (right): Fars region, Qashqai territory, 189 x 145 cm. Auktionshaus Dr. Fritz Nagel, Stuttgart (300/1971).

Illustrations 542 and 547 convey an idea of the change in layout that began during the latter part of the 18th century. In place of the rigid, clear designs, the ground became filled with a plethora of various filler motifs, to which in some cases even the central cruciform subsequently fell victim. The same principle applies here that applied throughout the Armenian areas of settlement: the loss of the sacred function of the carpet is attended by a change in the collection of traditional designs. These designs degenerate to the point where later they simply serve to fill up space (ill. 547). Interestingly enough, however, the cross motifs of these filler designs have been able to preserve to this day their apotropaic and votive function.

Group C X: Carpets from Central Asia I, known as Turkoman Carpets

At the outset of this book, the author pointed out that Erdmann, in his nomadic-tribal hypothesis, suspected the origin of the knotted-pile carpet to be in central Asia. The present author was able to make a reasonably strong case in support of the fact that no carpets were produced by the Turkish peoples in central Asia until the 12th century. In fact, by way of contrast, we can cite Ibn Battuta, who reported that carpets were exported into Turkish lands from Aksaray.

The scholarly study of the carpets of central Asia is, relatively speaking, most recent. It is interesting to note that the earliest publication by General Bogolyubov in 1908 gives no information whatsoever as to its possible producers. The ethnographer Valentina Georgievna Moshkova was the first to conduct expeditions, four in all, from 1929 to 1946; she participated in two others as well. This made it possible to take an inventory of the existing material from the first part of the present century. It was also Moshkova who, in 1946 with her article 'The Tribal Designs in Turkoman Carpets', influenced to no minor degree the way of thinking of almost all the researchers engaged in publishing material on this subject. She based her work on the hypothesis that each of the Turkoman tribes to which carpet production was attributed had one (or several?) of its own tribal-specific guls.

In his publication 'Turkoman Carpets' Werner Loges perceived what is essentially at issue here:[331]

"It is doubtful whether during the 18th century or the time before there existed clear features for distinguishing between the carpets of individual tribes. The visual material that has survived and can, with some degree of certainty, be dated to a time prior to 1800 is, by comparison, limited to such scant traces that we cannot even begin to imagine the range of variation in the knotted products nor the tribal-specific differences. There is a good deal of evidence to support the conclusion that during this rather confusing early period of the Turkoman carpet, numerous elements of design and production – which, with respect to products from the 19th century, are thought to be typical of certain tribes – were common heritage to all Turkomans. According to the historical sources, presumably all tribes originally lived together in the regions along the east coast of the Caspian Sea; in fact, they lived closer together and under more cramped conditions than was later to be the case.

It is therefore conceivable that a given carpet could be distinguished from others during this early period only according to the tribal-specific emblem it bore, that is to say its tribal gul. Yet even these guls of varying designs must have had a common source derived from the basic beliefs of the Turkmenian people. We can, after all,

Ill. 548 (left): BUIM no. 14785, 220 x 150 cm. Iparmüvészeti Müzeum, Budapest.

The SP-Holbein carpet of Group C II from the 16th century already shows the separation of the segments by colour typical of Group C X.

hardly assume that guls of this complexity, which we know from carpets that have survived, were purely the result of a more or less haphazard development of designs. Instead, certain parallels manifest in the basic conception of all the guls – the important principal of the four-way divided central pattern in particular – point to the common origin of the ornamentation: religious and cultic traditions."

Within the context of this book, our interest is events prior to 1800; and yet the author did resort to more recent work as well. In order to find out whether or not we are actually dealing with tribal-specific guls, it is important to determine how the guls are related. For this reason it is important to gather together the early guls for comparison and analysis, in order to be able to assess their origin, design-historical development, meaning and use. Illustrations 549 through 633 are shown here in order to provide a basis for this. First we find guls in the shape of eight-pointed star medallions. These are followed by a series of earlier guls that Thompson, strangely enough, referred to as 'lobed guls'. The present author fails to find anything here resembling lobes. What we have here is nothing more than somewhat flattened eight-pointed stars such as those already encountered in Groups B II and C II. The composition of the next groups is also based on an asymmetrical transformation of the eight-pointed star or, instead of an octagon, the reduced form of this star. The secondary guls, however, develop from the basic cruciform or the design of the light-symbol cross.

As we will see, it is a matter of only a few compositional types and their permutations, which now need to be discussed in the order of their appearance in this design-historical development:

Primary Guls

The basic design of group-type C X HG a:

Ill. 549 (page 412): basic design of group-type C X HG a. Diagram.

The reader should note here that this design is based on the Urartian and early Armenian-Christian cross design (ills. 54, 56).

C X HG a_1: 'Ersari medallion gul I'
outer shape: compressed eight-pointed star
centre: cross-star in Holbein gul
filling: blossom-shaped vestiges of the former light-symbol cross of the basic form type H_1.

Ill. 550: Leningrad no. KOB-205: 'Ersari medallion gul 1' from ill. 637.

C X HG a_2: 'Salor Medallion gul' of the Salor and Ersari
outer shape: compressed eight-pointed star
centre: cross-star in Holbein gul variant
filling: blossom-shaped vestiges of the former light-symbol cross of the basic form type H_1.

Ill. 551: 'Salor medallion gul' from ill. 638 with diagram.

Ill. 552: 'Salor medallion gul' from an antependium, 63 x 166 cm. Private collection.

Ill. 553: 'Salor medallion gul' from an antependium, 61 x 188 cm. Private collection.

Ill. 554: BMIK no. 84.898., 245 x 145 cm: central medallion.

Comparing this with ill. 551, we see that both are based on the same compositional scheme.

C X HG a_3: 'Arabach medallion gul'
outer shape: compressed eight-pointed star
centre: cross-star in the small eight-pointed star within the large eight-pointed star
filling: deformed vestiges of the 'blossoms' from C X HG a_1.

Ill. 555: 'Arabach medallion gul' from ill. 644.

C X HG a_4: 'Ersari medallion gul II'
outer shape: former eight-pointed star drawn out horizontally
centre: cross-star within octagon within drawn out eight-pointed star within drawn out eight-pointed star.
filling: eight cross-stars in place of the 'blossoms' of C X HG a_1.

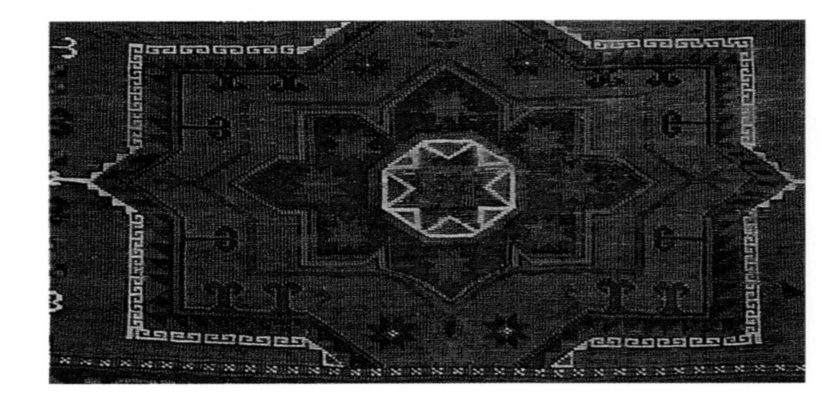

Ill. 556: 'Ersari medallion gul' from ill. 641.

C X HG a_5: 'Kizil Ayak medallion gul'
outer shape: decorated eight-pointed star
centre: rhomboid Kotshak cross in the Sary gul C X HG c_1
filling: Kotshak ends of the Sary gul, above and below.

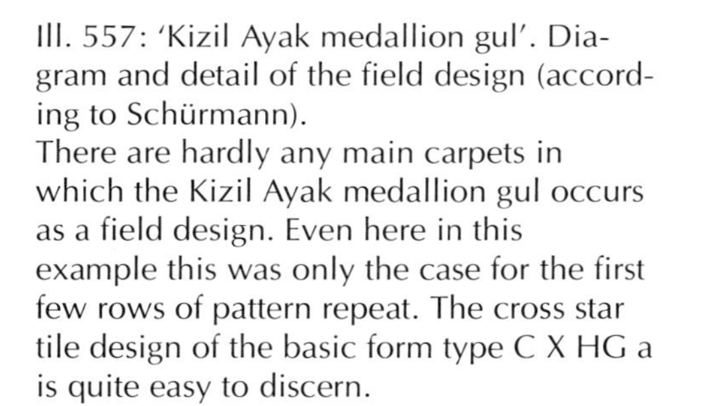

Ill. 557: 'Kizil Ayak medallion gul'. Diagram and detail of the field design (according to Schürmann).
There are hardly any main carpets in which the Kizil Ayak medallion gul occurs as a field design. Even here in this example this was only the case for the first few rows of pattern repeat. The cross star tile design of the basic form type C X HG a is quite easy to discern.

The basic design of the group-type C X HG b:

Ill. 558: Basic design of the group-type C X HG b. Diagram.

C X HG b_1: 'Salor gul'
outer shape: flattened, rounded eight-pointed star
centre: Greek cross within the eight-pointed star of the basic type cross-D_1
filling: the Armenian letter-symbol 'dd' in each quarter section of the eight-pointed star; emerging diagonally from the corners of the basic square are three-armed 'cloverleaf multiple crosses'.

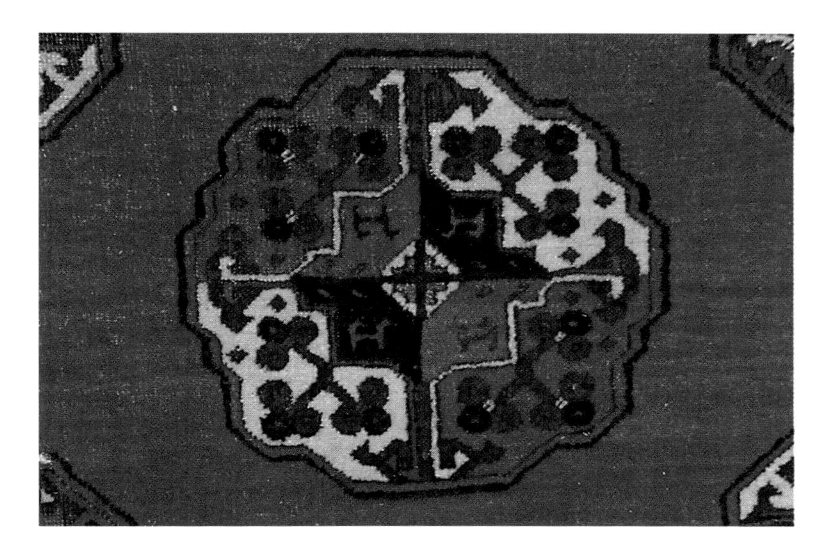

Ill. 559: 'Salor gul' from a carpet. 280 x 280 cm. Private collection.

C X HG b_2: 'Saryk-Ersari gul'
outer shape: flattened, rounded eight-pointed star
centre: Sagdak gul C X NG b within the eight-pointed star of the basic type cross-D_1; filling: cloverleaf-crosses originating from the former 'cloverleaf multiple cross', of the C X HG b_1-type, here disintegrated into two parts.

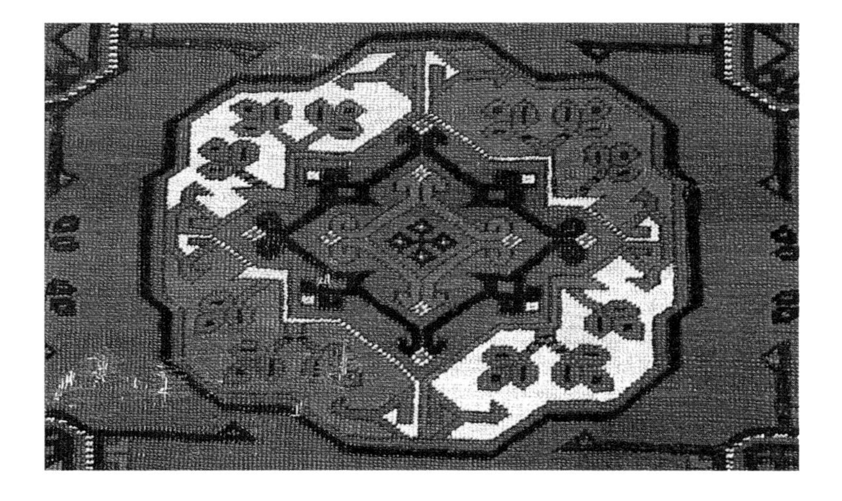

Ill. 560: 'Ersari-Saryk gul' of the Saryk from a carpet fragment, 229 x 160 cm. Private collection.

C X HG b_3: 'Ersari gul' I
outer shape: flattened, rounded eight-pointed star
centre: cross-star-Greek cross in Memling gul within an altered, former eight-pointed star of the basic form type D_1
filling: cloverleaf-crosses of the former 'cloverleaf multiple cross', of the type C X HG b_1, here disintegrated into two parts.

Ill. 561:'Ersari-Saryk gul' of the Ersari from the carpet in ill. 649.

Ill. 562: 'Ersari-gul' from ill. 648.

C X HG b_4: 'Tekke-Arabachi gul'
outer shape: flattened, rounded eight-point cross
centre: Greek cross within eight-pointed star of the basic form type D_1 cruciform
filling: three individual acorns on stems, protruding diagonally.

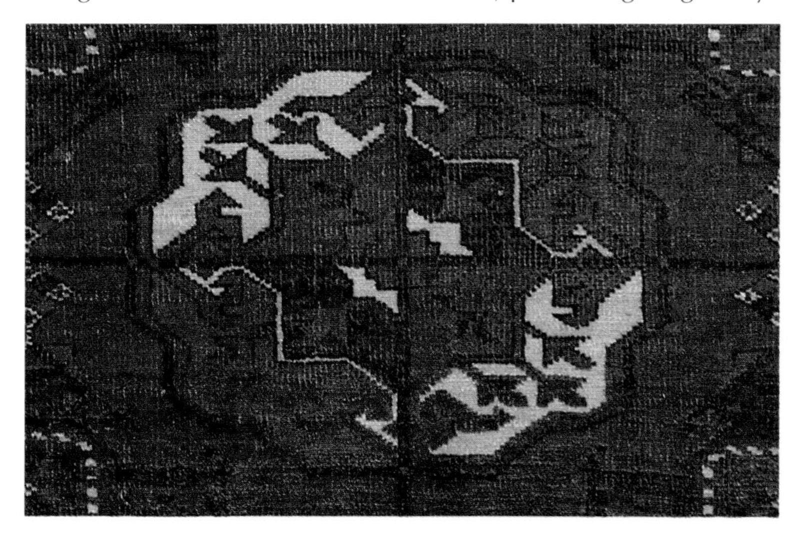

Ill. 563: 'Tekke gul' from a carpet, 310 x 225 cm. Private collection.

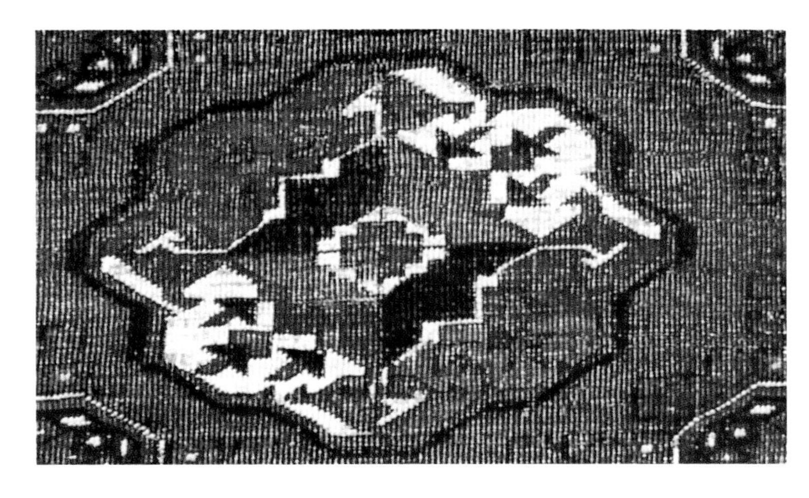

Ill. 564: 'Arabach gul' from ill. 645.

C X HG b_5: 'Ersari gul' II
outer shape: flattened, rounded eight-pointed star
centre: Sagdak gul C X NG b within the Greek cross of the reduced eight-pointed star of the basic type D_1 cruciform
filling: the animated Armenian letter-symbol › ԴԴ ‹ in each quarter section of the cross spandrels

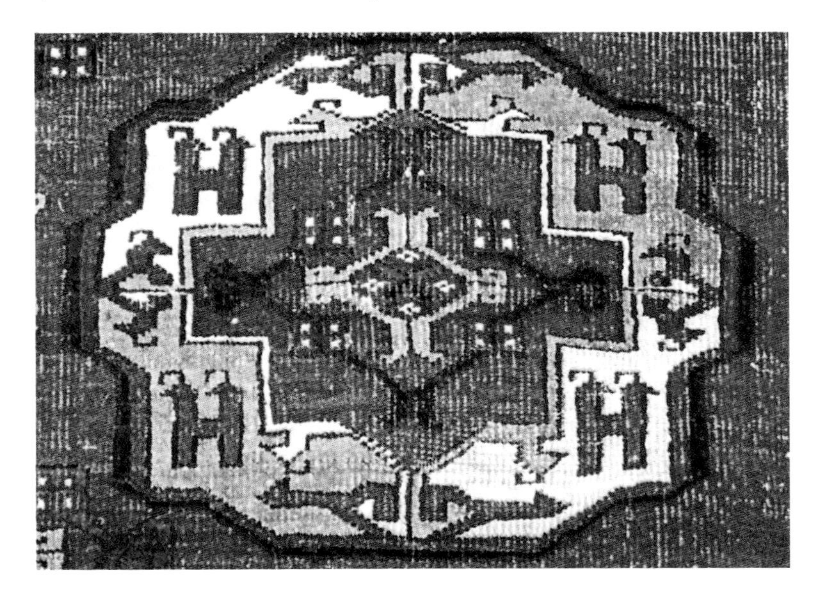

Ill. 565: 'Ersari gul' II from ill. 651.

C X HG b_6: 'Ersari gul' III
outer shape: flattened, rounded eight-pointed star
centre: cross-star within the basic type H_1 light-symbol cross
filling: cloverleaf-crosses on the arms of the light-symbol cross.

Ill. 566: 'Ersari gul' III, 177 x 128 cm; detail from a carpet. Museum für Völkerkunde, Munich, no. 78–300175. Hubel Collection 168.

The basic designs of the group-type C X HG c:

Ill. 567: Basic design of the group-type C X HG c. Diagrams.

At the right the complete cross star; the vestiges of this still discernible at the left.

C X HG c_1: 'Sary gul' of the Salors
outer shape: modified, asymmetrical eight-pointed star
centre: rhomboid lily cross in eight-pointed star within cross-star with cross arms of the basic form type D_1
filling: squares divided into quarter sections and protruding diagonally from the corners of the underlying square.

Ill. 568: 'Sary gul' of the Salor from ill. 640.

C X HG c_2: 'Sary gul' of the Saryks
outer shape: as in C X HG c_1
centre: as in C X HG c_1
filling: the four-part squares are no longer connected to the underlying square, filling instead the negative area around the outside of the underlying square.

Ill. 569: 'Sary gul' of the Saryk from a cushion (chuval), 90 x 113 cm. Private collection.

C X HG c_3: 'Sary gul' of the Beluch
outer shape: as in C X HG c_1 centre: modified Kotshak cross in a hexagon within an eight-pointed star within a cross-star with cross arms of the basic form type D_1.
filling: squares protruding diagonally from the corners of the underlying square; the ground either only white or only red.

Ill. 570: 'Sary gul' of the Baluch from a carpet, 130 x 88 cm. Private collection.

C X HG c_4: 'chuval gul I' of the Tekke
outer shape: as in C X HG c_1, slightly flatter; centre: Greek cross within a small eight-pointed star within a large hexagon (reduced octagon) made up of differently coloured quarters; all this then embedded in a cross-star with cross arms of basic form type D_1.
filling: isolated vestiges of squares

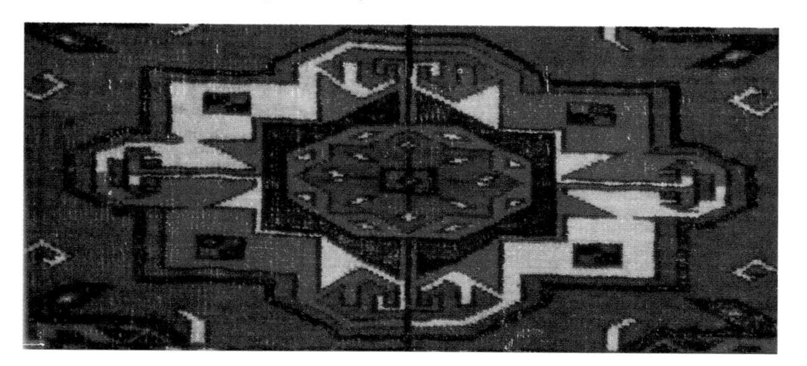

Ill. 571: 'chuval gul I ' of the Tekke from a cushion (chuval), 43 x 112 cm. Iparmüves-zeti Müzeum, Budapest, no. 24.434.

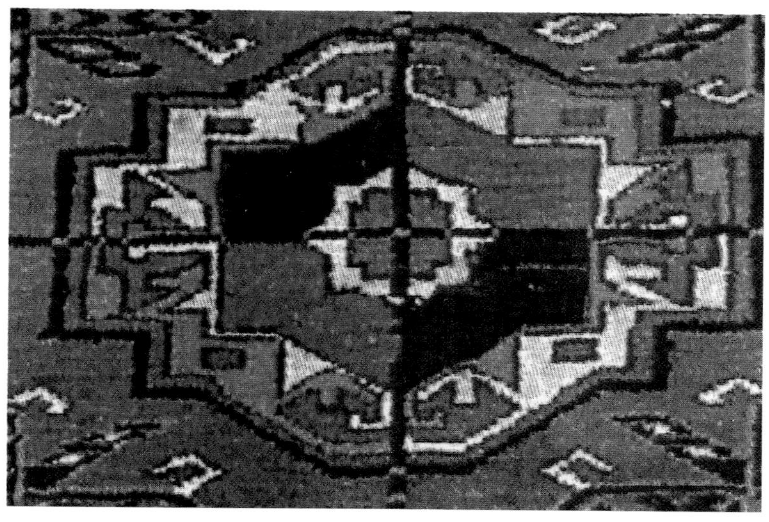

Ill. 572 'chuval gul I' of the Tekke from a carpet, 136 x 117 cm. Russian Museum, Leningrad, no. KOB-192.

C X HG c_5: 'chuval gul II' of the Tekke
outer shape: as in C X HG c_1
centre: Kotshak cross within a hexagon with cross arms of the basic type D_1
filling: none

Ill. 573: 'chuval gul II' of the Tekke from a cushion, 75 x 109 cm. Auktionshaus Dr. Fritz Nagel (314/3267).

C X HG c_6: 'cross-star-cross gul' of the Ersari
outer shape: rhomboid-like hexagon
centre: light-symbol cross H_1 with beams in the form of a cloverleaf multiple cross within a cross-star within a Greek cross enclosed within a hexagon with cross arms of the basic form type D_1.

Ill. 574: 'Cross-star-cross gul' of the Ersari from a carpet, 304 x 178 cm. Private collection.

Ill. 575: 'Cross-star-cross gul' of the Ersari from a carpet, 286 x 159 cm. Private collection.

C X HG c_7: 'Salor-chuval gul' of the Salor, Tekke and the Saryk
outer shape: octagon with and without the Kotshak ends of the basic form type E.
centre: four-part rhomboid-Kotshak cross.

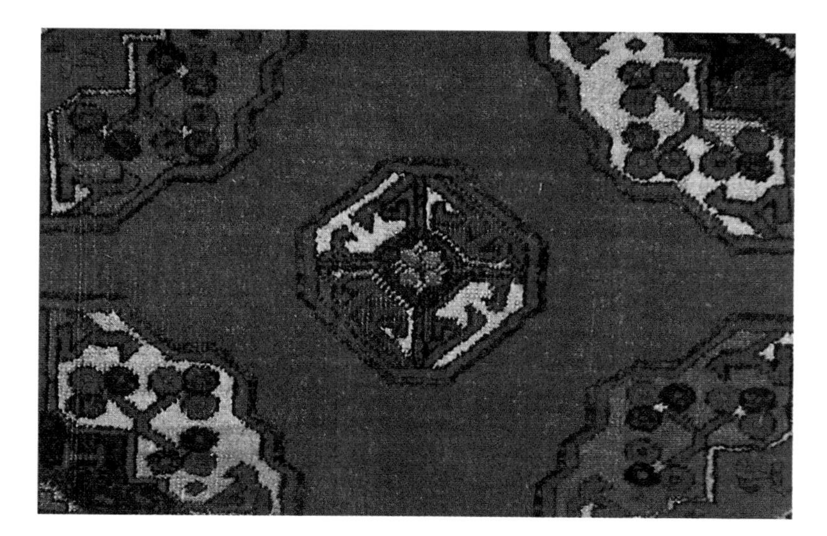

Ill. 576: 'Salor-Joval gul' from a Salor carpet, 293 x 241 cm.
Private collection.

Ill. 577: 'Salor-chuval gul' from a Tekke carpet, 326 x 250 cm.
Private collection.

The basic design of the group-type C X HG d:

Ill. 578: Basic design of the group-type C X HG d.

C X HG d_1: 'Gülli gul I' of the Ersari
outer shape: octagon
centre: rhomboid cross within an eight-pointed star with cross arms of the basic form type D_1
filling: cloverleaf-crosses analogous to C X HG b_2.

Ill. 579: 'Gulli gul I' of the Ersari (according to Moshkova).

C X HG d_2: 'Gülli gul II' of the Ersari
outer shape: octagon
centre: rhomboid multiple cross within a hexagon with cross arms of the basic form type D_1
filling: two cloverleaf-crosses protruding diagonally.

Ill. 580: 'Gülli gul II' of the Ersari (according to Moshkova).

The basic design of the group-type C X HG e:

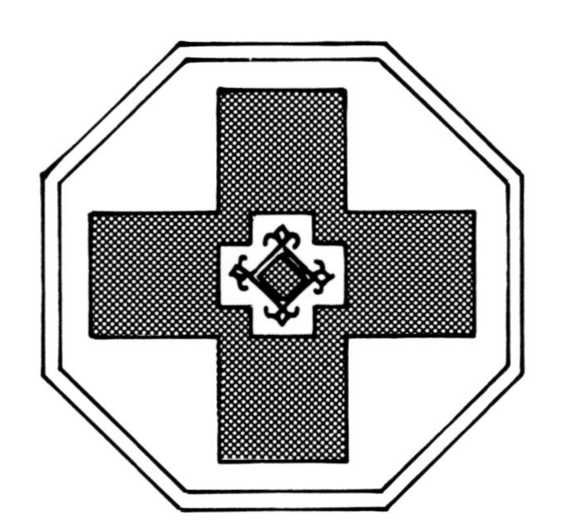

Ill. 581: Basic design of the group-type C X HG e.

C X HG e_1: 'Gülli gul III' of the Ersari
outer shape: octagon
centre: rhomboid-Kotshak cross within a small Greek cross within a large Greek cross
filling: three cloverleaf-crosses protruding diagonally.

Ill. 582: 'Gulli gul III' of the Ersari (according to Moshkova).

C X HG e_2: 'Gülli gul IV' of the Ersari
outer shape: octagon
centre: rhomboid-cross fourchée within a Memling gul within a Greek cross with two cross arms of the basic form type D_1.
filling: cloverleaf-crosses of the disintegrated 'cloverleaf multiple cross' and additional cloverleaf-cross, protruding diagonally.

Ill. 583: 'Gulli gul IV' of the Ersari (according to Moshkova).

C X HG e_3: 'Gülli gul V' of the Ersari
outer shape: octagon
centre: rhomboid knotted-light-symbol cross within a Greek cross; filling: three cloverleaf-crosses protruding diagonally.

Ill. 584: 'Gulli gul V' of the Ersari (according to Moshkova).

C X HG e_4:

'Tauk-Nuska gul' of the Yomud, Chaudor, Kizil Ayak, Ersari and Arabach
outer shape: octagon
centre: Kotshak cross within an octagon (or what was an octagon, now reduced to a hexagon)
filling: 8 animated Armenian letter-symbols › ԴԴ ‹ or 8 cruciform flowers.

Ill. 585: 'Tauk-Nuska gul' of the Yomud from a carpet, 271 x 159 cm. Auktionshaus Dr. Fritz Nagel, Stuttgart (304/375).

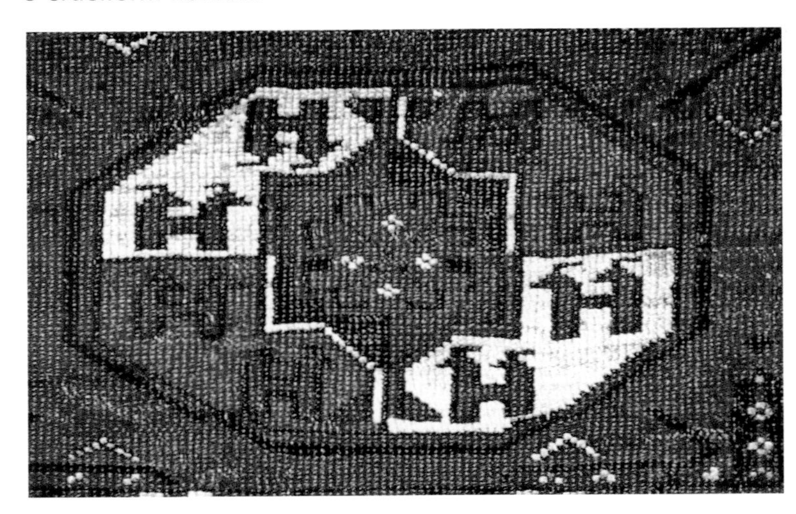

Ill. 586: 'Tauk-Nuska gul' variant of the Kizil Ayak from a carpet, 238 x 198 cm. Private collection.

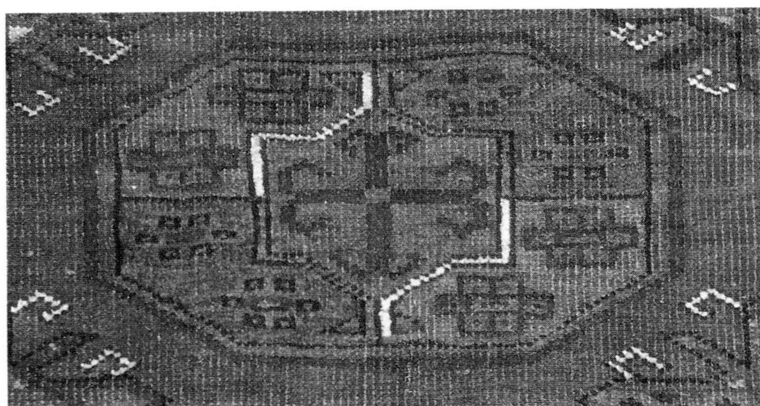

C X HG e_5:

'Temirchin gul' of the Saryk / 'Onurga gul' of the Ersari
outer shape: octagon
centre: cloverleaf multiple cross positioned diagonally within a rectangle with cross arms of the basic form type D_1
filling: a stylized tree of life in each quadrant.

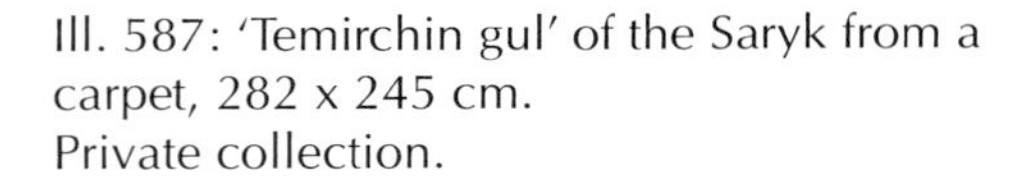

Ill. 587: 'Temirchin gul' of the Saryk from a carpet, 282 x 245 cm.
Private collection.

The basic design of the group-type C X HG f:

Ill. 588: Basic design of the group-type C X HG f.

C X HG f_1: 'Salor gul' of the Salor and Tekke, 'Mary gul' of the Saryk
outer shape: octagon
centre: cross-star within a Greek cross as a Kotshak cross of the basic form type D_1 within the square
filling: negative designs from the ornamentation of the squares.

Ill. 589: 'Salor gul' Detail from the fragment of a cushion, 78 x 44 cm. Private collection.

Ill. 590: 'Salor gul', detail from the fragment of a cushion, 30 x 60 cm. Museum of Fine Arts, Boston, no. 8.376.

C X HG f_2: 'Ersari gul'
outer shape: compressed octagon
centre: cross-star within a Greek cross within a square
filling: negative designs on stems, longer in comparison to previous design.

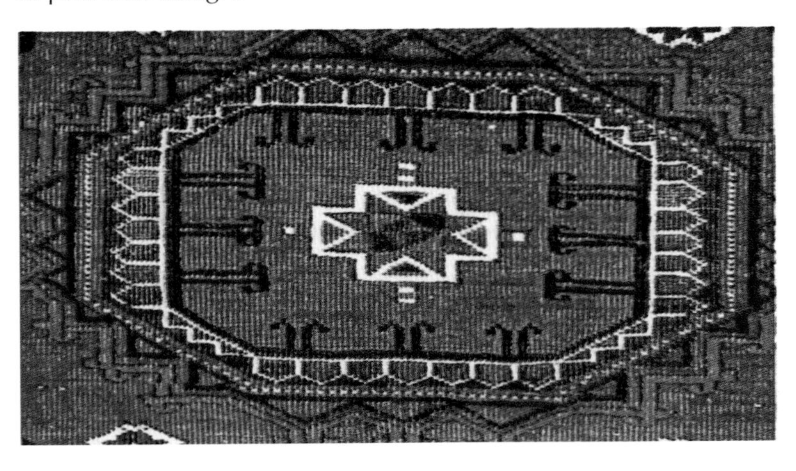

Ill. 591: 'Ersari gul' from a cushion (chuval), 146 x 50 cm. Private collection.

C X HG f_3: 'Ajakly gul' of the Kizil Ayak
outer shape: octagon
centre: anchor-cross within square of different colour
filling: as in C X HG f_1.

Ill. 592: 'Ajakly gul' of the Kizil Ayak (according to Moshkova).

C X HG f_4: 'Mary gul' of the Kizil Ayak
outer shape: octagon
centre: facetted Greek cross within square
filling: later design of C X HG f_1.

Ill. 593: 'Mary gul' of the Kizil Ayak (according to Moshkova).

C X HG f_5: 'Mary gul' variant of the Saryk
outer shape: octagon
centre: Salor-chuval gul of the type C X HG c_5
filling: as in C X HG f_1.

Ill. 594: 'Mary gul' variant of the Saryk from a fragment, 90.8 x 61.6 cm. Private collection.

C X HG f_6: 'shield gul' of the Salor, Saryk and Tekke
outer shape: octagon
centre: reduced chuval gul of the type C X HG c_3
filling: as in C X HG f_1.

Ill. 595: 'Shield gul' of the Tekke from a cushion (chuval), 72 x 129 cm. Private collection.

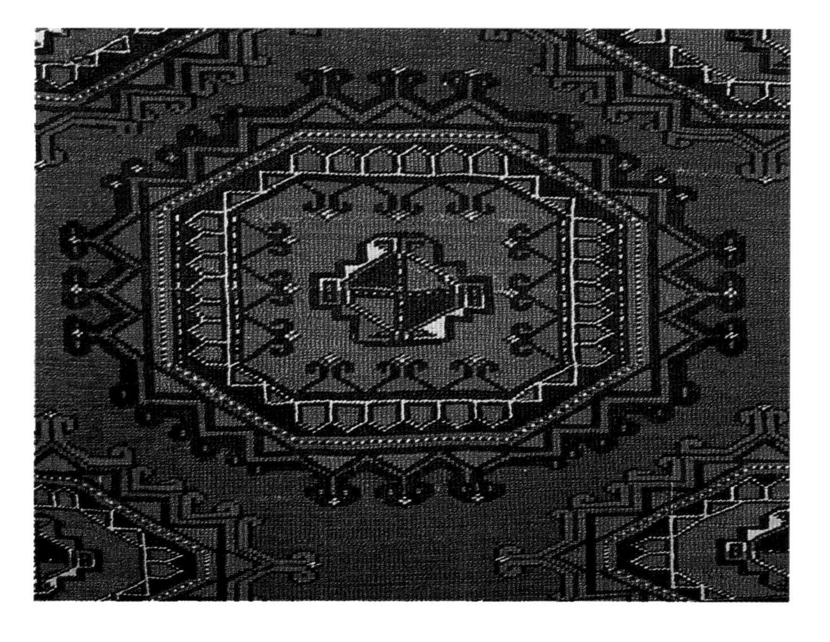

Ill. 596: 'shield gul' of the Saryk from a cushion (chuval), 93 x 165 cm. Private collection.

C X HG g: 'Memling gul' of the Salor and Tekke
outer shape: diamond-shaped octagon
centre: cross-star within a step-form cross

Ill. 597: 'Memling gul' of the Salor from a cushion (chuval), 47 x 111 cm.
Private collection.

C X HG h: 'Aina-Kotshak gul' of the Tekke and Beluch
outer shape: rectangle
centre: cross-star within Greek cross with cross arms of the basic form type D_1; filling: in each case either a dotted-cross, dotted-diamond or an H-shape.

Ill. 598: 'Aina-Kotshak gul' of the Baluch from a carpet, 149 x 86 cm.
Auktionshaus Dr. Fritz Nagel, Stuttgart (296/3151).

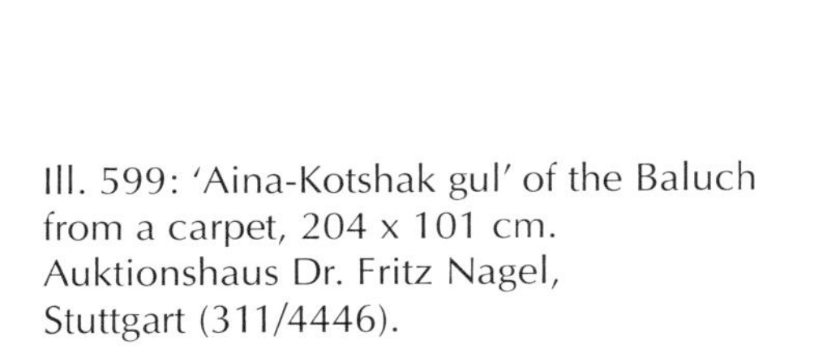

Ill. 599: 'Aina-Kotshak gul' of the Baluch from a carpet, 204 x 101 cm.
Auktionshaus Dr. Fritz Nagel, Stuttgart (311/4446).

C X HG i: 'Greek cross gul' of the Tekke
outer shape: diamond-shaped octagon
centre: cross of basic form type C_1 with three-pronged shafts within the Greek cross
filling: small triangles in the cross axes.

Ill. 600: 'Greek cross gul' of the Yomud from a cushion (chuval), 36 x 67 cm. Kunstauktionshaus Dr. Fritz Nagel, Stuttgart (325/4225).

C X HG k: 'Ak-Su design' of the Salors, Tekke and Chaudor
centre: Kotshak cross.

Ill. 601: 'Ak-Su design' of the Salor from a cushion (chuval), 41 x 114 cm. Private collection.

C X HG l: 'Kepse gul' of the Yomud
outer shape: diamond with distinctly dentelled edges
centre: cross of basic form type D_1 or cross-star within octagon. A late form of the secondary gul C X HG b, later to become a main gul.

Ill. 602: 'Kepse gul' of the Yomud from the carpet in ill. 654. Private collection.

The 'Kepse gul' represents a late permutation of the 'Tscharch-Palak gul' of ill. 618, which has here become the main gul. The cross-stars surrounding the central cross in the 'Tscharch-Palak gul' have become 'lilies of grace' here.

Ill. 603: 'Kepse gul' of the Yomud from a carpet, 283 x 183 cm. Private collection.

Ill. 604: 'Kepse gul' of the Yomud from a carpet, 306 x 172 cm. Galerie Ostler, Munich.

Ill. 605 'Kepse gul' of the Yomud from a carpet, 303 x 181 cm. Private collection.

C X HG m: 'Dyrnak gul' I of the Yomud and Ersari
outer shape: hooked diamond
centre: diamond-shaped lily cross.

Ill. 606: 'Dyrnak gul' I of the Yomud from a carpet, 304 x 195 cm. Auktionshaus Dr. Fritz Nagel, Stuttgart (325/4450).

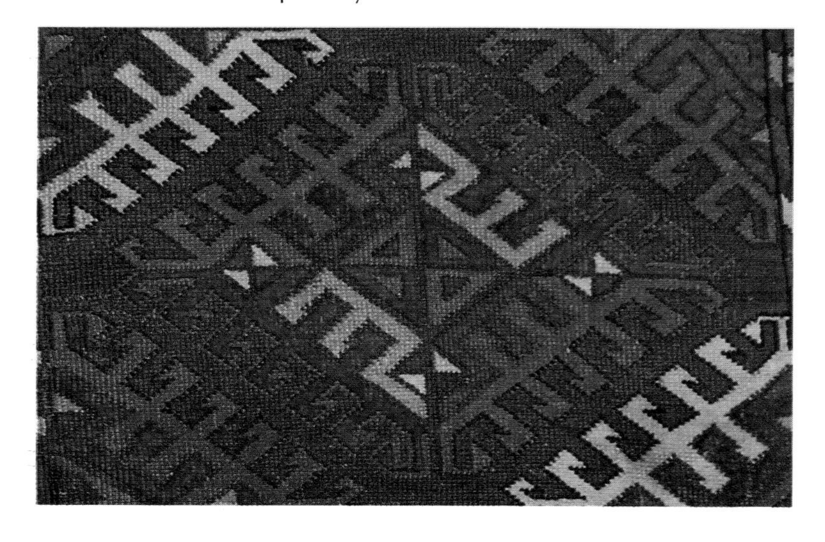

C X HG n: 'Dyrnak gul' II of the Yomud and Ersari
outer shape: hooked diamond
centre: four-part diamond
filling: vestiges of the negative designs still linked to or already isolated from C X G H m.

Both variants of the 'Dyrnak gul' generally alternate in compositions of nothing but diamonds.

Ill. 607: 'Dyrnak gul' II of the Yomud from a carpet. LV & A no. 272–1906. Victoria and Albert Museum, London.

Secondary Guls

The basic design of the group-type C X NG:

Ill. 608: Basic design of the group-type C X NG a.

C X NG a_1: 'Sagdak gul' of the Salors and Ersari
outer shape: cross-star of the basic type G_1 combined with a light-symbol cross of type H_2, with Kotshak ends all around
centre: lily cross gul C X NG e
peculiarity: in the Ersari example the squares at the ends of the arms of the former light-symbol cross offset here, each contain an inscribed cross.

Ill. 609: 'Sagdak gul' of the Salor from a cushion (chuval), with diagram, 47 x 111 cm. Private collection.

Ill. 610: 'Sagdak gul' of the Ersari, detail from ill. 651.

C X NG a_2: 'Chemche gul' of the Salors
outer shape: differentiated cross-star
centre: Kotshak cross within an octagon.

Ill. 611: 'Chemche gul' of the Salor from ill. 640 with diagram.

C X NG a_3: 'Gurbaka gul' I of the Tekke
outer shape: reduced cross-star
centre: cross-star within an octagon.

Ill. 612: 'Gurbarka gul' I of the Tekke from ill. 652 with diagram, 283 x 183 cm. Private collection.

C X NG a_4: 'Gurbaka gul' II of the Tekke and 'secondary gul' of the Ersari
outer shape: reduced cross-star
centre: cross-star within an octagon.

Ill. 613: 'Gurbarka gul' II of the Tekke from a carpet, 319 x 204 cm. Private collection.

Ill. 614: 'Gurbarka gul' II of the Tekke from a carpet with diagram, 301 x 225 cm. Private collection.

C X NG a_5: 'Gurbaghe gul' of the Ersari
outer shape: reduced cross-star
centre: cross-star within an octagon.

Ill. 615: 'Gurbaghe gul' of the Ersari from ill. 649 with diagram.

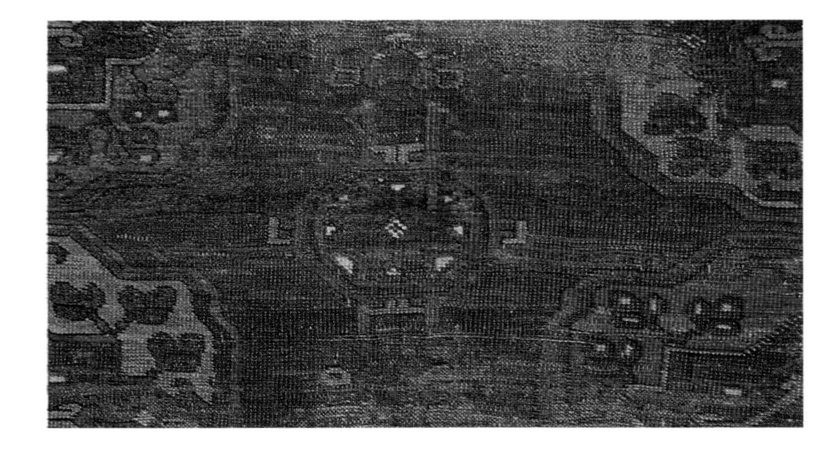

C X NG a_6: 'Gurbaghe gul' of the Saryks
outer shape: reduced cross-star
centre: cross-star within an octagon.

Ill. 616: 'Gurbaghe gul' of the Saryk from a carpet fragment with diagram, 229 x 160 cm. Private collection.

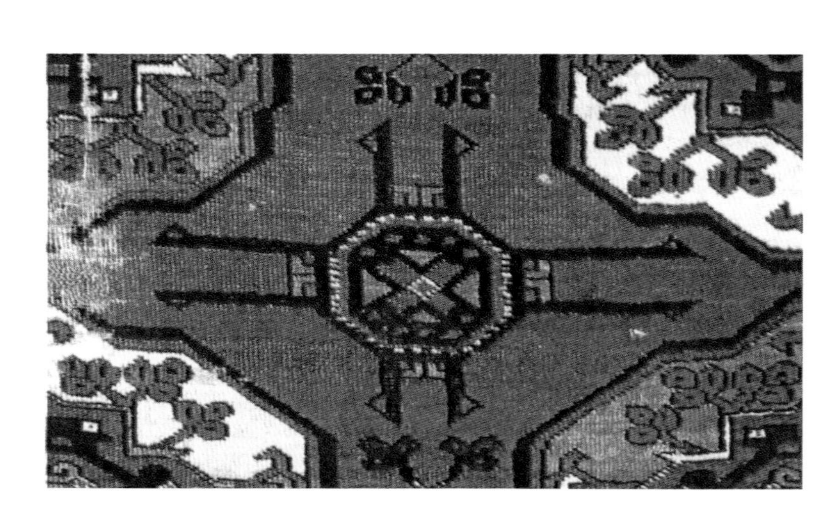

C X NG a_7: 'Gurbaghe gul' of the Arabach
outer shape: a combination of Greek and step-form cross
centre: cross-star variant in the manner of Group B II.

Ill. 617: 'Gurbaghe gul' of the Arabach from ill. 645 with diagram.

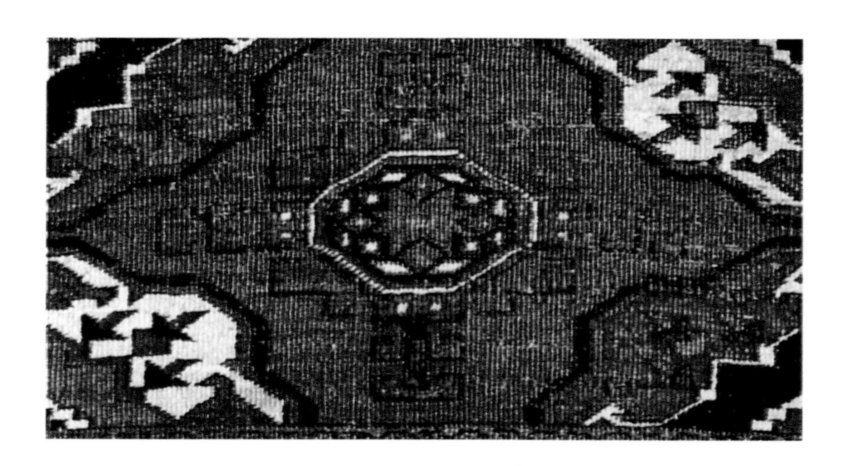

C X NG b_1: 'Tscharch-Palak (Greek cross) gul' of the Salors, Tekke and Saryks
outer shape: step-form cross
centre: Kotshak cross of the basic form type D_1 within a Greek cross within a step-form cross adorned with cross-stars.

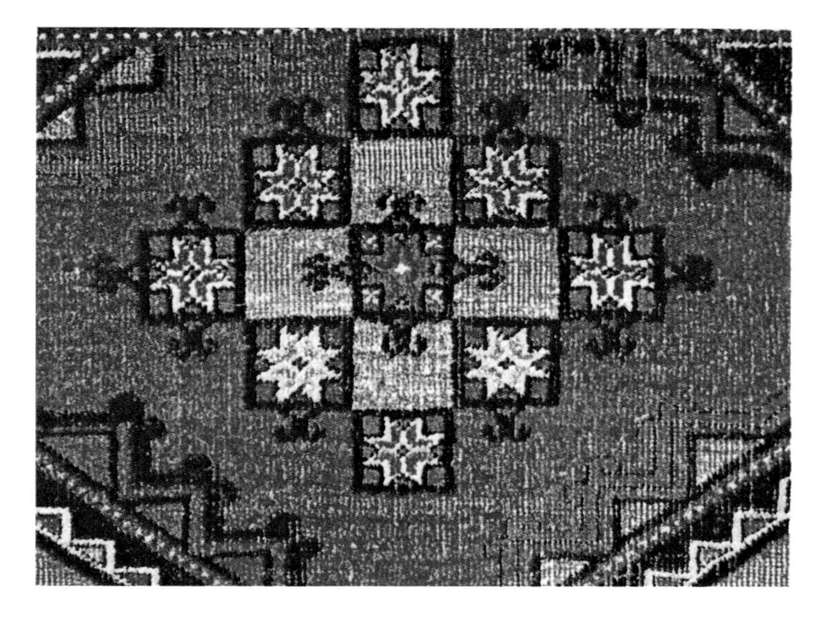

Ill. 618: 'Tscharch-Palak gul' of the Salor from ill. 642.

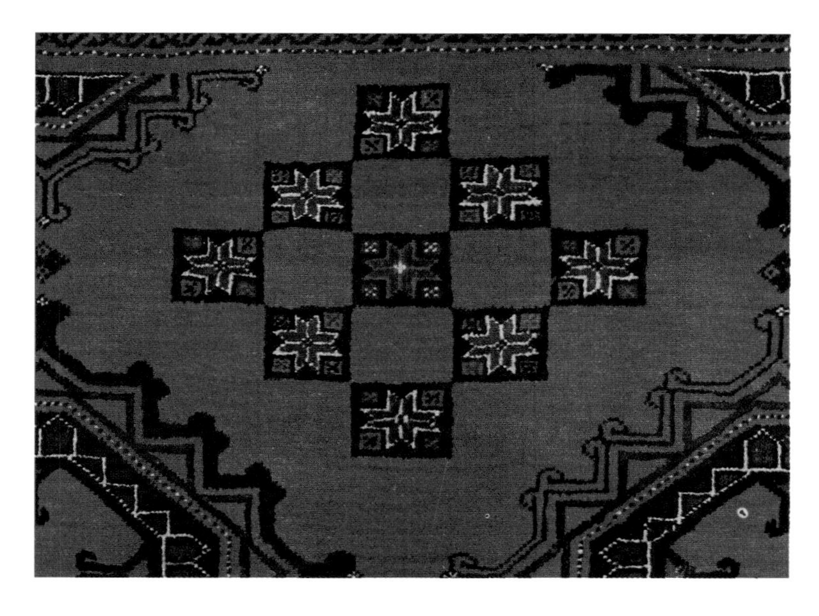

Ill. 619: Tscharch-Palak gul' of the Salor from a cushion (chuval), 90 x 152 cm, LV & A no. 394–1880. Victoria and Albert Museum, London.

Ill. 620: 'Tscharch-Palak gul' of the Tekke from a cushion (chuval), 72 x 129 cm. Private collection.

C X NG b_2: 'Tscharch-Palak (Greek cross) gul' "II" of the Tekke
outer shape: modified step-form cross
centre: 'shield gul' from C X HG f_6 within an octagon.

Ill. 621: 'Tscharch-Palak gul' II of the Tekke, detail from ill. 643.

C X NG b_3: 'Tscharch-Palak (cross-star cross) gul of the Yomud
outer shape: cross-star of the type G_2 with Kotshak ends
centre: cross-star.

Ill. 622: 'Tscharch-Palak-(cross star-Greek cross-)gul' of the Yomud from a cushion (chuval) with diagram, 78 x 120 cm. Bertram Frauenknecht, Nuremberg.

C X NG c_1: 'light-symbol cross gul' of the Salors, Imreli and Kizil Ayak(?)
outer shape: very clear light-symbol cross with Kotshak ends
centre: Four-part diamond, with or without a Kotshak cross.

Ill. 623: 'light-symbol cross gul' of the Imreli from a wall cushion (chuval) with diagram, 58 x 162 cm. Private collection.

C X NG c_2: 'Tschemtsche gul' of the Tekke, Yomud, Kizil Ayak and Arabach
outer shape: highly differentiated light-symbol cross with Kotshak ends
centre: cross-star or cross of the basic form type G_1.

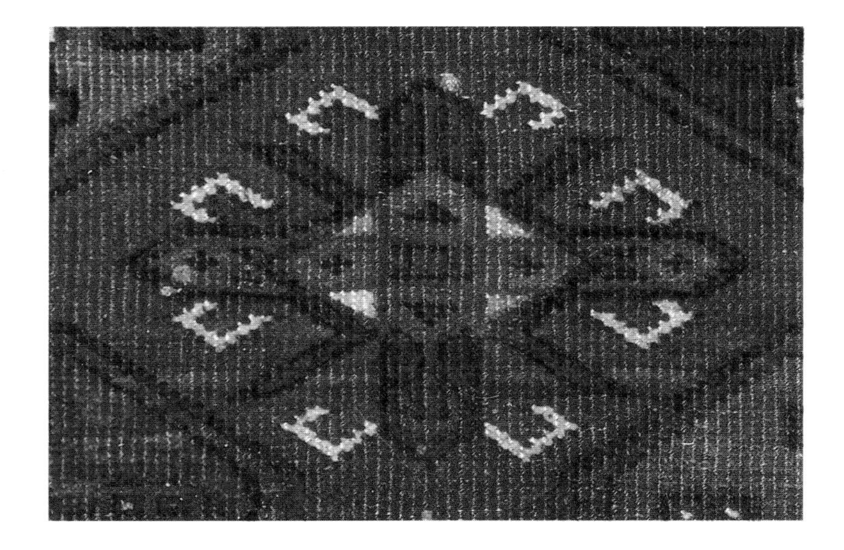

Ill. 624: 'Chemche gul' of the Kizil Ayak from a carpet with diagram, 238 x 198 cm. Private collection.

C X NG d: 'Erre gul' of the Yomud
outer shape: Greek multiple cross clearly set apart in colour on a square (rectangular) ground
centre: diamonds, one within the other.

Ill. 625: 'Erre gul' of the Yomud from a carpet with diagram.

C X NG e: 'Lily cross gul' of the Salors, Tekke and Ersari
outer shape: Kotshak cross of the basic form type E
centre: four-part diamond.

Ill. 626: 'Lily cross gul' of the Salors from a cushion (chuval) with diagram, 49 x 106 cm. Private collection.

Borders

C X B a: 'step-form cross border' of the Salors, Saryk and Ersari
Classic, clear examples of step-form crosses, one next to the other, with distinct multiple cross in the centre. Frequent alternation in the secondary borders between small Greek and St. Andrew's crosses.

Ill. 627: 'Step-form cross border' of the Salors from a carpet, 280 x 280 cm. Private collection.

C X B b_1: 'Kotshanak border' of the Salors, Tekke and Chaudor
The alternation between Kotshak diamond-crosses and multiple crosses achieved through colour changes, surprise effects and overemphasis of negative designs. The Armenian S-border is a frequent secondary border.

Ill. 628: 'Kotshanak border' of the Salors from ill. 642.

Ill. 629: 'Kotshanak border' of the Salors from a cushion (chuval), 63 x 166 cm. Private collection.

C X B b_2: 'Kotshanak border variant' of the Tekke(?)
Kotshak diamond-crosses, one next to the other. Changes of colour here also achieve an overemphasis of negative designs. The Armenian S-border used as secondary border.

Ill. 630: 'Kotshanak border variant' of the Ersari from a cushion (chuval), 146 x 52 cm. Private collection.

C X B c: 'cross border' of the Tekke, Salors

A row of coffers containing crosses of alternating colours of the basic form type A/D$_1$. The secondary border shows small step-form crosses.

Ill. 631: 'Cross border' of the Tekke from a cushion (chuval) fragment with diagram, 75 x 101 cm. Manfred Dayss, Stuttgart.

C X B d: 'lily-(Kotshak) cross border' of the Saryk, Kizil Ayak, Tekke, Arabach and Ersari

Lily crosses, and later Kotshak crosses linked together in hexagons or rhomboids, with the negative areas filled with their halves. Frequently the Armenian S-border used as secondary border. The Kotshak crosses can be replaced in later examples by step-form crosses (Chamtos border) or rosettes (Ersari).

Ill. 632: 'Cross border' of the Arabach from a cushion, ill. 645.

Ill. 633: 'Kotshak cross border' of the Ersari from a carpet, ill. 651.

The inventory of early decorative designs shows beyond any doubt that the vast majority of carpets, if in fact not all of those known to the present author, reveal elements of Christian ornamental art. What have been thought to be tribal-guls from the 19th century can all be traced back to just a few basic designs, which, moreover, are dependent on one another in their design-historical development. Jon Thompson[332] attempted to derive the guls from an invented 'cloud-collar' motif without realizing that this Chinese motif was an import from the west as well. Thus he proposes a chain of development which progresses as follows: 'cloud-collar' – 'cloud-collar gul' – 'Turkish motif' (from an Armenian carpet of the 16th century!) – 'archetypal guls' – 'lobed guls' – 'octagonal guls' – 'rhomboid guls' – 'Chemche gul' – 'medallion designs'.

A chain of development for the carpets of central Asia cannot be proposed in isolation and without reference to other known sources. Therefore we must draw upon the carpets from Groups A and B especially, as well as upon material depicted in paintings. We know that during the 13th century, in the wake of the Christianization of the Greater Mongolian Empire, though not only there, the cross-star tile design attained its widest distribution. In MBN no. 10/294 (ill. 251) we found a classic Armenian example, still adorned with a complete world-picture. Furthermore, in Group B II we were able to follow a development showing how the world-picture was gradually superseded by the cross or by the Gloria Crucis. We find this stage of development of the 15th/16th century in C X HG a_1 and in C X HG a_4: in the former the cross, and in the latter the Gloria Crucis. Ulrich Schürmann illustrates a carpet of the Kizil Ayak(?),[333] which, in spite of its very late date of production, kept the aforementioned cross-star tile design in the first two rows of pattern repeat (ill. 557). Here we see quite clearly that the so-called 'Kejebe' motif, fancifully interpreted by Elena Tzareva[334] in her glossary as a "wedding tent on the camel," is without a doubt part of this compositional scheme. And what is more, we see that both the 'Ersari' from ill. 637, as well as the 'Arabach' from ill. 644, have preserved the composition better than the comparable 'Salors' (ill. 639). In addition to this, we have to consider Amy Briggs' carpet depictions, collected from the Timurid period, and realize that at the beginning of the 14th century cruciforms such as those found in C X HG a_1 had emerged, as had already the shape of the compressed eight-pointed star toward the end of this same century. These designs were common during the 15th century, at the end of which there was a tendency toward the octagon, which naturally caused the deformation of any remaining eight-pointed stars. The Armenian example presented by Thompson shows this very stage of development from the first part of the 16th century.

Since the 'Holbein gul' itself is nothing more than a compressed eight-pointed star, we should also look to Group C II for comparison. It should come as no surprise to find there the same or similar problems or solutions, the same or similar details of design.

Thus in Groups C II a, C II c_2, C II d_1, C II e_2 and C II f we discover examples of how weavers attempted to give new life to the interior of the gul by changing its colour. In the beginning this was done only in individual guls. Not until the last example, in BUIM no. 147865 (ill. 548), do we find this colour change within the Holbein guls throughout the carpet, which is then typical of most of the guls in Group C X. This carpet represents a prototype for the textiles produced in central Asia.

In comparing the Salor-Torba in ill. 634 with a Holbein carpet, we notice that an entire section of the composition was borrowed: the Holbein gul with the four cross-star rosettes along the axes of the cross.

Ill. 634: Cushion (chuval) of the Salor, 86 x 137 cm. Sotheby's, New York; 1/12/1984.

The front side of the cushion shows the close connection in design with the SP-Holbein carpets of Group C II.

Certainly the guls of Group C X HG f are special reduced forms of Group C X HG a, although there are also parallels among the later representatives of Group B II that have been through a very similar or even the same development. This is different with respect to the 'Kotshanak border', which has been frequently cited here. C X B b_1 is completely identical with borders of Groups B II, C II and C VI. As far as we can see at the moment, this border only begins to show up in carpets from the 16th century, which should serve as an additional point of reference in dating.

We possess only one depiction in a European painting of a carpet supposedly produced in central Asia: the painting is entitled 'Woman Playing the Cittern' by Gabriel Metsu 1660/67 (ill. 635). It shows to the right a carpet serving as a tablecloth, which exhibits the colours typical of carpets from central Asia. The main gul corresponds roughly to the structure of Group C X HG b, as the reconstruction in ill. 636 is intended to show. This gul, its outer shape rounded, contains in the centre a lily cross within the rounded hexagon of the basic type D cruciform . It resembles, to a certain extent, the Tekke gul C X HG b_4 in its asymmetrical distribution of the outer cross arms. Half of the secondary gul, visible here, shows two lily blossoms enclosing the negative half of a cross. A narrow border, already torn, completes the carpet. The lily cruciform flower could be seen as connected to the cloverleaf-cross in the 'Ersari' shown in ill. 649, even though the negative design of the former carries no meaning.

A carpet exhibiting a gul of the design depicted in this painting has not been found to this day.

Ill. 635: Gabriel Metsu: Woman Playing the Cittern, detail; c. 1660. Gemäldegalerie, Kassel.

Ill. 636: Reconstruction of the field design from ill. 635.

Beyond the correspondences discussed thus far, there are two very weighty considerations that permit us to postulate possible origins for these so called Turkmen carpets. The first is provided by the frequently-mentioned S-border, which has received thorough treatment in these pages. The second concerns the make-up of the 'Salor gul' C X HG b_1, the 'Ersari gul II C X HG b_5 and the relatively late 'Tauk Nuska guls' C X HG e_4 of the Yomud, Chaudor, Kizil Ayak, Ersari and Arabach. In each segment of these guls there are between one and two Armenian › ԴԴ ‹-symbols, whose meaning we discussed on page 39. The fact that one finds Armenian symbols in the carpets of every Turkoman group credited with the production of carpets, the tribal name of which the present author has used here for the sake of clarity, should make us think.

Let us not forget that it is precisely the very early carpets that contain especially clear Christian symbols and also provide us with clues as to their Armenian production or exposure to Armenian influence. There is, for example, no early gul which does not contain a clear cruciform, whereas by the beginning of the 19th century this cross has been replaced.

Furthermore, we notice that until the middle of the 20th century – precisely the time of the study by Moshkova mentioned before – carpets originating in the regions of central Asia were all named in accordance with the production centres at the oasis regions. This is of importance. It is, moreover, striking that all the Turkoman names for the guls as well as for the carpet designs are exclusively descriptive in character, but give no information as to content. These facts call for critical thinking.

Let us take a moment to summarize what we know thus far. The early carpet in the central Asian-Turkmenian area is Christian in its symbolism, and exhibits features indicating its Armenian production or at least involvement. It was named after the oasis towns of its origin, as for example Bokhara, Khiva, Kerki, Merv, Beshir or Pende. In its ornamentation, part of which is the use of the Christian cross of victory as a central motif, it clearly belongs to a single line of design evolution. In some examples there are still clear and documented traces of cosmological systems analogous to those in the more western areas of Armenian settlement.

The group of carpets which have survived from before 1800 is comparatively small, yet they encompass a longer period of time than has been thus far suspected. The oldest textiles probably date as far back as the 16th or 17th century. So few of what are called main carpets, almost always nearly square, have survived that no attempt has ever been made to show a development. This is not the case with the group of large pieces, often referred to as 'Torbas', meaning tent bags. The evolution shown above is based in no small way on their inclusion. Loges points out that the function of these bags is yet unexplained, suspecting himself their use for 'decorative purposes, though not for pets but rather for the festive decoration of dwellings.'[335] The present author sees parallels in the one-sided frames of the antependia used in Europe, suspecting these Torbas to have fulfilled liturgical purposes. Many of them were later reworked into seat cushions, almost all of one size, as the majority of the pieces attributed to the Tekkes and the Ersaris evidence through the presence of creases. A group of carpets which has thus far gone unmentioned is what was referred to until recently as 'Hatschlu', but has now come to be known almost exclusively as 'Engsi'.'Hatschlu' means cross carpet, again a simple Turkmenian description of the design, 'Engsi' means the carpet curtain at the entrance to a tent. There are few truly old 'Hatschlus'. These show a clear Greek cross and small crosses or lilies filling the ground (ills. 655, 656). In other words, they have as their principle of composition the 'Gloria Crucis'. They must have had a function similar to that of many of the arch-form carpets: to adorn the lectern or the recess of the altar. It has been pointed out repeatedly that there is no documentation whatsoever to prove that 'Hatschlus' were used as 'Engsi' before the second half of the 20th century.

The question which still has to be answered concerns the regions of Armenian settlement in central Asia. We must note, independent of the following discussion, that Armenians were to be found at all times as artisans, dealers and clerics in all the larger settlements and towns engaged in trade. We know, beyond this, that during the time from 1220 to 1230 Genghis Khan settled Christian minorities, and among them a good many Armenians, in Khorassan and Mazandaran, which is to say in the regions south and south-east of the Caspian Sea. Despite the fact that over the course of centuries they were deprived of their own language as they became assimilated into the Persian culture, these 'settlers' continuously maintained close contact with their home country.

At the beginning of the 17th century, under Shah Abbas I segments of the Armenian population were once again forced to resettle in the same regions, as well as in the region of what is today Kabul in Afghanistan. Khorassan and Mazandaran constitute those regions we consider the actual home of the Turkomans to be. Discounting all the hypotheses concerning the production of carpets in this region, we must not overlook the fact that this is a mixed population, only part of which are Turkmen, the other part being Armenian. We can assume that the Christian minorities lost their identity as a result of the enforced Islamization of the 18th century, which, in fact, nearly all the remaining Christian communities there fell victim to. At the moment, the question as to whether the Salor clans from the regions of the Caucasus (about whom Moshkova wrote) were Armenian cannot be answered. What is more, the assumption that sometime during the middle of the 19th century the Salors gave up sheep herding in favour of farming, thus destroying the conditions necessary for carpet weaving, seems doubtful. It seems more likely that the artisans engaged in carpet manufacturing stayed in Pendeh, not joining in the move to the Serakic region. Nor is the ethnic origin of the Olam clear. As a splinter group, they lived together with precisely those groups of Turkmen whose names are associated with the early carpets, yet they deny a Turkmenian origin. Here again, we may be dealing with what was left of groups of Armenians within the original population, if they were able to survive at all. It would also be interesting to gain more insight into the connections between the Salors and the Kizil Ayaks, who, on the one hand, had been considered part of the Ersari since the 17th century, and yet they considered themselves related to the Tekke from Mery.[336] If, however, it is true that the Kizil Ayak are a subgroup of the Salors from Pendeh,[337] they would then be the link between Salors, Ersari, and Tekke. This would provide us with the means for explaining those design developments which are obviously dependent on one another.

By the same token, the dependence of design development on the kindred relationships between individual groups of different tribes would give even more significance to the question as to the ethnic affiliations of the group which actually manufactured the carpets. Such a dependence would make the hypothesis of tribe-specific guls, even for the 19th century, all the more doubtful.

The conquest of the Turkmenian regions during the 19th century at the hands of Czarist Russia, and their incorporation into the Greater Russian Empire, brought about what were probably, according to what we know today, the most significant changes for the manufacture of carpets. Even if we assume that at the oases, carpets had been made to order for centuries, the sudden increase in demand along with the colonial mentality of exploitation clearly caused a fundamental change in the production of carpets, a change much like the manifest development in Persia. During this time, the last remaining religious points of reference were lost; this becomes particularly clear when we look at the debasement of designs. The carpet had become a mere commodity.

This changed, islamicized attitude can be seen in other ways as well. Kalter illustrates a Tekke woman's coat,[338] which bears a very strong similarity to a priest's robe. Even the crosses from the end of what once was the stole of the robe are still present, decorating the collar and the trim of the upper part. And yet what a conceptual change! Knowing how Turkomans feel about the status of their women – who take their place last after any amount of household goods – the degradation of clothing a woman in priest's vestments could not be more graphically shown.

Ill. 637 (above): Cushion (chuval) of the Ersari, 64 x 168 cm. Russian Museum, Leningrad, no. KOB-205.

It is plainly evident here that the compositional elements are crosses and star-tiles. The so-called 'Kejebe' motif grows out of the reduced half-cross.

Ill. 638 (below): Antependium of the Salors, no dimensions (detail according to Neugebauer/Orendi 1909).

The star tile of this carpet, known only from the literature, constitutes for the time being the only one in which the negative shapes of the old cross design still maintain the correct angle in relation to one another.

Ill. 639 (above): Antependium of the Salors, 76 x 224 cm. Eberhard Herrmann, Munich.

Ill. 640 (below): Cushion (chuval) of the Salors, 83 x 112 cm. Ethnographical Museum, Leningrad, no. 87–20.

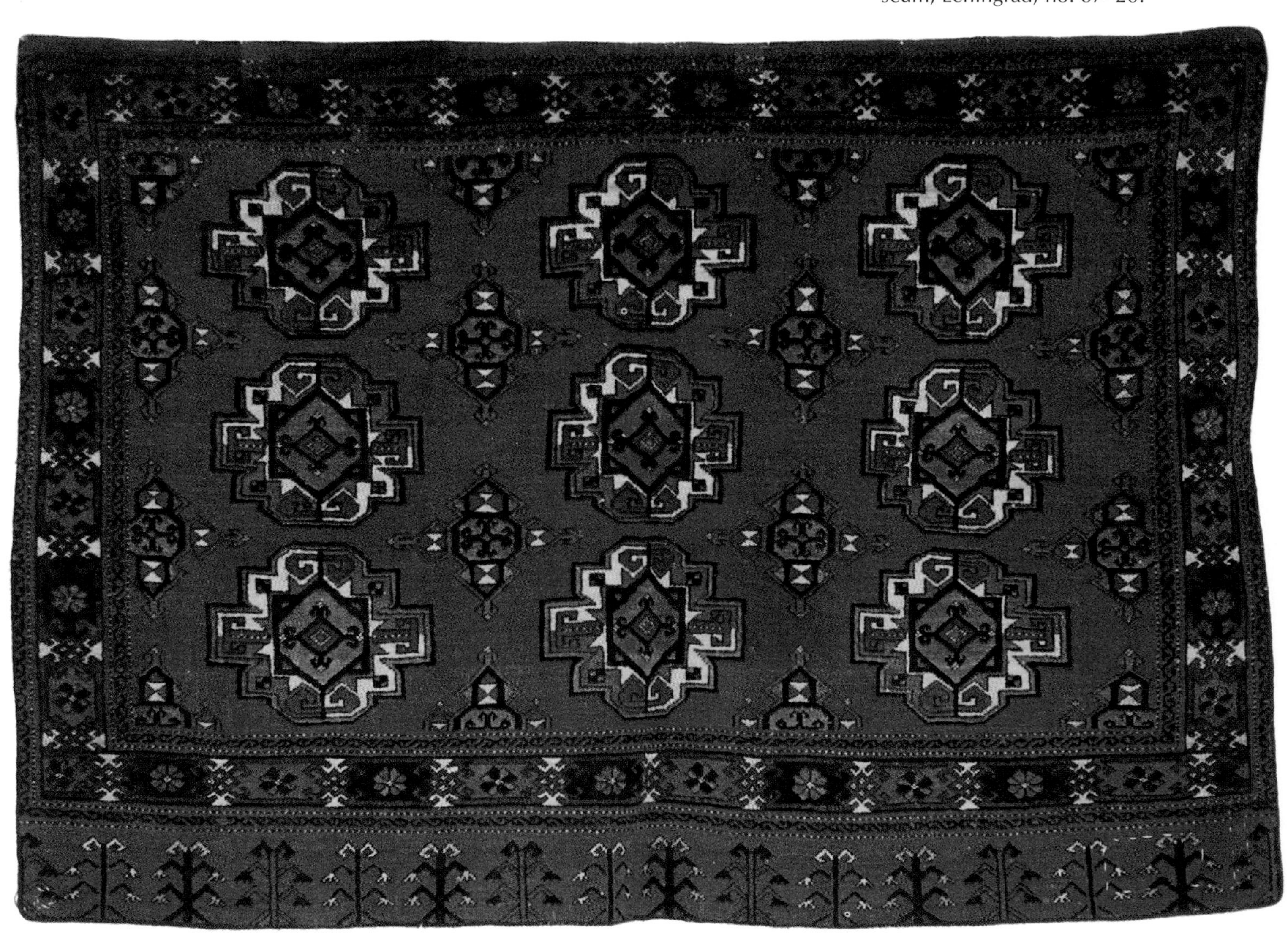

Ill. 641 (above): Cushion (chuval) of the Ersari, 52 x 143 cm. Private collection.

The star tile within a star tile becomes the single-star medallion.

Ill. 642 (below): Cushion (chuval) of the Salors, 78 x 142 cm. Staatl. Museum für Völkerkunde, Munich, no. 86–308014. The Woger Collection.

Ill. 643 (above): Cushion (chuval) of the Tekke, 74 x 117 cm. Private collection.

Here we find the rare variant of the 'Tscharch-Palak gul' of the Tekke as secondary gul.

Ill. 644 (below): Cushion (Torba) of the Arabach, 50 x 125 cm. Museum of Oriental Art, Moscow, no. 1265 III.

Even here the cross-star tile design is still intact.

Ill. 645 (page 451 below): Cushion (chuval) of the Arabach, 81 x 149 cm. Private collection.

Ill. 646 (page 451 above): Cushion (chuval) of the Tekke, 70 x 105 cm. Auktionshaus Dr. Fritz Nagel, Stuttgart (327/830).

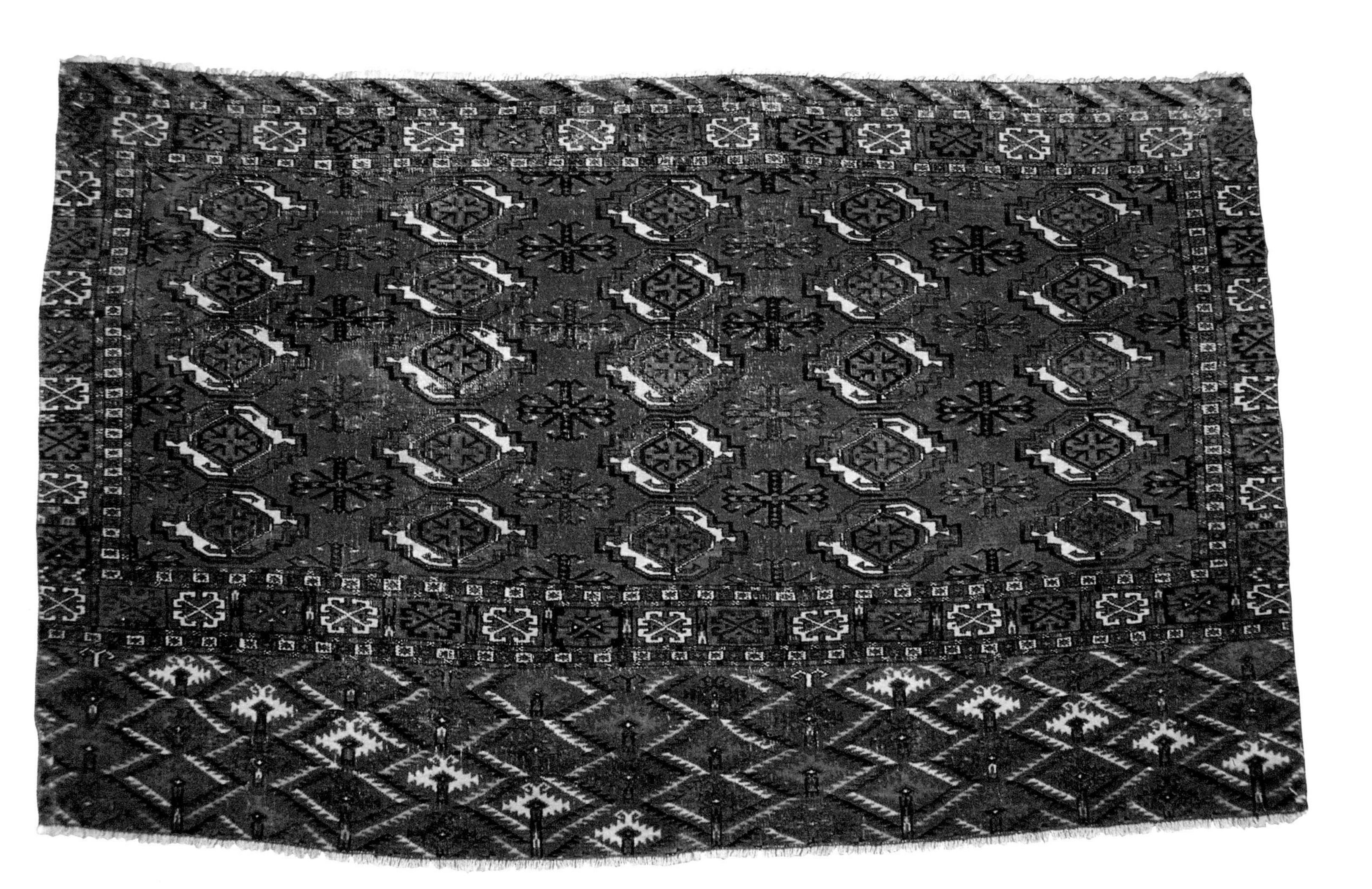

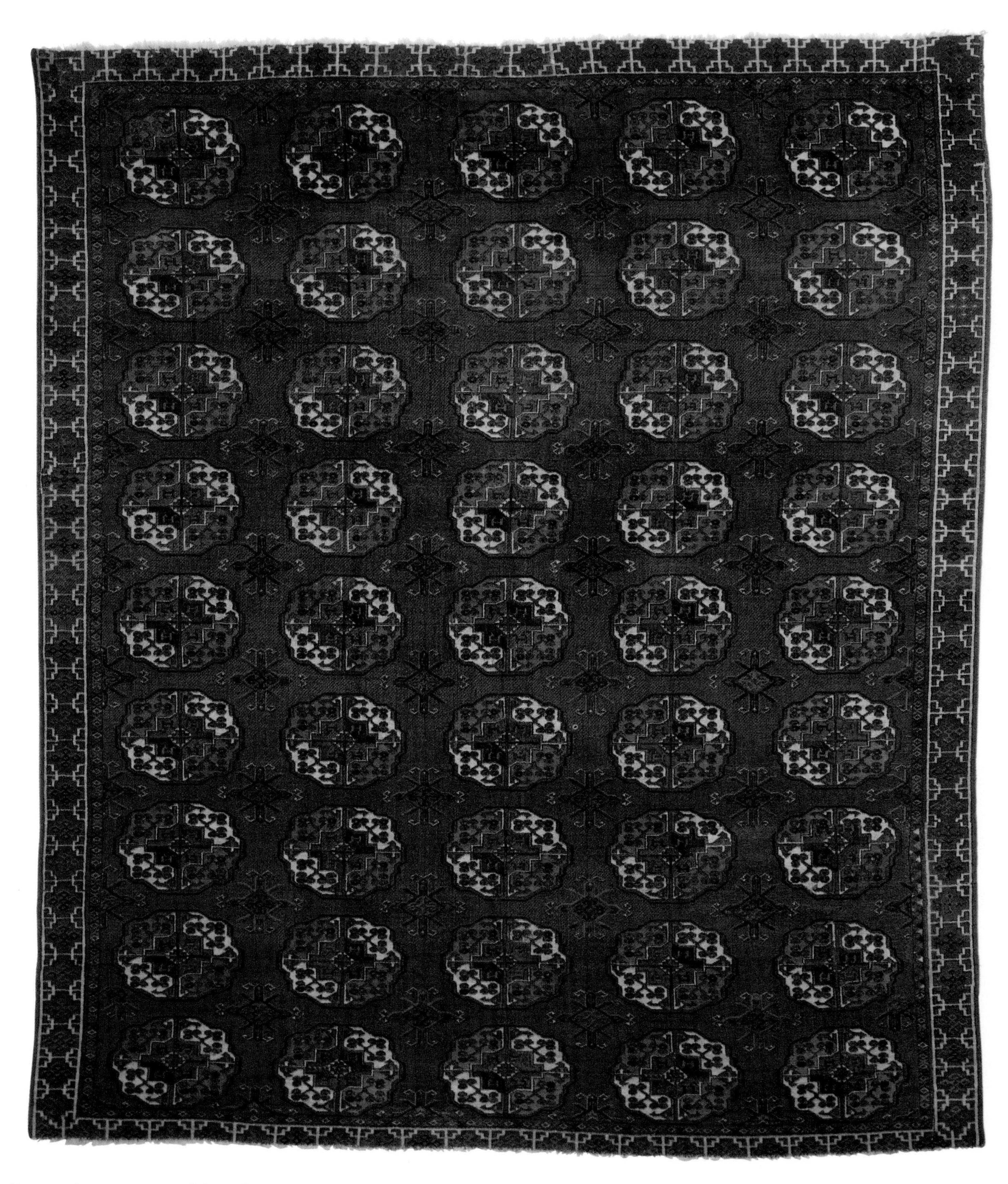

Ill. 647 (above): Carpet of the Salors, 258 x 209 cm. Private collection.

For the present, this carpet is the only one in which the old 'Chemche gul' has survived.

Ill. 648 (right): Carpet of the Ersari, 258 x 207 cm. Private collection.

Ill. 649: Carpet of the Ersari, 204 x 208 cm.
Private collection.

Ill. 650: Carpet of the Saryk, 211 x 201 cm.
Private collection.

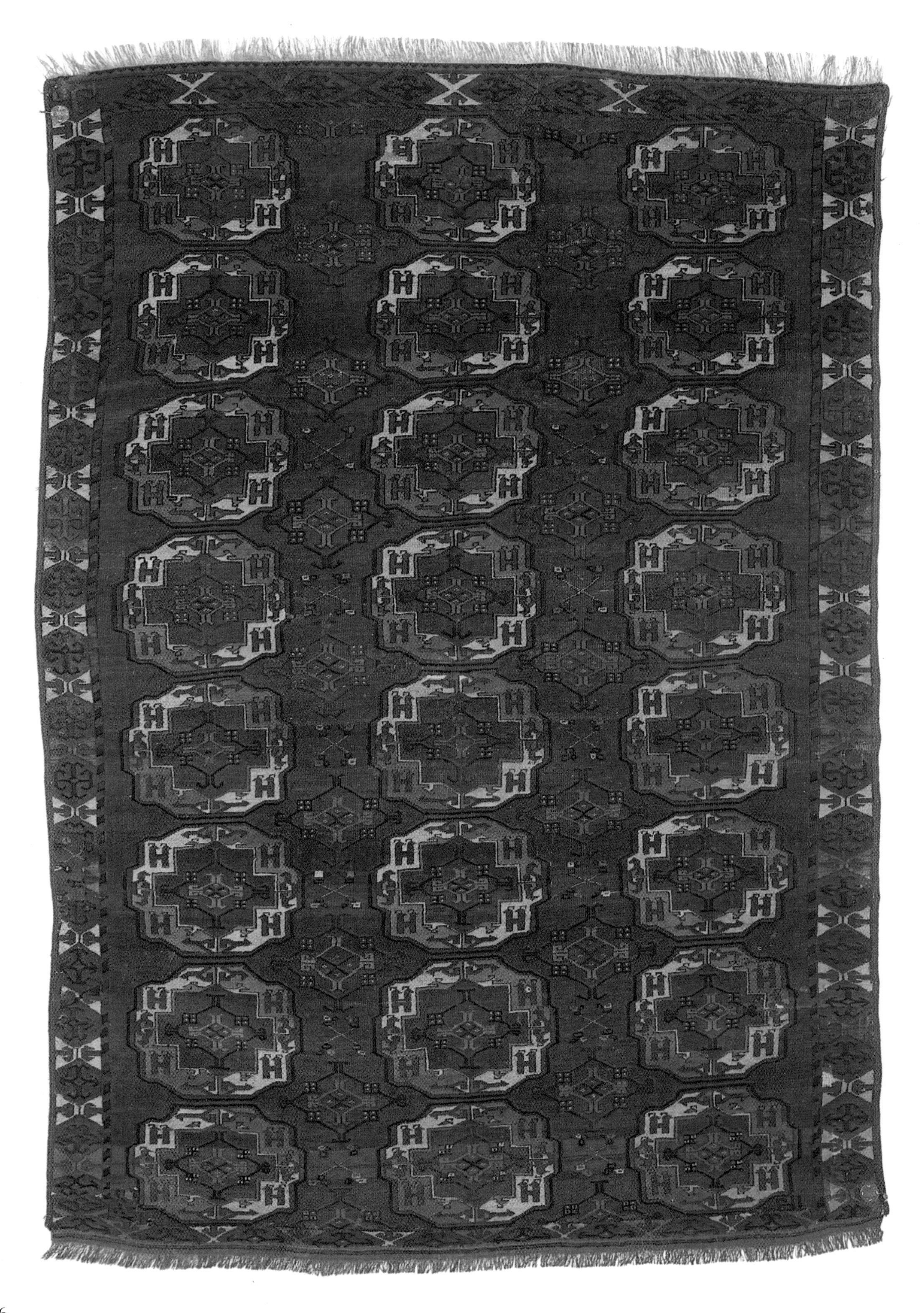

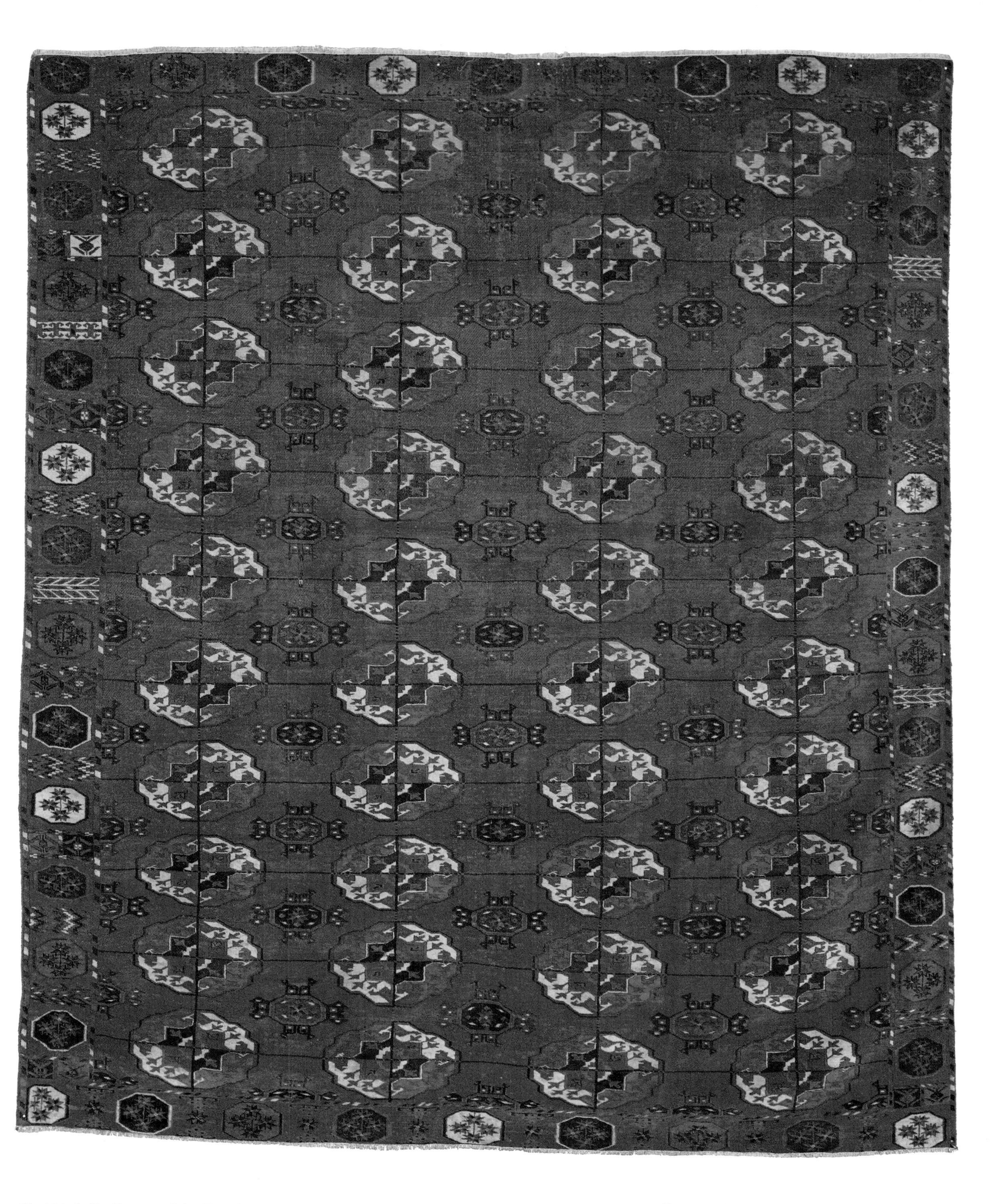

Ill. 651 (left): Carpet of the Ersari, 293 x 200 cm. Meyer-Müller Collection, Zurich.

Ill. 652 (above): Carpet of the Tekke, 237 x 193 cm. Private collection.

Ill. 653 (above): Carpet of the Saryk, 232 x 228 cm. Private collection.

Ill. 654 (right): Carpet of the Yomud, 292 x 176 cm. Private collection.

Of the Turkoman region this carpet is one of the most resplendent in colour. In contrast to all of the later 'Kepse gul' carpets, the guls are not arranged diagonally here.

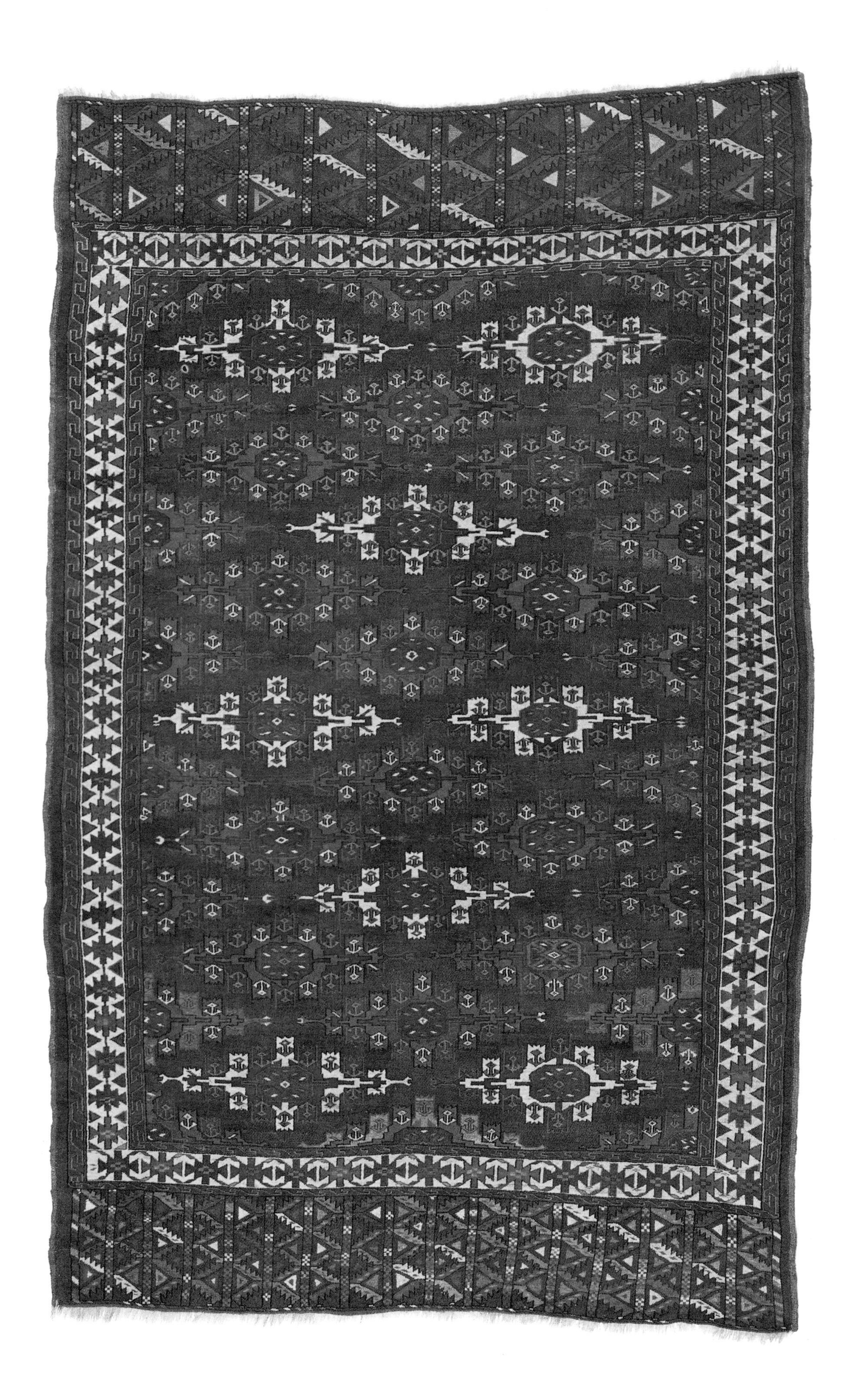

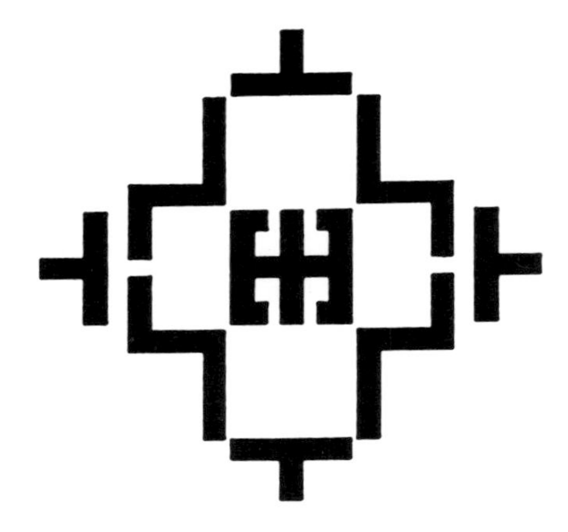

Group C XI: Carpets from Central Asia II – Carpets of the Uzbeks, Kirghizes and from the Oasis Towns of East Turkestan

The carpets that we know of today from the Uzbeks and the Kirghizes are so few in quantity and moreover so recent that they are actually too young to warrant treatment here. In terms of design, they show a close correspondence with Caucasian-Armenian products, without any special tribe-specific features being noticeable. Since both the Uzbeks and the Kirghizes were Christians into the 18th century, Christian symbols are predominant in the older examples. We encounter step-form crosses (ills. 657, 659), Kotshak- or diamond-crosses, Memling guls, as well as guls from Group C X. Attributing these carpets correctly is difficult in individual cases,

Ill. 655 (page 460): cross carpet (Hatschlu) of the Yomud, 157 x 119 cm. Peter Bausback, Mannheim.

Ill. 656 (page 461): cross carpet (Hatschlu) of the Yomud, 155 x 134 cm. Auktionshaus Dr. Fritz Nagel, Stuttgart (270/89).

Very few examples have survived which show the beams of the 'Gloria Crucis' radiating outward, diagonally, from the centre of the cross.

Ill. 657 (right): Main carpet of the Uzbeks, 153 x 134 cm. Peter Bausback, Mannheim.

especially since the existence of a spezialized manufacturing tradition, prior to the middle of the 19th century – though suspected by Moshkova – was never sufficiently substantiated. In spite of this, it is likely that these tribal groups did manufacture carpets both for their own use as well as for the markets in Samarkand and Buchara, looking to both the west and the east for models. The 'Julshirs' (ill. 658) from the region of Samarkand are amongst the few examples remaining of what was no doubt a very old tradition.

The situation was different for the old oasis cultures of East Turkestan. The mere existence of the Silk Route continually kept these regions abreast of the products and methods of manufacture in both the west and the east. Thus the carpets reflect this cultural overlap in their material as well as in their design and colour. In this context we will consider only Christian carpets, or those that were at least influenced by Christian traditions.

Ill. 658 (above): Julshir of the Kirghiz, 304 x 145 cm. Kunstauktionshaus Dr. Fritz Nagel, Stuttgart (300/2043).

This so-called Julshir, a thick sleeping mat of long pile, consists of three strips, approximately 50 cm in width, which were sewn together.

Upon reviewing the published material, a number of very interesting carpets caught the present author's attention, but the criteria which have heretofore been used to distinguish between their possible manufacturing areas – Yarkand, Kashgar and Khotan-have left him unconvinced. The differences in the appearance the carpets due in fact to the chronological evolution of their designs have commonly been seen as regional.

It would appear that the focal point for the production of Christian carpets was to be found in the regions located the furthest to the east, with Khotan in the Tarim basin perhaps even marking the most westerly point. We know that the inhabitants of the Tarim basin belonged to the centum Indo-European language group. Their settlements extended all the way into what is today the region of the Chinese province of Kansu. These people maintained close cultural and commercial contacts with the west, south-west and the south. The rich oasis towns constituted early targets for successful missionary activity. We can assume that, by the 5th century at the latest, the Nestorian form of Christianity had become firmly entrenched there, spreading then to western China with the same intentions. The same can be said of

Ill. 659: Carpet of the Kirghiz, 312 x 155 cm. Auktionshaus Dr. Fritz Nagel, Stuttgart (288/111).

The carpet contains little more than traces of the composition from ill. 667, and yet the Greek crosses, arranged vertically along the central axis, one on top of the other, define this as a religious image.

Buddhism, Islam and Manichaeism, the latter becoming the state religion of the Uighurian empire during the 8th century. During the second half of the 13th century, Marco Polo gave an account of the then still extant Christian kingdom in the Tenduk country, which, though subject to the Tatars, was ruled by princes of the tribe of Prester John.[339] The country of Tenduk, with its capital of the same name, was presumably located in the Ordos region, on the Yellow River. Although there is much to support the contention that the oasis towns were regions of religious tolerance for centuries, we know nothing to this day about the decline of Christian activity in this area.

The carpets handed down to us, however, the earliest of which may go back to the 16th century, bear silent witness to the Christian tradition through their ornamentation. These designs exhibit their dependence on, or correspondence with, western models – despite their having been influenced by eastern (commonly Chinese) features.

In his book "Art Rugs from Silk Route and Great Wall Areas", which has received hardly any recognition in Europe, Lee Yu-kuan[340] published what are perhaps the most interesting and earliest carpets. In spite of fundamental problems concerning dating and attribution, the illustrated material presented there is exceptional.

To begin with let us consider a carpet (ill. 660) which, on the one hand, shows the cross-block design filled with light-symbol crosses, numbering twelve, yet which exhibits also the East Turkestan variant of the Kotshanak border in its early design. The alternation between cross-rosettes and lilies in the border is of special interest.

We also find early designs, though of a different sort, in a double niche carpet (ill. 661) which may possibly contain the permutation of a world-picture. In the centre of the medallion we see the cross within the Greek cross; in the four cardinal directions there are lighter, smaller medallions which likewise form a cross; between these we find the stars of the celestial spheres accompanied by two sets of seven Greek-cross medallions. The composition contains parallels to the late example from Group B II: ARM no. 1975–147 (ill. 293). The inner border consists of positive and negative half-crosses in reciprocal alternation, with which we are already familiar from Christian oriental illuminations. In the main border we find 'E' designs, one after the other, as we have already found them in Armenian carpets. The question as to whether these stripes are intended to mean 'water', or whether they are merely imitations of those found in Caucasian carpets, cannot as yet be answered.

In ill. 662 we see the East Turkestan variant of the carpets of Group C V a (cf. ills. 448, 449, 454). Diamond poles connect octagons in which very beautiful Kotshak crosses are clearly recognizable. The inner secondary border corresponds to that on the relief in Norawank (ill. 136); the main border replaces the 'E' designs with lilies of grace.

Quite archaic is the composition of a silk carpet that was on display at Nagel's in 1978 (ill. 663). Despite the division into coffers, the cross-star tile design is still completely preserved there. Leaf-form crosses, showing a surprising resemblance to those of the 13th century (ills. 204, 205), stand out from the blue ground. In looking at the negative form of the star-tile, we see in its centre two step-form crosses of different colours, one inside the other. In the middle of these is a very clear cross fourchée. Around the centre of the star-tile we find small, diamond-shaped step-form crosses and rosettes placed in a way which is reminiscent of Group C V e. The inner secondary border is closely related to C III c_2 and c_3, with even the acorns still showing. The main border is nearly identical to that of the preceding carpet (ill. 662), the lilies of grace being replaced by cruciforms.

Ill. 660 (left): East Turkestan,
210 x 103 cm. Private collection.

Ill. 661 (right): East Turkestan, 287 x 148 cm. Private collection.

Ill. 662 (left): East Turkestan, 330 x 165 cm. Eberhard Herrmann, Munich.

Distinct Kotshak crosses fill the octagonals, which appear laid out here like tiles in the diagonal fashion typical of western carpets.

Ill. 663 (right): East Turkestan, 259 x 193 cm, silk. Auktionshaus Dr. Fritz Nagel, Stuttgart (273/99 a).

It is the large cross compositions in the negative areas in particular that are important in the evolution of designs.

Ill. 664 (left): East Turkestan, 280 x 157 cm. Private collection.

The cross-star tile design with its archaic details has been preserved here in unusual clarity.

Ill. 665 (right): East Turkestan, 295 x 168 cm. Victoria & Albert Museum, London, no. 1474–1883.

As is the case in the Caucasus and in Anatolia, the cross-star tile design undergoes a reduction in compartment-medallion carpets in East Turkestan as well.

Ill. 666 (left): East Turkestan, 233 x 130 cm. Textile Museum, Washington, no. R 56.2.2.

A cross carpet that has its parallels in the Hatschlus of the Turkoman region.

Ill. 667 (right): East Turkestan, 241 x 141 cm. Private collection.

We have already seen the Greek cross composition in the Kirgis carpet of ill. 659. The borders stem from Anatolian-Caucasian models.

Ill. 668 (left): East Turkestan, 470 x 190 cm. Private collection.

The carpet contains the so-called Afshan design of Caucasian carpets, here rendered in a different colour. Cf. ill. 478.

Ill. 669 (right): East Turkestan, 290 x 142 cm. Victoria & Albert Museum, London, no. T 244–1927.

Once again we find the cross-star tile design in ill. 664, the only difference being that in this case the star-tiles are dominant, with the cross tiles appearing only in the negative area of the ground. The border consists of coffered cross-rosettes.

In Group C XI, in much the same way as with Group B II (pp. 171 ff., ills. 250–260), elements of the composition were taken out of context and worked into medallion carpets. As an example of this let us cite the handsome two-medallion carpet of the V & A[341] (ill. 665). The star-tiles have become more imposing, each isolated in its own nearly square coffer. The inner structure of the star-tiles corresponds to that common in the Kasak region (see star Kasaks in ills. 352, 354). The design of the cross was clearly preserved, despite its being partially modified along floral lines. The inner edge of the main border is framed by a swastika border, which is set apart in colour, the outer edge by a step-form cross border. Both originate from previous Armenian prototypes. The main border represents a further development of that shown in ill. 663, except that the cross present in the latter has been superseded by the lily, the divine symbol of grace.[342] Despite some difference in design, the border detail bears a certain similarity to the 'tree of Jesse' found in Armenian work and could be an adequate representation of its Chinese counterparts.

Ill. 670: Western Chinese antependium, 99 x 314 cm. Eberhard Herrmann, Munich.

With reference to its Armenian-Christian counterpart in ill. 639, this Chinese antependium shows those features shared by both as well as what distinguishes them.

Illustration 667[343] shows yet another Christian carpet of this region. The field is filled with Greek crosses in endless repeat, which themselves contain flowery light-symbol crosses. The main border strikes us as Anatolian: two 'E'-shapes face into each other so that a cross results, and these appear in rows, one after the other. The secondary borders likewise have their origin in the west. Both in conception and design there are parallels in Christian-Kirghiz works (ill. 659) or, for example, in no. 34–32 of the Ethnographic Museum in Leningrad,[344] giving us reason to suspect this influence here.

Schürmann illustrates a 'Khotan'[345] (ill. 668) which was doubtless modelled after examples in Group C V d from the region of Armenia and south-eastern Anatolia. And yet such a carpet clearly shows how strong the Chinese influence can be on the arrangement of colour.

We see this influence also in another carpet (ill. 666) which corresponds to the 'Hatschlus', the cross carpets of the Turkmenian regions[346] (ills. 655, 656). This is even clearer in its representation of the 'Gloria Crucis' than comparable examples mentioned above.

We can find and follow evidence for details of design from nearly all carpet sources from the 17th and 18th centuries in the carpets of East Turkestan and western China:

for example, compositions covering the full extent of the field in the manner of the flowering cross (ill. 669), or the double niche or medallion carpets. It would take us beyond the scope of this book to demonstrate the fascinating transformation of originally Christian carpet designs by Chinese-Buddhist elements and the exchange of what were in part symbols of identical content. Let us cite one example as representative, this being a Buddhist antependium (ill. 670). A comparison with ill. 639 shows what is common to both as well as what is different. In the Buddhist example, the cross, inscribed in a circle and decorated with cloud-bands, is suspended in the middle above a spring. However, this is no longer the Christian cross of victory, but rather the Buddhist symbol of cosmic-divine harmony.

One thing, however, is obvious. In spite of the credit constantly given to the Islamic faith for exercising such influence with arts, particularly in the Tarim Basin, we in fact find no evidence of this anywhere in the early carpets. Thus we can conclude that the manufacture of carpets was not in the hands of Islamic nomads, but carried out rather by artisans located in the towns. This is underscored by the fact that the carpets were manufactured by master weavers, in other words, men.[347]

Various authors have often pointed to the influence of 'Timurid art' and to the influence of Chinese art brought about by it. The present author, however, is of the impression that this Chinese influence, without which what we today call 'Ottoman art' could not be understood, came about much more directly by way of the Silk Route and the transfer of designs carried out by means of it.

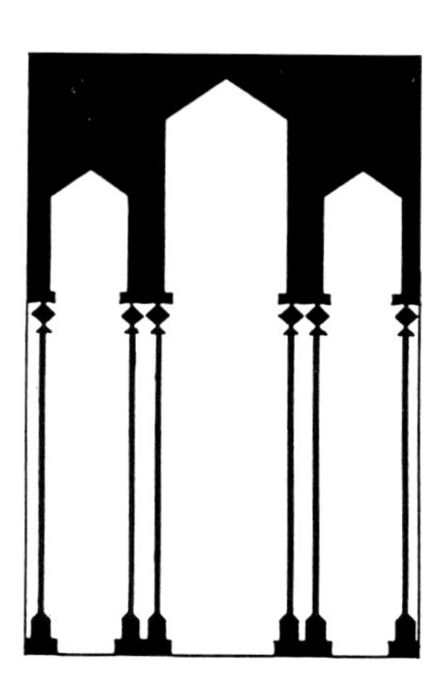

Group C XII: Arch-Form Carpets – Paradise-Gate Carpets

As has been mentioned elsewhere in this book,[348] the author suspects the idea of the arch-form carpet to have originated in Palestine. In the Jewish cult, we find the customary use of Torah-shrine curtains, and of curtains intended to cover the entrance to the temple, the 'holy of holies.' The floor mosaics of the Beit Shean synagogue offer an illustration of such a curtain from the 6th century (ill. 671). The oldest Christian arch-form curtain, from somewhat later in the 6th century, is a textile fragment woven by Copts (ill. 674), which first appeared in a publication by Swoboda in 1892[349] and which, in 1895, Alois Riegl linked to the arch-form carpets.[350] For the sake of completeness, the author would like to add here that in this fragment Swoboda believed himself to have identified one of the four curtains of the early Christian altar tabernacle, the ciborium (Tetravelum).

Whereas the Christian arch-form curtain can hypothetically be traced back to the Torah-shrine curtain, this tells us nothing yet about the representation of the arch. An arch can be seen in the positive or in the negative: the positive view being the arch as a piece of architecture, the negative view the arch as a passageway. In search of a design tradition, we find two examples of arches from pre-Christian times, the content of each entirely different. In the ruler steles of Mesopotamia, the arch as a miniature arch of triumph symbolized worldly and religious power, as did the carpet. This concept becomes clear in the depiction of the 'empty throne' (ill. 672), which originated in about the year 400 in Constantinople: it is a symbol of God's might. In the Phrygian grave steles, however, the arch represents the gateway to eternity. Both traditions merge in the arch-form carpet, a tradition that finds its expression in the design of the Armenian Katchkars (ills. 131, 708): the arch of triumph as a gateway to eternity, to paradise. It is only logical that in the early carpet examples, more than

Ill. 671 (above): Floor mosaic from Beit Shean; 8th century. Israel Museum, Jerusalem.

The arched cult niche here has its place in the temple; between its columns we see the curtain of the Torah Shrine.

Ill. 672 (left): The 'empty throne', c. AD 400 SMPK, Early Christian-Byzantine Collection, Berlin, no. 3/72.

The arched niche shows the 'empty throne' as a symbol of the rule of God.

Ill. 673 (right): Phrygian grave stele, 2nd/3rd century. SMPK, Early Christian-Byzantine Collection, Berlin, no. 4/69.

The Phrygian couple on this grave stone is depicted standing in the gateway to eternity. Above the gate there is a depiction of Christ(?); and, as symbols of faith, we see vines growing up the columns.

anywhere, this entrance to paradise should take on the form of a church with three aisles. With the lilies above the arch representing the 'grace of God on the Day of Judgement' (p. 482, ills. 675, 679), the meaning of the design becomes completely clear. These carpets uniquely symbolize complex concepts of the Christian faith, showing the believer how it is possible to receive God's grace through the church in order to triumph over death and enter into paradise on Judgement Day.

Carpets of this sort served to close off the entrance to the 'holy of holies,' which, as Swoboda suspects, may have been the Armenian altar tabernacle (Templum), much like the ciborium which was once present in almost all large cruciform domed shaped churches. It may, on the other hand, have been the niche which substitutes for this ciborium: located in the apsis area of smaller Armenian churches for the purpose of keeping the liturgical accoutrements, as was also the case with the Torah-shrine. Both ways of closing off the 'holy of holies' are confirmed by the inscription on the Gorzi carpet (p. 484). The present author was assured convincingly that this custom was still practised in Armenia until the genocide in Turkey in 1915 and indeed continued into the Stalin era.

Ill. 674 (right): Coptic curtain, reconstruction of a fragment from the KFM (according to Riegl).

This arched curtain used by Coptic Christians, in which we find the recurring motif of the 'Ankh cross', already contains the most important elements of Christian arch-form carpets. Like such Armenian carpets, this must have served as a means of closing off the entrance to the temple or the ciborium.

Group C XII a: Columned-Arch Carpets I

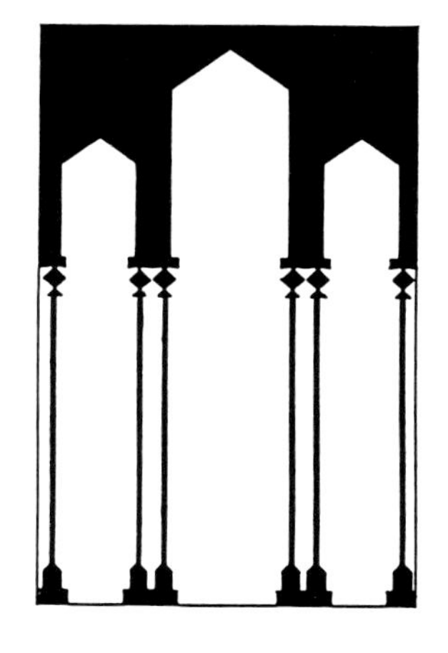

There prove to be a number of problems involved in positing a chronology for arch-form carpets. The oldest bears the date 1051 (AD 1602) or (1)651. Alois Riegl published this as an 'oriental carpet from the year AD 1202'[350] (ill. 680), transposing the year 651 into the Armenian calendar. This is most certainly not to be reconciled with the design evolution presented here.

For the time being, the author regards the arch-form carpet from the McMullan Collection in the MMA[351] (ill. 675) as the earliest representative. The inner panel of this carpet (in the literature it has come to be known by the term 'multi-column Ladik') shows three pediments supported by slender columns. Of these three, the

Ill. 675 (page 480): MMA no. 1974.149.19, 169 x 115 cm. The Metropolitan Museum of Art, New York. Gift of J.V. McMullan 1974.

The oldest surviving arch-form carpet shows quite clearly the cross section of a cruciform domeshaped church, symbolizing the gate to paradise. Above this the rows of lilies represent symbols of grace for the Day of Judgement.

Ill. 676 (left): Evangelistary from Ardjesh, dated 1303. Matenadaran, Erivan. Ms. no. 4052, F. 81r.

Here an apostle is shown against the background of what is, analogous to the carpet from the previous illustration, the cross section of a cruciform.

Ill. 679 (page 483): TMW no. R 34.22.1, 168 x 112 cm. Textile Museum, Washington.

Here the leaf ornamentation above the arch panels at the sides is to be compared with that in ill. 185.

Ill. 677 (below left): Cruciform domeshaped church from 1030, Samtawissi.

The façades of Armenian churches reflect, in relief, the composition of arch-form carpets.

Ill. 678 (below right): Church of the Holy Sepulchre from 1339, Norawank.

Particularly noteworthy is the depiction of the coupled columns – their capitals and their bases; they are identical to those on the early arch-form carpets.

middle one is the highest, as one would expect in a church nave. The composition is comparable to the evangelist-miniature painted in Ardjesh in 1303[352] (ill. 676). It may, however, be even more similar to the façade of the cruciform domeshaped church of Samtawissi (from 1030, ill. 677) or to that of the Church of the Holy Sepulchre of Norawank, consecrated in 1339 (ill. 678). In the carpet, located above this architectural symbol, we find a frieze of lilies. Oddly enough, these lilies are continually referred to in the carpet literature as (Ladik-) tulips, probably because the tulip was the chosen plant of the Ottomans. Yet, in this case, there can be no mistaking these for anything but lilies of the species Lilium candidum or white lily. This cultivated plant, known as far back as antiquity, originates in Lebanon. Here, as the divine symbol of grace, it represents the grace of God on Judgement Day.[353] The inner panel is framed by a main border consisting of differently coloured cartouches, placed one after the other. Each contains a cross formed by filigrane lilies. Even the arms of the light-symbol cross, set apart in colour, likewise bend to form plant stems in the shape of the 'H'. In the negative areas between the cartouches in the border we see cross-star halves as fillers on both sides. The outer secondary border contains Greek cross-rosettes, the inner border, the individual elements of a disintegrating scroll vine.

In summarizing the message of this arch-form carpet, we can say that the church is the gateway to eternity and paradise. One can enter by way of the arch of the triumph of faith with the help of God's grace on Judgement Day.

The carpet just described is one of the few knotted on a white ground. It can probably be dated to the first half of the 15th century. It was followed by those on a red

ground from the collections of Dr. von Hengel,[354] and likewise red those of the MMA from the McMullan Collection, from around 1500,[355] the Washington Textile Museum,[356] (ill. 679), the collections of Davonzati,[357] Danker, the Protestant church in Brasov,[358] the TIEM,[359] and those in private collections in Germany.[360] Those datable to the 16th century are the examples of Grote-Hasenbalg II.12,[361] of the Museum für angewandte Kunst in Vienna,[362] and the Iparmüveszeti Museum in Budapest,[363] all of which are on a white ground. Likewise attributable to this century, but on a red ground, are those of Cittone, those from the former collections of Schmutzler,[364] Kessler,[365] the Budapest Museum, at Lefevre's,[366] and Sotheby's,[367] as well as those of the Protestant church in Bistrita[368] and the Dumbarton Oaks Collection.[369] Here should also be mentioned the Vakiflar examples,[370] and those at Nagel's,[371] which expand the design architecturally by adding an upper floor and drawing in stairs, thus sacrificing the lilies. In comparing these examples – which are also referred to as 'Transylvanian carpets' – we notice that the lilies have grown smaller in size, in some cases completely disappearing. The round, cross-filled cartouches have changed their shape, becoming longish ovals with more lavish blossoms. In certain cases involving those carpets last mentioned new border designs were added. Yet through all this, the group of three pediments standing on coupled-columns was retained. This is also true of several examples dating from around 1600, for instance the carpet on a blue ground from the Parish Church in Bistrita.[372] Later on in this evolution, the outer columns are left out, as in the TIEM example[373] or in the piece cited initially, dated either 1602 or 1651.

This carpet (ill. 680) is of such great importance because it provides information concerning not only dating, but also the original purpose of the carpet. Taking into consideration its origin during the 17th century and the likelihood of Greek influence from the surrounding area, it is possible to read the Armenian inscription as follows:

Door curtain to the temple of the holy of holies of Saint Hripsime in the year of our Lord, 1051 (AD 1602) or (1)651. I Gorzi, the artist, made (or presented) this.

Each of these two possible manifestations of the 'holy of holies' (the 'altar tabernacle' – once often referred to as 'the temple', or 'the niche in the area of the apsis') was to be decorated as specified in the canon of Saint Sahak, in a manner worthy of their significance.

As the design tradition continued to evolve, the remaining columns began to disappear during the first half of the 18th century. From then on we may find them in either isolation or reduced to stumps. The lilies retain in part their original shape, even on into the early 19th century. From the increasing variety evident in the borders, we can conclude that there were a growing number of regions of production (ills. 688–690).

Now that this one continuous line of evolution has been demonstrated, it must be emphasized that this was not the only one. We can definitely assume that there were other centres of production throughout those regions densely populated by Armenians – that is, in the Caucasus, Anatolia, Persia and probably also in Greece. Geographically, the author places the group of columned-arch carpets just presented in the Armenian regions of the south-western Caucasus, and in eastern or south-eastern Anatolia, bearing in mind that over the centuries a certain amount of migration westward seems to have taken place. The carpet dated 1602 or 1651 must come from the southeast, that is to say, from the area of Aintap (known today as Gaziantep).[374] Assigning the later examples from the 19th century to Ladik, as is done time after time in the literature, is wholly unfounded. Moreover, they do not seem to coincide with the design repertoire, which is more eastern in appearance.

Ill. 680 (right): the 'Gorzi carpet', dated 1651. Formerly in Vienna, owned privately (according to Riegl).

Aside from the significance of its being dated to 1651, the 'Gorzi carpet', missing today, is so very important because it is the only one to document its use as a curtain covering the holy of holies in its inscription.

Group C XII b_1: Columned-Arch Carpets II

We now turn our attention to a group of arch-form carpets, the early representatives of which were attributed by many specialists to a manufactory at the Ottoman court in Bursa, Istanbul or Cairo due to their use of the asymmetrical knot. Later representatives which exhibit the symmetrical knot, and are likewise referred to as 'Transylvanian', split off in the 16th century from those presented in the preceding group and were probably produced in Caesarea, known today as Kayseri.

The carpets also have columns as a general rule, although aside from a few exceptions, only one pediment. In the case of early examples, in the main border, common to all of them, we find a curvilinear cross-star rosette supplanted by a 'tree of Jesse' which is surrounded by hyacinths and red carnations.

The structure of a silk carpet (ill. 682), knotted using the symmetrical knot, can best be understood when viewed within its overall context.[375] Here, in a double niche on a dark blue ground, we see two imposing trees of life, made up of different blossoms to look like cypresses. Placed at the gates of heaven, as it were, they symbolize eternal life. The artists behind this new compositional design were possibly influenced by the diamond-form carpet presented earlier (ills. 466, 681), which, judging by its signs of use, hung above an as yet unidentified object, 50 cm in width, such that only the double pediment shown in ill. 681 was visible. Even though there may not be complete agreement with respect to the individual details, there must be agreement with respect to the structure of the composition and the idea.

A second early example, probably from the last thirty odd years of the 16th century, is the famous arch-form carpet from the Ballard Collection in the MMA (no. 22.100.51, ill. 683). Knotted with the asymmetrical knot, in its structure it corresponds directly to the column carpets discussed earlier, with its use of three aisles as a symbol for the church, and the noticeable simplification of its lilies. What is new, on the other hand, is the oil lamp hanging from the middle arch and the bouquet-like plant representations.

Ill. 682 (page 487): Private collection, 167 x 120 cm, silk.

Enormous, stylized trees of life stand on either side of the column in the gate to paradise. In the border, cross-rosettes and the 'tree of Jesse' – shaped like the tree of life – are interconnected with roses, carnations and hyacinths: symbols of the Virgin Mary.

Ill. 681 (right): Private collection, detail from ill. 466.

Ill. 683 (page 488): MMA no. 22.100.51, 168 x 127 cm. The Metropolitan Museum of Art, New York. Gift of James F. Ballard, 1922. Photograph by Otto E. Nelson.

Ill. 684 (page 489): WÖMAK no. T 8327, 183 x 117 cm. Österr. Museum für angewandte Kunst, Vienna.

In terms of the history of designs, the carpet is to be placed in the 16th century. There is a close connection to the designs in the ceramics industry in Nicea (today Iznik); the designs for the carpet may in fact come from the very same source.

It must be made quite clear at this point that oil lamps were already standard elements in the decoration of Christian churches at a time when Islam had not yet even been heard of; in the absence of any other identifying features, it is completely incorrect to argue that the presence of such a lamp, or a 'hanging lamp', should be regarded as evidence of a Moslem prayer carpet. The bouquet-like plants represent roses, carnations, anemonies as well as lilies(?). They are all, as in central European panel painting (cf. ill. 448), symbols of the Virgin Mary.[376] The lilies(?) appear for the first time in the somewhat more advanced, though otherwise identical border. The question remains as to whether what we have been calling lilies(?) are in fact lillies or tulips. In this context tulips seem highly unlikely, even if one were to presume an Ottoman patron. The S-secondary border also identifies this work as belonging to the Armenian Christian tradition.

Ill. 685 (page 490): CAM no. 1980.31, 168 x 132 cm. Cincinnati Art Museum, Cincinnati. Centennial gift of Mr. and Mrs. Richard R. Markarian.

Ill. 686 (page 491): Topkapi no. 13/2037, 190 x 140 cm. Topkapi Palace Museum, Istanbul.

The carpet from the Mausoleum of Selim II does not make use of the symbols for the Virgin Mary and substitutes a green (Moslem) ground for what was red (Christian).

The same can be said of a number of arch-form carpets having only one column-supported arch: for instance, of the examples in East Berlin (no. 89.156), in Cincinnati (no. 1980.31, ill. 685) and Kuwait (The National Museum). The example from Vienna (no. T 8327, ill. 684), despite its being identical technically and in its use of colour with those just mentioned, appears to be the earliest in the evolution. Its border corresponds to that of the above-mentioned silk carpet, yet without the later lilies(?). The arch field is filled with blossoms, leaves and palmettes, quite similar in composition and detail to those designs used by Armenian artisans in Iznik in making the tiles for the Ottoman court in approximately 1560.[377]

The arch-form carpet from the mausoleum of Selim II[378] is also Armenian and datable approximately to the year 1575. This carpet (ill. 686), like the very similar example in Washington, TMW no. 1697.24.1, is the first non-Christian commissioned carpet in the Group XII b. To start with, it is distinguished by the colour of its ground, which is green – the prophet's colour. Red, in contrast to this, is the colour used to represent Christ. Furthermore, carnations, roses and hyacinths, symbols of the Virgin Mary, as well as the S-secondary borders were not included. The designs were generalized, leaving only details in the secondary borders to provide clues as to authorship and tradition.

The carpet in the Museum für Islamische Kunst in West Berlin (no. I.15.64) is quite unusual. It is the only one to be dated and in possession of a chronogram for the year 1610/11. On the one hand, it exhibits all the border details of the above-mentioned carpets in Berlin, Cincinnati and Kuwait (that is to say, all the symbols of the Virgin Mary as well as the Armenian S-secondary border); however, it also has a green niche. We should consider the possibility that this was the result of a misunderstood imitation from the 19th century.

A Jewish arch-form carpet from the 16th century with a red arch field, the so-called 'synagogue carpet', in the Textile Museum in Washington (no. R 16.4.4,ill. 687) also presents problems. It bears an inscription, in Hebrew, of Psalm 118:20:

"This is the gate of the Lord, into which the righteous shall enter."

Ill. 687 (page 493): TMW no. R 16.4.4, 186 x 155 cm. Textile Museum, Washington.

The Hebraic inscription cites Psalm 118:20: 'This is the gate of the Lord, into which the righteous shall enter.' In its content it is then clearly to be identified as a paradise-gate carpet from a Christian-Jewish community.

The conceptual closeness of its content to the interpretation of the Christian-Armenian arch-form carpet (p. 482) discussed above cannot be overlooked. Is it Christian or Jewish? We can be sure that this carpet would have been used in a Christian community of Hebrew speakers.

Erdmann suspected these carpets to have originated in Cairo,[379] and since then they have also been attributed alternately to a court manufactory in Cairo, Istanbul or Bursa. Istanbul is not entirely out of the question. Beginning with Mehmed II, Armenian craftsmen were settled there and provided with special privileges. Moreover, since 1461 Istanbul had been the seat of the Armenian patriarch, whom Mehmed II had called to there from Bursa. Under the influence of Rüstem Pasha (a patron of the arts from Cappadocia) not only did Sinan become court architect, but in addition, the Armenian influence from central Anatolia seems to have become increasingly felt.

It is altogether possible that in central Anatolia, as well as in workshops, for example in Istanbul or Bursa at the end of the 16th or during the first part of the 17th century, carpets were produced with nearly identical border designs but using different techniques. As a result of the conflicts between the Ottomans and the Safavids in West, central or East Armenia, some of the Armenians living in these regions were either forced to work in Istanbul and in the western regions of the Ottoman Empire or did so voluntarily, whereas others took jobs in that part of Persia ruled by the Safavids. This quite naturally would have had an effect on the technical quality of the carpets.

Ill. 688 (left): Vakf. no. E 61. Vakiflar Carpet Museum, Istanbul.

As in the case of other groups, the columns in this group are also reduced. In its development, this carpet corresponds to the 'Gorzi carpet' from 1651 and is in all probability its contemporary.

Group C XII b_2: Columned-Arch Carpets III, known as 'Transylvanian Niche-Form Carpets'

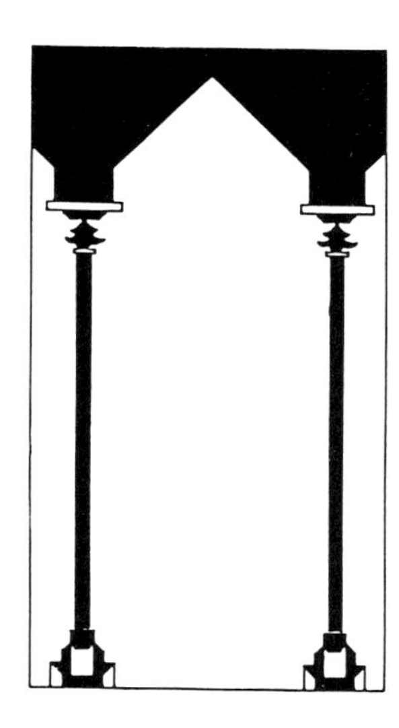

The continuation of the design-historical evolution is to be found in carpets from central Anatolia (Caesarea?) that were knotted with the symmetrical knot during the 17th century. Many of these were or are in the Protestant churches of Transylvania, which led to the term 'Transylvanian carpets.' The examples at Christie's,[380] in Grote-Hasenbalg,[381] Bernheimer,[382] and most of those published by Schmutzler,[383] all of which presumably originated during the 17th century, have a red ground (ills. 688, 689, 690). Not until the beginning of the 18th century do we find examples on an ochre ground, with what are often very degenerated border details. With these, as well as some on white ground, we must consider the possibility of their originating in eastern Europe.

Ill. 689: Private collection, 186 x 135 cm.

At the end of the 17th or the beginning of the 18th century, the columns become superfluous; with their function no longer 'weight-bearing', an understanding of their significance in relation to the whole is lost; ultimately they completely disappear.

Group C XII c: Arch-Form Carpets IV of the so-called Bellini Type

Here we are dealing with a relatively small group of arch-form carpets with one pediment in the upper part and an opening, or keyhole-shaped formation, in the lower part. In all of the known examples, a cross variant fills the middle. In the opening, or 'keyhole', of earlier examples, we also find a cross, cross-star, or later on, the 'tree of Jesse'. We find in the 'Breviaire d'Alaric'[384] (ill. 691) a piece strongly influenced by the Oriental Christian Church, a model for both the arch as well as the multiple-arch carpets.

Ill. 690 (left): Davide Halevim, Milan, 195 x 125 cm.

Ill. 691 (below): Breviaire d'Alaric. Bibliothèque Nationale, Paris. Ms. Lat. 4404, F. 1v-2r.

The examples from the Wher Collection[385] (ill. 692), the Museum für islamische Kunst in West Berlin[386] (ill. 693), the Islamisches Museum der Staatlichen Museen in Berlin,[387] the MMA in New York[388] (ill. 694) and the Victoria & Albert Museum in London[389] (ill. 695) all date back to the end of the 15th and the early 16th century. We may add the examples from the Keir Collection[390] (ill. 696) and those from the Islamisches Museum der Staatlichen Museen in Berlin[391] (ill. 697) dating from the second part of the 16th century. At first sight, this latter group does not appear to bear much resemblance to the former. The 'keyhole' design has been enlarged con-

siderably. In place of the cross-star or cross-rosette which filled it before, we now find the rather dominating symbol of the 'tree of Jesse', which we encounter similarly in the so-called dragon carpets. The central cross motif, though still present, has been considerably reduced in size.

There can be no doubt that the 15th century arch-form carpet from the Carpet Museum in Teheran, already mentioned (ill. 328), is to be included in the discussion of this group. Instead of the 'keyhole', it exhibits only the dominating cross-star in the lower part of the niche, and above this the representation of two ambos, or 'reading desks', found in eastern churches. The Arabian inscription is an admonition to repent and fast. This carpet is representative of the early East Armenian type, whereas those mentioned above are West Armenian.

Group C XII d: Multiple-Arch Carpets

Of interest to us here are three multiple-arch carpets, two of which are located in the TIEM and one in the Textile Museum of Washington.

TIEM no. 720 is the oldest of the three (ill. 698). The fragment shows us five arches, which have been preserved and a pediment variant that bears a strong similarity to the border designs discussed in connection with Group A II. The border enclosing each arch resembles that used in Armenian and Cilician architectural reliefs from the 13th century. These provide us with help in dating, though a later date, such as perhaps the 14th century, would not seem completely out of the question. Aside from the carpet itself, the fact that in each case the cross-stars in the lower openings were deliberately destroyed is worthy of note. Of course that leads to the question why. If we are correct in assuming that this arch represents a gate to paradise, and there is much to support this apart from the Hebraic inscription, then the deliberate destruction of Christian symbols at the entrance to paradise by later, Moslem owners is to be understood.
The fragment TMW no. R 34.00.2 (ill. 699) has three arches in contrast to each of the others, and its pediments are stepped. It is, in its layout, similar to the preceding; in many of its details it unifies traditions of East and West Armenia. We need only compare it with the arch-form carpet in the museum in Teheran, illustrated earlier (ill. 328), or with carpets from Group B II (ill. 292), with which it shares a border. It must have originated during the first part of the 15th century, or somewhat earlier.

TIEM no. 744 presents two rows of, in each case, eight pediments, one above the other (ill. 700), with clearly discernible crosses in each. The entire formation is framed by a border of type C II c_1, which makes its origin at the end of the 15th century appear likely. This carpet gives us occasion to consider the function of such multiple-arch carpets. Even today they are referred to in the literature as multiple 'prayer carpets' or 'saf'. Here it was assumed that these carpets were Moslem and that each arch delineated the prayer space for one individual. In TIEM no. 744 we see how absurd this idea actually is: the existing space in the arch fields would not even be sufficient for a new-born baby. This is not unusual. The dimensions of all those carpets made prior to the 19th century are such that this use cannot have been possible; not to mention the fact that arch-form carpets up to the 19th century do not show any signs of use that might specifically indicate their function as 'prayer carpets.' If, on the other hand, we assume that such multiple-arch carpets are primarily Christian, then we could also assume that they fulfilled quite a different

Ill. 692 (page 498): Wher Collection, 167 x 123 cm. Courtesy of the Wher Collection, Switzerland.

It is reasonable to presume that the keyhole-like representation at the bottom of this special type of paradise-gate carpet was once to have represented a baptistry; there are in this very example still indications of this.

Ill. 693 (page 499): BMIK no. 87.1368, 170 x 124 cm. SMPK, Museum für Islamische Kunst, Berlin.

In later carpets the 'baptistry' becomes the entrance to the 'holy district', at the centre of which there is always a cross.

Ill. 694 (page 500): MMA no. 22.100.114, 119 x 152 cm. The Metropolitan Museum of Art, New York. Gift of James F. Ballard, 1922. Photograph by Otto E. Nelson.

Ill. 695 (page 501): LV & A no. T 135–1911, 147 x 115 cm. Victoria & Albert Museum, London.

It is especially interesting to compare this carpet with those that follow. We can reconstruct how the area around the entrance is transformed into the 'tree of Jesse' and the large cruciform into the 'lily of grace', flanked by mythical creatures carrying the tree of life.

Ill. 696 (page 502): Keir no. 28, 155 x 112 cm. The Keir Collection.

Ill. 697 (page 503): BOIM no. I 24, 180 x 120 cm. Staatliche Museen zu Berlin, Islamisches Museum, Berlin.

Ill. 698 (left and below): TIEM no. 720, 126 x 424 cm. Türk ve Islam Eserleri Müzesi, Istanbul.

Arch-form carpets of this type were used not only to cover the parclose, but also the considerably higher altar platform. The deliberate defacement of the cross-stars in the entrance to paradise by subsequent Moslem owners deserves our attention.

Ill. 699: TMW no. R 34.00.2,
147 x 174 cm. Textile Museum, Washington.

purpose. We notice their shortness in width (height) and that they frequently show signs of having been used as hangings. We know from Indian miniatures that carpets of this sort were, for example, used to cover the outside of a throne.

Even as early as 1891 Alois Riegl recognized their use as 'wall carpets'.[392] The use of carpets in covering the altar, the parclose, and the choir stalls in the churches of Transylvania may be supportive evidence. Anyone who takes a moment to look around while walking through the Christian oriental churches that still exist (in the Turkish region of today, almost all those that were Armenian have been destroyed) will still find the holes for the hooks which were used to attach the textiles.

Ill. 700: TIEM no. 744, 130 x 311 cm. Türk ve Islam Eserleri Müzesi, Istanbul.

Crosses or cross-stars are located in the small arch panels, themselves reminiscent of row homes. Perhaps they represent tomb-stones, with the carpet serving as a votive gift in commemoration of a specific tragedy or armed conflict. It is at any rate ludicrous to imagine that we should be dealing with a prayer rug intended to accommodate repentant souls.

The Amida Carpet

Now, finally, let us briefly turn our attention to a non-Christian carpet, the 'Amida carpet' (ill. 707).[186] With respect to its design, it is one of the most interesting carpets which exists. In contrast to what has been the principal subject matter dealt with in this book, it does not contain any manifestly Christian symbolism. The heraldry found in the border as well as in the field connects the emblems of the Nisanid, Abu l-Qasim 'Ali from Amida, with that of the Orthokid, Kara Arslan from Kaifa. Considering that Amida was first subjugated by Ali in 1165, and that the region of Hisn-Kaifa was in the possession of the Nisanids only from 1170 to 1184; and considering, furthermore, that Ali had already died by 1178, this carpet must have been designed during the period from 1170 to 1178. The border depicts Ali the 'lion' subduing Amida the 'bull' (ills. 701, 702), and also shows the short-winged, crossed dragon heads of the Orthokids (ills. 705, 706). The inner panel (ill. 704) takes its orientation from the composition of the Mschatta façade (ill. 703). Here we see the over-sized lion, Ali, in front of the Amida bull. Amida is the present day Diyarbakir. Although the carbon-dating analysis suggests that this carpet did not originate until the 16th century, it could nonetheless be an original from the period suggested above. Its signs of wear indicate that it was used as a throne carpet.

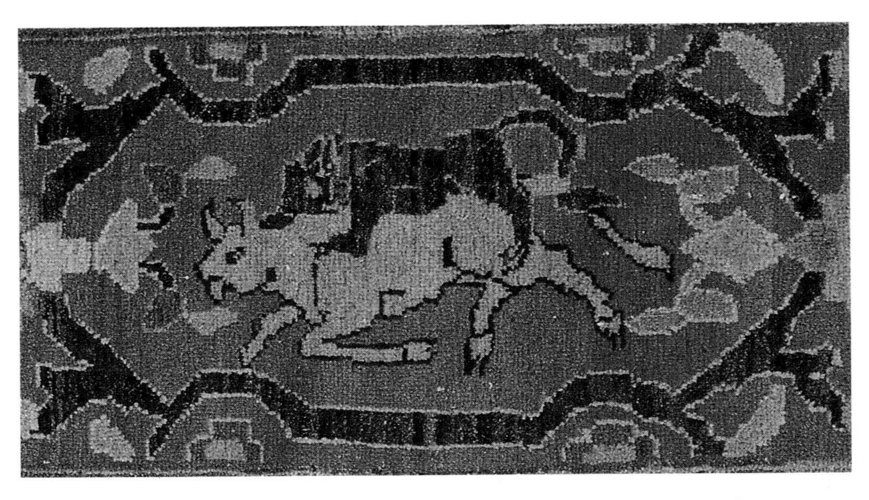

Ill. 701: Border from ill. 707 with the emblem of the Nisanid Abu l-Qâsim 'Ali of Amida.

Ill. 702: Heraldic emblem of the Nisanid Abu l-Qâsim 'Ali of Amida on the entrance façade of the Ulu Djami in Diyarbakir, relief dating from 1165.

Ill. 703: Façade of the desert castle Mschatta (Syria), detail, from 825–850. Staatliche Museen zu Berlin, Islamisches Museum, Berlin.

Ill. 704: Inner panel of the carpet in ill. 707.

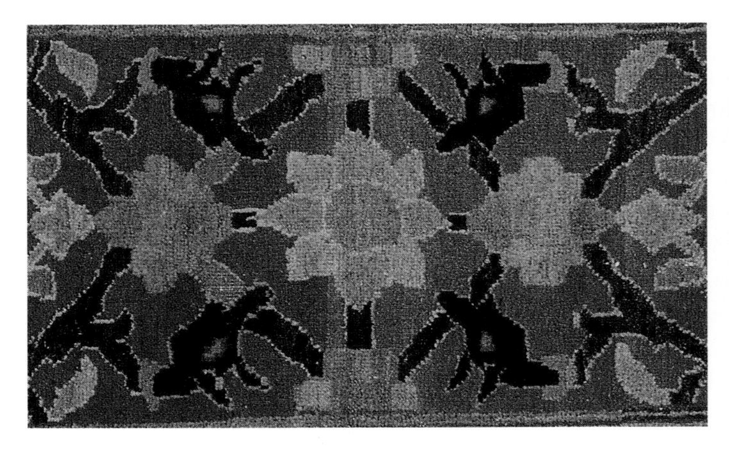

Ill. 705: Border from ill. 707, showing the emblem of the Orthokids.

Ill. 706 (above): Heraldic emblem of the Orthokid Kara Arslan, façade of the Citadel of Aleppo, second part of the 12th century.

Ill. 707 (right): The 'Amida carpet', 595 x 440 cm. Private collection.

Ill. 708: Tsaghats-Kar, Yeghegnatsor. Katchkar, dated 1041. St. Horhannes Church.

This Katchkar is intended to remind us once again of the fact that both Armenian carpets as well as Katchkars are characterized by a very similar approach to surface area design, one which is founded on the same traditions.

Summary and Outlook

The oldest surviving carpets have shown us that what we are dealing with are by no means hide-imitations; instead, we have seen that they were the products of a technically advanced, traditional craft from town or court manufactories. They seem to confirm the hypothesis that the knotted-pile carpet is a technical refinement of the older Soumak weave – a refinement which became necessary in order to represent more perfectly the designs in the carpet, which were intended as a medium for the conveyance of symbolic meanings.

The designs encountered in these carpets take their place, without exception, in a chain of traditional designs which extends all the way back to pre-Christian times. They represent a synthesis of elements from late Hittite, Urartian and Phrygian art. The objects originally bearing these traditional designs were reliefs, articles of everyday use and, more than anything else, mosaics. Within the Monophysitic Christian-oriental churches of the Armenians and Syrians, these traditional designs were adopted and continued in use without a modification of their content. The symbols and signs of this form of artistic expression in the early Christian church, which stood in complete and total opposition to the representational art of classical antiquity, were incorporated into the art of both the west and the east as a consequence of warfare, waves of emigration, programmes of relocation, and missionary work. Let us, in this connection, recall the Irish manuscripts from the second part of the 7th century, as well as the carpet-like backgrounds of Ottonian manuscripts dating from the 10th century.

A critical study of the existing source material makes clear that the hypothesis which posits the origin of the knotted-pile carpet in the Turkmenian region, and its import to the west by Turkic peoples such as the Seljuks, is completely unfounded. However, the production of such carpets within the sphere of Armenian cultural influence is documented as far back as the 8th century, with production at the centre in Murcia, Spain not beginning until the 10th century.

Carpets from Group A, as well as the fragments of their forerunners, take their place in the line of traditional designs, exhibiting an astonishing variety in design even in the early Middle Ages. What is striking at this point are not only the first signs of reduction, possibly resulting in the encodement of the language of signs by cutting designs in half or in fourths, but also the surprise-effects achieved by conscious changes in colour.

Whereas we are completely dependent on comparing designs and written sources as a way of deducing how the carpets that were produced prior to the beginning of the second millenium must have looked, this all changes with the advent of the High Middle Ages. In its function as a symbol of power and dominion, both in the secular and religious realm, the carpet then increasingly found its way into churches and the homes of rulers, and thus into the paintings of that time. We are now aware of paintings in Armenia beginning in the 11th century, and in Europe beginning in the 13th century, in which carpets are depicted. As a result of the great spread of the Christian faith in Asia during the middle of the 13th century, we find carpets exhibiting Christian ornamentation even in China during the Sung period, and from then on also in the paintings from the time of the Il-Khans and Timurids who followed. These depictions provide us with new insights into the development of carpets, and into important *termini ante quem,* even though no written information on the actual age of the carpets depicted is available. In illuminated manuscripts we also find important references to the meaning of the symbols used in the carpets.

The cross has been the central theme in all the groups of carpets treated here, whether it was used as a single, central design or as part of a larger pattern repeat. During the High Middle Ages this basic symbol might have taken the form of a world-picture or, later, might have been the centre of the Gloria Crucis. It might, however, also have been replaced by ciphers of equal meaning: by the S-shaped symbol for God, the E-shape symbol for Jesus, or by the vegetal symbol of the 'tree of Jesse.'

Drawing on the art terminology commonly applied to painting, and on other sources used for comparisons, the present author has attemped to propose groups for carpets related temporally and technically as well as in terms of their designs. Despite what often appear to have been only contemporary developments in design, we have found that these were, or tended to be, sequenced: the B groups originated during the High Middle Ages, whereas the subsequent C groups were produced during the period beginning in the late Middle Ages and extending to the 18th century and beyond.

Intellectually, all this began within the sphere of Armenian cultural influence, even at a time when that country was being torn apart by the drawing of new political boundaries. Waves of emigrants poured into western Anatolia in particular, as well as into eastern Europe and the countries of the Mediterranean. The enforced deportation of Armenians to Greece, Persia and central Asia led to the relocation of existing centres, and the establishment of new centres of production in both the west and the east. This reshuffling naturally caused a certain adaptation and change in the old traditional set of designs. It is significant that the Armenian Monophysitic Christian oriental church was condemned as heretical and subjected to persecution by both the Orthodox and the Catholic church; it was only under the protection of Moslem rulers that Monophysitic Christianity, closely related to Islam, was able to maintain itself.[393] Always loyal subjects, the Armenians, over the course of time, worked their way to the forefront in administration, education, culture, trade, and in the crafts. Thus they came to be regarded by the rulers as a most important pillar in society. It is only by understanding this situation that we can understand what we often find to be an almost inextricable connection between the designs of the Armenian, Islamic Ottoman, and Safavid cultures in the regions of Asia Minor and central Asia.

The carpets discussed in this book come from all regions of Asia and Europe, where we can be sure that Armenians made up what was often a very significant part of the population. The author has attempted to demonstrate the connections that existed between the central 'sphere of cultural influence' and the 'dependencies', that is, between West Armenia and its 'Turkish' dependencies, and East Armenia and its 'Persian' or 'Turkmenian' dependencies.

Special significance is to be ascribed to the fact that, thus far, all the so-called 'Turkmenian tribal guls' known in the carpets of central Asia belong to a single design evolution, one which was dependent on the developments in central and West Armenia, and whose stages are to be seen as sequential progressions rather than as concomitant. Since, however, these guls also belong to a design tradition that can be traced back to the area of Asia Minor-Caucasus, and to the beginning of the first millenium BC, the doubts voiced in my introduction concerning the traditional theories of carpet history are confirmed by the existing source material. We can now conclude, in agreement with the early texts, that the production tradition of the knotted-pile carpet originated in and was indigenous to the area we have referred to as having been most under the influence of the cultural sphere of Armenia. From there began the migration of designs into the regions where new production centres were being established as a result of emigration or enforced settlement of Armenian artisans there.

The present book can only be a beginning. The answer to each question conceals in itself a multitude of new, yet unanswered ones. Years ago, when the author felt convinced that indeed there had to be a Christian oriental carpet, he had no way of knowing just how extensive the material was he would be finding, nor how involved the necessary research over the years to come would be. When, in 1978, he began to work intensively on this problem and the preliminary results began to appear, the present study began to take shape. At first, much of what today is taken for granted seemed purely hypothetical. Later, after a large number of the carpets in museums around the world had been viewed personally, a lively exchange of ideas among a great many scholars began to take place. The stimulation resulting from this exchange and from the support which resulted have gone into this book. Extensive travel has played its part as well in clarifying peripheral issues, and contributing to a better understanding of the greater context implicit in the work.

The author now regards this volume as part of a complete revision of the history of the carpet. The fact that it will, at the same time, have an effect on the entire field of textile history (though not only on this) is but another outcome. After all, the entire subject of the ornamental arts of the Orient over the last 2,000 years is an area that has received virtually no attention – something which cannot be said of the millennia before Christ. The preliminary studies which led to this book have resulted in one of the largest collections of such material to be found to date. It is the intention of the author to continue with this research, the ultimate goal being the establishment of a data-bank in connection with an actively interested institution, in order to form the basis for continuing supplementary research.

The dividing lines between Christian oriental art and the art of Islam remain to be explored. Only as we come to know for certain all the material which has survived will scholars be in a position to identify real lines of development, and to make informed judgements and attributions in the future.

This book is to be regarded as a contribution to these ends.

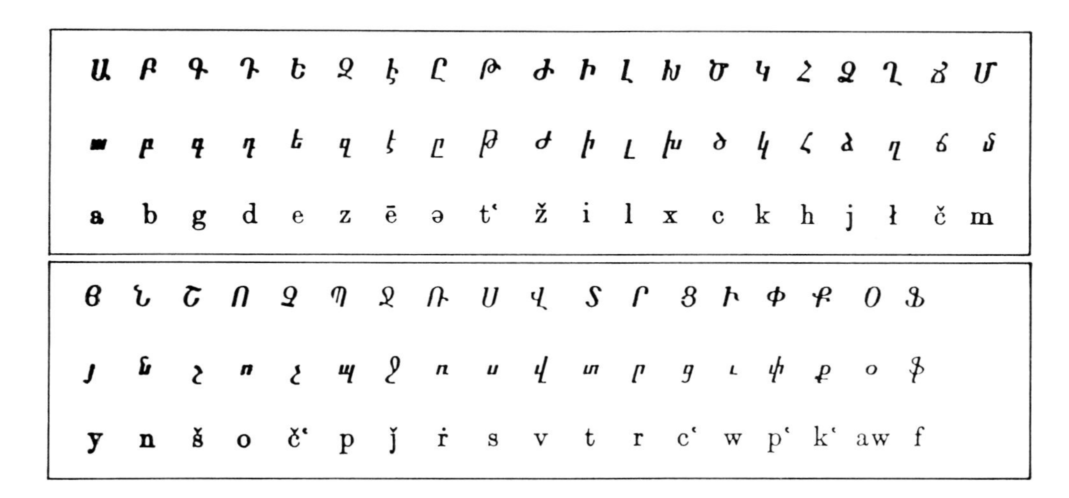

Ill. 709: The Armenian alphabet.

Appendix

Abbreviations

ARM	Amsterdam, Rijksmuseum
BA	Vatican, Biblioteca apostolica
BM	London, British Museum
BMFA	Boston, Museum of Fine Arts
BMIK	Berlin, SMPK, Museum für islamische Kunst
BOIM	Berlin, Staatliche Museen zu Berlin, Islamisches Museum
BUIM	Budapest, Iparmüvészeti Müzeum
CAM	Cincinnati, Art Museum
CLAM	Cleveland, Art Museum
DIA	Detroit, Institute of Arts
EM	Erivan, Matenadaran
FGA	Washington, Freer Gallery of Art
Keir	Keir Collection
KGM	Berlin, Kunstgewerbemuseum
LMHT	Lyon, Musée Historique des Tissus
LV & A	London, Victoria & Albert Museum
MBN	Munich, Bayrisches Nationalmuseum
Mevl.	Konya, Mevlana Museum
MMA	New York, Metropolitan Museum of Art
PHAM	Philadelphia, Art Museum
SLAM	St. Louis, City Art Museum
SMPK	Berlin, Staatliche Museen Preußischer Kulturbesitz
STSHM	Stockholm, Statens Historiska Museum
TIEM	Istanbul, Türk ve Islâm Eserleri Müzesi
TMW	Washington D.C., Textile Museum
UTB	Tübingen, Universitätsbibliothek
Vakf.	Istanbul, Vakiflar Carpet Museum
Wher	Wher Collection
WÖMAK	Wien [Vienna], Österreichisches Museum für angewandte Kunst

Notes

1
F. R. Martin, *A History of Oriental Carpets before 1800* (Vienna, 1908).

2
Ignaz Schlosser, *Der schöne Teppich in Orient und Okzident* (1960; Munich, dtv-edition, 1979), p. 21.

3
At the turn of the century the sales proceeds were considerably higher for Persian carpets than for those from the Ottoman Empire. There is no other explanation for the effectiveness of the story concerning Ardabil carpets – carpets which, due to their size, could never have been woven in Ardabil. Cf. Rexford Stead, *The Ardabil Carpets* (Malibu, 1974).

4
Kurt Erdmann, *Der orientalische Knüpfteppich,* 4th ed. (1955; Tübingen, 1975).

5
Kurt Erdmann, *Die Geschichte des frühen türkischen Teppichs* (Istanbul, 1957; London, 1977).

6
Marco Polo, travel account (original text in French: 1298).

7
Henry Yule, *The Book of Ser Marco Polo,* (London, 1875) vol. 1.

8
Arthur Upham Pope, "The Myth of the Armenian Dragon Carpets," *Jahrbuch der asiatischen Kunst* (Leipzig, 1925) II.

9
Hans Eckart Rübesamen, *Die Reisen des Venezianers Marco Polo* (Munich, 1983).

10
Erdmann, *Knüpfteppich,* p. 17: "We believe the Venetian merchant Marco Polo, who in 1271 traveled in Anatolia, when he writes of the world's best and most beautiful carpets being made *in the land of the Rumseljukian.* It is not certain whether he visited Konya. Yet we can be sure that the examples he saw in Sivas and Kayseri did not look any different from those in the mosque in Ala ed din."

Erdmann, *Geschichte,* p. 26: "Let us take this opportunity to refer once again to Marco Polo's account. Its English translation, by H. Yule, is commonly cited and can be rendered as follows: 'There are three classes in Turkmenia. The Turkomans live in the mountains and the plains, where they find good grazing land for their herds. The other two classes are composed of Armenians and Greeks respectively. They live *among the Turkomans* in the towns and villages and are engaged in trade and crafts. Here (!)(which is to say in the towns) the world's best and most beautiful carpets are made.' As we see, Marco Polo does not say – as it appears in Yule's translation – that the art of weaving was practiced by the Armenians and Greeks, but rather that the 'world's best and most beautiful carpets' were made in the towns within *the Rumseljukian Empire.* Of course, this does not exclude the possiblity that the weavers were of Greek or Armenian decent in part. It is, in fact, likely. Armenians and Greeks were good craftsmen, always in demand as workers. This, however, was the extent of their importance."
The passage from the Yule text quoted here has been appended to read *'among the Turkomans.'* When compared with the translation cited above, the resulting change in meaning is clear.
We see that the passages quoted from pp. 14–16 concur in their descriptions of the Turkomans: they are Moslems with their own language and customs; they are a crude, peasant-like people; they sometimes live in the mountains and sometimes in the valleys, depending on where good grazing is to be found; their livelihood is raising cattle, which they cherish; they have good horses and mules and, as the second passage points out, sheep, too. There is also concurrence in how the Greeks and Armenians are described: they live *together* in towns and forts, of which are there many. Here the world's best and most beautiful carpets are made, as are lovely and appealing silk garments richly woven with gold.

We realize now that it is much less a matter of whether the passages marked by Erdmann with (!) are translated 'they' or 'there'. A correct rendering here does not alter the meaning, whereas Erdmann's addition *'among the Turkomans'* distorts it entirely. The English translation by Yule, for one, is at fault for this misinterpretation, and Erdmann was familar with it as well as with Pope's interpretation.[8] The English original reads *'mixt with the former'* and the German *'together';* each passage refers only to the fact that the Greeks and Armenians lived together. This is also documented by the German Marco Polo texts of the last 600 years, which Erdmann, oddly enough (or deliberately?), did not consider. There is simply no other possible interpretation: *All* of the versions of the Marco Polo text state unanimously that Greeks and Armenians lived together in towns and obtained their livelihood from trade and industry. Then, as is done throughout the Marco Polo text, the most important goods produced by the afore-mentioned inhabitants are listed by name: in the case of the Turkomans these are horses and mules, for the Greeks and Armenians, however, carpets and silken garments woven with gold.

11
Marco Polo, *Il Milione,* Tuscan, so-called 'Ottimo-version' from 1309. Biblioteca Nationale, Florence, inv. no. II.IV.88.

12
Marco Polo, *Il Milione,* trans. Ulrich Köppen (Berlin: Propyläen, 1971).

13
Der Mittelalterliche Marco Polo, Codex Admont. 504, text: Horst von Tscharner, Berlin, 1935 (Stiftsbibliothek, Admont [Styria, Austria]).

14
Marco Polo, travel account, German trans. (Nürnberg, 1477).
15
Marco Polo, *Chorographia Tatariae,* German trans., located in Landesbibliothek, Stuttgart, Württemberg (Leipzig, 1611).
16
Erdmann also refers to a passage in Abulféda, where Ibn Sa'id, who died in 1274, is quoted: "Turkoman carpets are made in Aksaray and exported to all the countries throughout the world" (Erdmann, *Knüpfteppich,* p. 26.). The original text in Abulféda makes no reference to 'Turkoman' nor does it contain the addition 'and exported to all the countries throughout the world.' This addition, however, is confirmed in Ibn Battuta, whom Erdmann refers to as follows: "Ibn Battuta, who, at the beginning of the 14th century, travelled in Anatolia, also praises them, maintaining that they were exported to Egypt, Syria, Iraq, Persia, India and China" (Erdmann, *Knüpfteppich,* p. 18) or "likewise praises the carpets of Aksaray, which were exported to Egypt, Syria, Iraq, India, China and in the land of the Turks" [here he probably means Persia] (Erdmann, *Geschichte,* p. 14.). The original text by *Ibn Battuta,* who traveled in Anatolia in 1333, reads: "Carpets made of lamb's wool are produced there and named accordingly [after Aksaray by the present author]. There is nothing of compare in any other country. They are exported from there to *Syria, Egypt, al-'Iraq* [this is the Il-Khanid Empire, including Iran, Iraq and parts of eastern Anatolia; the author], *India, China and to the land of the Turks.* This city belongs to the King of al-'Iraq." (H. A. R. Gibb, *The Travels of Ibn Battuta* (Cambridge: 1962) vol. 2, p. 432.) In comparing this with the Erdmann quotations, we again see significant changes. In the first quotation there is no mention of the Il-Khanid Empire [al-'Iraq] – even though Iraq and Persia [Iran] are mentioned – nor of *the land of the Turks.* In the second quotation al-'Iraq becomes simply Iraq and Persia [Iran] is left out because it is needed as clarification for *the land of the Turks.*
17
Donald P. Little, "The Significance of the Haram Documents for the Study of Medieval Islamic History," *Der Islam* 57: 2 (1980).
18
In connection with the travel accounts mentioned above, Erdmann continually speaks of the *'Rumseljukian Empire'*, and he also tries to equate *Aksaray* with *Konya, 'the capital of the Rumseljukian Empire'. Marco Polo* was in Anatolia in *1271, Ibn Sa'id* prior to *1274, Ibn Battuta* not until 60 years later: in *1333.* The Seljuk Empire had already come to a close by *1243.* In the battle of Köse Dag the Seljuks were decisively defeated by the Mongolians. This marked the end of independence for the Seljuks, who, during the years previous to this, had made up a militant group of leaders. From this point on, they were taxable subjects of the Mongolian great Khan like all the other inhabitants of the country. During the middle of the 13th century there was a Seljuk governor still in residence, Qylyq Arslan IV, who, having been outcast by his brothers, received support from the Mongolians against them. He was considered so devoted to the great Khan that in 1269, following the death of Möngke Khan and the disintegration of the great Mongolian empire, he was strangled to death by the Il-Khanid governor. Before this, the empire of the Rumseljuks had already broken up into ten smaller emirates, all of which were subject to the Mongolian governor residing in Aksaray. Aksaray – the 'White Palace' – like Aksaray on the Volga, was the residence of the Mongolian Khans or their governors in central Anatolia. It is for this reason misleading to continue to speak of the 'Rumseljukian Empire' after 1243, seeking to equate Aksaray with Konya.
In 1982, while looking for the 'White Palace', the author discovered a number of interesting things. After a thorough examination of the building of the Ulu Cami, he came to the conclusion that this building must once have been the audience chamber of the Saray. The refectory-like inner room with its gallery in the back as well as large segments of the entrance façade (south-facing) all attest to an architectural style characteristic of the middle of the 13th century. The cross vaulting with its early Gothic appearance is reminiscent of Armenian buildings, or even more so of the architecture of the crusaders. The mihrab, the dome in front of the mihrab, as well as the bricked-in eastern south-wall, today without windows, are all obviously structural additions or alterations from the first part of the 15th century. They are not part of the original structure. The Ulu Cami of today served a completely different purpose before it was redesigned as a mosque. In essential points it corresponds to the palace of Möngke Khan, as described by the Franciscan Carpini (cf. B. Spuler, *Geschichte der Mongolen* [Zürich:1968] p. 136.). The question as to why the Aksaray of today should be so small and unimportant, which Károly Gombos addresses in his unpublished manuscript (1980) 'Anatolian Carpets/The Myth of the Seljukian Carpets,' proves superfluous in light of what has been said above. Yet it is *Aksaray* that we should stress, which is to say that we are concerned here with *Aksaray carpets.* These were carpets which, as Ibn Battuta made quite clear in his account, bore the name of their place of production, and which were also found under this name in an archive in Jerusalem. It is important that this be understood: Aksaray carpets are *not* Konya carpets, regardless of the fact that the Erdmann version was adopted by all of the subsequent authors, no questions asked. One might go so far as to say that these carpets were produced in a city which, during the middle of the 13th century (presumably until the great Mongolian empire was broken up) was the residence of the Mongolian governor. It is, then, in the eyes of the author, impossible to conclude a 'Seljuk origin' from this. For one thing, there is no record of the Seljuks having been engaged as craftsmen. According to Marco Polo they were 'simple, coarse, even peasant-like people,' who were dependent on cattle as their sole livelihood. Erdmann himself does not rule out Christian craftsmen, though he does regard them as insignificant. We know, however, in contrast to this, that the great Khan Hulagu was quite favorably inclined toward Christians and took great pains to see that craftsmen of this faith were well represented at his court. His head wife, the Doquz Chatun, was an adherent of the Christian-Nestorian faith, as was his highest general, Ketboga. His reign can be credited with having done the most to further the spread of Christianity in Asia. In addition, he saw Asia Minor flourish, experienced the arrival of the Syrian-Monophysitic renaissance, as well as the emergence of a largely Christian-influenced architecture and architectural ornamentation.
It is, therefore, no coincidence that those travelling at this time in this part of the world should make frequent mention of Aksaray, despite the fact that under the Il-Khans, who were continually involved in border disputes with the neighboring Karamanids, it no longer appears to have had the function of a residency. When, in 1333, Ibn Battuta journeyed from Karaman to Aksaray, a good many things had already changed. As editor of the English translation *The Travels of Ibn Battuta* Gibb sees an error in his commentary on his route 'Konya-Karaman-Aksaray'. In 1307, most likely with the help of the Mamluks, the Sultan of Karaman extended his holdings to include Konya as well, whereas Aksaray, like Kayseri and Sivas, continued to be directly under Il-Khanid rule. Hence, it is only logical that Battuta would first travel within one area of jurisdiction before crossing the border into another.
19
Further 'evidence' in support of a Seljuk origin for Anatolian carpets is seen by Erdmann in the fact that several of them were found in the Alâeddin-Mosque in Konya and the Esrefoglu-Mosque in Beysehir. Erdmann: "Despite this, they are truly splendid works, which we can, without hesitating, ascribe to the 13th century, or perhaps more precisely the 1250s. We are tempted, furthermore, to assume them to have been a donation of one of the Seljuk sultans who ruled in Konya; their provenance in the great mosque of the city would also support this." (Erdmann, *Knüpfteppich,* p. 17.) "Their provenance in the great mosque of the residence, Konya, supports the theory that they originated during the Rumseljukian period." (Erdmann, *Geschichte,* p. 7.) "They are in any case the products of a manufactory

that was capable of such large pieces of work by virtue of its location in a residence and its being supplied with orders from the court. This means that these carpets were, in all probability, produced in Konya. It means, furthermore, that these carpets represent a type that was in turn representative of the Rumseljukian art of weaving of the 13th century, be it that they entered the Ala el din-Cami as a donation of the Sultan or his vizier." (Erdmann, *Geschichte,* p. 11).
Erdmann's student Serare Yetkin adopts this hypothesis, writing: "The *greatest proof* that they were produced during the Seljuk period is their discovery in the great mosque at Konya. It is difficult to prove that they were ordered by the sultan to be presented to the mosque after its enlargement in 1221, but it is certain that these extraordinary carpets were woven at some time during the years 1221 to 1250, the period when Seljuk reign was at its strongest." (S. Yetkin, *Historical Turkish Carpets (Istanbul, 1981),* p. 15.)
Without having to provide extensive justification, might the author be allowed to elaborate briefly on just what does and does not constitute 'proof' in all academic fields, art history included. It is, for example, absurd to think that in finding movables in rooms to which the public has always been granted access, one has, as it were, found 'proof' as to where such movables originated and when. In fact, in the absence of additional evidence in the form of archival material, documents, etc., one can do little more than conjecture.

20
R. B. Serjeant, *ISLAMIC TEXTILES – Material for a History up to the Mongol Conquest* (Beirut: 1972).

21
Even the possiblity that we might be dealing with an example of cut pile-weave can be ruled out. Serjeant refers to such an example ('velvet like pile,' p. 19) using the Arabian term *mukhmal.*

22
Károly Gombos, *Anatolian Carpets/The Myth of the Seljukian Carpets,* ms. (Budapest, 1980), 92 pp. [poorly translated]

23
J. Iten-Maritz: *Enzyklopädie des Orientteppichs,* 2nd ed. (Zürich, 1977).

24
Topdschian, *Zeitschrift für armenische Philologie* II (1903): pp. 51–52.

25
Sergeant, p. 69.

26
It was particularly the blood relationships with Armenia, which were more developed in every respect, that were important; they have, to this day, not been given the attention they deserve in view of their art-historical relevance. Already those involved in the first crusade of 1095 married a number of Armenian women, as for example Count Balduin of Lothringen and Tankred the Norman with their retinues. The wives of Balduin II and Count Fulco V of Anjou were also Armenian, to name just a few. Precisely the association of the nobility in Armenia Minor with France, on the one hand – especially Lothringen and the house of Anjou – and with the Norman Empire in southern Italy was to be of exceptional importance; it was the actual beginning of the Romanesque period.

27
The New Testament, Matt. 21: 8–9, Mark 11: 7–10, Luke 19: 36–38.

28
John Mills, "The Coming of the Carpet to the West," *The Eastern Carpet in the Western World* (London, 1983), p. 11. (exhibition catalogue)

29
Meyer Schapiro, "The Miniatures of the Florence Diatessaron. Their Place in Late Medieval Art and Supposed Connection with Early Christian and Insular Art," *The Art Bulletin* 55 (1973), p. 514.

30
Viken Sassouni, "Carpets with Armenian Inscription," *The Armenian Review* XXXV, 4–140 (1982), p. 420 ff.

31
Mania Ghazarian, *Armenian Carpets* (Mocow, 1985), p. 61.

32
Meyers Enzyklopädisches Lexikon (Mannheim, 1973), 7, p. 156.

33
The old crosiers are without crosses, as for example that of the Metropoliten Parthenios of Kayseri in the Benaki Museum, Athens (Manolis Chatzidakis, *Benaki Museum* [Athens, 1975] ill. 29). In the case of earlier crosiers in the patriarchate of Echmiadzin, the cross was mounted later, whereas later examples were equipped with it originally.

34
Evangelistary, Akner (near Tarsus), dated 1287; Matenadaran, Erivan, codex no. 197, F. 341r.

35
Ernst Badstübner, Helga Neumann, and Hannelore Sachs, *Erklärendes Wörterbuch zur Christlichen Kunst* (Berlin and Leipzig, n.d. [1984?]), p. 328.

36
Badstübner, p. 68.

37
Evangelistary, Nakhichevan, dated 1304; Matenadaran, Erivan, codex no. 3722. Literature: L. A. Durnovo, *Ornaments of Armenian Manuscripts* (Erivan, 1978), plate 67 lower left.

38
At this point I would like to thank Mr. Armen Zarian for his help.

39
Helmut Uhlig, "Das Mandala," *Tantrische Kunst des Buddhismus* (Berlin, 1981), p. 75 ff. (exhibition catalogue)

40
Paul Huber, *Heilige Berge* (Zürich, 1980), p. 56 ff.

41
Huber, p. 98 ff.

42
Transcriptions from the 9th century (Biblioteca apostolica, Rome) and the 12th century (Biblioteca Laurenziana, Florence and the Sinai monastery library). See Huber, p. 56 ff.

43
According to information given the author by Prof. Dr. Mebus A. Geyh from the Niedersächsisches Landesamt für Bodenforschung [State Agency of Lower Saxony for Soil Research and Conservation], a sample of 80 mg is sufficient in determining age (20.12.84).

44
H. Kurdian, "Kirmiz," *Journal of the American Oriental Society,* vol. 61:2 (Baltimore, 1941),: p. 105 ff.

45
Serjeant, p. 206 ff.

46
Dr. Friedrich Parrot, *Reise zum Ararat* (Berlin, 1834), p. 106.

47
Thin-layer chromatography and letter from 3.11.1986.

48
Serjeant, p. 65.

49
Serjeant, p. 171.

50
E. Kühnel and L. Bellinger, *Catalogue of Cairene Rugs* (The Textile Museum Washington, 1955), p. 1.

51
Franco Brunelli, *The Art of Dyeing in the History of Mankind* (Vicenza, 1973), p. 188.

52
Ulrich Schürmann, *Der Pazyryk; Seine Deutung und Herkunft* (New York-Mannheim, 1982).

53
Gold der Skythen (München, 1984), p. 45. (exhibition catalogue)

54
Rainer Michael Boehmer, "Phrygische Prunkgewänder des 8. Jh. v. Chr., Herkunft und Export," *Archäolog. Anzeiger* 2 (1973).
55
Rodney S. Young, "Three Great Early Tumuli," *The Gordian Excavations Final Reports* 1, p. 310.
56
Ernst H. Gombrich, *Ornament und Kunst* (Stuttgart, 1982), p. 229 ff. IX Zierat oder Zeichen? See also the following paragraphs: LCI 2, p. 571 ff.

57
In what follows, frequent reference is made to Badstübner. This is not because the author was not familar with or did not have at his disposal other sources of reference such as the *Lexikon der Christlichen Ikonographie* (LCI). The reason is, in fact, that there is not a single such reference that takes into consideration the iconography and iconology of Christian oriental art and Armenian art in particular, simply because they were written in order to help people understand European art. The dictionary mentioned here, like no other, makes at least an attempt to address itself to the art of the Orthodox Church, though even here Armenian art is not included as such.

58
Agathangelos CII, 114 (Langlois, p. 157).
59
Maurice Chéhab, "Mosaiques du Liban," *Bulletin du Musée de Beyrouth,* vol. XIV (Paris, 1958).
60
Doro Levi, *Antioch Pavements* (Princeton, 1946).
61
Carl H. Kraeling, *GERASA, City of the Decapolis* (New Haven, Connecticut, 1938).
62
Ludwig Budde, *Antike Mosaiken in Kilikien* (Recklinghausen, 1972).
63
R. W. Hamilton, *Khirbat al Mafjar. An Arabian Mansion in the Jordan Valley. With a contribution by Dr. Oleg Grabar* (Oxford, 1959).
64
Hamilton, p. 331.
65
Kraeling, p. 316, ill. plate LXII b.
66
Kraeling, p. 317, 338 ff, ill. plate LXXXI a, b.
67
Hamilton, plate LXXXVIII (11).
68
Erdmann, *Knüpfteppich,* p. 30 ff, 47 ff.
69
Here the cross-star appears in connection with two 'medallion crosses' on the key stone in the vaulting.
70
Art Bulletin 50 (1968): pp. 119–140; *Art Bulletin* 55 (1973): pp. 494–531, 532–546.
71
Codex 57 (Trinity College, Dublin).
72
Cotton Ms. Nero D.IV (British Library, London).
73
Codex 24 (Stadtbibliothek, Trier).
74
Cividale del Friuli (Archäologisches Museum), codex CXXXVI.
75
Gabriel Mandel, *Die Buchmalerei der Romanik und Gotik* (Gütersloh, 1964), 16.
76
Erdmann, *Knüpfteppich,* p. 14.
77
Cf. in this connection a report by Albert von Le Coq: "Auf Hellas Spuren in Ostturkestan."
78
Edmund de Unger, "An Ancestor of the Mamluk Carpets," *HALI* (1982) 5:1.
79
HALI 8:4 (1986), p. 6.
80
Badstübner, p. 336.
81
Johanna Zick-Nissen, "Eine kunsthistorische Studie zum ältesten erhaltenen Knüpfteppich islamischer Zeit," *HALI* 1:3 (1978).
82
TIEM no. 685. This carpet, as well as others from Groups A I and A II, were found in 1930 in the Alâeddin Mosque in Konya, cf. Durul/Aslanapa, *Seljuklu Halilari* (Istanbul[?], n.d.[1974]).
83
Levon Azarian, *Armenian Katchkars* (Lisbon, 1973), ill. 22.
84
Hans Holländer, *Kunst des frühen Mittelalters* (Stuttgart, 1969; Herrsching, 1981), p. 22 ff. Although the quotation used here refers to early Christian illuminated manuscripts, later on the conception in Armenian art is identical to this.
85
Ilona Turánszky/Károly Gink, *Azerbaijan,* English trans. (Budapest, 1979), plate 47.
86
Serjeant, p. 66.
87
So-called 'Zili' (the Armenian 'zilu'?); Vakiflar Kelim Museum, Istanbul, no. YD 872.
88
Fresco on the outside of the west wall of St. Mary's Church of Hosios Loukas, today on the inside of the east wall of the Loukas church (from the 10th century). Literature: Paul Lazarides, *Hosios Loukas* (Athens, 1985).
89
Today in the Museo de Arte Cataluna, Barcelona (from the early 12th century). Literature: *ARTE – Kunstgeschichte der Welt,* (Lausanne, 1979), 3, p. 226 (ill.).
90
Georgios Lampakis, *Mémoire sur les antiquités chrétiennes de la Grèce* (1902).
91
Levi, plate CXII b.
92
Erdmann, *Geschichte,* pp. 32–36.
93
Azarian, ills. 26, 27.
94
See among others: Kurt Erdmann, "Orientalische Tierteppiche auf Bildern des XIV. und XV. Jahrhunderts," *Jahrbuch der preuß. Kunstsammlungen L* (1929). John Mills, *Carpets in Pictures* (London, 1975); John Mills, "Early Animal Carpets in Western Paintings – a Review," *HALI* 1:3, B. Scheunemann, *Anatolische Teppiche auf abendländischen Gemälden,* diss., Berlin, 1953. (no illustrations, inaccessible)

95
The Stories of St. Francis, Friar Agostino and the Bishop of Assisi's Vision of St. Francis, detail: lower right (Upper Church, Assisi).
96
Erdmann, *Tierteppiche,* pp. 265, 268.
97
Berlinghiero Berlinghieri (before 1242), *Crucifix,* Museo Civico, Lucca [Italy].

98
For example, the relief in the tympanum of the west portal in Areni; or the tympanum relief on the portal of the gawit of the main church in Norawank.
99
Giunta Pisano, *Crucifix,* S. Domenico, Bologna.
100
Cimabue, *Crucifix,* S. Francesco, Arezzo.
101
Duiccio, *The Presentation in the Temple,* Cathedral Museum, Siena.
102
Lombardesque, *Madonna with Child and Saints,* San Vincenzo, Galliano.
103
Paul von Limburg, *The Adoration of the Magi,* miniature from *Les Très Riches Heures* (1413–1416) of the Duc de Berry, Musée Condé, Chantilly F. 52.
104
Cf. Vakf. E 130
105
Master of S. Francesco, *Crucifix,* Pinacoteca, Pecarpetia.
106
The Stories of St. Francis, Christmas Mass at Greccio, detail: lower right (Upper Church, Assisi).
107
Giotto, *Bonifacius VIII Announces the Year of Jubilee,* S. Giovanni in Laterano, Rome, fresco.
108
Cf. Erdmann, *Tierteppiche,* p. 266.
109
The Stories of St. Francis, Pope Gregor IX's Vision of St. Francis, detail: below (Upper Church, Assisi).
110
Giotto, *Madonna with Child and Angels,* S. Giorgio alla Costa, Florence.
111
The Stories of St. Francis, The Sermon before Honorius III, detail: below (Upper Church, Assisi).
112
Vitale da Bologna, *A Story of the Holy Abbot Antonius,* Pinacoteca Nationale, Bologna.
113
Cf. 94.
114
Turkish scholars in particular would like to see the animal representations traced back to what may be totem symbols of the Oghuz.
115
The earliest depictions in European paintings are from the year 1317, which is comparatively late. The assumption is clearly related to the hypothesis of a nomadic-Turkoman origin.
116
Simone Martini, *St. Louis of Toulouse Crowning Robert of Anjou,* Museo di Capodimonte, Naples.
117
Sienese, 14th century, *The Annunciation,* formerly in the Schloßmuseum, Berlin. (whereabouts unknown)
118
Erdmann, *Tierteppiche,* ills. 6, 7.
119
The material from Serjeant's work, see 20, shows beyond any doubt that Armenians produced textiles of this sort. To this day, the author is not aware of any study that might have attempted to identify this group. Judging from the designs, the fabrics cited here, as well as the one to be discussed next, belong within the area of Armenian production. One need only compare the textiles from ills. 162–165 with those from ill.175 in order to notice just how closely related they are. Even the elephants from ill. 164 can be found there.
120
Sammitum, half silk; Italy [?], 13th [?] century, Deutsches Textilmuseum, Krefeld.
121
Achtamar, The Church of the Holy Cross from 915–921, relief (on west façade).
122
Erdmann, *Tierteppiche,* p. 285.
123
Enzo Orlandi, *Giotto,* German ed. (Stuttgart, 1975), p. 31 ff.
124
Jan van Eyck, *Lucca-Madonna,* before 1441, (Städtisches Kunstinstitut, Frankfurt). Jan van Eyck, *Mary with Child,* 1441–43, (The Frick Collection, New York). Jan van Eyck, *The Madonna of Kanonikus van der Paele,* 1436 (Municipal Gallery, Bruges).
125
Evangelistary of Gagik of Kars, 11th century (Armenian Patriarchate, Jerusalem) codex no. 2556.
126
Evangelistary, 11th century (Matenadaran, Erivan).
127
Evangelistary, Drasak in Cilicia, dated 1193 (University Library, Tübingen) codex Ma XIII 1.
128
Viken Sassouni, "Carpets with Armenian Inscription," *The Armenian Review* XXXV: 4–140 (1982), p. 420 ff.
129
Evangelistary, presumably from the 13th century (University Library, Tübingen) codex Ma XIII 4.
130
Evangelistary from Teodosiopolis, dated 1232 (San Lazzaro, Venice) codex no. 325/129.
131
Cf. ill. 151.
132
Evangelistary, dated 1235; Freer Gallery of Art, Washington: acc. no. 44.17.
133
Evangelistary, dated 1315; Bibliothek der Mechitaristen Congregation, Vienna, codex 460.
134
Cf. star-tiles from the 'Kubadabad Palace' in Beysehir. *The Anatolian Civilizations* (Istanbul, 1983) III: 30 e.g. D 22, 13th century. The name Kubadabad Palace most probably comes from the Mongolian governor Kudabanda; it served as his summer residence.
135
Carpet Mevl. 860/861/1033, collection of the Mevlana Museum, Konya, on exhibit in the Ethnographic Museum of Konya.
136
Evangelistary, *c.* 1220 (The British Museum, London) codex add. 7170, F. 197v. Evangelistary, 1219–1220 (Biblioteca apostolica, Vatican) codex Syr. 559.
137
See **136:** London, F. 197r and F. 199r; Vatican, F. 180r and F. 183r.
138
Lectionary, dated 1577, from a drawing from 1285 (Biblioteca apostolica, Vatican) Borgia 169, F. 40.
139
Gibb, *Travels* (cited in 16).
140
Hanna Erdmann, "Die Beziehung der vorosmanischen Teppichmuster zu den gleichzeitigen Ornamenten," *HALI* 1: 3(1978), p. 228 ff. Jan Bennet, *Teppiche der Welt,* German ed. (Gütersloh, 1978), p. 182.
141
Chen Chü-Chung Wen Ji Kuei Han: *The Return of Lady Wen Chi to China.* Single painting? Li Tang Wen Ji Kuei Han: *The Return of Lady*

Wen Chi to China. Single painting? Sung Hui-Tsung Shih Pa Hsüeh Shih: *The Story of Lady Wen Chi,* scroll. All located in the National Palace, Taipei, Taiwan.
142
Wen Fong, *The Story of Lady Wen Chi,* scroll (Metropolitan Museum of Art, New York).
143
Kurt Erdmann, "Kairener Teppiche; Teil I: Europäische und islamische Quellen des 15.-18. Jahrhunderts," *ARS ISLAMICA* VI (1939), p. 179 ff; "Teil II: Mamluken- und Osmanenteppiche," *ARS ISLAMICA* VII (1940), p. 55 ff.
144
Cf. B. Spuler, *Geschichte der Mongolen* (Zürich, 1968); and J. Saunders, *The History of the Mongol Conquests* (London, 1971).
145
For the Chinese, woollen products were considered 'barbaric'. Cf. Bennett, *Teppiche,* p. 189 (cited in 140).
146
Demotte Shah-nameh, Tabriz or Baghdad, *c.* 1330 or earlier (Freer Gallery of Art, Washington), no. 23.5.
147
Richard Ettinghausen, "New Light on Early Animal Carpets," *Festschrift für Ernst Kühnel* (Berlin, 1979), p. 93 ff.
148
Cf. p. 88 ff.
149
Durnovo (cited in 37), no. 50 (13th century), no. 65 (1294), no. 72 (1323).
150
Durnovo no. 37, 71, 72, 74 (all from the beginning of the 14th century).
151
Amy Briggs, "Timurid Carpets," *ARS ISLAMICA* VII (1940), p. 20 ff.
152
Briggs, ill. 48.
153
Herbert Kühn, *Die vorgeschichtliche Kunst Deutschlands* (Berlin, 1935), p. 87 ff.
154
Badstübner, p. 146.
155
Durnovo, no. 54; lectionary for Prince Hetum, dated 1286 (Matenadaran, Erivan) codex no. 979.
156
Brentjes, Mnazakanjan, and Stepanjan, *Die Kunst des Mittelalters in Armenien* (Berlin, 1981) ill. 237: evangelistary from 1275–1300 (Matenadaran, Erivan) codex no. 9422, F. 162r.
157
Carl Nordenfalk, "An Illustrated Diatessaron," *Art Bulletin* 50 (1968), p. 120. (already cited in 70)
158
Ernst H. Gombrich, *Ornament und Kunst; Schmucktrieb und Ordnungssinn in der Psychologie des dekorativen Schaffens* (Stuttgart, 1982), p. 224.
159
Fragment with border, used to cover a Renaissance chair, Bernheimer Collection, Munich. Further fragments in the Victoria and Albert Museum, London and in the Keir Collection.
160
Christine Klose, "Ein anatolischer Sternteppich des 16. Jahrhunderts," *WELTKUNST* 56: 16 (1986), p. 2178 ff.
161
e.g. *The Eastern Carpet in the Western World* (London, 1983).
162
Azarian, no. 27 ff.
163
A point of reference for dating the border can be provided by Domenico Ghirlandaio, *Enthroned Madonna,* from the mid-15th century (Galleria degli Uffizi, Florence).
164
Andrea Mantegna, *Lodovico III Gonzaga with Wife and Royal Suite,* fresco 1465/74 (Camera degli Sposi, Castell San Giorgio, Mantua). We find the border from ill. 368 on the lower left and, at the same time, in the lower middle section that from ill. 369. This is also an important dating reference for Groups C II b_2 and C II c_1.

165
Carlo Crivelli, altar, *Annunciation with St. Emidius, c.* 1480 (National Gallery, London). The carpet depiction at the upper right is all in all very informative: it is combined with the peacock (immortality), the lily ('immaculate' conception) and the dove (hope, chastity). The pseudo-Kufic forms depicted in the outer border represent a late form in the development of Kufi-borders (C II d_2 and d_3) and is thus an important *Terminus ante quem.*
166
Holländer, pp. 58–73.
167
Lemyel Amirian, "On the Origin of the Dragon and Phoenix Carpet in Berlin," *HALI* 4: 1, p. 31.
168
Donald King, "The Carpets in the Exhibition," in the catalogue from the exhibition *The Eastern Carpet in the Western World* (London, 1983), p. 49.
169
George Ferguson, *Signs and Symbols in Christian Art* (New York, 1961).
170
Cf. remarks pp. 37/38. The carpet was purchased in Rome by Bode and is said to have come from a church in Italy.
171
Achtamar.
172
Ferguson, pp. 15, 17.
173
Physiologus: writings in natural history and religion from the 2nd – 4th century. This is the primary source of Christian animal symbolism. The oldest surviving illustrated example is the Physiologus of Smyrna from the 11th century.
174
Domenico Ghirlandaio (cited in 163).
175
A carpet from the former Pohlmann Collection, Berlin. Often published e.g. in Bode-Kühnel or Erdmann.
176
Erdmann, *Kairener Teppiche.*
177
F. Sarre, "Neue Forschungen und Dokumente zur türkischen Kunstgeschichte," *Kunstchronik N. F. XXXI* (1920).
F. Sarre, "Die ägyptische Herkunft der sogenannten Damaskus-Teppiche," *Zeitschrift für bildende Kunst XXXII* (1921).
178
Rıfkı Melûl Meriç, *Nakış Tarihi Vesikaları* (Ankara, 1952), vol. II-III.
Rıfkı Melûl Meriç, *Türk Nakış San'atı Tarihi Araştırmaları* (Ankara, 1953), vol. I.
179
"Abu Salih," ed. Evetts and Buttler *Anecdota Oxoniensia,* sem. series VII.
180
Josef Strzygowski, *Die Baukunst der Armenier und Europa* (Vienna, 1918), pp. 731/732.
181
Badstübner, p. 366, 367. Ferguson, pp. 39, 40.
182
As for example in the carpet BOIM no. 91.26 (no illustration).

183
Robert Pinner, and Michael Franses, "The East Mediterranean Carpet Collection (in the Victoria & Albert Museum)," *HALI* 4: 1. King.
184
Mark Whiting, "The Red Dyes of some East Mediterranean Carpets," *HALI* 4: 1, pp. 55, 56.
185
Cf. John Eskenazi, *Il Tappeto orientale dal XV al XVIIII secolo* (London, 1981), plate 3. Now: The Christopher Alexander Collection, Berkeley.
186
First publication: 'Amida-Carpet' (ill. 707) 595 x 440 cm warp: cotton Z4(3)S, light, light layering weft:
cotton Z3S, light, 1–2 shoots, not continuous but running back and forth, 25–30 cm in length, loops hooked using the Gobelin technique.
pile: goat hair 2Z, knots asymmetrical to the left, pile height 4–9 mm, V=22, H=25 *c.* 550 knots/dm^2
sides: original goat hair-selvage over 3 warps
top and bottom end: traces of the original warp band
colours: 15(?) (white, beige, ochre, light brown, Venetian red, umber, rust, gray, light blue, moderate blue, dark blue, black, yellowish green, yellowish brown and pink).
C^{14}-analysis: material taken from a mend, Institute for Environmental Physics, Universität Heidelberg, 30.8.83
sample number: C^{14}-sample HD 7779–7996
Allowing for a margin of error of 1 sigma, the amount of C^{14} was found to be 96.9 + 0.4%, which corresponds to the C^{14} age of 260 ± 30 years before 1950.
At a probability of 95%, the age measured here of 260 ± 30 years is equal to a dendro-chronological age of: AD 1500–1660.
Private collection.
187
W. Bode and E. Kühnel, *Vorderasiatische Knüpfteppiche aus alter Zeit,* 4th ed. (Braunschweig, 1955), p. 76.
188
Erdmann, *Knüpfteppich,* p. 28.
189
Kurt Erdmann, *Siebenhundert Jahre Orientteppich,* ed. Hanna Erdmann (Herford, 1966), ill. 124.
190
Kühnel, *Catalogue,* p. 65 ff.
191
Robert Pinner, and Michael Franses, p. 41.
192
Serjeant, p. 67.
193
F. R. Martin, "A Shiraz Carpet of the Fifteenth Century," *Burlington Magazine* XVI (1909), pp. 130/131.
194
Serjeant, p. 27 ff.
195
Serjeant, p. 173.
196
The Quedlinburg knotted-pile carpet, Quedlinburg, Lower Saxony, c. 1200; Protestant church St. Servatius in Quedlinburg. Literature: *Die Zeit der Staufer* (Stuttgart, 1977) 1, p. 641.
197
Erdmann, *Siebenhundert Jahre,* p. 236.
198
Bennet, *Teppiche der Welt,* p. 265.
199
Erdmann, *Knüpfteppich,* p. 77, cf. ills. 272, 283.
200
Museum für Kunsthandwerk, Frankfurt; no. 12975/3889. Christopher Alexander Collection, Berkeley. In private ownership. (The latter is cited in Bennet, *Teppiche der Welt,* p. 6.)
201
Cf. the final pages of the Armenian evangelistary MS no. 8205, 11th century, Matenadaran, Erivan.
202
Erdmann, *Siebenhundert Jahre,* ill. 96 (p. 88).
203
Luise W. Mackie, "Native and Foreign Influences in Carpets woven in Spain during the 15th century," *HALI* II: 2 (1979), p. 92.
204
Doris Eder, *Kaukasische Teppiche,* Orientteppiche 1 (Munich, 1979), p. 378.
205
Evangelistary of the Syrian-Orthodox Bishop of Mardin, 13th century; F. 5v and F. 6r. Literature: *Les Manuscrits Syriaques à Peintures,* (Paris, 1964), p. 137.
206
Carlo Crivelli, *Annunciation with St. Emidius,* second half of the 15th century (National Gallery, London).
207
"Editorial Feature I: Star-Kazaks," *HALI* 3: 1 (1980), p. 17.
208
Erdmann, *Siebenhundert Jahre,* p. 136.
209
Robert Pinner and Jackie Stanger, "'Kufic' Borders on 'Small Pattern Holbein' Carpets," *HALI* 1: 4, p. 335 ff.
210
Stuttgart Holbein Carpet: first publication.
The results of the analysis conducted by the Institute for Environmental Physics, Heidelberg Universität were as follows:
sample number: C^{14}-sample HD 7779–7996
Allowing for a margin of error of 1 sigma, the amount of C^{14} was found to be 93.6 ± 0.4%, which corresponds to a C^{14}-age of 530 ± 35 years before 1950.
The age measured here of 530 ± 35 years can be equated with two possible dendro-chronological ages:

At a probability of 68%	AD 1330–1345
	AD 1390–1430
At a probability of 95.5%	AD 1320–1370
	AD 1390–1440

Technical details: 279 x 190 cm
warp: cotton Z5(4)S, light, no layering
weft: cotton Z5(4)S, light and light blue, two shoots
pile: wool 2Z, pile height 4–6 mm, in places less symmetrical knots, V 30, H 26 = 780 knots/dm^2
sides: dark red wool over 3 warps, light red wool over 3 warps added later
top and bottom end: traces of a dark brown woolen kilim, with 3–5 rows of knots missing in places colours: 10 (natural white, yellowish white, ivory-yellow, moderate brown, dark brown, ruby, pink, light blue, dark blue, grayish green) texture: soft, smooth
condition: nearly complete
In the possession of the previous owner's family since the end of 1880s (acquired before 1890).
In spite of the results of the C^{14}-analysis, a date of production during the latter part of the 19th century is to be expected because 'azo dye' – presumably 'congo red', allegedly not discovered prior to 1884 – was found in the carpet.
211
Emil Schmutzler, *Altorientalische Teppiche in Siebenbürgen* (Leipzig, 1933). Plate 10 illustrates the upper part.
212
Végh, Layer, and Dall'Oglio, *Turkish Carpets in Transylvania* (Crosby Press, 1977). Plate 1 illustrates the lower part.
213
Schmutzler plate 11. The border C II c_2/C III d_2, together with C II b_2, can already be found before 1474 depicted by Andrea Mantegna in the Camera degli Sposi, Castell San Giorgio in Mantua.

214
Besim Atalay, *Türk Halıcılığı ve Uşak Halıları* (Ankara, 1967).
215
Bode/Kühnel, p. 35.
216
Erdmann, *Knüpfteppich,* p. 51 ff.
217
Erdmann, *Kairener Teppiche,* p. 188.
218
King, p. 69.
219
Charles Grant Ellis, "The 'Lotto' Pattern as a Fashion in Carpets," *Festschrift für Peter Wilhelm Meister* (1975), p. 19.
220
Rose Hempel and Maritheres Gräfin Preysing, *Alte Orient-Teppiche,* Museum für Kunst und Gewerbe Hamburg (1970), p. 12

221
Schmutzler, plate no. 16. The border type can already be found depicted before 1556 by Girolamo dal Libri (1474–1556) in the painting 'La Madonna dall Ombrello', appearing as the border of a carpet of Group C III. Museo Castelvecchio, Verona.
222
Schmutzler, plate no. 18.
223
Végh, Layer, and Dall'Oglio, plate 5.
224
Thus far there are no illustrations available in the literature. Author's archives.
225
Erdmann, *Knüpfteppich,* ill. 143.

226
TIEM no. 867 is currently not available in publication; it was on display at the First International Congress on Turkish Carpets (Istanbul, October 1984).
227
Herbert Reichel, *Berühmte Orient-Teppiche aus historischer Sicht* (Rheinberg, 1969). No. 47, colour plate p. 189.
228
Islamische Kunst exhibition (Berlin, 1981), catalogue no. 116, colour plate p. 273.
229
Friedrich Spuhler, Hans König, and Martin Volkmann, *Alte Orientteppiche, Meisterstücke aus deutschen Privatsammlungen* (Munich, 1978), no. 6.
230
Belkis Balpinar and Udo Hirsch, *Vakiflar Museum Istanbul: Teppiche* (Wesel, 1988). No. 37 and no. 38.
231
Joseph V. McMullan, *Islamic Carpets* (New York, 1965), no. 68.
232
Charles Grant Ellis, *Oriental Carpets in the Philadelphia Museum of Art* (London, 1988).
233
Islamische Kunst exhibition (Berlin, 1981), catalogue no. 116, colour plate p. 273).
234
Erdmann, *Knüpfteppich,* p. 30 ff.
235
King (cited in 141: no. 42 ill.).
236
Erdmann, *Knüpfteppich,* colour plate VIII.
237
King, p. 71.
238
King, p. 73.
239
Österr. Nationalbibliothek, Vienna. – It is interesting to note in this context that in the case of this earliest depiction of the 'Memling gul' we are dealing with a picture connected with René of Anjou. Frequent reference has been made here to the familial ties existing between the house of Anjou and the Kingdom of Armenia Minor in Cilicia.
240
The reverse side of the portrait of a young man; Thyssen Collection, Lugano-Castagnola. It seems important here that the still life, analogous to the symbolic function of certain plants in the borders (see p. 492), is interpreted as a symbol of the Mother of God (the Virgin Mary). The iris and the lily stand for innocence, the columbine for a yearning to be with God. On the significance of still lifes see, among others: G. Langemeyer, "Das Stilleben als Attribut," *Stilleben in Europa* 80 (Münster, Baden-Baden, 1979), p. 221 ff.
241
Eder, pp. 126, 128, 129, ff.; 220, 221.
242
W. Brüggemann and Hans Böhmer, *Teppiche der Bauern und Nomaden in Anatolien* (Munich, 1982), p. 60 ff.
243
Museum for Anatolian Civilizations, Ankara. The depiction is not only interesting with respect to the 'Kotshak-cross' as a symbol of the sun and as the possible proto-design of the later 'tree of Jesse' compositions. The two eagles flanking the Kotshak-cross hold hares in their beaks; they are not dead. It is conceivable that the tradition of depicting believers as hares – a tradition that played an important role in the symbolism of early Christianity – can be traced back to this.
244
Historical Museum of Armenia, Erivan. Ill. 385
245
Museum for Anatolian Civilizations, Ankara.
246
This example shows quite clearly that symbols have to be seen in their overall context, which includes the relevant historical and theological background. Otherwise, as we see here, the Nestorian cross of triumph of Mongolian warriors may be turned into an 'old-Turkish' motif of the Oghuz.
247
Iten Maritz, p. 318.
248
Eder, pp. 278, 279, 280, 281.
249
Erdmann, *Knüpfteppich,* p. 45, ills. 96, 97 ff.
250
Şerare Yetkin, *Early Caucasian Carpets in Turkey* (London: 1978) II: 47, ill. 169. Here the carpet in the collection of Prince Roman Sanguszko is to be found.

251
Eskenazi, p. 47, fig. 2. Here the carpet is said to be located in the Art Institute of Chicago. During the summer of 1984, when the author visited the Art Institute of Chicago, no one knew anything about this carpet. It was neither on exhibit nor in storage. Dr. Pinner of *HALI* informed the author in 1985 that Michael Franses had supposedly seen it in the 'basement of the museum' in 1973. So far the museum has not responded to an inquiry into this matter. In 1985 even Michael Franses was not able to find the carpet any more.
252
HALI 6: 2, p. 212, ill. no. 8. Here the carpet is incorrectly referred to as a 'Hereke carpet' by its owners. Origin: Dr. G. Nordenson, Stockholm. Exhibition 1946, National Museum, Stockholm. Literature: "Orientaliska Mattor – Svenske Orientsällskapets," *Nationalmusei Utställningskatalog* no. 124, 25. Arsjubileum 1946, no. 45, ill. IV. Private collection.

197 x 145 cm
warp: cotton Z3S, light, heavily layered
weft: cotton Z3S, light, 2 shoots
pile: wool 2(?)Z, height of pile 1–3 mm, symmetrical knot, V=43–47, H=50, *c.* 2250 knots/dm^2
sides: not original top and bottom end: original
colours: 9 (white, gray, yellow, yellowish-orange, golden ochre, dark brown, red, greenish-yellow, bluish-green).

253
Gigi Pagnano, "L'Arte del Tappeto Orientale ed Europeo dalle Origini al XVIII Secolo," (Busto Arsizio, 1983), no. 62.

254
Martin Volkmann, *Alte Orientteppiche* (Munich, 1985) no. 12.

255
Martin, *A History,* p. 116.

256
Heinrich Jacoby, *Eine Sammlung orientalischer Teppiche* (Berlin, 1923), p. 39 ff.

257
Pope, *Myth.*

258
Pagnano, no. 54.

259
Pagnano, no. 63.

260
Charles Grant Ellis, *Early Caucasian Rugs* (Washington, 1976), plate 12.

261
Ellis, *Caucasian Rugs,* plate 7.

262
Ellis, *Caucasian Rugs,* fig. 3, p. 13.

263
Ellis, *Caucasian Rugs,* plates 9, 6, 13.

264
Erdmann, *Knüpfteppich,* ill. 96.

265
Martin, *A History,* p. 116.

266
Pagnano, no. 55.

267
Ellis, *Caucasian Rugs,* plate 11.

268
Badstübner, p. 162. The hare appears for the first time in Urartian art, symbolizing believers (cf. **243**, ill. 451) as it does in early Christian art as well. We can assume that the hare, often shown eating grapes and thus a symbol of the holy baptism – like the majority of Christian symbols – has its origin in Armenian tradition. In Christian oriental art it carries a positive meaning; it is only in the secular iconography of the Renaissance that this meaning becomes negative. The hares on either side of the tree of life symbolize eternal life in this case.

269
Ellis, *Caucasian Rugs,* p. 52.

270
The border (detail in ill. 310) contains the mirror-image of the same elements of design as MBN no. 10/294 (ill. 308) of Group B I. The design corresponds to contemporary borders of the Renaissance, as found for example in the floor of the Biblioteca Laurentiana in Florence by Michelangelo (1514).

271
First publication:
347 x 261 cm
warp: cotton Z5S, light, light layering, 88–90 kn/10 cm
weft: cotton Z5S, light, 2 shoots
pile: wool 2Z, height of pile 1–3 mm, symmetrical knots
V=51, H=44, *c.* 2240 knots/dm^2
sides: not original
top and bottom end: --, several rows of knots are missing
colours: 9 (white, yellow, red, dark purple, moderate brown, green, blue, bluish gray, black).
C^{14}-analysis: Institute for Environmental Physics, Universität Heidelberg, 4.12.1984
sample number: C^{14}-sample HD 8951–8926
Allowing for a margin of error of 1 sigma, the amount of C^{14} was found to be 94.2 ± 0.7%, which corresponds to the C^{14} age of 480 ± 55 years before 1950. The age measured here of 480 ± 55 years is equal to a dendro-chronological age of:

at a probability of 68%	AD 1410–1450
at a probability of 95.5%	AD 1390–1490

Author's commentary: considering the present state of research, design-historically, an origin prior to 1500 does not seem possible. However, if we raise our margin of error to 2.5 sigmas, an origin at around *AD 1610* becomes probable, in addition to those listed above. This would correspond quite well to the design-historical evolution postulated here.

272
Ellis, *Caucasian Rugs,* plate 16.

273
Yetkin vol. 1, plate 36.

274
Ellis, *Caucasian Rugs,* plate 17.

275
Sailer, Salzburg 1982; 215 x 425 cm.

276
Erdmann, *Knüpfteppich,* ill. 106.

277
Yetkin vol. I, plates 35, 34, 31, 28.

278
Ellis, *Caucasian Rugs,* plate 18.

279
Museum of Fine Arts, Boston, no. 64.2101.

280
Ellis, *Caucasian Rugs,* plate 22.

281
Mania Ghazaryan, *Armenian Carpets* (Moscow, 1985), ill. 25.

282
Ghazaryan, ills. 24, 23.

283
Ellis, *Caucasian Rugs,* plate 27.

284
Ellis, *Caucasian Rugs,* plates 28/29. Both from the mid-17th century (!).

285
Ghazaryan, ill. 22. 18th century.

286
Erdmann, *Knüpfteppich,* plate VI.

287
Erdmann, *Knüpfteppich,* ill. 105.

288
MMA no. 1970.302.10.

289
Yetkin vol. II, plate 182.

290
Vakiflar Museum, Istanbul; no. A 136.

291
Museum of Fine Arts, Boston; no. 53.156.

292
Yetkin, plate 45 ff.

293
Ghazaryan, p. 46.

294
Schmutzler

295
Julius Lessing, *Altorientalische Teppichmuster nach Bildern und Originalen des XV.-XVI: Jahrhunderts* (Berlin, 1877), ills. 13 and 14.

296
Volkmann, no. 18.
297
Brüggemann, no. 52.
298
Knotform-crosses have been a part of Armenian manuscript illumination since the 11th century at least, cf. Durnovo, no. 16, 20, 85. Since knotform-crosses are already represented in early Christian mosaics (e.g. Constantinople, Ephesus, Bodrum, Misis, Antioch, Gerasa), we can expect to find an uninterrupted tradition of this design.
299
L. Coen, *The Oriental Carpet,* no. 24.
300
McMullan, no. 96.
301
Marino and Clara Dall'Oglio, "A Discovery at Sion," *HALI* 7: 3, p. 37, ill. 1.
302
Antike Anatolische Teppiche aus österreichischem Besitz (Vienna, 1983), no. 25.
303
Erdmann, *Knüpfteppich,* ill. 39.
304
Galerie Koller, Zürich: Auction 5.10.85, no. 1320, plate 21, 228 x 130 cm.
305
Erdmann, *Knüpfteppich,* ill. 38.
306
McMullan, no. 98.
307
King, no. 18.
308
Bezalel Narkiss, *Armenische Kunst; Die faszinierende Sammlung des Armenischen Patriarchats in Jerusalem* (Stuttgart, 1980), p. 11 ff.
309
Erdmann, *Siebenhundert Jahre,* ill. 115.
310
King, no. 21.
311
King, no. 20 and 23.
312
King, no. 22.
313
Pagnano, no. 24 and 27.
314
Volkmar Gantzhorn, "Wurde ein Großteil der sogenannten persischen Safividen-Teppiche des 16. Jahrhunderts in der Türkei hergestellt?" Ms. *The First International Congress on Turkish Carpets,* Istanbul, October 7–14, 1984 (Istanbul, 1985).
315
Eskenazi, p. 47, plate 28.
316
Christopher Alexander Collection, Berkeley.
317
Caluste Gulbenkian Museum, Lisbon, no. I. 97.
318
Arthur U. Dilley, *Oriental Carpets and Carpets* (New York – London, 1931), plate VI.
319
King, no. 59.
320
Arthur Upham Pope, "A Survey on Persian Art," vol. XI. CARPETS: Chapter in *The Art of Carpet Making* (London, 1938/39), plate 1120.
321
Suha Umur, *Osmanlı, Padişah Tuğraları* (Istanbul, 1980), pp. 111, 121.
322
HALI 5: 1.
323
Ulrich Schürmann, *Teppiche aus dem Orient* (Wiesbaden, 1974), plate 23.
324
King, no. 61.
325
Walter B. Denny, "Ten Great Carpets," *HALI* 1: 2 (1978), p. 156.
326
King, no. 57.
327
Giovanni Curatola, *Teppiche* (München, 1981), p. 33, no. 76.
328
Ulrich Schürmann, "Dragon Carpets and Vase Carpets," *11th Textile Museum Carpet Convention,* October 1985. Published in *ORIENTAL CARPET REVIEW* VI: 2 (1986), p. 4, 28A.
329
Karapet Karapetian, *Isfahan-New Julfa, The Houses of the Armenians* (Rome, 1974).
330
Pagnano, for example. To date, the dispute has not been settled as to whether these are Persian, Indo-Persian or Indian carpets. Nor have any criteria for classification yet been defined. In view of the evolution of designs, the author considers it possible that the carpets mentioned here were produced sometime between 1600–1633, that is, during the time when export with India rested solely in the hands of the Armenians.
331
Werner Loges, *Turkmenische Teppiche* (München, 1978), p. 137.
332
Jon Thompson and L. W. Mackie, *Turkmen Tribal Carpets and Traditions* (Washington, 1980), p. 63.
333
Ulrich Schürmann, *Zentralasiatische Teppiche* (Frankfurt, 1969), no. 58, p. 118.
334
Elena Tzareva, *Teppiche aus Mittelasien und Kasachstan* (Leningrad, 1984), p. 23.
335
Loges, p. 47.
336
V. G. Moshkova, *Die Teppiche der Völker Mittelasiens im späten XIX. und frühen XX. Jahrhundert* (Tashkent, 1970), German ed. (Hamburg-Berlin, 1977), p. 303.
337
S. A. Milhofer, *Die Teppiche Zentralasiens* (Hannover, 1968), p. 203.
338
Johannes Kalter, *Aus Steppe und Oase* (Stuttgart, 1983), p. 87, ill. 68.
339
Rübesamen, ch. 55 and 56, pp. 96, 97.
340
Lee Yu-kuan, *Art Carpets from Silk Route and Great Wall Areas* (Tokyo, 1980) plate 100 – text p. 182; plate 35 – text p. 151, nearly identical to plate 36.
341
Schürmann, *Zentralasiatische,* no. 87.
342
Badstübner, p. 68.
343
Lee, plate 63 – text p. 165.
344
Tzareva, no. 136.
345
Schürmann, *Zentralasiatische,* no. 86.
346
Schürmann, *Zentralasiatische,* no. 90.
347
Milhofer, p. 265.

348
Volkmar Gantzhorn, "Der christlich orientalische Teppich – ein Aspekt armenischer Kunst," *The Fourth International Symposium on Armenian Art, Theses of Reports* (Erivan, 1985), p. 111 ff.

349
Heinrich Swoboda in *Römische Quartalsschrift für Archäologie und Kirchengeschichte* VI, p. 95 ff.
350
Alois Riegl, *Ein orientalischer Teppich vom Jahre 1202 n. Chr. und die ältesten orientalischen Teppiche* (Berlin, 1895).
351
McMullan, no. 91.
352
Matenadaran, Erivan: Ms. 4052, F. 81b.
353
Badstübner, p. 68; LCI (cited in 57) III, p. 100 ff.
354
Erwin Gans-Ruedin, *Orientalische Meisterteppiche* (Bern, 1954), plate 1.

355
McMullan, no. 90.
356
L. W. Mackie, *Prayer Carpets* (Washington, 1974), no. XII. Textile Museum Washington no. R 34.22.1.
357
Lefevre Auction, 27. 4. 1979.
358
Végh, Layer, and Dall'Oglio, no. 25.
359
Volkmann, et al., no. 15.
360
TIEM no. 822.
361
Grote-Hasenbalg, *Meisterstücke orientalischer Knüpfkunst* (Berlin, 1921).
362
No. T Or. 361.
363
Végh, Layer, and Dall'Oglio, no. 26.
364
Schmutzler, no. 29.
365
Végh, Layer, and Dall'Oglio, no. 24.
366
Lefevre Auction, 25.1.1974, no. 1.

367
Jan Bennet, *Schönheit echter Orientteppiche* (München, 1974), no. 42. (Sotheby's)
368
Schmutzler, no. 22.
369
Mackie, *Prayer Carpets,* no. XIII.
370
Vakiflar Museum Istanbul, No. E 17.
371
Nagel Stuttgart, 308. Auction, no. 3285.
372
Schmutzler, no. 21.
373
Iten-Maritz, J., *Der anatolische Teppich* (München, 1975), p. 47.

374
Borders of this type were used in this region for a long period of time. (Mania Ghazaryan)
375
First publication:
167 x 120 cm
(With the carpet framed behind glass, an investigation is only possible to a limited extent.)
warp, weft, pile: silk
symmetrical knot, V=9/cm, H=6/cm, *c.* 54 knots/dm^2
sides: as originally, golden-ochre coloured selvage over 4 warps
top and bottom end: as originally, golden-ochre coloured kilim border *c.* 2 cm, partially damaged and at the top missing in places
colours: 12 (ivory, gray, golden-yellow, orange, dark ochre, moderate brown, dark brown, rust, peach, moderate blue, dark blue, black).
Private collection.
376
cf. 240, e.g. Ghirlandaio, *Enthroned Virgin;* ill. 472/S. Badstübner, p. 68; Ferguson.
377
cf. Katharina Otto-Dorn, *Türkische Keramik* (Ankara, 1957), plate 12.
378
Ernst Kühnel, *Die Sammlungen türkischer und islamischer Kunst im Tschinili Köschk* (Istanbul), (Berlin and Leipzig, 1938), plate 37.
379
Erdmann, *Kairener Teppiche.*
380
Christie's Auction, 19.4.79, London.
381
Grote-Hasenbalg, ill. I.3.
382
Bernheimer, *Alte Teppiche des 16. bis 18. Jahrhunderts der Firma L. Bernheimer,* München (Munich, 1959), no. 55.
383
Schmutzler, no. 33.
384
Bibliothèque Nationale, Paris, Ms. Lat. 4404, F. 1v-2.
385
Türkische Kunst und Kultur aus osmanischer Zeit, catalog on the exhibition, Frankfurt (Recklinghausen, 1985) II, p. 209.
386
King, no. 16.
387
No. T I. 6930.
388
No. 22.100.114 (Ballard Collection).
389
No. T 135–1911.
390
Pagnano, no. 35.
391
Erdmann, *Knüpfteppich,* ill. 158.
392
Alois Riegl, *Altorientalische Teppiche* (Leipzig, 1891), p. 86 ff.
393
The protection enjoyed by Armenian Christians began with Mohammed and the first caliphs and was upheld – despite their being incorporated as a work force by the Safavids and Ottomans, who annexed them – on up to the beginning of this century. Concomitant with the weakening and annihilation of the Ottomans, who had provided caliphs since 1517 and had also been the guardians of the key to the Kaaba in Mekka, this protection consequently lapsed.

Bibliography

Preliminary Note: Over the course of the past ten years the author has attempted to work through all the available literature on the subject of carpets or textiles and in preparation for this volume to record the pieces presented in colour illustrations there. A complete list of these works is provided in the publication by Marc-Edouard Enay and Siawosch Azadi: *Einhundert Jahre Orientteppich-Literatur, 1877–1977.* 152pp. Hannover: 1977. In the following bibliography the reader will find only those works listed to which special reference was made in the present volumne.

Amirian, Lemyel. On the origin of the Dragon and Phoenix Rug in Berlin. HALI 4: 1.

The Anatolian Civilisations. 3 vols. Exibition catalogue. Istanbul, 1983.

Akurgal, Ekrem. Kunst in der Türkei. Würzburg, 1980.

Atalay, Besim. Türk Halıcılığı ve Uşak Halıları. Ankara, 1967.

Avi-Yonah, Michael, and *Aharon Kempinski.* Syrien-Palästina II. Munich, 1980.

Azadi, Siawosch, and *Rüdiger Vossen.* Türkmenische Teppiche und die ethnographische Bedeutung ihrer Ornamente. Hamburg, 1970.

Azadi, Siawosch. Turkman Carpets and the Ethnographic Significance of their Ornaments. Fishguard, 1975.

Azarian, Levon. Armenian Katchkars. Lisbon, 1973.

Badstübner, Ernst, Helga Neumann and *Hannelore Sachs.* Erklärendes Wörterbuch zur Christlichen Kunst. Berlin; Leipzig, n.d. [1984?].

Balpinar, Belkis, and *Udo Hirsch.* Teppiche des Vakiflar-Museums Istanbul. Wesel, 1988.

Balty, Janine. Mosaiques Antiques de Syrie. Brussels, 1977.

Bauer, Elisabeth. Armenia. Lucerne, 1977.

Bausback, Peter. Antike orientalische Knüpfkunst. (Annual catalogues of the exhibitions in Mannheim).

Bennet, Jan. Schönheit echter Orientteppiche. Munich, 1974.
Bennet, Jan. Teppiche der Welt. Gütersloh,1978.

Bernheimer. Alte Teppiche des 16. bis 18. Jahrhunderts der Firma L. Bernheimer. Munich, 1959.

Bode, Wilhelm, and *E. Kühnel.* Vorderasiatische Knüpfteppiche aus alter Zeit. 4th ed. Braunschweig, 1955.

Boehmer, Rainer Michael. "Phrygische Prunkgewänder des 8. Jh. v. Chr. Herkunft und Export." Archäolog. Anzeiger 2 (1973).

Bourguet, P. du. Die Kopten. Baden-Baden, 1980.

Brenk, Beat. Spätantike und frühes Christentum. Berlin, 1977.

Brentjes, Mnazakanjan, Stepanjan. Die Kunst des Mittelalters in Armenien. Berlin, 1981.

Brentjes, Burchard. Mittelasien – Kunst des Islam. Leipzig, 1979.
Brentjes, Burchard. Drei Jahrtausende Armenien. Leipzig, 1973.

Briggs, Amy. Timurid Carpets. ARS ISLAMICA VII (1940).

Brüggemann, W. and *Hans Böhmer.* Teppiche der Bauern und Nomaden in Anatolien. Munich, 1982.

Brunello, Franco. The Art of Dyeing. Vicenza, 1973.

Budde, Ludwig. Antike Mosaiken in Kilikien. Recklinghausen, 1969.

Buschhausen, Heide, and *Helmut Buschhausen.* Armenische Handschriften der Mechitaristen in Wien. Vienna, 1981.

Carswell, John. New Julfa, The Armenian Churches and other Buildings. Oxford, 1968.

Chéhab, Maurice. Mosaiques du Liban. Paris, 1958.

Christie's London. Auction house catalogues.

Cramer, Maria. Das altägyptische Lebenszeichen im christlichen (koptischen) Ägypten. Wiesbaden, 1955.
Cramer, Maria. Koptische Buchmalerei. Recklinghausen, 1964.

Curatola, Giovanni. Teppiche. Munich, 1981.

Dall'Oglio, Marino, and *Clara Dall'Oglio.* "A Discovery at Sion." HALI 7:3.

Denny, Walter B. Ten Great Carpets. HALI 1:2.

Dev Manuelian, Lucy and *Eiland Murray:* Weavers and Kings, Kimbell Art Museum, Fort Worth 1984

Dilley, Arthur U. Oriental Rugs and Carpets. New York-London, 1931.

Durnovo, L. A. Ornaments of Armenian Manuscripts. Erivan, 1978.

Durul/Aslanapa. Selçuklu Halıları. Istanbul, 1974.

Eder, Doris. Kaukasische Teppiche. Munich, 1979.

Ellis, Charles Grant. The 'Lotto' Pattern as a Fashion in Carpets. Festschrift for Peter Wilhelm Meister, 1975.
Ellis, Charles Grant. Early Caucasian Rugs. Washington, 1976.
Ellis, Charles Grant. Oriental Carpets in the Philadelphia Museum of Art. London, 1988.

Erbstösser, Martin. Ketzer im Mittelalter. Stuttgart.

Erdmann, Hanna. Die Beziehungen der vorosmanischen Teppichmuster zu den gleichzeitigen Ornamenten. HALI 1:3 (1978).

Erdmann, Kurt. Der orientalische Knüpfteppich. 4th ed. Tübingen, 1955.
Erdmann, Kurt. Die Geschichte des frühen türkischen Teppichs. Istanbul, 1957; London, 1977.
Erdmann, Kurt. Orientalische Tierteppiche auf Bildern des XIV. und XV. Jahrhunderts. Jahrbuch der preuß. Kunstsammlungen L 1929.
Erdmann, Kurt. Kairener Teppiche. ARS ISLAMICA VI (1939) Part I; VII (1940) Part II.
Erdmann, Kurt. Siebenhundert Jahre Orientteppich. Herford, 1966.

Eskenazi, John. Il Tappeto orientale dal XV al XVIII secolo. London, 1981.

Ettinghausen, Richard. New Light on Early Animal Carpets. Festschrift for Ernst Kühnel. Berlin, 1979.

Ferguson, George. Signs and Symbols in Christian Art. New York, 1961.

Frankfurt: Türkische Kunst and Kultur aus osmanischer Zeit. Recklinghausen, 1985.

Gans-Ruedin, Erwin. Orientalische Meisterteppiche. Bern, 1954.

Ghazaryan, Mania. Armenian Carpets. Moscow, 1985.

Gibb, H. A. R.. The Travels of Ibn Battuta. Cambridge, 1962.

Gold der Skythen. Catalogue on the exhibition in Munich, 1984.

Gombos, Károly. Anatolische Teppiche/Die Mythe der Seldschuk-Teppiche. Ms. Budapest, 1980.

Gombrich, Ernst H. Ornament und Kunst. Stuttgart, 1982.

Grabar, André. Byzanz. Baden-Baden, 1964.
Grabar, André. Die Mittelalterliche Kunst Osteuropas. Baden-Baden, 1968.

Grote-Hasenbalg, Werner. Meisterstücke orientalischer Knüpfkunst. Berlin, 1921.

Guyard, M. Stanislas. Geographie d'Aboulfeda. Tome II.

HALI, Internationale Zeitschrift für Orientteppiche und Textilien. London since 1978.

Hamilton, R. W. Khirbat al Mafjar. Oxford, 1959.

Havret, H. La Stèle chrétienne de Si-ngan-fou. Shanghai, 1895–1902.

Hempel, Rosa, and *Maritheres Gräfin Preysing.* Alte Orientteppiche. Hamburg, 1970.

Holländer, Hans. Kunst des frühen Mittelalters. Stuttgart, 1969; Herrsching, 1981.

Huber, Paul. Heilige Berge. Zürich, 1980.

Hutter, Irmgard. Frühchristliche Kunst, Byzantinische Kunst. Herrsching, 1981.

Iten-Maritz, J. Der anatolische Teppich. Munich, 1975.
Iten-Maritz, J. Enzyklopädie des Orientteppichs. Zürich, 1977.

Jacoby, Heinrich. Eine Sammlung orientalischer Teppiche. Berlin, 1923.

Kalter, Johannes. Aus Steppe und Oase. Stuttgart, 1983.

Karapetian, Karapet. Isfahan-New Julfa, The Houses of the Armenians. Rome, 1974.

Kawerau, Peter. Die jakobitische Kirche im Zeitalter der syrischen Renaissance. Berlin, 1955.

Kayser, Felix. Kreuz und Rune. Stuttgart.

King, Donald. The Eastern in the Western World. The Carpets in the Exhibition. London, 1983.

Kitzinger, Ernst. Byzantinische Mosaiken in Israel. Milan, 1965.

Klose, Christine. Ein anatolischer Sternteppich des 16. Jahrhunderts. WELTKUNST 56: 16 (1986), p. 2178 ff.

Korchmasjan, Drampjan, and *Akopjan.* Armenische Buchmalerei des 13. und 14. Jahrhunderts aus der Matenadaran-Sammlung, Erivan. Leningrad, 1984.

Kraeling, Carl H. GERASA, City of Decapolis. New Haven, Connecticut, 1938.

Kühn, Herbert. Die vorgeschichtliche Kunst Deutschlands. Berlin, 1935.

Kühnel, E. and *L. Bellinger.* Catalogue of Cairene Rugs. The Textile Museum Washington, 1955.

Kurdian, H. Kirmiz. Journal of the American Oriental Society 61: 2. Baltimore (1941).

Kutzli, Rudolf. Langobardische Kunst. Stuttgart, 1974.
Kutzli, Rudolf. Die Bogomilen. Stuttgart.

Lampakis, Georgios. Mémoire sur les antiquités chrétiennes de la Grèce. 1902.

LCI: Lexikon der Christlichen Ikonographie. Freiburg, 1968.

Le Coq, Albert von. Auf Hellas Spuren in Ostturkestan.

Lee Yu-kuan. Art Rugs from Silk Route and Great Wall Areas. Tokyo, 1980.

Lefevre London. Auction catalogues.

Lehmann-Haupt, K. F. Materialien zur älteren Geschichte Armeniens und Mesopotamiens. Göttingen, 1907.

Leroy, Jules. Les Manuscrits Syriaques à Peintures. Paris, 1964.

Lessing, Julius. Altorientalische Teppichmuster nach Bildern und Originalen des XV.-XVI. Jahrhunderts. Berlin, 1877.

Lewi, Doro. Antioch Pavements. Princeton, 1946.

Little, Donald P. "The Significance of the Haram Documents for the Study of Medieval Islamic History." Der Islam 57: 2 (1980).

Loges, Werner. Turkmenische Teppiche. Munich, 1978.

Mackie, Louise W. Prayer Rugs. Washington, 1974.
Mackie, Louise W. Native and Foreign Influences in Carpets woven in Spain during the 15th Century. HALI II: 2 (1979).

Mandel, Gabriel. Die Buchmalerei der Romanik und Gotik. Gütersloh, 1964.

Martin, F. R. A History of Oriental Carpets before 1800. Vienna, 1908.
Martin, F. R. A Shiraz Carpet from the Fifteenth Century. Burlington Magazine XVI (1909).

Mazal, Otto. Schatzkammer der Buchkunst. Graz, 1980.

McMullan, Joseph V. Islamic Carpets. New York, 1965.

Meriç, Rıfkı Melûl. Nakış Tarihi Vesikaları. II-III. Ankara, 1952.
Meriç, Rıfkı Melûl. Türk Nakış San'atı Tarihi Araştırmaları. I. Ankara, 1953.

Meyer Schapiro. The Miniatures of the Florence Diatessaron. Their Place in Late Medieval Art and Supposed Connection with Early Christian and Insular Art. The Art Bulletin 55 (1973).

Milhofer, S. A. Die Teppiche Zentralasiens. Hanover, 1968.

Mills, John. The Coming of the Carpet to the West. The Eastern Carpet in the Western World. London, 1983 (exhibition catalogue).
Mills, John. Carpets in Pictures. London, 1975.
Mills, John. Early Animal Carpets in Western Paintings. HALI 1: 3.

Moshkova, V. G. Die Teppiche der Völker Mittelasiens im späten XIX. und frühen XX. Jahrhundert. Tashkent, 1970.

Nagel = Kunstauktionshaus Dr. Fritz Nagel. Auction catalogues, Stuttgart.

Narkiss, Bezalel. Armenische Kunst. Stuttgart, 1980.

Neubecker, Ottfried. Heraldik. German ed. Frankfurt, 1977.
Neubecker, Ottfried. Wappenkunde. Munich, 1980.

Nordenfalk, Carl. An Illustrated Diatessaron. Art Bulletin 50 (1968).

Nova, Alessandro. Michelangelo, der Architekt. Stuttgart, 1985.

Orlandi, Enzo. Giotto. German ed. Stuttgart, 1975.

Otto-Dorn, Katharina. Kunst des Islam. Baden-Baden, 1964.

Otto-Dorn, Katharina. Türkische Keramik. Ankara, 1957.

Pagnago, Gigi. L'Arte del Tappeto Orientale ed Europeo dalle Origini al XVIII Secolo. Busto Arsizio, 1983.

Parrot, Dr. Friedrich. Reise zum Ararat. Berlin, 1834.

Pinner, Robert, and *Michael Franses.* The East Mediterranean Carpet Collection (in the Victoria and Albert Museum). HALI 4: 1.

Pinner, Robert, and *Jackie Stanger.* 'Kufik' Borders on 'Small Pattern Holbein' Carpets. HALI 1: 4.

Pjotrowski, Boris. Urartu. Munich, 1980.

Pope, Arthur Upham. The Myth of the Armenian Dragon Carpets. Jahrbuch der asiatischen Kunst II (Leipzig, 1925).
Pope, Arthur Upham. A Survey on Persian Art. (ch. XI. CARPETS) The Art of Carpet Making. London, 1938/39.

Reichel, Herbert. Berühmte Orient-Teppiche aus historischer Sicht. Rheinberg (Rheinland), 1969.

Restle, Marcell. Die byzantinischen Wandmalereien in Kleinasien. 3 vols. Recklinghausen, 1967.

Rice, David Talbot. Morgen des Abendlandes. Munich, 1971.

Riegl, Alois. Altorientalische Teppiche. Leipzig, 1891.
Riegl, Alois. Ein orientalischer Teppich vom Jahre 1202 n. Chr. und die ältesten orientalischen Teppiche. Berlin, 1895.

Roll, Eugen. Ketzer zwischen Orient und Okzident; Patarener, Paulikianer, Bogomilen. Stuttgart, 1978.

Rübesamen, Hans Eckart. Die Reisen des Venezianers Marco Polo. Munich, 1983.

Ry, Carel J, du. Die Welt des Islam. Baden-Baden, 1970.

Saeki, P. Y. The Nestorian Documents and Relics in China. Tokyo, 1951.

Salih, Abu. Anecdota Oxoniensia. Eds. Evetts and Buttler. Sem. series VII.

Sarre, Friedrich. Neue Forschungen und Dokumente zur türkischen Kunstgeschichte. Kunstchronik N.F. XXXI (1920).
Sarre, Friedrich. Die ägyptische Herkunft der sogenannten Damaskus-Teppiche. Zeitschrift für bildende Kunst XXXII (1921).

Sassouni, Viken. Armenian Church Floor Plan – a hitherto unidentified design in Oriental Rugs. HALI 4: 1.
Sassouni, Viken. Rugs with Armenian Inscription. The Armenian Review XXXV: 4 (1982).

Saunders, J. The History of the Mongol Conquests. London, 1971.

Schlosser, Ignaz. Der schöne Teppich in Orient und Okzident." Munich, 1960; dtv, 1979.

Schlumberger, D. Der hellenisierte Orient. Baden-Baden, 1969.

Schmidt, H. and *M. Schmidt.* Die vergessene Bildersprache christlicher Kunst. Munich, 1981.

Schmutzler, Emil. Altorientalische Teppiche in Siebenbürgen. Leipzig, 1933.

Schürmann, Ulrich. Zentralasiatische Teppiche. Frankfurt, 1969.
Schürmann, Ulrich. Teppiche aus dem Orient. Wiesbaden, 1974.

Schürmann, Ulrich. Der Pazyryk. Seine Deutung und Herkunft. New York – Mannheim, 1982.

Schug-Wille, Christa. Byzanz und seine Welt. Baden-Baden, 1969.

Serjeant, R. B. Islamic Textiles. Beirut, 1972.

Sotheby's London and New York. Auction catalogues.

Spuhler, Friedrich. Islamic Carpets and Textiles in the Keir Collection. London.
Spuhler, Friedrich. Die Orientteppiche im Museum für Islamische Kunst Berlin. Berlin, 1987.

Spuler, Bertold. Geschichte der Mongolen. Zürich, 1968.

Stierlin, Henri. Architektur des Islam. Zürich, 1979.

Strzygowski, Josef. Die Baukunst der Armenier und Europa. Vienna, 1918.

Thompson, Jon, and *L. W. Mackie.* Turkmen Tribal Carpets and Traditions. Washington, 1980.

Turánszky, Ilona, and *Károly Gink.* Azerbaijan. Budapest, 1979.

Tzareva, Elena. Teppiche aus Mittelasien und Kasachstan. Leningrad, 1984.

Uhlig, Helmut. Das Mandala. Tantrische Kunst des Buddhismus (exhibition catalogue) Berlin, 1981.

Umur, Suha. Osmanlı Padişah Tuğraları. Istanbul, 1980.

Unger, Edmund de. An Ancestor of the Mamluk Carpets. HALI 5: 1 (1982).

Végh, Gyula, Károly Layer, and *Marino Dall'Oglio.* Turkish rugs in Transylvania. Crosby Press, 1977.

Viale, M. e. V. Arazzi e Tappeti Antichi. Turin, 1948.

Volkmann, Martin, Friedrich Spuhler, and *Hans König.* Alte Orientteppiche, Meisterstücke aus deutschen Privatsammlungen. Munich, 1978.

Volkmann, Martin. Alte Orientteppiche. Munich, 1985.

Whiting, Mark. The Red Dyes of some East Mediterranean Carpets. HALI 4: 1.

Whitting, P. D. Münzen von Byzanz. Munich, 1973.

Yetkin, Şerare. Historical Turkish Carpets. Istanbul, 1981.
Yetkin, Şerare. Early Caucasian Carpets in Turkey. London, 1978.

Young, Rodney S. Three Great Early Tumuli. The Gordian Excavations Final Reports I (Philadelphia, 1981).

Zick-Nissen, Johanna. Eine kunsthistorische Studie zum ältesten erhaltenen Knüpfteppich islamischer Zeit. HALI 1: 3 (1978).

Zier, Wilhelm. Morgenröte des Abendlandes. Stuttgart, 1981.

Sources of Illustrations

The photographic material for the carpets, paintings, illuminations and art objects from public collections is from the studios of the institutes mentioned or from the picture agencies SCALA (133, 138, 141, 148, 152, 154, 162, 388, 429, 482) and ARTOTHEK (171). The VAC-Archive of the author represents all other pieces from private collections or businesses. This material was made available to the author for this publication only on trust and with the guarantee of absolute anonymity. This excludes any further use of this material. The VAC-Archive has acquired material over a period of several decades, thus making it impossible in certain cases to establish former or current ownership.